UNDERSTANDING
OCEANIA

CELEBRATING THE UNIVERSITY OF THE
SOUTH PACIFIC AND ITS COLLABORATION WITH
THE AUSTRALIAN NATIONAL UNIVERSITY

UNDERSTANDING
OCEANIA

CELEBRATING THE UNIVERSITY OF THE
SOUTH PACIFIC AND ITS COLLABORATION WITH
THE AUSTRALIAN NATIONAL UNIVERSITY

**EDITED BY STEWART FIRTH
AND VIJAY NAIDU**

Australian
National
University

PRESS

PACIFIC SERIES

ANU PRESS

Published by ANU Press
The Australian National University
Acton ACT 2601, Australia
Email: anupress@anu.edu.au

Available to download for free at press.anu.edu.au

ISBN (print): 9781760462888
ISBN (online): 9781760462895

WorldCat (print): 1101142803
WorldCat (online): 1101180975

DOI: 10.22459/UO.2019

Cover design and layout by ANU Press

Contents

Acknowledgements

Books are the work of many people and this one is no different. The editors owe an enormous debt of gratitude to Kathryn Skorkiewicz in the Department of Pacific Affairs at The Australian National University (ANU). Kathryn was responsible for organising the copyediting, checking the permissions and for making a reality of one reviewer's suggestion— one we accepted—that we not only provide biographical information about contributors but also give them the opportunity to describe their personal academic journey at the University of the South Pacific (USP) and ANU. We would also like to thank the copyeditors Cathy Johnstone and Sarah Jost for their careful work in rendering the collection publishable on a number of platforms by ANU Press. And we pay tribute to Emily Hazlewood at ANU Press for seeing our collection through to publication with her characteristic high standards and attention to detail.

Finally, this collection would not have been published without the financial support of the Department of Pacific Affairs through the Australian Government's Pacific Research Program and the personal support of Nicole Haley, Program Convenor.

Acronyms

ACP	African, Caribbean and Pacific
ADB	Asian Development Bank
AIDAB	Australian International Development Assistance Bureau
AKA	Aelon Kein Ad
AOSIS	Alliance of Small Island States
APEC	Asia-Pacific Economic Cooperation
AusAID	Australian Agency for International Development
AV	alternative vote
CAMV	Conservative Alliance–Matanitu Vanua
CCF	Citizens' Constitutional Forum
CDF	Commodity Development Framework
CIS	Centre for Independent Studies
DAWN	Development Alternatives with Women for a New Era
DECRA	Discovery Early Career Researcher Award
DFAT	Department of Foreign Affairs and Trade
DWFN	distant water fishing nation
ECP	Enhanced Cooperation Programme
EIMCOL	Equity Investment Management Company Limited
FDB	Fiji Development Bank
FFA	Forum Fisheries Agency
FLNKS	Front de Libération Nationale Kanak et Socialiste
FLP	Fiji Labour Party
FSM	Federated States of Micronesia
GATS	General Agreement on Trade in Services

GNI	gross national income
HRPP	Human Rights Protection Party
IAS	Institute of Applied Sciences
ICT	information and communications technology
IGC	Intergovernmental Committee on Intellectual Property, Genetic Resources, Traditional Knowledge and Folklore
IMR	Institute of Marine Resources
IOE	Institute of Education
IPR	intellectual property rights
IPS	Institute of Pacific Studies
IRETA	Institute of Research, Extension and Training in Agriculture
JICA	Japan International Cooperation Agency
MIRAB	migration, remittances, aid and bureaucracy
MSG	Melanesian Spearhead Group
NCDS	National Centre for Development Studies
NFL	National Football League
NGO	non-government organisation
NRL	National Rugby League
NSC	National Sports Council
NZAID	New Zealand Agency for International Development
NZMFAT	New Zealand Ministry of Foreign Affairs and Trade
ODA	official development assistance
ODT	Oceania Dance Theatre
PACER	Pacific Agreement on Closer Economic Relations
PaCE-SD	Pacific Centre for Environment and Sustainable Development
Pacific TAFE	Pacific Technical and Further Education
PacLII	Pacific Islands Legal Information Institute
PANG	Pacific Network on Globalisation
PIAS-DG	Pacific Institute of Advanced Studies in Governance and Development

PICs	Pacific Island countries
PICTA	Pacific Island Countries Trade Agreement
PIDF	Pacific Islands Development Forum
PIF	Pacific Islands Forum
PNA	Parties to the Nauru Agreement
PR	proportional representation
PSIDS	Pacific Small Island Developing States Group
RAMSI	Regional Assistance Mission to Solomon Islands
RNZAF	Royal New Zealand Air Force
RPCR	Rassemblement pour la Calédonie dans la République
SDL	Soqosoqo Duavata ni Lewenivanua
SGDIA	School of Government, Development and International Affairs
SNTV	single non-transferable vote
SVT	Soqosoqo ni Vakavulewa ni Taukei
THA	temporary housing area
TOL	temporary occupation licence
UDP	United Democratic Party
UNDP	United Nations Development Program
VLV	Veitokani ni Lewenivanua Vakarisito
VP	Vanua'aku Pati
WHO	World Health Organization
WIPO	World Intellectual Property Organization
WTO	World Trade Organization

Contributors

Matthew G. Allen is a professor of Development Studies at the University of the South Pacific. He is a human geographer with over 20 years' experience working in the Melanesian Pacific. His diverse research interests include natural resource governance, rural development, state–society relations, and peace, conflict and development. In addition to his scholarly research, Matthew has undertaken advisory work for the World Bank, the Asian Development Bank, AusAID/DFAT and the government of Solomon Islands. He previously held a number of academic appointments at The Australian National University (ANU) and was an Australian Research Council DECRA Fellow from 2014 to 2017. Matthew has published several books and around 50 peer-reviewed articles, chapters and reports. His most recent book is *Resource Extraction and Contentious States* (Palgrave Macmillan, 2018).

Alumita Durutalo (25 January 1960 – 8 October 2018) was the coordinator of the Pacific Studies Programme at Te Tumu, School of Māori, Pacific and Indigenous Studies at the University of Otago. She was a graduate of the University of the South Pacific (USP) and The Australian National University (ANU). She taught Politics at USP 1997 to 2001, gained her PhD from ANU in 2006, and returned to USP to become Acting Director in Politics in the Diplomacy and International Affairs Programme. From 2006 to 2009, she was a Commissioner on the Fiji Public Service Commission. She was the author of a number of publications on Pacific Islands politics and her research interests included political parties, foreign policy, elections and democratisation in the Pacific Islands states; indigenous leadership and development in the Pacific Islands; and indigenous languages, culture and identity amongst Pacific Islands migrants in the First World. She possessed a dignity, empathy, generosity and modesty that is much missed.

Stewart Firth is a research fellow at the Department of Pacific Affairs, College of Asia and the Pacific, The Australian National University (ANU). He was a professor of politics at the University of the South Pacific, Suva, 1998 to 2004 and greatly enjoyed the experience. He co-edited *From Election to Coup in Fiji: The 2006 Campaign and Its Aftermath* (2007), *Politics and State-Building in Solomon Islands* (2008), and *The 2006 Military Takeover in Fiji: A Coup to End All Coups?* (2009), all published by ANU E Press. He is the author of *Australia in International Politics: An Introduction to Australian Foreign Policy*, 3rd edn (Allen & Unwin, 2011). He is chair of the Pacific Editorial Board for ANU Press, and he co-teaches an ANU undergraduate course on Pacific politics. His research focuses on the international relations of the Pacific Islands.

Miranda Forsyth is an associate professor in the School of Regulation and Global Governance (RegNet) in the College of Asia and Pacific at The Australian National University (ANU). The broad focus of Miranda's research is investigating the possibilities and challenges of the inter-operation of state and non-state justice and regulatory systems. She also works on the issue of how best to localise or vernacularise foreign legal norms and procedures. In July 2015, she completed a three-year Australian Research Council Discovery–funded project to investigate the impact of intellectual property laws on development in Pacific Island countries. Prior to coming to the ANU, Miranda was a senior lecturer in criminal law at the Law School of the University of the South Pacific, based in Port Vila, Vanuatu for eight years. Miranda is the author of *A Bird that Flies with Two Wings: Kastom and State Justice Systems in Vanuatu* (ANU E Press, 2009) and co-author of *Weaving Intellectual Property Policy in Small island Developing States* (Intersentia, 2015). Miranda is currently working on a multi-year research project investigating ways to overcome sorcery accusations and related violence in Papua New Guinea.

Joseph D. Foukona is a lawyer and has considerable experience in his chosen field of land legislation and reform in the Pacific. He has been a lecturer at the School of Law, University of the South Pacific since 2004, and obtained his PhD at The Australian National University (ANU). His research focus matches closely his keen personal interest in finding solutions to the seemingly intractable problem of the alignment in Melanesia between customary land tenure systems on one hand and state legislation, land administration and commercial demands on the other. He has worked with non-government organisations and local communities and consulted for international and regional organisations.

He was educated in Solomon Islands, Fiji, Vanuatu, Papua New Guinea, New Zealand and Australia, with a PhD on land law reform from ANU. He continues to be involved in ANU projects in the Pacific.

Jon Fraenkel is a visiting fellow with the Department of Pacific Affairs, College of Asia and the Pacific, The Australian National University (ANU), and a professor of comparative politics in the School of History, Philosophy, Political Science and International Relations at Victoria University of Wellington. He was formerly a senior research fellow based at ANU (2007–12) and taught at the University of the South Pacific in Fiji (1995–2007). He is Pacific correspondent for *The Economist* magazine. His research focuses on the politics of the Pacific Islands region, institutional design in divided societies, electoral systems, political economy and the economic history of Oceania.

Greg Fry is an honorary associate professor in the Asia Pacific College of Diplomacy in the Coral Bell School of Asia Pacific Affairs at The Australian National University (ANU). He is also currently an adjunct associate professor in the School of Government, Development and International Affairs at the University of the South Pacific (USP). He was formerly Academic Co-ordinator of Graduate Studies in Diplomacy and International Affairs at the USP from 2011 to 2015. Prior to that, he was for 23 years the Director of Graduate Studies in International Affairs at the ANU. In 1981, he taught politics at USP in the School of Social and Economic Development. Greg's research focuses on the geopolitics and international politics of the South Pacific region, conflict and conflict resolution in the Pacific Island states, and the politics of regionalism and regional diplomacy. He is co-editor of *Australia's Regional Security, Contending Images of World Politics* (with Jacinta O'Hagan; Red Globe Press, 2000) and *Intervention and State-Building in the Pacific* (with Tarcisius Kabutaulaka; Manchester University Press, 2008). His most recent publication, *The New Pacific Diplomacy*, was co-edited with Dr Sandra Tarte of USP and published by ANU Press (2015).

Epeli Hau'ofa (7 December 1939 – 11 January 2009) was born of Tongan missionary parents in Papua New Guinea and gained his PhD on the Mekeo people of Papua at The Australian National University (ANU) in 1981. He was head of the Department of Sociology at the University of the South Pacific (USP) from 1983, and later head of the School of Social and Economic Development. In 1997, he became the founding director of USP's Oceania Centre for Arts and Culture, which quickly became a hub of Pacific artistic expression and intellectual activity. He and his wife Barbara made Fiji their home. As the late Ratu Joni Madraiwiwi wrote of Epeli, he 'was a larger than life figure. His beard and genial visage were reinforced by an ever-present twinkle in his eye. He had a boundless capacity for humour, as well as an understated tongue-in-cheek manner'. More than any other Pacific Islander of his generation, he offered a new and positive conceptualisation of Pacific development and identity, emphasising the way in which the ocean connected rather than separated Pacific peoples.

Tarcisius Kabutaulaka is currently the director of the Center for Pacific Islands Studies (CPIS) at the University of Hawai'i at Manoa. He is a political scientist with a PhD from The Australian National University (ANU) and undergraduate and master's degrees from the University of the South Pacific (USP). He joined the CPIS in 2009. Prior to that, he worked for six years as a research fellow at the East-West Center's Pacific Islands Development Program. Before moving to Hawai'i in 2003, he taught history and political studies at the USP in Fiji. Over the years, Kabutaulaka has also done consultancy work for governments and regional and international organisations. He is the editor for the Pacific Islands Monograph Series and the founding editor of *Oceania Currents*. He is also a member of the editorial board of *The Contemporary Pacific*. Kabutaulaka comes from the Weather Coast of Guadalcanal in Solomon Islands.

Labasa-born **Brij Vilash Lal** went to the University of the South Pacific (USP) in 1971 on a government scholarship to prepare for a career as a high school teacher of English and history. Instead, in 1974 he became USP's first-ever graduate to do postgraduate studies overseas—at the University of British Columbia. He returned to teach briefly at USP before going to The Australian National University (ANU) to do a PhD. He returned to USP for three years before accepting an appointment at the University of Hawai'i in 1983. He joined ANU in 1990 and retired from there as professor of Pacific and Asian history in 2016, receiving along the way many honours and awards for his scholarship and contributions to the humanities, including Australia's Centenary of Federation Medal, Fellowship of the Australian Humanities Academy, and Member of the Order of Australia. He remains ever grateful to USP for the great start he got there from fondly remembered inspirational teachers.

Vijay Naidu's future was moulded by the establishment of the University of the South Pacific (USP). In 1974, he completed his bachelor's degree with a 'cafeteria combination' of sociology, politics, geography, history and economics. He then began tutoring in Foundation Politics and Advanced Pacific History courses. On a part-time basis, he completed his master's degree in political sociology. In 1989, he completed his doctoral degree in the sociology of development at the University of Sussex, UK. Over the last 44 years, he has worked at USP as tutor, lecturer, reader, professor, head of school, dean, pro-vice chancellor and acting vice chancellor. He has served as professor and director of Development Studies at USP and at Victoria University of Wellington. He has worked with colleagues at ANU including David Hegarty, Stewart Firth, Greg Fry, Jon Fraenkel and Brij Lal. Over the last 30 years, he has attended a number of conferences and seminars convened by ANU scholars. A number of his conference papers have been published in books and journals. He is on the editorial board of a number of international scholarly journals. He has served as consultant to government, non-government organisations (NGOs) and United Nations agencies. He has served in various Fiji Government Commissions. He is active in a number of NGOs.

Steven Ratuva is director of Macmillan Brown Centre for Pacific Studies and professor of anthropology and sociology at the University of Canterbury. He is a former fellow at The Australian National University (ANU) and worked at the University of the South Pacific for 11 years as head of sociology and a senior fellow in development and governance. With a PhD from the University of Sussex, he has published widely on development, conflict, political change, coups, social protection, elections, ethnicity, security, military, affirmative action, gender and nationalism. He has also published widely on the politics of Fiji.

Claire Slatter retired from academia in 2018 after 23 years of teaching politics at the University of the South Pacific (USP). She also set up (with Dr Margaret Mishra) and taught ethics for close to three years at the Fiji National University. Claire did her first degree in politics and sociology at USP, her master's at The Australian National University (ANU) under an ANU scholarship, and her PhD at Massey University (Albany Campus). She is a gender and development specialist, a founding member and current board chair of the Global South feminist network of scholar activists, Development Alternatives with Women for a New Era (DAWN), and a founding and active member of the Pacific Network on

Globalisation (PANG). She is also a founding member of the Citizens Constitutional Forum of Fiji. Claire's research and publications have mainly focused on the politics of development in the Pacific region.

Sandra Tarte is an associate professor and head of the School of Government, Development and International Affairs, Faculty of Business and Economics at the University of the South Pacific (USP). She has been a lecturer and senior lecturer at USP since 1995 and has held various roles, including head of the School of Social Sciences. Sandra graduated with a PhD in East Asian Studies from The Australian National University (ANU) in 1996. Her PhD thesis, 'Japan's Aid Diplomacy and the Pacific Islands', was co-published by the National Centre for Development Studies at ANU and USP's Institute of Pacific Studies in 1998. Sandra has written widely on regional cooperation in the Pacific, with a focus on fisheries management and conservation. She has also consulted for the South Pacific Forum Fisheries Agency, the South Pacific Regional Environment Program, the International Development Centre, Tokyo, and Greenpeace Pacific.

Katerina Martina Teaiwa is an associate professor in the School of Culture, History and Language, College of Asia and the Pacific at The Australian National University (ANU). Born in Fiji, she spent many years on the Suva campus of the University of the South Pacific (USP), where her mother, Joan Teaiwa, worked in extension services and her sister, Teresia Teaiwa, was a lecturer. Professor Epeli Hauʻofa was a close mentor and introduced Katerina to Seiuli Allan Alo Vaʻai. Together they founded the Oceania Dance Theatre (ODT), which is now part of the performing arts programme of the Oceania Centre for Arts, Culture and Pacific Studies at USP. Allan and Katerina developed the ODT's first international shows for Canberra and Honolulu titled Boiling Ocean I and II shortly after the Fiji coup of 2000. They collaborated for many years, including on a field school involving USP, National University of Samoa, and ANU students in 2013. Katerina's research is on histories of phosphate mining in Kiribati and the relocation of Banabans to Fiji. She has also been a consultant with UNESCO and the Secretariat of the Pacific Community on cultural policy in Oceania. She is author of *Consuming Ocean Island: Stories of People and Phosphate from Banaba* (Indiana University Press, 2015). In 2017, she converted her research into a visual arts exhibition, Project Banaba, for Carriageworks, Sydney. Katerina is currently vice president of the Australian Association for Pacific Studies.

Morgan Tuimaleali'ifano is an associate professor in history, former head of the School of the Social Sciences, and former coordinator of the history discipline in the Faculty of Arts, Law and Education, at the University of the South Pacific (USP). His current research lies in three areas: the evolution of Indigenous leadership within Western frameworks, the influence of the Pacific diaspora on Indigenous society, and framing a pan-Pacific identity. His PhD was supervised at The Australian National University by Drs Niel Gunson, Donald Denoon and Deryck Scarr, and awarded by USP in 1997. It resulted in the publication of *O Tama-a-Āiga: The Politics of Succession to Samoa's Paramount Titles* in 2006 (Institute of Pacific Studies, USP) and a series of articles. He is a member of the Pacific History Association, having served as its past president and convenor of two conferences in 2002 in Samoa and 2008 in Fiji.

Joeli Veitayaki is from Gau Island, Fiji, and has been associated with the University of the South Pacific (USP) since 1979. He completed his undergraduate and master's degrees at USP and has worked there since 1990. Joeli attained his PhD in environment and development from The Australian National University in 2000 and has maintained his connections with mentors and colleagues there. He is currently an associate professor at the School of Marine Studies and as well as the director of the International Ocean Institute – Pacific Islands Operational Centre and co-chair of the Korea South Pacific Fisheries Forum. Joeli has published papers in the areas of customary marine tenure, capacity building, Law of the Sea, marine resources management, community-based resource management, and regional cooperation. He has worked and collaborated with trainers and researchers in most of the Pacific Island countries as well as in Australia, Canada, the US, South Africa, Portugal, Japan, France, Norway, Korea, and Scotland.

R. Gerard Ward first did research on land use studies in Fiji in 1958. This was followed by completion of land use maps of the main islands based on aerial photograph interpretation. These were published in 1964, and a volume entitled *Land Use and Population in Fiji* was published by Her Majesty's Stationery Office, London, in 1965. He continued to conduct research in and on Fiji in subsequent years and maintained connections with the University of the South Pacific from soon after it was established. His studies in the Pacific Islands began in Samoa when he was a member of staff in the Department of Geography at Auckland University College, continued at University College London (1961–67), University of Papua New Guinea (1967–71), and subsequently at The Australian National

University (ANU). He was director of the Research School of Pacific Studies at ANU from 1980 to 1993. He formally retired in December 1997, but has remained a professor emeritus.

Christine Weir studied history at the University of Cambridge, trained as a history teacher, and in 1976 accompanied her husband Tony to the University of the South Pacific (USP), where he was employed as a physics lecturer. During eight years in Fiji, she taught in Fiji schools, learned about Pacific history, and did some tutoring at USP in social science and education. During the following years, while resident in Canberra, she returned to study at The Australian National University (ANU), completing a master's in anthropology and then a PhD in Pacific history (2003) on missionary ideas about work in Fiji and Solomon Islands. In 2007, Christine returned to Fiji to take up the position of lecturer in history at USP, which she held for seven years, teaching a variety of courses in Pacific and world history, supervising several research students, and researching colonial and contemporary Christianity in the Pacific. Since returning to Canberra in 2014, she has continued her research as an honorary lecturer in the College of Asia and the Pacific at ANU and is currently working on a biography of Bishop Jabez Bryce, the first Indigenous Bishop of Polynesia.

1

Themes

Stewart Firth

Stewart Firth: Personal Journey

I arrived at the University of the South Pacific (USP) in Suva in 1998 and was delighted to be back in the Pacific. Thirty years earlier I had taught in Port Moresby—in the first years of the University of Papua New Guinea—and I knew that, in order truly to know the Pacific, one had to live there. My expectations were fully justified. I knew I would learn a great deal from the students, and so it proved, as my romantic preconceptions about Fiji fell away in the face of the country's uncompromising politics and deep divisions. And I knew Fiji and the region would prove endlessly interesting, as indeed they did. Most rewarding of all, I had the opportunity to return to teaching Pacific history—my starting point in doctoral research—and to mine the immense research resources at The Australian National University (ANU) on Pacific history to inform my teaching. ANU and USP thus came together in a tangible way in the classrooms and lecture halls of the old School of Social and Economic Development building, where students would discuss the legacy of Sir Arthur Gordon or the Indo-Fijian experience or Maasina Rule in the Solomon Islands or the Mau movement in Samoa—subjects that in a real sense belonged to them. I had marvellous colleagues at USP and my time there will always live with me.

The University of the South Pacific (USP) is the inspiration for this collection, which brings together contributors who have all been students, lecturers or researchers there during its 50-year history. This volume is sponsored by The Australian National University's (ANU) Department of Pacific Affairs, through the Australian Government's Pacific Research Program, as a celebration of the Pacific's best-known university 50 years after its founding and its collaboration—personal and intellectual—with Australia's national institution of learning and research.

For many years it was a common career trajectory for young lecturers at USP to undertake doctoral research at ANU, almost always on a Pacific Islands topic. Twelve of our 19 contributors gained their doctorates at ANU, most of them before or after being students and/or teaching staff at USP. They are Matthew Allen, Alumita Durutalo, Miranda Forsyth, Joe Foukona, Epeli Hau'ofa, Tarcisius Kabutaulaka, Brij Lal, Sandra Tarte, Katerina Teaiwa, Morgan Tuimaleali'ifano, Joeli Veitayaki and Christine Weir. Greg Fry and Claire Slatter, both of whom taught and researched at USP, are ANU graduates with involvement in USP extending over decades. In all cases the award of an ANU postgraduate degree was merely the springboard for academic careers that included many other achievements and distinctions over decades. The fit between the two institutions is a natural one, with USP being a premier institution of learning in Oceania and ANU the centre of Pacific Islands expertise, teaching, and research in Australia.

The connections to USP and ANU of the remaining five contributors are various: Vijay Naidu's career has been defined by USP as he rose from being a student there in the 1970s to occupying a succession of senior roles and becoming professor of development studies. He has worked closely with the ANU over the years in research, conferences and publication; Stewart Firth was professor of politics at USP for six years before moving to the ANU; Jon Fraenkel spent 11 years at USP before becoming a research fellow at the ANU and is now professor in comparative politics at Victoria University of Wellington; Steven Ratuva was a student at USP, later head of sociology, spent time at ANU, and is now professor in the Department of Anthropology and Sociology at the University of Canterbury; Gerard Ward retired in 1998 after a distinguished academic career, which included being foundation professor of human geography at the ANU as well as undertaking pathbreaking geographical research in Fiji and serving USP in a number of review capacities.

Contributors have been asked to make their own choice for an article or chapter, already published elsewhere, to be republished here. Only in one case—Epeli Hau'ofa, perhaps the greatest mind associated with USP since its founding and who died in 2009—did we as editors make our own choice. 'The Ocean in Us', his remarkable article from the late 1990s, called for a coherent identity for the Pacific Islands and Pacific Islanders, one that he saw deriving from the Pacific Ocean itself and the close relationship of Pacific peoples with the sea. Alumita Durutalo was looking forward to the republication of her chapter 'Defending the Inheritance: The SDL and the 2006 Election' before her sudden tragic death in October 2018.

This voluntary approach to organising the volume led, perhaps unexpectedly, to the emergence of a number of common themes, not least about USP itself.

In his commentary on the history of the institution, Vijay Naidu points to both its success and its limitations: success as a regional university which is a key institution of learning for the Pacific and which has vastly increased in numbers of campuses, students and staff over 50 years; and limitations imposed by a top-down model of governance, a focus on training for employment at the expense of a wider education, and by political events in Fiji.

In his account of the road from Laucala Bay, Brij Lal revives the sense of liberation that accompanied the founding of USP. He writes:

> The opening of the University of the South Pacific was a monumental achievement in the modern history of the Pacific Islands, a genuine turning point, much like the impact of the Second World War, or the beginnings of decolonisation in the 1960s. It placed higher education within the reach of all school children who passed the appropriate exams with requisite marks, not only those who (or whose parents) could afford it, or the select few who went overseas on a small number of government scholarships.

Lal remembers new people and new ideas: lecturers such as Tony Chappell, Ron Crocombe and Ahmed Ali, fellow students such as Vijay Naidu, Jone Dakuvula, and Amelia Rokotuivuna, as well as writers who charted the Fiji Indian experience such as Ken Gillion and Raymond Pillay. Vanessa Griffin described the part-European experience and Albert Wendt raised disturbing questions about history and literature. USP in the 1970s was a crucible of fresh thinking about decolonisation, the place of the Pacific Islands in the wider world as well as key political issues such as French nuclear testing.

Balancing Tradition and Modernity

Gerard Ward, a distinguished geographer and the oldest of our contributors, visited three Fijian villages in 1958 and 1959—Saliadrau, Sote and Nabudrau—and returned there in 1983. During that time the population of Fiji had almost doubled. In the quarter century between these visits, thatch roofs and bamboo walls had given way to iron, timber and concrete, and many people had many material possessions. Roads had reached two of the villages and bananas as a cash crop had disappeared. At the same time the informality that had characterised relations between landowning *mataqali* (landowning group) and non-landowning villagers had yielded to more formal, legalised relationships as land grew more scarce and the commercial imperative grew stronger. Ward observed 'much greater variation in wealth and income within villages' and correctly predicted a loosening of the bonds between chiefs and commoners.

'*Matai* Titles and Modern Corruption in Samoa' gives Morgan Tuimaleali'ifano an opportunity to describe what happens when a *saofa'iga* (title installation ceremony) and the gifting that accompanies it 'is taken out of the public and into the private and individualised arena'. He does this through the lens of a ceremony in which a title was bestowed upon him and his family, showing the extent to which previously reciprocal exchanges are being reduced to the payment of cash and 'shameless public demands' for more cash are being made by the orators of the village. Capitalism, Tuimaleali'ifano tells us, is undermining the essence of the *fa'a Samoa*.

In 'Making Room for Magic in Intellectual Property Policy', Miranda Forsyth reminds us that the arid assumptions of the market economy are made even by those who wish, with the best of intentions, to recognise traditional knowledge in order to protect Pacific cultures against misappropriation. Whereas traditional knowledge is embedded in social relationships, modern Western knowledge has been reduced to purely economic and legal instruments that ignore this difference in dealing with intellectual property. Forsyth suggests ways of ameliorating this problem: by recognising the dynamic character of indigenous knowledge and innovation; by using vernacular languages in legal instruments to capture the 'different epistemological frameworks at play'; by using indigenous institutions to regulate traditional knowledge; and by taking account of the values inherent in that knowledge.

Politics and Political Economy

Politics, political institutions and diplomacy are the themes of our third section, which begins with a classic survey of Pacific political institutions by Jon Fraenkel. He points to the variety of ways in which Pacific Islanders have dealt with the eternal dilemmas of politics: how to accommodate ethnic diversity and other sources of conflict, adapt modern government to tradition, build states where none existed before, and provide for women's representation. Just as electoral systems vary throughout the region, so do the political systems that owe their origins to Westminster, Washington or Paris. And the relationships between island territories and metropolitan powers are diverse. As Fraenkel notes, 'In between the extremes of independence and incorporation, the Pacific Islands are host to a range of hybrid political arrangements between island territories and former colonial rulers'. At the same time, there are region-wide commonalities—in the weakness of political parties, for example, and the readiness of elected representatives to change sides.

A number of contributions place Fiji and the Fiji economy in the broader context of globalisation and the turn to neoliberalism in economic policy, both of which have affected Fiji profoundly since the late 1980s. At the height of international enthusiasm for neoliberal economic policy, the Pacific Islands, as Claire Slatter shows, were supposedly in need of firm management by the World Bank, the Asian Development Bank, aid donors and policy experts in order to shape up as competitors in the global economy. This broad issue of the place of small Pacific Island states in a globalised world is one that has occupied the intellectual energies of staff and students at USP over many years and continues to do so.

In her chapter on the Soqosoqo Duavata ni Lewenivanua (SDL) party's victory in the 2006 elections, Alumita Durutalo takes us to a moment in time that now seems remote: after the election, with Laisenia Qarase confirmed as prime minister, but before the coup that ushered in a newly dominant role for the Republic of Fiji Military Forces and its commander Frank Bainimarama. Back then it seemed as if the traditional appeal to indigenous Fijians of *vanua* (domains of chiefly rule and Fijian identity), *lotu* (the church) and *matanitu* (traditional government) in the election of a government had been reconfirmed and would continue to form the basis of political strategies by the parties—over the decades the Alliance, Soqosoqo ni Vakavulewa ni Taukei (SVT) and SDL—that had the support of the majority of iTaukei. Four out of every five iTaukei, after all, voted for the SDL in 2006, ensuring its success. But as Durutalo warned at the time, there was no guarantee that this formula for political victory would endure. And so it proved.

Reimagining

A key theme of this collection is the Pacific in the imagination, and the gap between image and reality in the region.

Tarcisius Tara Kabutaulaka examines it in his chapter on Melanesia. Notions of a ladder of evolutionary development deeply influenced the European way of looking at the Pacific Islanders. Europeans could recognise themselves in Polynesia, with its hierarchy, aristocracy and relatively large-scale political organisation. Some Polynesian island groups were on the way to becoming states already and their customs of respect based on rank seemed to mirror those of Europe. The Europeans had a similar reaction to Fiji, where Fijian chiefs quickly adapted to the service of the British colony established in 1874, becoming instruments of the new state structure. In the rest of Melanesia, however, the Europeans encountered a bewildering array of languages, senses of identity and communities, all on a small scale and none suited to be building blocks of coherent colonial administration. European notions of race, as Kabutaulaka emphasises, were fundamental in the way the Pacific Islanders came to be categorised and to the inferior place accorded to Melanesians in the Pacific racial hierarchy. The prejudice extended to gender and Kabutaulaka draws on the work of Margaret Jolly and Marata Tamaira to remind us that Europeans tended to depict Polynesian women as more attractive and alluring than Melanesian women. He sees Pacific Islanders as having internalised these European prejudices in their attitudes towards each other, with some Polynesians, for example, looking down upon Melanesians and Melanesians discriminating among themselves on the basis of skin colour. The argument Kabutaulaka brings us, though, runs counter to this history of denigration, because he sees a contemporary movement to embrace Melanesia in positive terms as the basis for a cultural and political reinvigoration.

Steven Ratuva finds another need for reimagining. He focuses on an issue that has been a lively source of debate in the classrooms of USP and that addresses a key question often raised by iTaukei students—namely, what accounts for the differential development of their community compared with that of others in Fiji, especially Fijians of Indian descent? Did British protection of the iTaukei community over the whole period of British colonial rule stifle their opportunities in the modern world and leave them behind at independence and beyond? Ratuva takes the case of Ratu Sir Lala Sukuna, the best-known indigenous Fijian of the 20th century and a man held up as an unqualified hero of the Fijian people to generations of iTaukei. His 'concerns and deeds', as he reminds us, 'were beyond reproach' in his time, but need to be reevaluated in the light of Fiji's history. With his deep attachment to chiefly Fiji and to keeping people in the village, Sukuna can now be seen, in Ratuva's view, as a conservative force standing in the way of the emergence of commoner Fijians into the modern world; his efforts to protect the iTaukei 'had the effect of disempowering and undermining their potential for progress' and kept them 'politically and culturally submissive'.

We need to reimagine Indo-Fijian history as well as iTaukei history. We tend to overlook the importance of Christian schools in the education of Fijians of Indian descent, yet as Christine Weir points out in her chapter on All Saints Primary School in Labasa, in the 1940s and 1950s almost a third of Indian children were attending Christian mission schools, Anglican, Methodist and Catholic. Not many converted to Christianity, but their parents liked the education these schools offered. They played their part in the rapid upward mobility of generations of Indo-Fijians, reflected also in their higher education at USP from the late 1960s.

Rethinking Development

In some parts of the Pacific, especially the small island states, development is almost synonymous with development assistance, which assumes an enormous importance in budgets and political calculations. In his chapter on 'Development Assistance Challenges', Vijay Naidu places the aid process in its wider economic and political context, emphasising the extent to which aid conditionalities are designed to remake Pacific Island economies in the service of market competitiveness. But Naidu goes further, setting the aid scene in the context of the years after September 11, when Western donors became keener than ever to ensure that aid served security purposes. The aid flows from Australia, New Zealand and the US to the Pacific Islands were 'geopolitical rent', he observes, paid to Island governments for the purpose of bringing stability and a pro-Western orientation to the region. Much the same still applies except for the rise of China, which has complicated the strategic calculations of longstanding Pacific partners such as Australia and New Zealand. Writing in 2006, Naidu saw China 'emerging as a major player in the region', one whose presence would be welcomed by Fiji. Twelve years later, we can see that Naidu was right. When USP opened in 1968, China was convulsed by its Cultural Revolution and played almost no part in Pacific affairs. Fifty years later, China is a presence to be reckoned with, above all through its investments, trade, tourism and thousands of new Chinese migrants, but also because of its highly visible soft loan and aid program. Naidu is also right to remind us of the strategic origins of development assistance, clearly on view in Australia's recent shift towards closer engagement with the region, an initiative driven by alarm in Canberra about the growth of China's influence.

Just as development has an international dimension, so it also has a domestic one. While the standard of living for many Fijian villagers had improved by the 1980s, rural development remained slow in the decades that followed. Writing in the wake of the 2006 coup, Joeli Veitayaki connects Fiji's succession of coups to a lack of rural development for indigenous Fijians. The discontent of rural iTaukei, he suggests, was a political resource seized upon by coup leaders who knew that the promise of a better life would bring iTaukei support. But the affirmative action policies of the 1990s and the early 2000s, introduced by indigenous Fijian governments, had few positive effects in the villages, where 'poor performance in rural development' remained. The main beneficiaries of affirmative action, he argues, were indigenous Fijian elites in a position to access these programs of assistance. The corollary is that genuine rural development will break Fiji's coup culture.

The most contested of all development resources in the Pacific Islands is land and in their chapter on urban land in Solomon Islands, Joseph Foukona and Matt Allen examine the complex interplay of law, the market, migration, squatter settlements and an ideology of customary land ownership in conflict with the law. Their conclusion is that, even after the long peace since the so-called 'Ethnic Tension' of 1998 to 2003, 'a spectre of ethnoterritorial violence' continues to hang over the city and that 'the formal rules governing land and property rights often bear little resemblance to on-the-ground realities', where issues of land ownership are determined by personal patronage networks and personalised politics. Just as legal claims to the land of Honiara have been contested since the 1920s, so that contestation will continue in a cultural framework that lends legitimacy to tradition.

Into the Future

In his classic commentary on Pacific regional identity, Epeli Hauʻofa offers USP as an example:

> In a very real sense the University of the South Pacific is a microcosm of the region, and many aspects of its history, which began in 1968 in the era of decolonisation of island territories, mirror the developments in the regional communities it serves. The well-known diversity of social organisations, economies, and cultures of the region is reflected in the student population that comprises people from all 12 countries that own the university, as well as a sprinkling from other regions.

Writing in the 1990s, Hauʻofa saw USP as the 'premier hatchery' of regional identity. He pleaded for the most expansive concept of this identity, one that would be genuinely postcolonial and independent:

> The issue of what or who is a Pacific Islander would not arise if we considered Oceania as comprising people as human beings with a common heritage and commitment, rather than as members of diverse nationalities and races. Oceania refers to a world of people connected to each other … As far as I am concerned, anyone who has lived in our region and is committed to Oceania is an Oceanian.

The single common heritage of all Oceanians is the sea itself, the same sea lapping on the shores of every Pacific Island country. Hauʻofa's call for an Oceanic identity remains more urgent than ever as the region faces a common and existential security threat in climate change. What is needed is new and more effective regional diplomacy.

This 'new Pacific diplomacy' is addressed by Greg Fry and Sandra Tarte. Fifty years ago only two Pacific Island countries were independent— Samoa and Nauru, with Cook Islands having moved into free association with New Zealand—and even the possibility of a distinctive Pacific diplomacy did not exist. And for decades afterwards, Pacific diplomacy on numerous issues from decolonisation to tuna fisheries and nuclear testing was refracted through an Australia/New Zealand lens, one that gave expression to Pacific Island interests within limits. Those limits were on display at the 1997 meeting of the then South Pacific Forum, when agreement on a weak statement on climate change as desired by Australia was reached in the face of concerted opposition from Pacific countries. Since then much has changed. The seas have begun to rise, the largest cyclones ever recorded have battered Pacific countries, and Pacific Islanders' concern about climate change has intensified. Driven by urgent national interests, Pacific Island states are taking the initiative on climate change without reference to Australia through groups such as the Pacific Islands Development Forum and the Pacific Small Island Developing States group at the UN.

Katerina Teaiwa takes us outside the Pacific to the Pacific diaspora in Australia, and specifically to the strikingly dominant participation of Pacific Islanders in sport, where 'it is the Pacific Islander male, and more specifically Polynesian male, who is the most visible'. In the Australian diaspora, Teaiwa notes that, 'participation in sport and popular culture is a particular area of visibility and success for Pacific peoples that holds great meaning for minority communities', and the links between *mana*, masculinity and sport become evident. The arena is one in which men can show their *mana*, defined as 'being strong, efficacious, prosperous, successful, having "status and prestige"' and performing mighty acts. These mighty Pacific sportsmen uplift whole communities of Pacific Islanders in a situation where 'I' is the same as 'we' and the individual can bring respect to the many.

The Afterword looks forward to the continuing and emerging Pacific contexts that will inform the teaching and research of the USP and ANU in the years ahead.

2

A Commentary on the 50-Year History of the University of the South Pacific

Vijay Naidu

Vijay Naidu: Personal Journey

For the past four decades I have been an engaged Pacific scholar and, during this time, I have read and been influenced by the work of some pioneering scholars from The Australian National University (ANU), worked closely with ANU colleagues, and enjoyed longstanding friendships with several who were at ANU at some point in their working lives.

My undergraduate class of 1971 at the University of the South Pacific (USP) included Brij Lal and Kesaia Seniloli (both of whom later completed their PhD studies at ANU, and Brij would later become a distinguished professor at ANU), Rajesh Chandra (former vice chancellor of USP), and Justice Daniel Fatiaki (former chief justice of Fiji and currently judge of the Supreme Court in Vanuatu). Among our lecturers in subsequent years were Professor Ron Crocombe and Dr Ahmed Ali, both of whom had ANU connections. Studying Pacific history and societies, Pacific Islands development and migration, and ethnicity in Fiji meant that from my undergraduate days I was exposed to the scholarly writings of Jim Davidson, E.K. Fisk, Gerry Ward, Harold Brookfield, Ken Gillion, Neil Gunson, Deryck Scarr, Dorothy Shineberg and Oskar Spate.

I worked closely with Professor Ron Crocombe as his tutor in the Advanced Pacific History course he taught at the third-year level. I owe my fortuitous entry into academia to him and Professor John Harre especially.

In addition to Brij Lal, other ANU scholars past and present with whom I have enjoyed friendship over the years, and/or whose work I have read and been influenced by, are Ahmed Ali, Stewart Firth, Greg Fry, William Sutherland, Ron Duncan, Ropate Qalo, Sandra Tarte, Scott MacWilliam, Stephanie Lawson, Katarina Teaiwa and Jon Fraenkel.

Research collaboration and attendance at seminars and conferences have resulted in a number of chapters in books published by ANU. David Hegarty, the former director of the State, Society and Governance in Melanesia program became a close associate and friend.

Introduction

The year 2018 marks the 50th anniversary year of the University of the South Pacific (USP)—a significant historic milestone and a proudly celebratory year. USP is one of two regional universities in the world, the other being the University of the West Indies (UWI). The notion of 'regional' has a specific meaning for these unique institutions as they are owned and financed by a number of small island states in a geographic region: the South Pacific for USP and the English-speaking Caribbean islands for UWI. Until 1991, USP had 11 member states. In that year, the Republic of Marshall Islands became the 12th member state and, with that milestone, the USP began serving the northern Pacific. Given the wide scatter of Pacific Island states in 'our sea of islands', the university serves a region spread over 33 million square kilometres of the Pacific Ocean. It is genuinely the University of Oceania. The significant and almost indispensable support of the United Kingdom, Australia and New Zealand, as well as other donor country assistance that USP has received since its birth in 1968, is acknowledged at the outset.

USP's 50th anniversary is worthy of the designated year-long celebration. It provides an opportunity for reflection on the institution's evolution, to flag its remarkable achievements and pay homage to those who have helped build it. It is also a time to think about contemporary issues and challenges that face the university and to peer into its future prospects and challenges in the coming decades. In the introduction of one of the commemoration books produced for the 25th anniversary of USP, the seminal *A New Oceania: Rediscovering Our Sea of Islands*, the then head of geography department, Professor Eric Waddell, remarked:

> On this our 25th anniversary we need not only celebrate our past but reflect on our future; set, if necessary, a new agenda, revise our goals. Is this not the real mission of the School of Social and Economic Development: to contribute to the designing of a Pacific future? (Waddell, Naidu and Hau'ofa 1993)

The mission of contributing to the design of a Pacific future should, in fact, be one for the university as a whole.

A Peace Dividend

Today USP has 14 campuses and 10 centres, with three campuses in Fiji and a campus each on the remaining 11 member states. As will be shown, student numbers have increased several thousand fold. However, it all began on the grounds and buildings of the former Royal New Zealand Airforce (RNZAF) base in Laucala Bay in Suva. The end of the Pacific war, the last theatre of war in the Second World War, meant that New Zealand and its allies did not need the base anymore. The idea of a regional university in vogue at that time coincided with the availability of more than 70 hectares of undulating land from the coast to the crest of the Muanikau hills. The British colonial government of Fiji agreed to make the land and all its buildings and facilities, including the largest wooden aircraft hangar in the southern hemisphere and a swimming pool, available for the new university. This peace dividend became the site of the headquarters of the USP, the premier higher education centre for the region and the cradle of the regional anti-nuclear and independent Pacific movement, building the campaign against nuclear weapons testing in French Polynesia and, later, the nursery for independence and pro-democracy movements.

Brief History

The history of USP and some of its achievements in the first two-and-a-half decades of its existence are well covered in the book *Pacific Universities: Achievements, Problems, Prospects* written by former staff of the university (Crocombe and Meleisea 1988), and the 25th anniversary publication

A Garland of Achievement (USP 1993). The first substantive vice chancellor of the university, the late Dr Colin Aikman, who served USP from 1968 to 1974, wrote in the latter book, 'We set out to turn a dilapidated flying boat base at Laucala Bay into the campus of a viable regional university', constructing university buildings and facilities in member countries. Dr Aikman justified USP's establishment on the grounds that students from the regional university would return to serve their countries upon graduation, and contribute to social and economic development. He went on to say:

> Everywhere you look in the region USP graduates have prominent positions in government, in education and in other walks of life. There is, too, the USP 'mafia'—the USP graduates throughout the South Pacific who maintain valuable contacts with one another (Aikman 1993:5).

The university has been contributing to the creation and growth of a pan-Pacific identity through its students becoming more aware of the wider USP region, and that Oceania has shared histories and cultures as well as common challenges and possibilities. As noted by the late Professor Epeli Hau'ofa, there is considerable scope for enhancing both this supra-national identity and solidarity.

In his introduction to USP's 1999 Annual Report, the university's fifth vice chancellor and the first 'regional' person at the helm, Esekia Solofa succinctly summarised the university's growth:

> The development of USP since its formal constitution by charter in 1970 saw the 70s decade as a period of building and establishment, followed in the eighties by a period of rationalization and consolidation. USP had come of age by the end of the eighties. It entered its third decade with youthful zest and confidence, ready to tackle the various challenges facing the development of its member countries and the region, through the provision of higher education. The nineties saw considerable expansion in the university as areas of study widened and new programmes were added; as support services were upgraded and new innovations introduced in their operation; as total enrolments grew, new buildings [were] constructed, and more staff recruited (Solofa 2000:1).

The first 19 years of the new millennium have seen the continued expansion of buildings and facilities on nearly all campuses and centres of the university, as well as a growth in student numbers in virtually all modes of undergraduate studies and in postgraduate enrolments. Of special significance is the Japan–Pacific Information and Communications Technology (ICT) Centre, which houses the university's ICT hub, and a large multipurpose lecture theatre as well as conference, IT labs and office facilities. Former vice chancellor Savenaca Siwatibau (2001–03) began the negotiations towards having this complex built. This edifice is an addition to previously built structures such as the library, the Japanese-funded Marine Studies complex on the 'lower campus' at Laucala, and the Australian-funded lecture theatres on the 'upper campus'. All these facilities, together with the three faculty buildings, enhance the university's modern outlook and complexity. Visiting USP alumni bringing their children to enrol have been heard to remark that they no longer recognise the campus because of this transformation.

New buildings and campus upgrades have been completed in regional campuses and centres, although progress has been uneven. Kiribati, Marshall Islands and Nauru have been the most recent sites of expanded facilities. A major new campus is planned for the Solomon Islands where the new School of Public Health will be located. The state of the present Honiara campus leaves much to be desired.

Noteworthy too are the efforts by the university to continuously upgrade its ICT facilities and the USPNet that links the campuses and centres. This is vital both for communication and exchange of data. Professor Rajesh Chandra, the former vice chancellor and president of USP, can be credited for his push to make the university's ICT facilities among the best in the South Pacific, and for the leap forward to online teaching and learning.

The university's development has not all been rosy. It has coped reasonably well with the demands of 12 member states, and their changing human resources needs, along with addressing difficult financial and resource constraints. External factors such as relative stagnant economies of member states, and in particular political instability and military coups in Fiji and the 'tensions' in the Solomon Islands, have affected the university. The Fiji coups of 1987, 2000 and 2006 have been especially disruptive as they increased the sense of insecurity among staff and students. The presence of armed soldiers of the Republic of Fiji Military Forces on Laucala campus, and the detention and torture of academics after the 1987 coups, traumatised the university community. In the Solomon Islands, the fighting in Guadalcanal and the overthrow of government in 2000 accompanied by lawlessness not only disrupted the lives of most Islanders but particularly affected schools and tertiary institutions, including USP's Honiara campus and the Institute of Marine Resources on Guadalcanal.

The late Geoffrey Caston, USP's fourth vice chancellor (1983–92) stood steadfast in keeping the university open during the unprecedented period of instability in 1987. He declared that the university was 'involved now in the defence of a bridgehead for our values' (Caston 1987:5) and, in the trying circumstances of military dictatorship, sought to keep alive academic freedom. His successor, Esekia Solofa (1992–2001), identified another significant role for the university. In 1993 he opened the first national dialogue in Fiji between political and civil society leaders to address the constitutional crisis in the country. The event was organised by the Citizens Constitutional Forum (CCF). He said the university campus should always be an open and 'safe space' to dialogue on matters of serious national importance for member countries (CCF 1993:1). The University Council considered whether to spread more of the university 'real estate' across other member countries to reduce the risks posed by political turmoil in any one country. There was talk about relocating the university headquarters from Fiji to another member state.

University staff and students were further traumatised by the ethnically motivated insurrection of May 2000 led by George Speight and his group against the Fiji Labour Party–led government of Mahendra Pal Chaudhry. Chaudhry and the government ministers and backbenchers were taken hostage for 56 days, during which time there were periods of 'mob rule' in parts of the country. Schools and the university opened and closed depending on rumours about gangs of rebels heading towards Suva's central business district or to the campus. Academic freedom was seriously compromised when the university administration decided to shut down the website of its journalism students' newspaper *Wansolwara*, which provided excellent coverage of the unfolding political instability and the military coup, on 29 May 2000 because of 'security reasons' (Robie 2000).

Following the December 2006 coup, the university became somewhat complicit in gagging academic staff from openly criticising government policies, and eventually compelled a leading economics professor to relinquish his position. The university also adopted a policy that sets out to restrict staff from communicating directly to the media. This restriction is accompanied by another prohibition that seriously compromises the governance of the university; staff have been prohibited from communicating with members of the University Council and its Chair if they have complaints and grievances that remain unresolved through normal university processes. Complaints about the vice chancellor and president need to be made to the vice chancellor and not to Council.

In short, even though USP continues to pay lip-service to its commitment of academic freedom, the political environment in Fiji has made the university not particularly enthusiastic about promoting healthy debates and discussions about Fiji politics, economy and government policies.

USP Member States

The 12 member states of USP are Cook Islands, Fiji, Kiribati, Marshall Islands, Nauru, Niue, Samoa, Solomon Islands, Tokelau, Tonga, Tuvalu and Vanuatu. As co-owners of the university, their representatives sit in the USP Council together with representatives of donor countries, university officials and academics. The council makes policy decisions as well as deciding matters relating to university finance, the appointment of the chancellor, pro-chancellor and vice chancellor. As in other universities that follow the British model, the chancellor is the symbolic head of the institution. The position is rotated each year among the heads of state of USP member countries. Up to the end of June 2018, the President of the Republic of Fiji was the Chancellor. The current Chancellor is the President of the Republic of Kiribati, Taneti Maamau.

The new chancellor, USP's 25th, is His Excellency Taneti Maamau, the President of the Republic of Kiribati. The pro-chancellor is elected by council and has the responsibility of chairing university council meetings. The vice chancellor and president (the nomenclature 'president' is a recent addition to the vice chancellor title) is the principal head of the university and is responsible for the daily operation of the institution. On completion of the eighth Vice Chancellor Professor Rajesh Chandra's term (2007–18), the position was filled by Professor Pal Ahluwalia who had previously been Pro-Vice Chancellor Research and Innovation at the University of Portsmouth in England.

Member states of the university contribute to its funding based on a formula that seeks to apportion financial subventions according to the benefits that accrue to each member state. As Fiji has the largest campus, it has most of the students, its citizens form the biggest pool of employees, it is the largest recipient of USP tax revenue, and it has historically been the largest contributor. Other sources of funding include student fees and donor contributions, both of which have increased significantly in recent years.

Like other Council of Regional Organisations in the Pacific (CROP) member agency boards, the USP Council has tended to rubber stamp the policies that the head of organisation and the senior management team have proposed. They also tend to listen and accede to advice by non-member state and donor country representatives. In recent years, this tendency has become more marked, and especially disturbing is the relative passivity of representatives of member states in contrast to the active role played by Australia and New Zealand representatives. As aid from the latter countries to the university has increased, there has been a parallel increase in how much say they have in the affairs of the university. Australia and New Zealand government representatives who have been university vice chancellors have sought to make USP in the image of their own universities. This approach has eroded the unique and special features of USP's regional and Pacific character (see Naidu 2004 for further discussion on seeking equality of partnership between aid donors and recipients citing USP as an example). The path taken by USP, like so many other universities, has been to focus on making and/ or saving money, becoming accredited or ranked, rather than fulfilling its educational objectives. Issues related to this trend will be addressed under some of the sub-headings below.

USP's Reach as a Regional University

As mentioned earlier, the member states of the university are spread over a huge expanse of the Pacific Ocean, posing daunting challenges of communication and transportation.

University campuses are located in each one of these countries' capitals, and in some instances there are university centres in the outer islands— as in the case of Vanuatu, which has four such centres. Besides Laucala campus, which has the university's three faculties—Faculty of Arts, Law and Education, Faculty of Business and Economics and Faculty of Science, Technology and Environment—there are two other large campuses. These are Alafua campus in Apia, Sāmoa, which is the home of the School of Agriculture and Food Technology and the Institute of Research, Extension and Training in Agriculture (IRETA); and the Emalus campus in Port Vila, Vanuatu, where the School of Law and the Pacific Languages Unit are located. Fiji hosts two other campuses in Lautoka and Labasa.

Almost from its very inception the university set out to be the higher education institution for the region by progressively establishing university centres for distance learning and teaching in all its member states. USP has been recognised as a world leader in the use of satellite communication (initially, the Pan-Pacific Education and Communication Experiments by Satellite program, or PEACESAT) in connecting these centres to Laucala campus. Over some three decades, distance and flexible learning was provided with the use of print materials and visits by mainly Suva-based tutors. Given the tyranny of distance and associated transportation of mail bags, the university overcame considerable challenges in the delivery and receipt of course materials, assignments, test papers and examination scripts.

Since the advent of computers and the internet, the university has adopted the use of online facilities for teaching and learning. Serious challenges do remain because of the relative paucity of privately owned computers, computer lab facilities and internet access or connectivity issues in some of the member states. In these countries there are also infrastructural limitations (such as bandwidth) and regulatory bottlenecks. Students in countries outside of Fiji struggle to access course materials and related resources. Online teaching of courses has increased staff workloads as many staff also teach the same courses face-to-face, and there are challenges regarding coordination of teaching and learning with numerous tutors and markers across member states. The availability of lecture slides on the internet has also meant that, in some courses, student attendance in face-to-face classes has significantly dropped.

The University Library

As in the case of regional centres and campuses, the university recognised from the beginning that having a good library was pivotal to learning, teaching and research. University librarians, Esther Williams, Sin Joan Yee and Elizabeth Reade-Fong and their staff, have been at the forefront of establishing a world-class library. The university library has grown in tandem with the university, with state of arts facilities and thousands of books and hundreds of journals. With the IT revolution, it has become the information hub for students, staff and the wider public alike. Library staff have also offered courses and programs of study in librarianship and related information technology. The main USP library has digitised collections and subscribes to search engines that allow wide access to scholarly journals. This library is also linked to and facilitates other libraries in the 15 campuses. The Pacific Islands Marine Resources Information System is based in the marine studies complex, but is part of a network of libraries and information centres of regional organisations and government departments involved in fisheries and marine resource work.

Besides the special collection of books, journals and writings on the Pacific in the Pacific Collection of the USP Library, the university also has the South Pacific Regional Herbarium and Biodiversity Centre, which has thousands of Fiji and Pacific plant materials in its care. The university's School of Law (Emalus campus, Port Vila) established the Pacific Islands Legal Information Institute (PacLII) so that students from across the region could have easier access to legal materials. It is now used by governments, non-government organisations, legal scholars and professionals, students and members of the public—and is seen as an example of excellence for providing legal information.

Institutes and Centres

The university has been changing its form and component structures together with some of its functions over the years. A good illustration of such changes is the creation and phasing out of institutes and centres. The flamboyant second vice chancellor of USP (1975–82) was Dr James Maraj, a Trinidadian and former head of the Commonwealth of Learning, who created a number of institutes and centres to enhance the university's research and consultancy activities. These were the Institute of Pacific Studies (IPS), the Institute of Applied Sciences (IAS), the Institute of Education (IOE), the Institute of Marine Resources (IMR), the Institute of Research, Extension and Training in Agriculture (IRETA) and the Institute of Social and Administrative Studies. These institutes were linked to the schools of the university. A Centre for Applied Studies in Development, a Centre for Appropriate Technology and Development and an Atoll Research Centre were also established, but none of the centres proved viable and were disbanded. Of the six institutes, only four have variously survived: the IAS, IMR, IOE and IRETA. The Pacific Institute of Advanced Studies in Development and Governance was also short-lived. The Pacific Centre for Environment and Sustainable Development (PaCE-SD), a relative newcomer, has become a dynamic hub of postgraduate research and advocacy on climate change, aided by a healthy boost of funding and a passionate director.

A major challenge to self-funded entities such as these centres and institutes has been the capacity of member state governments, businesses and civil society organisations to pay for services rendered. Generally speaking, international financial institutions and other multilateral agencies, including the UN system, have opted to use the services of Australian and New Zealand institutions and companies to do work in Pacific Island countries (PICs).

USP Restructuring

Among the variety of changes that the university has undergone are those that have strengthened its teaching and research capabilities and those that have detracted from these core functions. USP began 50 years ago with three interdisciplinary schools. While there were recognised disciplines, the objective was to promote interdisciplinary and multidisciplinary teaching and research. Ten years on from this orientation and thanks to senior academics who came from 'traditional universities', departments emerged with their own heads and the rise of separate silos. The schools continued to exist (two with name changes) and did try to encompass the earlier objective of cross-disciplinary work. This model existed until the new millennium. From the early 2000s, the schools were replaced by faculties: Arts, Law and Education; Business and Economics; and Science, Technology and Environment. Each of these faculties are led by a dean.

The Pacific Technical and Further Education (Pacific TAFE) has been recently added to provide vocational programs and has incorporated the university's pre-degree foundation programs.

A marked shift in the processes of decision-making and the relative size and influence of administrative units of the university has accompanied this restructure. Academic staff including professors have little say in policy decisions because the former school boards of study have been abolished and executive power resides in the office of deans and in the vice chancellor and president's office. The latter position has considerable power bestowed on it and, in many ways, the senior management team has become the main decision-making body of the university. The University Senate, the apex academic forum is a shadow of what it had been before the restructure. The trend has been towards top-down management.

The restructure also phased out the internationally renowned Institute of Pacific Studies (IPS), which published the largest number of works of Pacific Islanders and virtually on all Pacific Island countries, and the region as a whole. IPS was replaced by the poorly resourced USP Press.

University Staff

USP is home to the largest pool of well-qualified academics in the South Pacific Islands. In 1969 there were 31 academic staff, today there are over 300. In the very early years of the university, a majority of the senior staff including the vice chancellor, registrar and heads of schools and professors came from New Zealand. Very quickly, however, the mix of nationalities became more diverse with Australians, British, Americans (including Peace Corps volunteers, and former volunteers), Canadians, Indians, Cook Islanders, Fijians, iKiribati, Samoans and Tongans joining as academics and administrators. This mix was further enhanced with Solomon Islanders, Ni-Vans, Niueans, Tuvaluans, Africans and other nationalities. Indeed, it was noted at a conference in the mid-1990s in Melbourne on the internationalisation of education, that USP was only second to the University of Singapore in its openness to recruiting academics internationally. By this stage, the university comprised staff from more than 30 nationalities (Naidu 1997).

A major challenge for the university, however, has been the recruitment and retention of quality staff, both regional and foreign, male and female. USP emoluments have never been competitive with those offered in neighbouring Australia and New Zealand. With the adoption of more market-based policies and the removal of subsidies in housing and other support, the university has not been able to attract and retain good-quality mid-career academics, let alone those who are at the top of their career. Various incentives and inducements have generally failed to entice staff for the long haul, especially from Australia, New Zealand and United Kingdom. There has been an increasing reliance on shorter term appointments of retired expatriate professors, and academics from South Asia.

With some exceptions, even well-qualified regional staff from USP member states have not continued their employment with the university. The reasons for this lack of stability in staffing according to Sarojini Pillay, a former registrar, have been 'insecurity inherent in a contract system, national immigration policies, high taxation, lack of competitiveness of USP salaries with those overseas and few employment opportunities for spouses'(1993:92). The longstanding three-year contracts did not help either. Although Fiji's direct personal taxation is now below the international average, USP's emoluments remain uncompetitive, and there are extremely limited opportunities for spouses of expatriate staff to be gainfully employed.

The university has recently moved towards offering five-year contracts to a few selected academic staff, but it has continued to refuse to institute tenure, despite tenure being a standard practice in comparative universities that USP benchmarks itself against. It is unsurprising, given USP terms and conditions of employment, that academic staff numbers have declined in recent years whilst student numbers have increased. In 2016 there were 425 academic staff but in 2017, that number had declined to 332 staff (USP 2017:22). It is also of concern that fewer quality appointments are being made at the professorial and associate professorial levels. Senior academic staff (senior lecturers, associate professors and professors), as a proportion of the staff establishment, have decreased from the envisaged 40 per cent to 35 per cent; tutors, teaching assistants, assistant lecturers and lecturers now predominate (statistics derived from USP annual reports up to 2017 and earlier staff policy documents). USP's current staff–student ratios are largely at variance with internationally accepted ratios for quality teaching and learning.

Meanwhile, USP's glossy annual reports have been winning prizes for corporate annual reports.

Students: A Home Away from Home and a Place of Diversity

The university began with a little over 150 students mainly in pre-university level, Preliminary 1 (form 6 equivalent) and Preliminary 2 (form 7 equivalent) programs. In 1969, of the 249 students, only 12 per cent were in degree studies, but by 1974 the situation had changed with almost 37 per cent of the 981 students undertaking degree studies, and a further 36 per cent enrolled in Diploma in Education programs (Aikman 1988:41). By 1993, student numbers had increased to 8,000, and by 1999 to a little more than 10,000. In 2017, the number was close to 30,000 with almost equal numbers studying in the face-to-face mode as in distant and flexible modes.

The students are mainly from member countries with Fijian students comprising over 70 per cent and other country student numbers reflecting their relative population size. The Solomon Islands, for instance, has the next highest number. Diversity is the hallmark of the student body. To begin with, students from the member states represent the geographical and supposed cultural regions of Melanesia, Polynesia and Micronesia, and bring with them considerable cultural diversity. However Solomon Islander, ni-Vanuatu and Fijian students are the most culturally diverse. The cosmopolitan nature of the larger campuses are added to by international students from Australia, New Zealand, Canada, the United States of America, Europe, China, India, Japan, Korea and African countries, as well as countries of the Caribbean region such as Barbados, Belize, Guyana, Jamaica and Trinidad, who come under exchange schemes. International students make up less than 5 per cent of the USP student body.

There is relative gender parity in student numbers, and in recent years there have been more women graduates than men. Women are also taking up studies in those disciplines that have long been dominated by men, such as engineering and physics. Students have generally got on well and in the larger campuses of Laucala, Alafua and Emalus, regional students feel at home because of similarities in cultures and the relationships that they have with each other and with staff members.

Over the last five decades, the university has produced more than 50,000 graduates and certificate and diploma holders. It has also trained hundreds of Islanders in shorter training programs to build capacity in the public services of member states. Among its graduates, the university can count presidents and prime ministers of PICs, members of parliament, ministers of state, diplomats, senior public servants, teachers, lawyers, engineers, economists and social scientists, chemists, biologists, accountants, medical doctors, physicists and energy experts, regional and international bureaucrats, academics and researchers. In virtually every regional organisation and forum, it is inevitable these days to come into contact with USP alumni.

Having contributed enormously to the human resource needs of member states from the 1990s onwards, the university began to pay increasing attention to postgraduate programs of study and research degrees. It also sought to enhance its profile as a centre of research excellence in all aspects of the Pacific. Postgraduate diplomas, course work–based masters qualifications as well as research degrees at the masters and doctoral levels have emerged over the last three decades. These are both discipline-based (for example, MSc in Chemistry, MA in Education and MCom in Economics) and interdisciplinary. These latter programs of study include development studies, environmental studies, marine studies, tourism studies, and Pacific studies. The Graduate School of Business has been offering diplomas and the MBA degree in business-related specialisms. There are more than 1,000 successfully completed masters and doctoral dissertations (932 masters and 92 PhDs) in the university library's care.

While the spirit of volunteerism appears to have died among the elected officials of the USP Student Association, who pay themselves fortnightly stipends and sitting allowances for every council and committee meetings they attend, other students volunteer their services for charitable causes and for humanitarian relief and rehabilitation work after natural disasters. The long history and shared experiences of such volunteer efforts provide another basis for solidarity and the formation of an Oceanic identity.

Remembering the Ancestors

At every commemorative event in Oceania, the ancestors are acknowledged and homage is paid to them. Scores of staff—from those holding academic leadership positions to those responsible for secretarial support, maintaining the grounds of campuses and the cleaning and maintenance of facilities—have helped the university thrive. A good number have passed on. It is impossible to name all the people who have made USP prosper, but a few more prominent persons can be mentioned beginning with those at the helm. Former vice chancellors Colin Aikman, James Maraj, Frank Brosnahan and Savenaca Siwatibau who started the building of the university and contributed immensely to its growth have passed away but their legacies remain. For example, the negotiations for the construction of the Japan–Pacific ICT centre began with Mr Siwatibau.

Vice chancellors Esekia Solofa and Rajesh Chandra have also overseen the consolidation and further expansion of the university. Among academics, the late Dr Ahmed Ali, Dr Uday Raj, Dr Alfred Liligeto, Dr Ajit Singh, Dr Prem Prasad, Dr William Kenchington, Professor Ron Crocombe, Professor Epeli Hauʻofa, Professor William Clark, Mr Tony Chappell, Mr Simione Durutalo, Dr Sadaquat Ali, Dr Michael Davis, Mr Lionel Gibson, Mr Kisor Chetty, Mrs Barbara Hauʻofa, Professor Asesela Ravuvu, Professor Bob Hughes, Professor Bob Briscoe, Professor Michael White and Professor William Aalbersberg taught and supervised generations of students and enhanced the reputation of the university through their research, writing and leadership. Their remarkable achievements have been paralleled by those of Professors Albert Wendt, Wadan Narsey, Patrick Nunn, Subramani, Subramaniam Sootheswaran, Konaiholeva Thaman and Randy Thaman.

To the list of distinguished scholars could be added the names of Professors Eric Waddell, John Morrison and Stewart Firth, as well as Dr Claire Slatter. Professor Crosbie (Croz) Walsh has been a dynamic teacher and researcher who inspired several cohorts of students in geography and development studies. Professor John Harre, who continues to be active in higher education circles, was known as a brilliant teacher and someone who inspired so many students to do well in their studies. The late Dr June Cook who specialised in European history inspired Professor Brij Lal to take up history and to become the most prominent scholar among the graduates of the university. Now retired from The Australian National University (ANU), Brij Lal has distinguished himself as a leading Pacific historian.

Other scholars and administrators who have contributed in their disciplinary and specialist areas of work include Dr Howard van Trease, Dr Clare Mathewson, Dr Richard Wah, Dr William Sutherland, Dr Surend Prasad, Associate Professor Greg Fry, Professor Biman Prasad, Professor Don Patterson, Marjorie Crocombe, Professor John Lynch, Professor David Harrison, Professor Robbie Robertson, Professor Robin South, Professor Nii-K Plange, Dr Kesaia Seniloli, Dr Martin Baker, Dr Ganesh Chand, Pio Manoa, Philip Rama, Sarojini Pillay, Seona Smiles, Dr Gunu Pillai, Professor Srinivasiah Muralidhar, Sundari Muralidhar, Paddy O'Sullivan, Filimoni Fifita, Lilly Vesikula, Tito Isala, Walter Frazer, Mela Vusoniwailala, Lillian May, Lillian Bing, Associate Professor Morgan Tuimaleali'ifano, Eileen Tuimaleali'ifano, Associate Professor Joeli Veitayaki, Professor Malama Meleisea and Professor Penelope Schoffel.

A Beautiful Cemetery

In *A Garland of Achievement*, Professor Epeli Hau'ofa, who led the Department of Sociology and the School of Social and Economic Development and then became the founder and iconic Director of the Oceania Centre for Arts and Culture, referred to the university's Laucala campus as a 'beautiful cemetery'. He said, 'The university is a beautiful cemetery—an intellectual cemetery. There is nothing on culture and the larger issues about where we are going' (1993:81–82). This perception emerged from his observation of the sharp contrast of Laucala campus before the 1987 coup and following the coup. Before the military overthrow of the month-long Fiji Labour Party Government led by Dr Timoci Bavadra, the campus had been a reflection of the changes taking place in the region as countries gained their independence. There was cultural ferment reflected in creative writing of poetry and plays, as well as other writing that related to 'our identity and to important social and political issues' (ibid.).

The post-coup interim government's free market system orientation and the end of the cold war had serious consequences for the university:

> Other things, like training for management and computing and accounting were even more emphasized. I think that had more damaging effect on intellectualism ... than the coup itself ... Talking about larger issues of social concern became of little value (ibid.).

There is much truth in what Epeli Hau'ofa observed regarding intellectual life of the university before and after 1987. In one sense, USP's redirection to business studies and computing was a response to the human resource demands of member countries in the throes of globalisation—the coup and its 'free market' aftermath possibly expedited the process.

While the Laucala campus has not returned to the cultural ferment of USP's first 20 years, a number of sparks of intellectual and cultural life have reemerged. Generally, public lectures and seminars on all kinds of subjects are being held almost on a daily basis in the schools and faculties on Laucala campus. Particular entities and schools have been especially active, including the now-named Oceania Centre for Arts, Culture and Pacific Studies. This centre has continued Hau'ofa's legacy of keeping an open door for people to show and enhance their potential as artists without any formal academic training or accreditation. The teaching of Pacific cultures and societies continues in Pacific Studies, and the centre has gained renown for its visual, music and performing arts, which combine Pacific cultural themes with modern designs, choreography and rhythms. Hau'ofa had himself sought new forms of creativity and fusion of old and new.

USP has also introduced four general courses that are compulsory for all undergraduate students. Two of these courses seek to inculcate language, research and computer literacy. More significantly, two other courses introduce wider social and political issues that Hau'ofa was so dismayed were no longer being addressed. At the second-year level, these courses cover cultural, historical, environmental, social and political changes in Pacific Island countries and the region, as well as ethics and governance more broadly. The latter courses are designed to generate greater awareness among all students about Pacific issues and the importance of ethics in all aspects of their lives. In the Schools of Social Sciences and Government, Development and International Affairs, teaching and learning as well as research and outreach are centred on political, economic, social and psychological issues in Oceania and more globally.

Since the 1990s, environmental changes have become much more significant with atoll states facing existentialist threats from rising sea levels, and all countries of the region increasingly subject to extreme weather events. PaCE-SD has been playing a leading role in postgraduate training, research and advocacy relating to climate change. This vanguard role has also seen the birth of 'Pacific Climate Warriors 350' formed by, among others, graduates of PaCE-SD. The Schools of Marine Studies and Geography, Earth Science and Environment have also taken up the challenge to teach and research on marine resource management, oceanic changes, terrestrial resources and environmental concerns.

The School of Language, Arts and Media has been active in not only teaching literature and language, but also producing a range of creative writing including poetry and short stories. The media component of the school continues to teach crucially important journalism courses. Journalism students continue to practice their knowledge and skills in the production of their newspaper *Wansolwara*, which addresses topical matters inside and outside the university.

The Faculty of Science, Technology and Environment has actively researched renewable energy, including a 'wave solar energy harvesting device', wind turbine engineering and a mobile cane for blind and visually impaired persons, with patents registered for the energy-harvesting device and the mobile cane. At the School of Agriculture and Food Technology, experiments in more climate-resilient crops and livestock breeds have been undertaken with some positive results.

While the student body as a whole has been fairly dormant for several years and has continuing governance issues, the Marshall Islands Students Association (MISA) has in the last few years taken up the cudgels for environmental and social justice for their country, Micronesia and Oceania as a whole because of the ongoing effects of radioactive fallout from nuclear weapons testing by the United States. MISA has rekindled awareness and interest in the nuclear tests and their consequences for health and other impacts, as well as the 'dome' on Runit Island where, as sea levels rise, the release of radioactive materials into the sea will have an impact on the Pacific Ocean.

Social and political justice is also sought by some staff and students for West Papua. Human rights violations by Indonesia security forces are monitored and shared via social media. Periodic talks and updates are held on the struggle for self-determination in that occupied country, with visiting West Papuans providing the most recent information regarding the experiences of the indigenous people there.

The courage of a handful of individual academics to speak up on social and political issues during periods of media censorship and other restrictions should also be acknowledged. They have maintained the longstanding ethos of any self-respecting university as the critic and conscience of society. Epeli Hauʻofa would have been proud of them as they challenge his perception that Laucala campus had become a beautiful cemetery.

The Future

In his message on the silver jubilee of the university, the then vice chancellor Esekia Solofa acknowledged and honoured the achievement and contributions of staff and students, and said among other things that:

> The University's role is essentially to assist in the development of its member countries. To do that properly, the University as a matter of necessity must have their support … The next 25 years will see the demands of the region and the needs of the communities grow in complexity and sophistication. Many problems that now exist will remain, and there will be new obstacles and barriers to overcome. The University will need to be more dynamic,

innovative and creative in its responses. The successes of the past could not have been possible without the active support of member countries. The future should not be any different (Solofa 1993:3–4).

However, the support of the member states of the university in the coming 25 years is not so assured by what has transpired in some member states, and globally in recent times.

New Universities

Fifty years ago there was no university in USP member countries (the University of Papua New Guinea was established in 1965) and USP upon its establishment in 1968 became the very first such institution for its 12 owning states, and the second such institution for all of Oceania, south of the equator. As universities are often seen as national symbols (like the national flag and airline), three member states have established their own universities in the last 25 years: the National University of Samoa, Fiji National University and Solomon Islands National University. These universities have become the priority consideration for their respective governments and it is likely that over time the support for the regional university may decline when it comes to tough decisions about funding. Indeed, in recent years, the funding from member states to USP has been relatively stagnant when compared to revenue raised in student fees, donor country contributions and other sources of income.

While the support of USP member states will remain crucial, the university has been compelled to seek alternative and complementary revenue streams. This has been most challenging given that per-capita income of member states together on average is still below US$5,000. Student fees have been regularly raised and with the emergence of the new universities (in Fiji there are four universities now), the question of fees is increasingly competitive. Some revenue is generated from commissioned research and consultancies. This area has potential for further growth but competitors for commissioned research and consultancy work come from better resourced Pacific-rim countries, particularly Australia and New Zealand. The Pacific TAFE appears to be doing well in providing vocational certificates and diplomas at the pre-degree level. USP can also seek to become the regional higher education centre of excellence in postgraduate teaching and research. This will be in accord with its efforts to promote a research culture in the institution.

Australia and New Zealand have been the largest donors and source of support for the university. Their funding support to USP has increased over time and, in recent years, there has been a greater reliance on aid funds for recurrent expenditure. As mentioned earlier, both Australia and New Zealand have representatives in the University Council, and they have become increasingly influential in the affairs of the institution. This trend has affected to some extent the ethos of USP. Instead of promoting Pacific values, epistemologies and ontologies, there has been a tendency to become like any other internationally recognised university desperately trying to get into the international university league table. A side effect of this trend has been a pronounced disdain for publishing its own books and journals that seek to serve member states and promote not only Pacific cultures and values, but also Pacific interests. This attitude must change if the unique character of USP is to be maintained and enhanced.

Besides budgetary issues, the other major and related challenge is the recruitment and retention of quality staff. Without attractive terms and conditions that will draw good academics to USP and make them want to stay for more than one contract, the university's future as a quality institution will be bleak. Very positively, after almost 50 years of employing academics on three-year contracts, the university is at last moving to five-year contracts. However, there is still no tenure track. The university has also abandoned its formerly effective staff development program of sending especially bright young staff for PhD studies abroad, often relying on scholarships and fellowships provided by donor countries and international organisations such as the Commonwealth. Today most young staff at the university struggle to complete their postgraduate studies as they carry disproportionately heavy teaching and marking loads. Additional extra workload comes from vacancies at senior levels remaining unfilled for long periods. This is most ironic because a good number of the senior regional academics at USP only obtained their PhDs through its staff development program.

Conclusion

Universities are expensive entities to establish and operate successfully. Over the last 50 years, a set of favourable circumstances beginning with the peace dividend of the former RNZAF base, member state support, donor funding, growing student numbers and dedicated staff have made USP a successful institution and an asset of the people and governments of Oceania. The university has been on top of its game by being a regional university of and for Oceania and by responding creatively to the changing demands in higher education and research in the region. It has had a long head start compared to its national-based counterparts, and has an incomparably superior reputation, at the heart of which are the achievements of its academic staff and students. The restructure of the institution has had negative consequences for academic staff who carry out the primary functions of teaching and research, but decision-making processes can be reviewed and corrected.

However, two longstanding hurdles will continue to affect USP: its funding and its capacity to recruit and retain quality staff. The major challenge for the university at this point in its history is to closely reexamine its core business of teaching and learning, research and community outreach in the context of Pacific realities, needs and interests.

References

Aikman, C. 1988. Establishment 1968–74. In Crocombe, R and M. Meleisea (eds), *Pacific Universities: Achievements, Problems, Prospects*. Suva: Institute of Pacific Studies, University of the South Pacific, 35–52.

Aikman, C. 1993. Of Bricks and Mortar. In *A Garland of Achievement: 25 Years of Learning and Serving Together. The University of the South Pacific 1968–1993*. Suva: University of the South Pacific, 5–6.

Caston, G. 1987. Address to Students and Staff of the University of the South Pacific, Suva, 30 June (in author's possession).

Caston, G. 1988. Consolidation. In Crocombe, R. and M. Meleisea (eds), *Pacific Universities: Achievements, Problems, Prospects*. Suva: Institute of Pacific Studies, University of the South Pacific, 75–96.

Citizens Constitutional Forum (CCF) 1993. The Vice Chancellor's Address. In *Report of a Consultation on the National Agenda*, 17–18 December. Suva: School of Social and Economic Development, University of the South Pacific.

Crocombe R. and M. Meleisea (eds) 1988. *Pacific Universities: Achievements, Problems, Prospects*. Suva: Institute of Pacific Studies, University of the South Pacific.

Hauʻofa, E. 1993. A Beautiful Cemetery. In *A Garland of Achievement: 25 Years of Learning and Serving Together. The University of the South Pacific 1968–1993*. Suva: University of the South Pacific, 81–82.

Naidu, V. 1997. Internationalization of Higher Education in the South Pacific. In J. Knight and H. deWit (eds), *Internationalisation of Higher Education in Asia Pacific Countries*. Amsterdam: European Association for International Education, IDP Australia and the Programme on Institutional Management in Higher Education of the OECD, 147–60.

Naidu, V. 2004. Aid in the Pacific: What Works and Why? *Development Bulletin* No. 66 (September). Development Studies Network. Canberra: Research School of Social Sciences, The Australian National University, 117–24.

Pillay, S. 1993. Staff and Staffing. In *A Garland of Achievement: 25 Years of Learning and Serving Together. The University of the South Pacific 1968–1993*. Suva: University of the South Pacific, 92–94.

Robie, D. 2000. Pacific Journalism Online Website Censored. Pacific Media Watch – Pacific Nius. *Scoop*, 2 June. www.scoop.co.nz/stories/WO0006/S00012/pacific-journalism-online-website-censored.htm

Solofa, E. 1993. A Strength of Will. In *A Garland of Achievement: 25 Years of Learning and Serving Together. The University of the South Pacific 1968–1993*. Suva: University of the South Pacific, 3–4.

Solofa, E. 2000. Introduction. *The University of the South Pacific 1999 Annual Report*. Suva: University of the South Pacific.

University of the South Pacific (USP) 1993. *A Garland of Achievement: 25 Years of Learning and Serving Together. The University of the South Pacific 1968–1993*. Suva: University of the South Pacific.

University of the South Pacific (USP) 2006–2017. *Annual Reports*. Suva: University of the South Pacific. www.usp.ac.fj/index.php?id=archivepublications

Waddell, E., V. Naidu and E. Hauʻofa (eds) 1993. *A New Oceania: Rediscovering Our Sea of Islands*. Suva: University of the South Pacific with Beake House.

3

The Road from Laucala Bay

Brij V. Lal

Brij V. Lal: Personal Journey

Two institutions bookend my career. One is the University of the South Pacific (USP) and the other The Australian National University (ANU). One is where I began my academic journey and the other where I completed it four decades later. My gratitude to both is inestimable. One taught me the alphabets of scholarship and the other helped me bring it to fruition. The purpose of education, I learned in my undergraduate years, was the betterment of society. It was deliberately, unequivocally instrumental in nature: scholarship as a means to an end and not an end in itself. Engagement and attachment were essential aspects of our role as educated citizens and leaders of our developing island nations. These values have remained with me after all these years. At ANU, I continued my pursuit of engaged scholarship unfettered by ideology and theoretical dogma and passing intellectual fashion. I learnt the value of living within my own history, not above or outside it. And I did so in the company of men and women of profound scholarship whose affectionate commitment to the Pacific Islands region was inspirational. Their names are legion: Jim Davidson, Harry Maude, Oskar Spate and many more who combined scholarship with practical engagement. At the USP, that role was assumed by Ron Crocombe, the indefatigable promoter of Pacific Island scholarship. They are my inspiration and my role models. It is pleasing that the once-fledging relations between the two institutions that have shaped my life are now flourishing, and the prospects for continued collaboration look brighter by the day. I begin this essay with the place where I began my journey, which led to an improbable scholarly career.

Lal, B.V. 2013. The Road from Laucala Bay. In L. Crowl, M. Tuainekore Crocombe and R. Dixon (eds), *Ron Crocombe: E Toa! Pacific Writings to Celebrate his Life and Work*. Suva: USP Press.

Republished with the kind permission of USP Press.

You who will emerge from the flood
In which we have gone under
Remember
When you speak of our failings
The dark time too
Which you have escaped
—Berthold Brecht, 'To Those Born Later'

It is now exactly 47 years since I went to the University of the South Pacific to undertake an undergraduate degree in history and English. I was on a government scholarship to prepare for a career as a high school teacher. The humanities were for the no-hopers, some people in the village said; bright students did law and medicine and other status-enhancing subjects that secured good marriages and prosperous careers. But for me at that time, just getting into university was an achievement of singular importance. I was the first one in my entire extended family throughout Vanua Levu ever to complete high school and the first to head for tertiary education. A career as a high school teacher was nothing to scoff at: it paid well, teachers had a good reputation in the community as exemplars of proper moral behaviour, and the prospect of promotion up the ladder of the educational bureaucracy looked bright. For the generation before us, a lowly career in the colonial bureaucracy was all that could be hoped for at best. Otherwise, it was back-breaking work in the cane fields. The timing was right for us. Fiji had just become independent (in 1970) and there was need for skilled manpower to propel the engine of postcolonial development. We would be the torchbearers of the independence generation.

The opening of the University of the South Pacific was a monumental achievement in the modern history of the Pacific Islands, a genuine turning point, much like the impact of the Second World War, or the beginnings of decolonisation in the 1960s. It placed higher education within the reach of all school children who passed the appropriate exams with requisite marks, not only those who (or whose parents) could afford it, or the select few who went overseas on a small number of government scholarships. It was, in its own way, a great leveller of hierarchy based on wealth and status. Unsurprisingly, university education on offer was unequivocally utilitarian, explicitly advertised in the names of the three foundational clusters of academic activity: the School of Social and Economic Development, the School of Natural Resources and the School of Education. All this did not matter to those of us lucky enough to get admission to the university in the first place; getting to the Laucala Campus was quite an achievement in itself. What a time it was. 'I sing of our youth', New Zealand historian Keith Sinclair once wrote, 'And the fierce gladness of being in at the beginning' (1963, cited Stead 2008:8).

Towards the end of my second year, after I had demonstrated a capacity for academic achievement, at least as measured in the final grades, the thought began to enter my head that an academic career might be worth contemplating and not beyond the realms of possibility. Reading in the library for endless hours was enthralling. What could be better than a life devoted to it? In this thought, I was anything but discouraged by some of the faculty, especially by my history lecturer June Cook, the chain-smoking Cambridge graduate who had come to the university after a stint in the United Nations (and who, I was to learn much later, had gone on to bat for me with people like Ron Crocombe, whom she was tutoring in French). The occasional nod of acknowledgement from some of the academics in the corridors, the chance encounter in the dining room, occasionally being called by your first name (after high school, where we remained anonymous, seldom recognised individually) suggested that perhaps one was being noticed, or at least making a small impression.

The university was a liberating experience in many ways: escaping the confining ways of village life in Labasa, encountering new people from other Pacific Islands, the new freedoms and opportunities. Intellectually it widened our horizons in previously unimaginable ways. In high school, we had no local history. For our higher exams, we had studied the great themes of European history: the unification of Germany and Italy, the causes of the First World War, the Russian Revolution, the rise of fascism in Italy and Germany. In earlier grades, we had studied aspects of New Zealand history: the economic policies of Sir Julius Vogel, the rise of the Liberal Party, the life of Sir Apirana Ngata. At university, Tony Chappell's year-long course introduced us to Pacific history, broadly including the cultural anthropology of Pacific Island societies comprising Melanesia, Polynesia and Micronesia. Ron Crocombe, the lean, lanky professor of

Pacific studies, deepened that knowledge through an extensive reading and anecdote-rich course in Advanced Pacific History. As I have said elsewhere, Ron was not a disciplined teacher, but he was an electrifying one who spoke with deep personal knowledge of the people he had met and the places he had visited. He seemed to know virtually every scholar who mattered in Pacific studies. And as a teacher, he took us seriously, perhaps more seriously than we deserved. I recall vividly Ron giving me a brand-new copy of *Pacific Islands Portraits* edited by Jim Davidson and Deryck Scarr (1970) and asking me to write a review of it.[1] Such confidence in one's ability to say something meaningful when one was merely learning the alphabets was daunting at the time, but it was also thrilling. Ron was already publishing third-year research papers as small monographs under the auspices of the South Pacific Social Sciences Association, which he founded. Some essays found an outlet in *Pacific Perspective*, a new journal he started, typically with the collaboration of senior undergraduates and edited by a junior Islander academic.[2] It's now gone. I tried to follow Ron's example in my own teaching career.[3]

Suddenly, history did not appear remote or unrelated. I remember distinctly the faces of our Solomon Island colleagues lighting up when the topic of the Pacific Islands labour trade was discussed and names of such places as Kolombangara and Choiseul were mentioned. These were not just names on paper, but names of places intimately familiar to the students. The mention of Efate or Tanna evoked a similar response among the ni-Vanuatu crowd when the history of the sandalwood was discussed. Ahmed Ali's course on colonialism in the Pacific introduced us briefly to aspects of Fijian colonial history, complete with names of familiar people and places, such as Sir Henry Marks, after which Marks Street in Suva was named and familiar to us as the place for affordable Chinese food. John Harre's lectures on the social anthropology of family and kinship

---

1   Those 'portrayed' were Peter Dillion, the Henrys of Tahiti, King George Tupou I of Tonga, Cakobau and Ma'afu, Xavier Montrouzier, John Coleridge Patteson, Kwaisulia of the Solomon Islands, Lauaki Namulau'ulu Mamoe, Baiteke and Binoka of Abemama, Pacific beach communities, the Pacific labour trade and the planter community in Fiji.

2   Sione Tupouniua was the editor, and editorial committee members included Isoa Gavidi, Lionel Brown, John Samy, Finau Tabakaucoro and Gary Finaly, besides academics Peter Stone and Brian Lockwood.

3   I published a set of senior prize-winning graduate essays at the University of Hawai'i titled *Wansalawara: Soundings in Melanesian History* (University of Hawai'i at Mānoa Center for Pacific Islands Studies, Occasional Paper 31, 1987) and Honours essays done under my supervision at the ANU in my *Chalo Jahaji: On a Journey Through Indenture in Fiji* (The Australian National University Division of Pacific and Asian History and Suva: Fiji Museum, 2000).

led us to Adrian Mayer's incomparable *Peasants in the Pacific* (1973), whose description of rural Fiji Indian society was as authentic as it was real. The rituals and ceremonies he described were a part of our life in rural Labasa. Ken Gillion's *Fiji's Indian Migrants* (1962) introduced us to the history of our people, their origins, and early settlement. Ahmed Ali once lent me his thesis to read. More impactful than the subject matter, a history of race and electoral representation in Fiji, was the artefact itself: to see in a perfectly bound volume of several hundred crisp pages neatly typed words about our own history (Ali 1973). All of a sudden, everything became real. The thesis and the books we read whetted my appetite for history and planted the seeds of ambition that I too might try my hand at it one day. But it remained a private ambition, riddled with doubt about its actual realisation. I wasn't very good at transformational grammar, which was a compulsory course in English. Discussion of alpha clause and beta clause left me cold. And I was, after all, on a scholarship to become a high school teacher of English and history.

We were undergraduates at the university at a time of great political optimism in the region. Our islands were in the process of gaining independence, and some amongst us were already marked for great things in the future, such as Barak Sope, who would go on to a mixed political fortune in his native Vanuatu, and the frequently shirtless, tennis-playing Teburoro Tito, who would become the president of Kiribati. Others would become diplomats, senior administrators and educators, a veritable 'USP Mafia' in the region. The atmosphere at university was suffused with the sense that, with the right kind of leadership, ordinary people could make a difference to the nation building that was under way after nearly a century of colonial rule. This was nowhere more evident than at the Social Issues in National Development conference, which Ron Crocombe organised at the university in 1974 (Tupouniua et al. 1975). The occasion was genuinely participatory, featuring international luminaries such as the anthropologist Sir Raymond 'Tikopia' Firth, local academics (Ahmed Ali), political practitioners (Fiji's Karam Ramrakha) and students (Vijay Naidu, Jone Dakuvula and Amelia Rokotuivuna). This emphasis on inclusiveness and Islander participation, on dissolving differences of hierarchy and status, was pure Ron, and it was stirring. The problem of development was considered from a variety of perspectives: anthropological, sociological, economic, historical, political. There was no contrived coherence of themes, no scripted choreography. This too was Ron, assertively multidisciplinary. 'What kind of life do we want for ourselves?' Amelia asked (ibid.). One that promoted human dignity and equitable development, she answered. 'We people of the Pacific Islands are in the enviable position of being able to make a choice since most of our nations are just beginning the journey of nationhood' (ibid.). Dakuvula pleaded for 'freedom to examine and criticise,' as the 'unorthodox and the ruled are worth trusting and listening to' (ibid.). Such innocence of those salad days seems so touching in the light of subsequent developments in Fiji and the region generally. After the 2006 military coup in Fiji, Jone, the youthful anarchist, was working for the military regime. Disillusioned, he is now at Fiji's new national university as its Registrar.

The same spirit of innocence was evident in scholarship as well. In 1973, three senior students at the university, Sr Mary Stella, Asesela Ravuvu and Raymond Pillai, all Ron's students, published a joint paper, 'Pacific History and National Integrity', which provided a distillation of thought current at the time. 'An objective study of Pacific history', they wrote, 'will contribute greatly towards overcoming the myth of white superiority which has so discouraged the Pacific peoples from asserting themselves' (Stella et al. 1973:1–7). An important function of history, and scholarship generally, was to instil confidence in people 'eager to make their own contribution' (ibid.). History thus had a constructive role to play 'in promoting the rehabilitation of the Pacific peoples because it restores their confidence and self-respect, and enables them to take their place in a new and changing world' (ibid.). They went on:

> If the Pacific peoples are to avoid the pitfalls that have plagued the progress of more complex civilisations, they must glean the pages of history and profit from the experiences of those who have gone before. Leaders in the Pacific need such knowledge in order to make soundly based decisions in their dealings with their own people and with other nations. History will not provide ready made solutions, but the process of analysing the past can be fruitfully applied to the present (ibid.).

Such optimism about the relevance of the past to the present was not confined to USP students and faculty. It was part of the general currency at the time. Delivering the presidential address to the Australia and New Zealand Association for the Advancement of Science in 1970, Harry Maude of ANU too had proclaimed that history:

> has a very practical and therapeutic role to enact in assisting the rehabilitation of the Pacific peoples at the end of a traumatic era of European political, economic, and technological ascendancy by renewing

their self-respect and providing them with a secure historical base to play their part as responsible citizens of independent or self-governing communities in a new world (Maude 1971:24).[4]

Subsequent history would prove that noble sentiment to be sadly misplaced. Once entrenched in power, political leaders disdained discussion and suppressed dissent. As Thomas Jefferson once said, 'Whenever a man has cast a longing eye on offices, a rottenness begins in his conduct'. Pacific leaders were no exception. University graduates were expected to be pliant cogs in the wheels of government bureaucracy, agents of state-sponsored development programs, not independent critics of its policies. Former students who later became political leaders themselves breached the principles of freedom of expression they had so stoutly championed in their youth. And not everywhere in the Pacific was there a single unitary tradition that could be utilised in nation-building efforts. The Papuans were seeking separation from the New Guineans, there was a breakaway movement in the Western Solomon Islands, the ni-Vanuatu were grappling with the divided legacy of colonial rule bequeathed by the British and the French. In Fiji, Fijians and Indo-Fijians had sharply divergent views about the colonial past that seemed only to harden with time.

The age of innocence of the earlier years about the role and importance of history is now gone. History, as a discipline, is taught in schools as part of an amorphous, mind-numbing social science unit rather than as a separate subject in its own right. It is a devalued currency in modern education in the islands. In universities, the sanctity of disciplinary boundaries is rejected as archaic. We now speak of 'histories' in the plural, contested, problematised, intersected along a myriad lines by a variety of concerns, interests, understandings and authorial subjectivities. We now live with the certainty that scholarship is partial in both senses of the term.[5] I accept these new developments intellectually, though I am also troubled by them. Doubt in small doses is salutary, but it can be disabling when taken to excess. Pluralism, diversity and fragmentation can be liberating, but so too can an exercise in synthesis, an overarching connected narrative to understand the larger shape of the human experience. I also tire quickly of the endless language games scholars play, usually for the edification

---

4   Maude retired to an academic career after a lifetime as a colonial civil servant. His academic colleague J.W. Davidson was active in advising Island people during their transition to independence.
5   For more on this, see Thomas (1990).

and amusement of each other. The habits of thought I acquired in my undergraduate years about the place of the humanities in the broad cultural life of a civilised society have persisted. I am comfortable with that.

There were several other things about my USP background that I observed quietly at the time but whose full importance I did not grasp. Among them was the literary renaissance that was taking place at the university in the 1970s and 1980s. Students and creative writers were beginning to write imaginatively about their own societies. Their works appeared first in the student journal *Unispac* and later in *Mana*, the publication of the South Pacific Creative Arts Society started by Marjorie and Ron Crocombe and Albert Wendt, among others. I was particularly fascinated by stories about the Indo-Fijian community, about which so little had been written, almost as if the world we came from was not worthy of literary exploration and critical engagement. We read pieces by Raymond Pillai, Anirudh Singh, Dhurup Chand, Sashi Kant Nair, Sulochana Chand, and others. Raymond was everyone's favourite.[6] He wrote with unerring clarity and authenticity about the world of rural Indo-Fijians. We understood perfectly what he meant about the stillness of village life being a 'cloak, like the veil a woman wears before strangers, hiding private life full of tragedy and violence' (Pillai 1980:15). When he wrote about Bangaru being black as a *baigan* (eggplant), we knew exactly what he meant. There was a Bangaru in every village. Vanessa Griffin introduced us to the world of Fijians and part-Europeans. Her word pictures were so true: 'This Fijian woman, any Fijian woman, was a common sight on the sea wall, sitting couched, with faded cotton skirt billowing in the wind, or standing against the sky,' with a 'basket plaited out of green coconut leaf' containing her bait (Griffin 1973:91).

The voices that Raymond, Vanessa and others captured were not found in archival documents so beloved by historians. It seemed to me then, and the conviction has deepened with time, that these writers were better able to capture the lived experience, its mystery, its rich daily texture, far better than conventional scholars. These creative pieces and the idea that our people had such wonderful stories to tell lodged deep at the back of my mind, and I have the lingering suspicion that they had something to do with my own efforts at creative writing later in my career. Sadly,

---

6   His two published collections of short stories include *The Celebration* (Suva: Mana Publications and South Pacific Creative Arts Society, 1980) and, posthumously, *The End of the Line* (Suva: Fiji Institute of Applied Studies, 2008).

though, the promise of a literary renaissance at the Laucala campus was short lived, ruptured by the coups of 1987 when the leading artists left for other shores or stopped writing altogether. It was revived in the mid-1990s by the Niu Waves group only to be disrupted by George Speight's insurrection in 2000. After the latest coup in 2006, a culture of silence and self-censorship has descended on Fiji's creative community, sadly with the silent support of its pliant academic hierarchy.

The idea of literature providing a window into the truth of the lived human experience was expressed most powerfully by Albert Wendt. Two things he said stayed with me. The first was the notion that there is no one perfect way to write history, that it could be written from a variety of perspectives. 'A novel is a history,' he wrote, 'an analogue of the real world, written by someone for whom life is a perpetual question and for whom there are no sacred truths'. The world the novelist sought to create 'attempts to explore all his possibilities, tries to be total, to include even the dreams/fantasies/smells/prophesies/and diseases of a particular place which exists outside time'. The difference between the two was that 'a historian tries to recreate a world that, according to historical evidence, was, and save it for all time'. But it was still fiction 'because it is selective recreation, and Art being selection ain't life'. Both were custodians and creators of memories as mythographers and mythmakers who 'explore our possibilities: the novelist through supposedly "imaginary" people and situations, the historian through people who supposedly existed. And in a world where the gods are dead, they both create their own meanings in the hope that those meanings will sustain them' (Wendt 1987:78–92).

At the time, Wendt's contentions seemed heretical, unsettling to those of us just beginning to learn the alphabets of academic disciplines. We were taught to believe that the past had a reality of its own that could be revealed through the use of proper methods of enquiry. We had our own codes and distinctive protocols of research, just as other disciplines had theirs. We were not in the business of 'creating our own meanings', but telling objective truths ascertained through verifiable evidence, this being one of the central tenets of historical scholarship.[7] The idea that historians were mythmakers seemed strange to us, disturbing; on the contrary, we fancied ourselves as myth busters, setting the record straight. But over time, I have come to accept the essential truth of Wendt's contention, though not

---

7　See, for instance, Novick (1988).

perhaps all of it. And I have also become more mindful of historian Ken Inglis's observation that 'a lot of history is concealed autobiography' (Inglis 1983:1). We live within, not outside, the histories we write. We end up creating texts that are partial. We reject the notion of value-free research in its entirety and of linear, one dimensional truth. We accept the role of imagination in the construction of human knowledge. And we readily acknowledge the distinct possibility of becoming a footnote in someone else's text in our own lifetime rather than penning transcending, timeless texts.

The other disturbing question Albert Wendt asked touched on issues of the representation of the past. It was not so much a question of who should or should not be allowed to write history. 'The crucial question,' Wendt argued, was, 'Can a historian ever get into the brain and blood of someone whose culture is so different from his own, and write from inside that person? And should he pretend he can?' These are important questions and I am not sure I have a clear or adequate response to them. Meanwhile, I do have questions to raise. Is it ever possible for *anyone* to get into the blood and bones of people long dead and gone? Isn't the past a foreign country to all of us? Is it ever possible to know the 'really real'? Insider cultural knowledge certainly confers some advantages, but cultural traits are learned not innate, and there are ample examples in Pacific studies of scholars writing sensitively about indigenous cultural matters and accepted as such by the people themselves. Think of Roger Keesing, David Hanlon and Marshall Sahlins, to take just three examples.

Over time, I have come to question some of the assumptions and parameters of positivist scholarship characteristic of an earlier generation. I do not deny the enormous value of archival research, but I have also become aware of its many limitations. Documents about the past are not neutral pieces of paper. They were written by people in particular contexts for particular purposes. They are instruments of and for power and authority. They have an agenda of their own. Those who questioned the foundations of the duly constituted architecture of power were dismissed as madmen, misfits and mavericks. Students of Fijian history would know the fate of the Fijian rebel Apolosi Nawai. In the 1960s, the Indo-Fijian leader A.D. Patel was subjected to sustained attacks for demanding independence. So it is important to read the historical records not only for what they say, but, perhaps equally importantly, what they leave out. Sometimes, the silence can be deafening.

Archival research privileges a particular kind of historical narrative. The written word provides the foundation of the project, enlivened wherever possible with oral and anecdotal evidence, although, until recent decades, non-written sources that could not be properly authenticated or verified were not accorded much weight. But what about histories of pasts where memory is not properly archived and written evidence does not exist? What, in other words, about the histories of unwritten pasts and peoples? Let me give a concrete example of what I have in mind. I grew up in a rural settlement in Fiji in the 1950s and 1960s. People had begun to settle on haphazardly leased pieces of land in the settlement soon after the end of indenture in 1920. Of little interest to the government except for purposes of rudimentary administration, the Indo-Fijians had to rely on their own cultural resources to establish families and farmsteads, create institutions that regulated social life in the villages, adjudicated disputes, celebrated life and mourned its passing. It was in these settlements that the main features of Indo-Fijian culture were fashioned from bits and pieces of the remembered past and the accumulated experience of the new environment. I came from this world that formed me and the people of my generation, but there was hardly anything written about it. It was almost as if that world did not exist, or did not matter. How to write truthfully about this past began to preoccupy me more and more. Albert Wendt's advice about capturing the spirit of the place, not only its dry facts, kept returning to me.

To make some sense of my lived reality, I began to write what I have termed 'faction', where I try to capture the actual lived experience in fictional or quasi-fictional terms.[8] I write about things I have observed or experienced, about stories I have been told: a family quarrel, the politics of running local schools, religious and cultural tensions—and I write about them creatively but with disciplined imagination. Unlike a novelist, I cannot conjure something out of thin air. I work with material given to me by experience or observation, and from that I create a connected narrative. Perhaps this is what novelists do as well, I do not know. My concern is to capture the inner truth rather than the factual accuracy of an experience. The experiment has worked for me over the years. I have received dozens of appreciative messages from readers across the world who have found my factional pieces authentic, reflecting their own

---

8   See my *Mr Tulsi's Store: A Fijian Journey* (Canberra: Pandanus Books, 2001) and *Turnings: Fiji Factions* (Lautoka: Fiji Institute of Applied Studies, 2008).

experiences.[9] Understandably, there will be many who will question the scholarly 'value' of this kind work. The truth of what I write in factions cannot be verified as a piece of archival evidence might be, but that is the best way I know how to get to the truth of an unwritten experience, to the blood and bones of the people I write about. And the truth, as they say, lies in the taste of the pudding.

Albert Wendt's point about the possibility of writing the history of another culture also raises pertinent questions with which I have grappled in my own work. I recall Ron Crocombe once telling me that he vowed not to conduct research on Fiji when he took up his appointment at the university. He wanted complete freedom to research and write about things that mattered to him without having to worry about the renewal of his work permit. If he could not write the truth as he saw it, he wouldn't even try. He kept his word. For a very different reason, I made a conscious decision from very early on to write about my own people and my own country. I do not want to be an intruder on someone else's past. There have been occasions when I have written about other places, but the primary site of my scholarly investigation has been Fiji. I am moved by a strong sense of belonging and attachment. It is where my head and my heart come together. I am a part of the history I write about. I may get things wrong, but at least it is my place and my history. I will bear the burden of my errors. I have a deep sense of responsibility and obligation to it. I care about the region of which I am a part, but not with the same passionate intensity that I feel about Fiji. My choice is political, not intellectual. I see no reason why an outsider cannot feel passionately involved about the place of his or her research endeavour. Nor do I feel particularly possessive about my site of research. The more research we have the better. It is the quality of engagement, not the colour of skin, that will matter in the end.

For a while, the 'ownership' of scholarship was a deeply contested and politically contentious issue in Pacific studies.[10] Did outsiders have the right to 'appropriate' someone else's history? Some saw scholarship as a deeply political act, and the involvement of outsiders as complicit in the process of academic imperialism. I encountered this most directly at the University of Hawai'i while teaching there in the 1980s, where

9   *Mr Tulsi's Store* was selected as one of the Ten Notable Books of Asia Pacific by the San Francisco–based Kiriyama Prize in 2002, and chosen as Highly Commended for ACT Book of the Year in 2002.
10   See, for example, in addition to Nicholas Thomas (footnote 5), Routledge (1985) and Hezel (1988).

issues of dispossession, marginalisation and indigenous sovereignty were acute and dominated public discourse. Unless history was taught from a particular ideological standpoint, deployed in the cause of indigenous empowerment, however defined, it was unacceptable and therefore to be rejected outright. Emotions were aroused and brought into sharp focus in an exchange between the anthropologist Roger Keesing and the Hawaiian scholar and activist Haunani-Kay Trask. Trask accused Keesing of being an academic 'colonialist', part of a 'colonising horde' who sought to 'take away from us [natives] the power to define who and what we are, and how we should behave politically and culturally' (Trask 1990:159–67). Arguing that 'anthropologists without natives are like entomologists without insects', she accused Keesing and other expatriate anthropologists of profiting from native cultures by studying and writing about them in academic institutions (ibid.). Keesing accused Trask and others like her of romanticising the past of Pacific cultures and drawing too rigid a line between outsiders and insiders.

> The time is long past where those who are friends of Pacific Islanders and Islands and those who are enemies can be sorted out on the basis of their genes or skin colours: there are plenty of 'insiders' many with Swiss bank accounts, busily selling their forests, their minerals, their fish—the lives and environments of the village cousins and their own children and grandchildren—to foreign interests (Keesing 1990:168–71).

Similar issues about representation and legitimacy were raised elsewhere in the Pacific, again producing rather more light than heat.

But these debates, which were once so animated and controversial, have lost their relevance and potency now. The boundaries of knowledge and power are more porous now, as are dated essentialised notions of cultural identity. The traditional gatekeepers of knowledge have had their function usurped by modern technology. Many practitioners of Pacific studies today are Pacific Islanders themselves, some in positions of power and influence.[11] Given the paucity of serious scholars engaged in serious study of the islands, people are grateful for knowledge and insight irrespective of their origin. In the scholarship produced in recent years, there has been a great degree of emphasis on local context and agency, on indigenous epistemology, with the result that some of the older criticism of

---

11   Vilsoni Hereniko is Director of the Center for Pacific Islands Studies at the University of Hawai'i; Teresia Teaiwa is Convenor of Pacific Studies at Victoria University of Wellington and Katerina Teaiwa is Convenor of Pacific Studies at The Australian National University.

imperialism and insensitivity has lost its effectiveness. It is also important that the geographical boundaries of the Pacific Islands have greatly expanded, thereby necessitating a re-thinking about what constitutes the 'real' Pacific.[12] There are many more Pacific Islanders—Samoans, Tongans, Cook Islanders, Niueans, Tokelauans—who now make their homes in Australia and New Zealand, thus complicating the outsider/insider paradigm. On the present evidence, these diasporic communities will gain in strength and influence in the future. The centre of gravity of island writing and scholarship is shifting to metropolitan locations. Further, some of the romance associated with the study of the Pacific Islands that suffused the earlier generation of Pacific scholarship has now vanished in the face of the trouble and turbulence that is an enduring part of the contemporary Pacific. Pope John Paul's 1985 declaration of Fiji as 'the way the world should be' would now be seen by most people as a cruel joke.

The journey I began at the University of the South Pacific all those years ago was influenced by people who taught us by their example and inspiration. It should be clear by now how much this has been a factor in my own intellectual development. We were trained to be generalists, and there was no provision for academic specialisation in the university curriculum. Karl Popper, Karl Marx and Max Weber made brief appearances in some courses, but there was no sustained engagement with their ideas. There were thus big gaps that had to be filled through private study. Scholarship in the western academy, or at least where I have worked, is organised along disciplinary lines with the result that a lot of time had to be spent simply learning the discipline's history, philosophy and development, the sort of thing that better undergraduate students in history in western universities would have encountered much earlier in their education (such as Lord Acton, R.G. Collingwood, E.H. Carr, G.R. Elton and E.P. Thompson). And the field's literature too had to be mastered. Pacific history could not be learned or taught in isolation from the histories of other regions or cognate areas about which we knew very little. We had no anthropology at the university and yet it was a discipline with special relevance for the study of the Pacific. The practice of reading for the sake of general knowledge and for sheer pleasure had to be cultivated, which was never

---

12   See, for instance, essays by Epeli Hau'ofa and others in Waddell, Naidu and Hau'ofa (1993).

easy for people coming from non-literate, oral cultures. Now reading is an integral part of my being, indispensible to sanity. For me, most knowledge still comes from the written text, not the latest technology.

People of my generation had no sense of entitlement that some now seem to have. Education in Australia is big business, and universities regularly compete for foreign students. Special help is assigned to them to improve their literacy and research skills. Everyone naturally wants to preserve the goose that lays the golden egg. But there was none of this for people of my vintage. We were expected to pick up the skills on our own as we went along by reading journals and books. And when it came to writing the dissertations, we were again very much on our own. I recall my designated advisor, Ken Gillion (my formal supervisor was Anthony Low who was then the vice chancellor), telling me that if after six months of reading in the library I was not on top of my subject, the most knowledgeable person in the world, I should not be doing graduate work. That kind of confidence could be debilitating, but it was fairly standard fare then. Students who had arrived on scholarship to pursue graduate work had gone through a rigorous process of selection, and the best thing that could be done for them, it was thought, was to leave them alone to get on with their work. And it worked.

After three years of labour, we were expected to submit three hardbound copies of our dissertation for examination by three scholars who were leaders in the field and had had no contact with the candidate. We were expected to make a distinctive and significant contribution to knowledge by the 'highest standards of contemporary scholarship'. The dissertation had to be as perfect as we could make it. Too many spelling errors and we could expect the examiners to reject it outright. Nothing could be worse for a young postgraduate student contemplating an academic career than to have his or dissertation rejected. There was a certain stigma attached to a dissertation that required re-submission. Word was quick to get out, and chances of securing a decent job at a decent university could be at risk. I was horrified some years ago when a candidate whose dissertation I had examined, pointing out numerous spelling and stylistic errors, told me the advice his supervisor gave him. The examiners, he had said, would point out the errors, which the student could then incorporate in his revision before the final submission. Such advice would have been unthinkable in our day. Now, it seems, many (but by no means all) students expect to make corrections after examination as a matter of course.

Graduate research is now fairly commonplace, at least in Australia, and doctorate is not in as short a supply as it once used to be. But 30 years ago, the criterion for admission to graduate work was fairly strict. Scholarships, by convention, were given to students not much over 30; anything beyond that age required special pleading. At least in the humanities and the social sciences, it was expected that students would go on to an academic career, not an unreasonable expectation at a time when universities were expanding rapidly. At any rate, graduate training was a prelude to a career. That is not universally the case now. There are now more mature age students in universities who pursue graduate work more out of interest rather than with any expectation of an academic career in prospect. Indeed, an academic career may not be the most lucrative either. In Australia at least, opportunities in the public sector can be financially and professionally more rewarding. Even those who pursue an academic career are now routinely resigned to the possibility of moving on to several jobs in a lifetime.

The research culture has also changed. 'Curiosity driven research' was the order of the day when I entered the academy, and for me it has remained that way. We were expected to work on topics that interested us and to make significant original contributions. Historical research was essentially an individualised enterprise. That was the strength of the work. The accounts we wrote were influenced by the moral and ideological position of the author, not something devised by a committee. Articles were useful in alerting the world to our work, but, ideally, historians were expected to write books at respectable intervals that would make a decisive intervention in the field and would have a longer shelf life. We might be expected to make the occasional foray into the public domain on some important event or controversy, but too much media exposure was not deemed desirable. It detracted from detachment and objectivity. Now, media monitoring is a regular part of a university's public relations exercise. We are expected, indeed obliged, to go beyond the lecture hall to make our expertise available to the wider public. In appropriate doses, this is a healthy and welcome development as part of general public education and engagement, but the demands increase daily for briefing and commentary. Salesmanship and showmanship are increasingly becoming an integral part of a scholar's life. I suppose it could be argued that reaching the general public is an important obligation of taxpayer-funded universities. There are other new developments to which we have to respond. Now scholars are routinely expected to apply for research grants. Indeed, in some cases, the ability to attract grants becomes a criterion in appointments and promotions. Grants not only support individual research, they also sustain the infrastructure of an academic department.

On paper, the pursuit of grants seems fair, but upon closer inspection much more problematic. To start with, grants are advertised with particular agendas in mind and focus on strategic areas with some relevance to the broader concerns of the Australian community: border protection, national security, asylum seekers, and so on. Areas that fall outside the prescribed parameters find it harder to get up. 'Cutting-edge research' is often an important factor in assessment. Although it is not stated, the truth is that research that does not somehow fit in with the reigning theoretical paradigm or conceptual category would not ordinarily count as cutting-edge research. Sometimes what is cutting-edge research today is yesterday's news tomorrow. It would seem to me that this requirement is more appropriate to policy-oriented, outcome-driven research. We were brought up in the tradition of humanities requiring a deep immersion in the culture, language and traditions of the people about whom we wrote, our research informed by a lifetime's work. That tradition is now in jeopardy, which is a pity because the finest research on the Pacific Islands came from those scholars who pursued individual research projects.[13] I am not convinced, on present evidence, that large grant-supported research necessarily produces more insightful or enduring scholarship, especially when the outcomes have to be produced in a hurry. I see some serious problems in historians and other practitioners of the humanities being forced to march at the pace and tune set by economists and other social scientists whose intellectual agendas and approaches are significantly different. Reviewing a recent biography of historian Sir Keith Hancock, Geoffrey Bolton, himself an Australian historian of note, remarked how long it took the author to publish the book. 'How fortunate', he wrote, '[that Jim] Davidson's university did not insist that he should instead churn out numerous articles in refereed journals as index of research productivity' (Bolton 2010). How fortunate indeed. The question remains: Is the day of the big book, the fruit of a lifetime's learning and scholarship, over? Are we publishing more and more about less and less?

---

13   The names are legion: J.W. Davidson, H.E. Maude, Dorothy Shineberg, O.H.K. Spate, Deryck Scarr, Hank Nelson. These are all people associated with ANU.

The pressures to conform are not likely to cease anytime soon. In a globalising world, higher education is increasingly interconnected. International ranking systems matter. Universities high in ranking and prestige attract more funding and better faculty as well as graduate students. Universities run on paper, and the more peer-reviewed paper is produced the better. In Australia, academic journals are ranked and the research published there rewarded. The precise criterion of ranking is not clear, but their influence is beyond doubt. Emphasis on excellence in writing and research is vital and should receive priority in every academic institution worth its name. There is, moreover, a certain professional satisfaction in being published in peer-reviewed places. But sometimes this becomes an end in itself, which leads to the question: What and for whom is the research being done? For fellow researchers, to be sure, but for those of us working on non-western regions such as the Pacific Islands, the question is more complicated, touching on the issue of ethical responsibility we have towards people about whom we write. Books published by prestige publishers are invariably beyond the reach of most of the reading public and most high-ranking journals unaffordable.

So we end up being caught between two sets of loyalties: loyalty to the institutions where we work and their demands and expectations, and the needs and expectations of the people and places where we conduct our research. Sometimes the issue is complicated by the absence of any scholarly outlet in the islands themselves where our research could be published. There were once many, now there are few. There is, for instance, not a single scholarly journal in the humanities coming out of USP, a curious regression considering that there were several two decades ago. Fortunately, the timely intervention of technology has helped; that is, the phenomenon of the internet and e-publishing. Works published by ANU Press, for instance, are available free of charge to everyone. Readers can download particular items in a book or the entire book itself. Electronic publishing may be the way of the future. It has not acquired the prestige of conventional publishing, but it is a matter of time. I understand and accept the reality of the changed circumstances of scholarly publishing, but it still takes some getting used to for people of my vintage for whom printed books are cherished cultural artefacts that occupy a privileged niche in the intellectual life of society and, as someone once said, like telescopes, compasses and sextants 'help us navigate the dangerous seas of human life'.

I have sometimes been accused by friends and foes alike of being an unrepentant elitist, once an insider but now looking austerely and judgmentally at the local scene from the comfort of a privileged chair from the outside. There may be a grain of truth in this perception, but it does genuinely dismay me to see opportunities not grasped and potential not realised among people who have much to contribute. It is particularly disheartening to see students being short-changed by their mentors when what they most need is role models of scholarly excellence. Exalted polemic is no substitute for solid scholarship. I accept that a university is a not a social security institution. It is, as it has to be, an inherently elitist institution that rewards merit and meritocracy above all else. My creed is best expressed in the inspiring words of the late great historian and public intellectual Tony Judt:

> Universities *are* elitist: they are about selecting the most able cohort of a generation and educating them to their ability—breaking open the elite and making it consistently anew. Equality of opportunity and equality of outcome are not the same thing. A society divided by wealth and inheritance cannot redress this injustice by camouflaging it in educational institutions—by denying distinctions of ability or by restricting selective opportunity—while favoring a steadily widening income gap in the name of free market. This is mere cant and hypocrisy (Judt 2010:6).

I believe that scholars have a vital role to play in society, none being more important than a willingness to speak truth to power. We should guard against the temptations of power, maintain a certain distance and detachment from it that keeps us alert to the ways in which public memory is hijacked in the service of those who govern our lives. Am I being unduly optimistic, hopelessly idealistic? 'Still bent to make some port he knows not where/ Still standing for some false impossible shore' (Arnold 1855)? But what, in this levelling world, is the alternative when, as New Zealand literary polymath C.K. Stead writes, 'universities which once set stiff requirements for entry now advertise for students and compete for market share' (Stead 2008:8)?

Over time, I have become much more attuned to the political interests and concerns that underpin a lot of academic activity. Nothing is ever so simple or neutral as it seems. The day of the 'God Professors' who once ran academic departments with unfettered power, influencing individual destinies and broad directions of research, is over. So, too, is the once common practice of 'tapping someone on the shoulder' for a job. The academic practice is much more open and transparent, at least on paper.

But ideas of what is valid and proper vary from place to place. At USP, the question most often asked at appointment times was: how many Pacific Islanders are there on the staff, as opposed to expatriates or 'Indians'. Few raised questions about gender equity. Ethnicity of regional origin was the primary marker of identity. In Australia, certainly at my own university, gender equity is a very serious consideration in any appointment process. Women are often alerted to new employment opportunities and encouraged to apply. I am not sure if we seriously ask how many Pacific Islanders or Asians there are in centres of Asian and Pacific learning in Australia. These are important issues, and they speak to different political and cultural concerns and contexts. I just hope that in our quite legitimate concerns for social equity, we do not lose sight of what, in the end, the true purpose of a university is.

There is no shortcut to success. The journey was much harder for my generation, moving from the world of pre-literacy to literacy within the span of a single lifetime. Being an academic is not only an occupation, it is a sacred responsibility, a distinctive way of life with its own overarching cultural codes, protocols and rituals. To succeed, it requires discipline, a cultivation of solitude, cultural re-invention and a deep humility. As Longfellow said a long time ago, 'The talent for success is nothing more than doing what you can do well, and doing well whatever you do without a thought for fame' (Longfellow 1887). Our tasks ahead are clearly defined. We must continue to produce and publish research that adds a vital sentence to the larger global conversation of scholarship. There is no substitute for excellence. We owe that to those who laid the foundations for us in those distant and difficult days, and to those who will inherit the torch from us in uncertain and demanding times. We must engage critically and sensitively with the outside world, breaking the mould of self-referential, 'ghettoising', inward-looking academia. Our natural home should be the interface between the world of scholarship and the world of the lay public. And finally, in this era of galloping globalisation, we should do everything in our power to revive the centrality of the humanities in the cultural life of humankind and in deepening our understanding of the human condition, past and present. As Stephen Garton and Elizabeth Webby argue, 'If our innovation culture is to prosper, it needs to be embedded in a deep understanding of humanity and cultural difference. This is why humanities are fundamental to human progress' (Webby and Garton 2010:4).

References

Ali, A. 1973. *Fiji and the Franchise, 1900–1937.* PhD thesis, unpublished, The Australian National University.

Arnold, M. 1855. A Summer Night. *Poems: Second Series.* London: Longman, Brown, Green, and Longmans.

Bolton, G. 2010. History's wily liberal endures. *The Australian,* 3 April.

Davidson, J.W. and D. Scarr (eds) 1970. *Pacific Islands Portraits.* Wellington: A.H. & A.W. Reed.

Gillion, K. 1962. *Fiji's Indian Migrants: A history to the end of indenture in 1920.* Melbourne: Oxford University Press.

Griffin, V. 1973. Marama. *The Mana Annual of Creative Writing.* Suva: South Pacific Creative Arts Society, 91.

Hezel, F.X. 1988. New Directions in Pacific History: A Practitioner's Critical View. *Pacific Studies* 11(3):107.

Inglis, K.S. 1983. *This is the ABC: The Australian Broadcasting Commission, 1932–1983.* Melbourne: Melbourne University Press, 1.

Judt, T. 2010. Meritocrats. *The New York Review of Books,* 6.

Keesing, R.M. 1990. Reply to Trask. *The Contemporary Pacific* 3(4):168–71.

Longfellow, H.W. 1887. *Hyperion.* London: George Routledge.

Mayer, A.C. 1973. *Peasants in the Pacific: A Study of Fiji Indian Rural Society* (2nd ed.). Berkeley: University of California Press.

Maude, H. 1971. Pacific History—Past, Present, Future. *Journal of Pacific History* 6(1):24. doi.org/10.1080/00223347108572180

Novick, P. 1988. *That Noble Dream: The 'Objectivity Question' and the American Historical Profession.* New York: Cambridge University Press.

Pillai, R. 1980. Muni Deo's Devil. *Celebration: A Collection of Short Stories.* Suva: South Pacific Creative Arts Society, 15.

Routledge, D. 1985. Pacific History as Seen from the Pacific Islands. *Pacific Studies* 8(2):81–100.

Stead, C.K. 2008. *Book Self.* Auckland: Auckland University Press, 8.

Stella, M., R. Pillai and A. Ravuvu 1973. Pacific History and National Integrity. *Pacific Perspectives* 1(2):1–7.

Thomas, N. 1990. Partial Texts: Representation, Colonialism and Agency in Pacific History. *Journal of Pacific History* 25(2):139–58.

Trask, H. 1990. Natives and Anthropologists: The Colonial Struggle. *The Contemporary Pacific* 3(4):159–67.

Tupouniua, S., R. Crocombe and C. Slatter (eds) 1975. *The Pacific Way: Social Issues in National Development*. Suva: Institute of Pacific Studies.

Waddell, E., V. Naidu and E. Hau'ofa (eds) 1993. *A New Oceania: Rediscovering Our Sea of Islands*. Suva: University of the South Pacific School of Social and Economic Development.

Webby, E. and S. Garton 2010. Editors' Introduction. *Humanities Australia* 1(4):4–5.

Wendt, A. 1987. Novelists and Historians and the Art of Remembering. In A. Hooper, S. Britton, R. Crocombe, J. Huntsman and C. Macpherson (eds), *Class and Culture in the South Pacific*. Suva: Institute of Pacific Studies, University of the South Pacific, 78–92.

PART 1: BALANCING TRADITION AND MODERNITY

4

Change in Land Use and Villages—Fiji: 1958–1983

R. Gerard Ward

Gerard Ward: Personal Journey

I began my links with the Pacific Islands region, which the University of the South Pacific (USP) now serves, in 1956 when I worked on a study of land use in Western Samoa. In the late 1950s, I undertook research on land use and population in Fiji, and it has remained a major site for my studies ever since. After USP was established, its library became a valuable resource for me and a number of its staff became close collaborators. Thus, when asked to be a member of the 1991 review team, it was a most welcome opportunity to renew contacts and contribute to USP itself.

A further opportunity occurred in 2003 when USP invited me to write a vision statement for the university: 'A Regional University of Excellence—University of the South Pacific', completed in 2004.

Ward, R.G. 1984. Change in Land Use and Villages 1958–1983. In *Symposium UGI No. 33 Developpement Rural dans les Pays Tropicaux, Bordeaux 22–24 August 1984, Travaux et Documents de Géographie Tropicale*. Centre d'Etudes de Géographie Tropicale, 55:109–20.

Republished with the kind permission of R. Gerard Ward.

Fiji, an archipelagic state of some 250 islands, of which about 70 are inhabited, lies 2,500 kilometres from its nearest larger neighbours, Australia and New Zealand. Of its population of over 600,000, 43 per cent are ethnic Fijians, 51 per cent Fiji Indians. Population is increasing at about 2.2 per cent per year, a fall from the rates of between 3 and 3.5 per cent that occurred in the 1950s. There is a considerable degree of economic specialisation between ethnic groups with Fijians concentrated in mixed subsistence–commercial agriculture and the public service, and Indians in smallholder sugar-cane growing and commerce. Although these occupational contrasts are decreasing, different distribution patterns result, though both major ethnic groups are well represented in the urban areas, which now have about 37 per cent of the total population.

Total population increased by 93 per cent between 1956 and 1982. Agriculture remains the main employment sector. With increasing population, expansion of emphasis on commercial farming and experience, and the drive for increased exports of sugar, the last 25 years have seen a rapid increase in the area of land in use. New levels of land use competition have emerged. Further increases in the numbers of people supported directly by agriculture and forestry will depend increasingly on intensification of land use. Soil surveys show that only about 30 per cent of the land area is suitable for agricultural and pastoral use (Twyford and Wright 1965). The greater part of the country is steep land largely unsuited for any productive use except conservation forests. Despite these limits on the expansion of farming, the limited range of alternative development opportunities engendered by small size and distance from markets or major sources of tourists leads the government to policies of maintaining a major rural sector and keeping people on the land.

There are also important land tenure constraints, which mean that a free land market does not operate except in restricted areas. Eighty-two per cent of the land is 'native land', owned by Fijian clan groups. In 1874 the British colonial government, concerned at the speed at which Europeans had been buying land, forbade the further sale of Fijian land to non-Fijians in order to protect the Fijians' access to the means of agricultural production. In fact, this was virtually the first act of the new colonial government. Eight per cent of the land is freehold. This represents land that Fijians had sold before 1874 and can be bought and sold. Needless to say, scarcity pushes up the market price of such land, often to levels beyond that at which agriculture is really economic. Nine per cent is Crown or government-owned land.

Fijian Indian farmers obtain land by purchasing freehold land, by leasing land from the government or by leasing native land through the Native Land Trust Board, which handles all leasing of Fijian land. About 30 per cent of the country (or 40 per cent of the native land) is in reserve and cannot be leased to any non-Fijian.

Thus the tenure class of any land is an important determinant of who can use it. As land quality also varies within each tenure class, the relationship between tenure and quality is important. Because the early European settlers sought and purchased high-quality land, 30 per cent of freehold land is Class I, and only 16 per cent of little use. But of the unleased native land only 16 per cent is Class I and 44 per cent is of not productive use (Class IV).

In the remainder of this paper I shall consider changes in land use and related matters over the last 25 years at two scales. The first is for the whole of the largest island, Viti Levu, which makes up 58 per cent of the country's land area. The second is at the micro level of three Fijian villages in Viti Levu.

Between 1958 and 1960 I completed a land use survey of most of Fiji at a scale of 1:50,000 using aerial photograph interpretation and ground checking (Ward 1965). In 1978 the Fiji Department of Agriculture completed a similar survey at the same scale. Figure 1 shows the land in use in 1958, the land developed and put into use between 1958 and 1978, and the land which in 1978 was already committed to future development.

In Viti Levu, the area of land in use increased by 233 per cent between 1958 and 1978 (and by 283 per cent if committed land is included), while the rural population of the island increased by 31 per cent between 1956 and 1976. Expansion of the area in use has continued since 1978. The fact that the increase in area in use has not been matched by comparable increases in rural population highlights some key characteristics of land use development over the past quarter century.

By 1958 the greater part of the Class I and II land (suitable for arable farming) was already occupied, primarily by sugar cane farms. Cane farms on the best land (Class I) in the late 1950s could support population densities of about 270 persons per square kilometre. On marginal land, the figure was closer to 40 per square kilometre. The dramatic increase in the area of land under cane, which took place during the late 1970s, mainly occurred on Class II or even Class III land. The latter is suitable for use only after major improvement. New sugar cane farms average 20 hectares compared with about 4 hectares on the best land of older cane areas. In other words, most of the expansion of land use since 1958 has been onto second-class and marginal land, which cannot support densities comparable to those on land already occupied by 1958.

A great deal of the expansion of land use has been through the establishment of the Fiji Pine Commission's pine plantations and the Department of Forestry's hardwood and other plantations. Both developments are in the main on lower-quality land and, as extensive forms of land use, are unlikely to support high densities of rural population. The major pastoral settlement scheme at Yalavou provides about 100 farms averaging approximately 240 hectares each and, apart from the farm families, is likely to generate about 50 additional rural jobs. Therefore, schemes like this are unlikely to support population densities of more than about four per square kilometre. Farms on cattle schemes in the wet zone of the east are generally smaller, but even here holdings average about 35 hectares and are unlikely to support more than about 30 persons per square kilometre.

Thus the general tendency has been for new land development to be for less-intensive farming, matching the generally lower quality of the unused land compared with that which was in use in the late 1950s. It would be unrealistic to expect most of Fiji's currently unused but useable land to support rural population densities of an order higher than between 20 and 40 persons per square kilometre.

In the case of native land occupied under customary tenure and used for mixed subsistence–cash crop agriculture, the assessment of 'carrying capacity' is much more complex. Under a purely subsistence system, and on good-quality land, a predominantly root crop agricultural system incorporating adequate fallow periods might support population densities of the order of 100 to 150 persons per square kilometre if no land is needed for forestry, firewood or hunting areas. In fact, densities of this level will be achieved rarely because of variable land quality. Nevertheless, the high yields attainable from root crops for relatively low labour inputs make this a theoretical possibility if there is little need to purchase food and consumer goods. When cash crops are added to, or replace, the subsistence crops, the land requirement per family increases. The increase is obviously greater with conversion to low-intensity forms of commercial farming such as grazing or copra production.

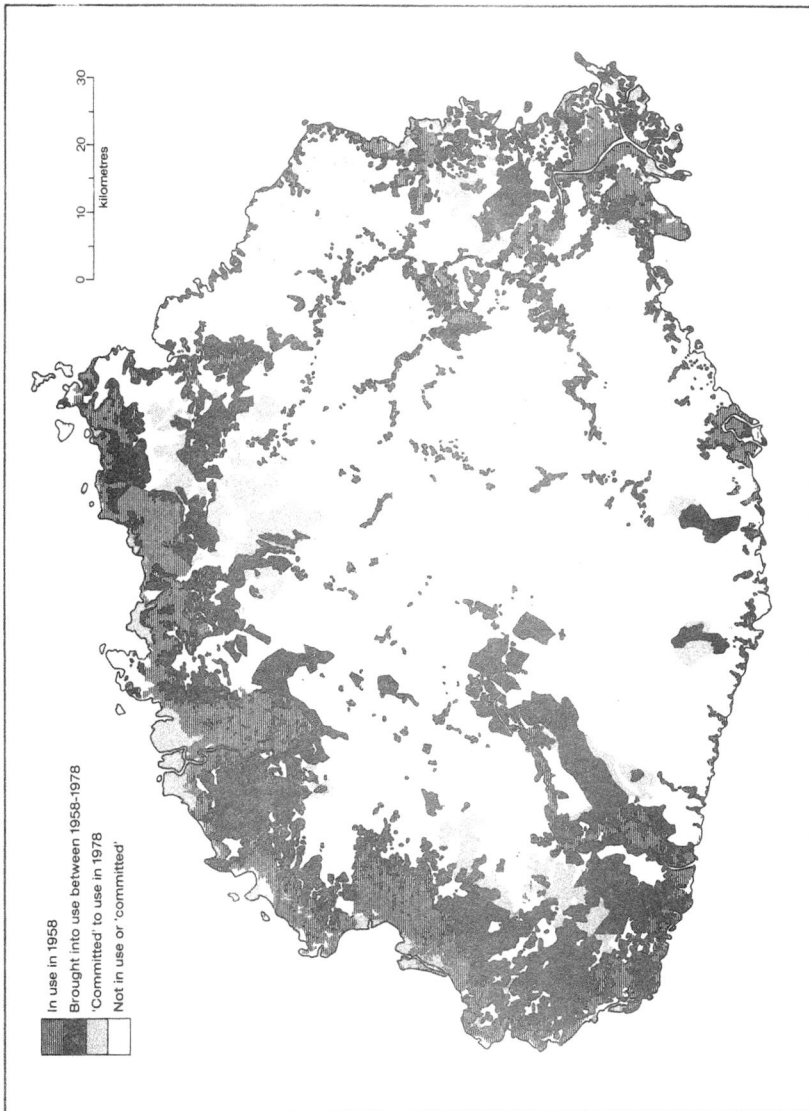

Figure 1. Viti Levu: Area of land use in 1958 and 1978.

Source: Based mainly on 1958 and 1978 land use surveys (see text). Originally prepared for Fiji Employment and Development Mission.

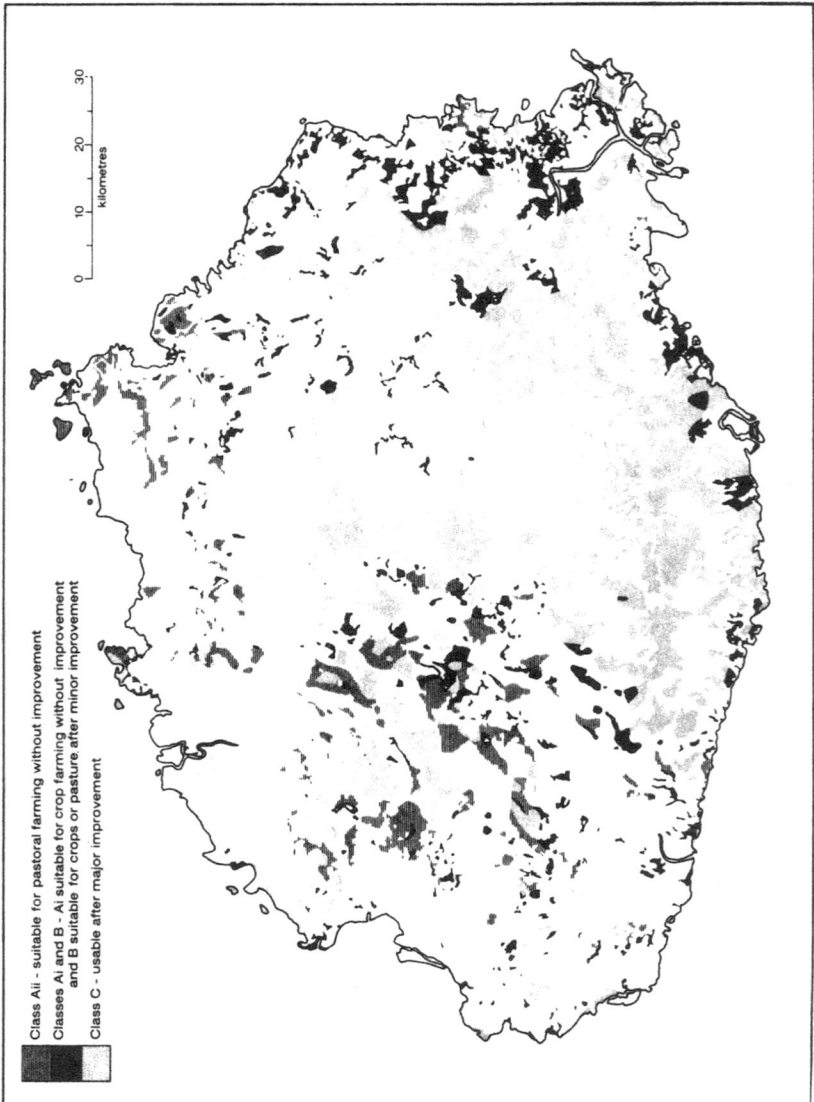

Figure 2. Viti Levu: Land unused in 1978 that is suitable for use.
Source: Based on data from Twyford and Wright (1965) as well as 1958 and 1978 land use surveys (see text). Originally prepared for Fiji Employment and Development Mission.

In the 1970s Fijian villages absorbed considerable numbers of people who might otherwise have been forced to seek work in the urban areas where unemployment is already considerable. This rise in village population has been possible because of some important features of traditional land tenure. But, as will be shown below, trends in rural villages suggest this possibility may not continue.

Figure 2 shows the land in Viti Levu that is suitable for use but that was not in use in 1978. The greater part of the unused or uncommitted land is of Class III quality, with soils suited to permanent agriculture or pastoral use only after major improvements. These improvements include major soil conservation measures on the steeper land, major drainage schemes on poorly drained areas or heavy regular fertiliser applications on infertile soils. The implication in terms of support of population is that future land use will be extensive on such areas with low population densities. In western Viti Levu, the areas of unused land are likely to be most suited to extensive grazing or pine afforestation, although distance to processing plants may be a problem in the latter case. The unused land of the south is generally hilly and the cost of providing access will be relatively high. There may be prospects for tree crops, grazing and perhaps further planting of hardwoods on land that is generally not under native reserve.

The best prospects for expansion of agriculture and pastoral farming in Viti Levu are in the east and there is more unused Class II land here than in other parts of the island. This needs only minor improvement. However, it must be noted that in this area very rapid expansion of pasture, crop production (for example, ginger) and cacao planting has occurred in the period since 1978. This expansion is not allowed for in the map and thus part of the area shown as unused or committed has in fact already been put into use.

This discussion of the area and quality of available land is at a very broad scale. The key point is that the last 25 years have seen a remarkable expansion in the area of land under economic use, but the reserves of land suitable for continuation of this trend are now limited, fragmented and generally of poor quality. Infrastructure costs per new farm will rise, and the time is approaching when these costs will outweigh the potential benefits. Thus future strategies for rural development will have to be based on greater intensification of land use, although a contradictory trend of increasing farm size may also become more obvious as higher standards of living are sought by farmers. It seems unlikely that the next 20 years will see as great an increase in rural population as occurred in the 1960s and 1970s and, as a consequence, the urban and non-agricultural sectors will be called on to provide a higher proportion of the necessary new jobs than they have provided in recent years. As long as the majority of Fijians have the opportunity to use customary land for subsistence cropping, and for some cash cropping, then village communities will be able to absorb some additional population in the largely non-monetary economy and provide a security net for those unable to find urban or other wage employment. A number of trends suggest that this condition will not be maintained for much longer.

Land is not distributed with any degree of equality between owning groups. In part this simply reflects the inequalities existing at the time of survey and registration of native land. In the decades since clan (*mataqali*) holdings were registered, the differential growth, or decline, of owning groups has led to greater divergence between the size of these groups and the areas of land held. Thus, some groups with few members now hold large areas while others, with many members, have little land. Where traditional systems of allocating land for use applied, such divergence in legal holdings was of limited significance. Members of *mataqali* with little land, or whose holdings were located at some distance from the village, were able to use the land of more fortunately placed groups. Recompense, made through customary processes, was non-monetary and usually not very demanding. In areas with little pressure on land, no significant material recompense was necessary.

Studies in the late 1950s showed that in villages that were close to urban areas or were otherwise firmly locked into commercial farming or other monetary activities, landowners were reluctant to allow other members of their own village who were short of land to have access to garden land through traditional mechanisms. In such areas, the monetary value of land, realisable by leasing or through cash cropping was fully recognised and 'lending' land to members of other *mataqali* was rarely practised (Ward 1960). Elsewhere, this was not the case and many Fijian farmers planted freely on the land of other *mataqali*. In the north-east, many of the villagers are members of *mataqali* who had left their own lands in the hills to the east and west of the main Wainibuka River valley and moved, by customary agreement, to live close to the river (and later the road) and use the land of other villagers.

In 1983 I revisited three villages in which I had worked in 1958 and 1959. In 1958, Saliadrau was very isolated with access only by foot or on horseback. Sote was more accessible by road and river. Nabudrau, while close to the capital Suva, could only be reached by boat and foot and had not had land suitable for commercial agriculture. Survey results on these villages were published in 1960 and 1965 (Ward 1960 and Ward 1965:271–95).

The changes in material conditions in the three villages are representative of those that have occurred generally. In 1958–59, all houses in Saliadrau, most in Sote and some in Nabudrau were built of local material (such as reed and split bamboo walls) and had thatch roofs. In 1983 all houses had iron roofs, most had sawn timber walls and in some concrete blocks were used. Water-sealed pit latrines or well-constructed covered pits were the norm in 1983 and all three villages have piped water, whereas only Nabudrau had this facility in 1959.

One of the most striking changes is in the material possessions of households. Furniture in houses now commonly includes beds, tables and chairs, food and clothing cupboards, and curtains. Some houses are subdivided into separate rooms or sleeping areas. Radios are commonplace. In the technical field, the greater use of motor mowers, chemicals for agriculture, a plough in one village, trucks (in two villages), outboard motors and other equipment reflects the much deeper involvement in the commercial economy. Altogether, these changes suggest a considerably higher material level of living than in the late 1950s.

The extension of rural roads has benefited Saliadrau and Sote. The former was reached by all-weather road in 1981, while a farm access road ends close to Sote although river transport to the main highway is still used for most movement of market produce. Nabudrau, in the lower Rewa Delta, is still dependent on outboard motor boats to provide the link to roads that in turn provide access to Suva, and thus suffers from high transport costs despite being close 'as the crow flies' to Suva.

The principal farming system in both years was swidden cultivation, usually with taro being the initial crop, though often interplanted with *yaqona* (*Piper methysticum*), which would then remain in the garden until harvested several years later. The dried root of *yaqona* is used to make a drink that is a mild narcotic, of ceremonial importance and relatively high value. Yams were of declining importance and cassava was a recent introduction to provide emergency food after the 1952 hurricane. The average area planted per household (excluding pasture and coconuts) in 1958 was 0.41 hectares, or 0.08 per head.

Gardens were well scattered, with some about 2 kilometres from the village. Some were on the restricted area of alluvial terraces near the village, but most were on steep land with slopes of up to 45 degrees. Apart from the *yaqona,* all production was for consumption within the village. Very little purchased food was used, although a tiny cooperative store had been established.

In 1983, although population was higher and there were more gardens, the total planted area was lower. The area planted per household (excluding pasture and coconuts) had fallen to 0.25 hectares and 0.05 hectares per head. However, in addition to *yaqona,* taro was now sold regularly in Navua and Suva markets, being carried in about one-and-a-half hours in a truck owned by one of the village families. But the most striking change was the increase in the area under cattle pasture, most being on a formal lease that covered much of the alluvial terrace adjacent to the village. A second lease had been applied for by another villager. The general pattern of garden location was much the same in 1983 as in 1958, except that more gardens were being planted on the ridges to the south of the village and on the opposite side of the river where the road is located. The alluvial flats could no longer be used because of the cattle farm.

In Sote village the changes in land use were rather more marked. Bananas, which had been the village's main cash crop in 1959, have virtually disappeared. This followed the general collapse of Fiji's export banana industry in the 1960s. Disease, shipping difficulties and hurricane damage all played a part in the demise of the industry. In Sote, root crops are now the main cash crop. The pattern of garden location has changed, with less emphasis on the small alluvial terraces where bananas were formerly planted. Some of this land is now under pasture, both on formal leases and under more customary arrangements. Recently, a number of cacao blocks, each of about 0.8 hectares, have been planted under forest shade, but most trees are still immature.

Less obvious, but of considerable importance, are changes in cultivation practices. In 1959 most taro gardens in Sote contained a number of taro varieties, sometimes six or seven in the one plot. Today, growers concentrate on the two varieties that are most popular in the Suva and

Nausori markets. A new 'Malayan' variety of *Saccharum edule* has been introduced; it flowers twice a year and thus is more productive for the market. At least one grower is using hormone treatment to induce out-of-season production of pineapples. Ploughing has been used by several farmers. The planted area (excluding coconuts and pasture) had fallen from 0.14 hectares to 0.1 hectares per head of population.

Livestock farming has become important and there are six cattle enterprises (three on formal leases) on village land, with a total area of 63.5 hectares under pasture. In addition, three members of the village have leases in a cattle development project to the north of the village. A commercial piggery has been set up, using purchased feed for the most part. The locking up of large areas in pasture is now a potential constraint on garden location. Several farmers have moved out of the village to live close to their own gardens for most of the time, and others are considering following suit.

In the latter half of the 1950s, Nabudrau was a village in decline. Its population had fallen to 57 in 1956 (from 155 in 1891). In 1958 there were only seven men in the village available for full-time agricultural work, while 52 men were working away from the village. A history of involvement in wage labour going back to the 1920s, as well as the restrictions of a low-lying swampy site, meant that there was virtually no cash cropping in Nabudrau. In both 1959 and 1983, 0.04 hectares were planted (excluding coconuts) per head of population. In 1983 there was still no significant cash cropping, and the subsistence gardening practised was little different from that of 1959. Almost all the food consumed in the village was grown there, although fish was obtained in an old exchange relationship with a nearby fishing village. Root crops were given in exchange.

Despite there being no significant cash income from agriculture, Nabudrau in 1983 was a much more active and much less depressed village than in 1959. A number of middle-aged men who had retired with pensions from public service or army positions had returned to live in the village. The school had expanded, serving several nearby villages. Instead of village children being sent to school in Suva (to take advantage of better facilities), some Suva residents of Nabudrau origin were now sending children to live in the village and attend school as this was somewhat cheaper than keeping them in Suva.

In 1958–59 in all three sample villages, three-quarters or more of the gardens were located on land that did not belong to the planter's kin group (Figures 3, 4 and 5). It was possible to predict in the early 1960s, as the commercial imperative (or, in another terminology, the penetration of capitalism) continued, that this rather laissez-faire attitude to the relationships between ownership and use of land would change. This has happened. Studies carried out in 1982–83 for the Fiji Employment and Development Mission showed clearly that intra-village disputes of land were becoming much more common and that villagers were less and less willing to allow non-members of a *mataqali* to use that *mataqali*'s land except through formal leases or following informal rent payments. In 1959, 74 per cent of the gardens in Sote were on land that did not belong to the planter. In 1983 in this village, the most committed of the three sample villages to commercial farming, the proportion had dropped to 37 per cent. In Nabudrau, where commercial agriculture was not significant, the situation was unchanged.

The case of Saliadrau, where the degree of commercial involvement had increased markedly only within the last two years (before 1983), the change compared with Sote had not been so great. But the position needs elaboration. A considerable proportion of the Saliadrau gardens (23 per cent in 1958; 36 per cent in 1983) were located on land to the south of the village belonging to a related *mataqali* resident in a neighbouring village, but with rather difficult access from that village. That village was not short of planting land in 1959 and, although a couple of its members are now planting in the general area used by Saliadrau, the flexible use situation has continued until the present. If one were to exclude this area from calculations, the 1958 figures would be 69 per cent of gardens on land that did not belong to the planter's *mataqali,* and only 46 per cent in 1984. It can be suggested that the pressures to relate use to ownership are also appearing in Saliadrau.

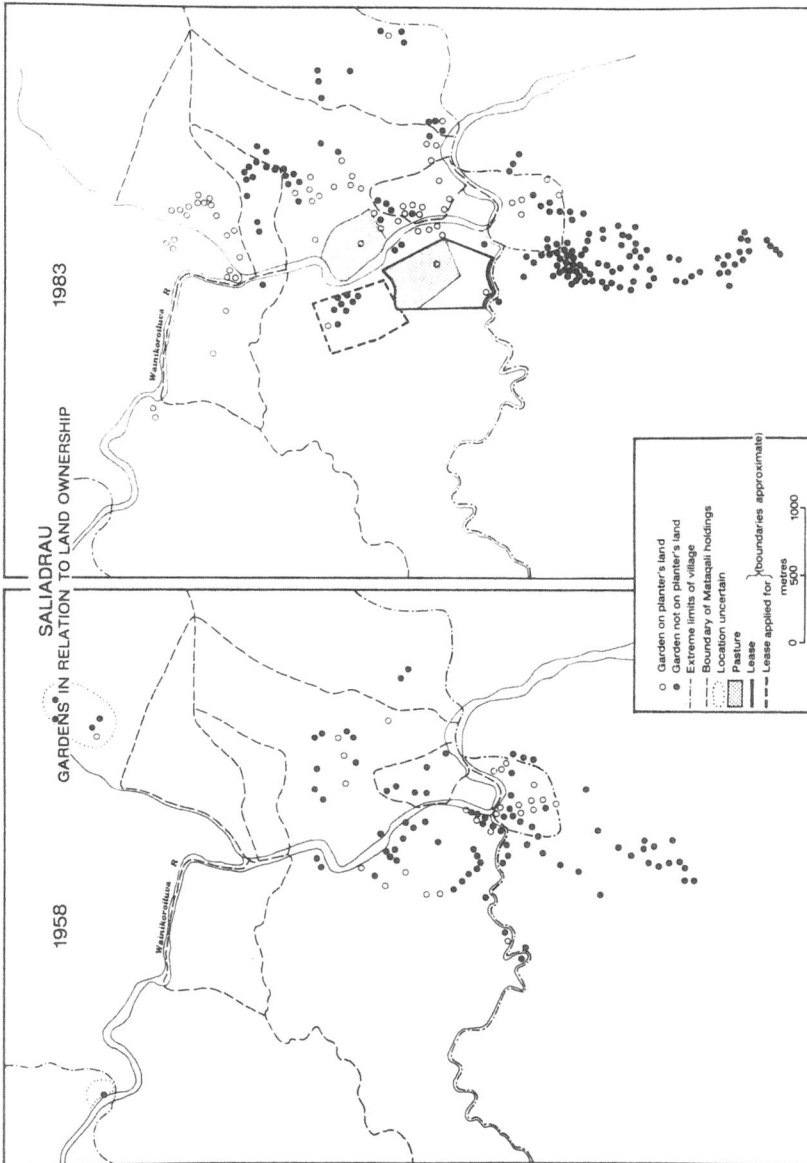

Figure 3. Location and tenure of gardens, Saliadrau village, 1958 and 1983.

Source: Author's fieldwork, 1958 and 1983.

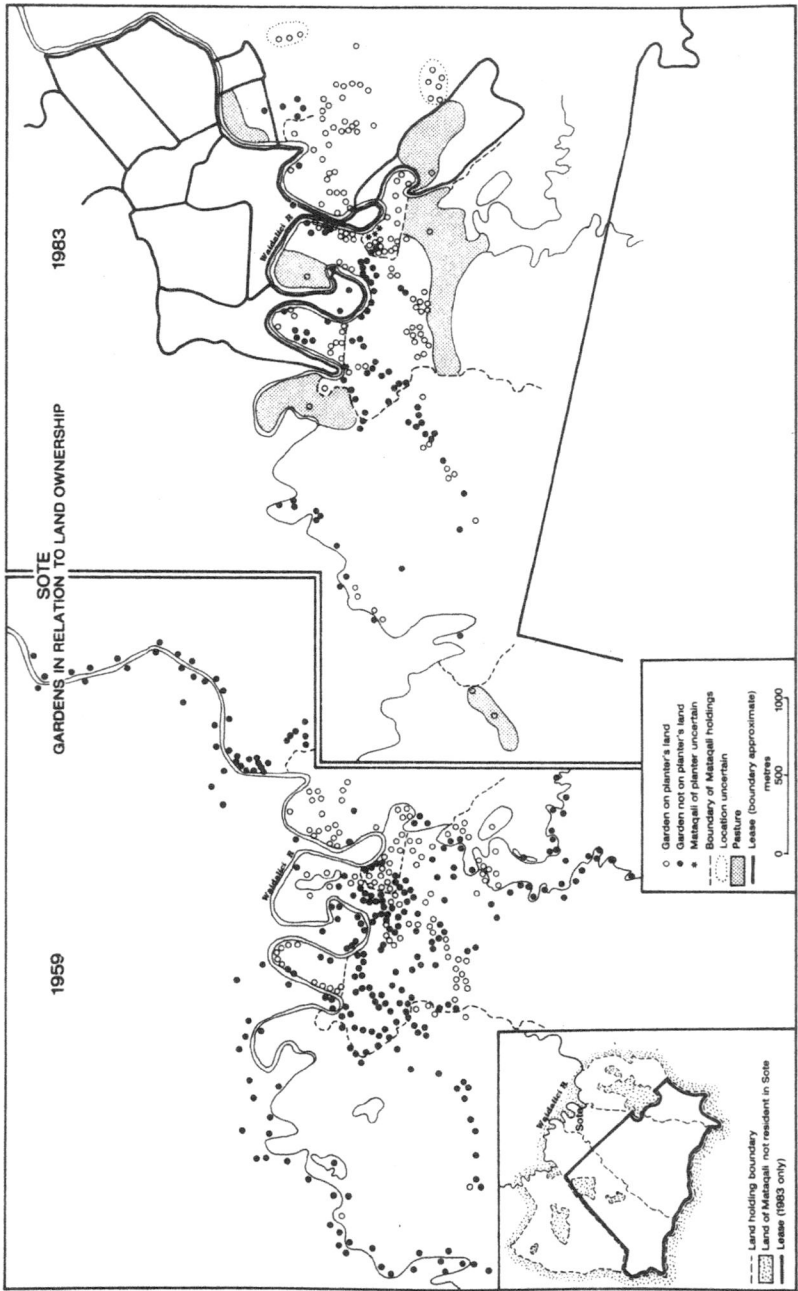

Figure 4. Location and tenure of gardens, Sote village, 1959 and 1983.
Source: Author's fieldwork, 1959 and 1983.

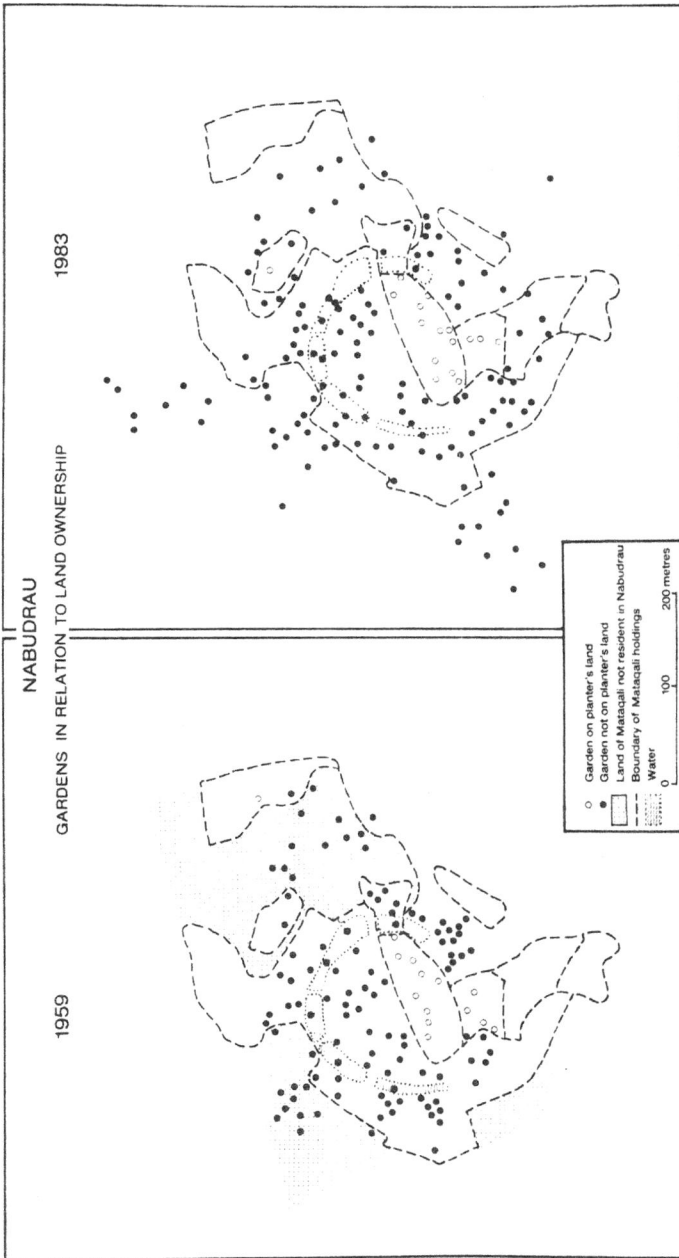

Figure 5. Location and tenure of gardens, Nabudrau village, 1959 and 1983.

Source: Author's fieldwork, 1959 and 1983.

Other changes are also evident in both Sote and Saliadrau. Since the 1960s it has been possible for Fijians to take out formal leases over the land of either their own or other *mataqali*. The leases are processed by the Native Land Trust Board with the agreement of the owning *mataqali*. Once leased the land lies outside the area of possible use under customary practices, and such leases are normally taken up for commercial purposes. The Sote example is instructive. To the north of the village, where Sote people formerly grew bananas on the land of another village, the leases of the cattle project now commit the land to cattle pasture. At least three Sote people live on their individual cattle farms within the scheme. To the south of the river that forms the northern boundary of village land, three formal leases and three other cattle farms on unleased land lock up 63.5 hectares under pasture. These pastoral farms constrain the area that can now be used for food or cash crop gardens. In addition, Sote people have leased 2,652 hectares to the government for mahogany plantations. As yet the removal of this land from the commercial pool has not had serious effects. Nevertheless, when combined with the increasing reluctance to allow non-owners to use customarily held land, especially for cash crops, the implications for land-short *mataqali* are quite clear.

Changes of the type described in the above paragraphs reduce the capacity of the Fijian village to accommodate people regardless of the extent of their legal landholdings. It was this capacity that allowed the villages to absorb many of the growing number of younger people who, in the late 1970s and early 1980s, would otherwise have been forced into urban employment or unemployment. In many villages, the trends described here have gone much further than in the sample villages. It is not unreasonable to suggest that, if present trends continue, another 10 years will see the end of the land tenure/land use flexibility that has persisted so far.

It is clear that the social and economic situation in Fijian villages has changed considerably over the last quarter century, and a number of trends are closely linked to the land use and land tenure changes described above. The first is the increasing number of tasks that are now performed by the nuclear family or household rather than by wider kin groups. As more farmers establish consolidated holdings on leases or on unleased *mataqali* land this trend will continue. Wage labour of varying degrees of formality within villages is increasingly widespread. So too is daily or weekly commuting from villages to urban or rural non-farm jobs. The improved road network of the last decade has facilitated this but it is not a new development, though now much more common. The withdrawal of this labour from farming does have implications for certain agricultural practices and crop choices. It also brings more cash and information into the villages. Daily papers and radio news broadcasts keep people informed of national events, even in villages like Saliadrau. Market information is now spread much more quickly.

It is also clear that there is now much greater variation in wealth and income within villages. In the case of Saliadrau, one man—a commoner—who stood out in 1958 solely because he had a few more garden plots than anyone else, is now the owner of the only truck in the village, has a cattle holding (on a formal lease) and a plantation of mahogany, was the first to build a sawn timber and iron-roofed house, is about to build a concrete-block house, has more furniture than anyone else, and is clearly en route to becoming a 'big peasant'. Meanwhile, the traditional village leaders of Saliadrau are not so well placed economically. Brookfield (1975) and others have noted the increasing presence in villages of people who are destitute or have very low real incomes. The individualisation of economic activity, the changing degree of access to land and cash, and the decline in the efficacy of mobilising assistance through kinship networks have detrimental as well as beneficial effects on different people. And the social security net of the 'traditional' social system is becoming much less effective. Spate, in his extremely perceptive report to the government, published in 1959, foresaw most of these trends.

In conclusion, some matters of policy importance may be noted. It should be recognised that a 'new frontier' approach to land development will not be practical for more than a few years as the supply of unused land will be inadequate. The ability of the subsistence component of the rural economy to absorb more people is questionable both because of rising expectations and the process of privatisation of land tenure. The rapid expansion of pastoral farming on village land may need to be questioned as there is a growing tendency for cattle to be grazed on the easily accessible alluvial flats, and for subsistence or commercial root crops to be forced onto steep land that cannot sustain prolonged cultivation. Rural villages within reach of urban areas or other wage employment areas will become increasingly dormitory centres for wage workers, with a destabilising effect on the role of the village in farming, and particularly production for market. The polarisation between the richer and the poorer in rural society will become more marked, perhaps with important consequences for the bonds that formerly held the Fijian society of chiefs and commoners together.

References

Brookfield, H.C. 1975. Preliminary Report on the Taveuni Resource Base Survey. Report to the Permanent Secretary for Fijian Affairs and Rural Development. Suva.

Spate, O.H.K. 1959. *The Fijian People: Economic Problems and Prospects*. A Report for the Legislative Council of Fiji, Council Paper No. 13. Suva: Government Printer.

Twyford, I.T. and A.C.S. Wright 1965. *The Soil Resources of the Fiji Islands*. Suva: Goverment Printer.

Ward, R.G. 1960. Village Agriculture in Viti Levu, Fiji. *New Zealand Geographer* 16(1):33–56. doi.org/10.1111/j.1745-7939.1960.tb00292.x

Ward, R.G. 1965. *Land Use and Population in Fiji: A Geographical Study*. London: Her Majesty's Stationery Office.

5

Matai Titles and Modern Corruption in Samoa: Costs, Expectations and Consequences for Families and Society

Morgan Tuimaleali'ifano

Morgan Tuimaleali'ifano: Personal Journey

I attended primary and secondary school in Auckland and Wellington, New Zealand. In December 1973, I returned to Samoa with hopes of undergraduate studies in New Zealand. With an eye on a government scholarship, I was told my application was late but I suspected it was the C bursary that carried no monetary reward. I was considering returning to New Zealand as a private student, but the then highly respected first native Secretary to Government, Tuala Karanita Enari, mentioned the University of the South Pacific (USP). With about 30 other students funded by New Zealand and Australia, we landed at Nausori in February 1974, and bussed to Laucala campus (the former Royal New Zealand Air Force base established during the Second World War) to meet Warden Joe Nailati who dished out linen, room keys and *sasa* brooms.

I signed up for survey courses in sociology/anthropology, economics and, argument/evidence, but was interested in history, particularly Pacific history because, apart from new options opening up on the Pacific in Auckland, I had gone through the New Zealand school system learning virtually nothing about the Pacific Islands. Graduates from The Australian National University's (ANU) Department of Pacific (and Southeast Asian) History dominated teaching and research in Pacific history: Ron Crocombe (first director of the New Guinea Research Unit at ANU), Peter Stone, Ahmed Ali, Brij Lal, Anthony Chappelle, Howard Van Trease, Asesela Ravuvu, as well as ANU economists Brian Lockwood, Bruce Knapman and others. After graduation in 1977, I worked in the USP registrar's office as an administrative assistant, then returned to complete an MA in 1987 and taught Pacific history in 1988, drawing largely from the expertise and resources of the Research School of Pacific and Asian Studies at ANU.

Although it did not start out this way, my PhD apprenticeship became a joint USP–ANU affair.

I was admitted to ANU in 1992 but without funds—just leave from USP and a small allowance adequate for irregular visits to Canberra from Armidale in New South Wales (where my wife was a PhD candidate at the University of New England). It would be fair to say that I was an orphan at the Department of Pacific and Asian History because no funds were transferred between USP and ANU. As a USP staff member, I registered at USP with the then head of History/Politics Department, Doug Munro, as administrative anchor in Laucala. At ANU, Donald Denoon, Niel Gunson and Deryck Scarr were effective supervisors providing access to superb facilities, student/staff seminars and welcoming homes. In 1997, I believe I was the first ANU-supervised PhD graduate in history enrolled at USP.

Even as I pen these short lines, the way in which my journey intertwines with these institutions, USP and ANU, which in turn shape and reshape our region, continues to excite, humble and overwhelm me.

Tuimaeali'ifano, A.M. 2006. *Matai* Titles and Modern Corruption in Samoa: Costs, Expectations and Consequences for Families and Society. In S. Firth (ed.), *Globalisation and Governance in the Pacific Islands*. Canberra: ANU E Press.

Republished with the kind permission of ANU Press.

On a bright October Saturday morning in 2005, I could make out his outline in front of the R.C. Manubhai hardware store in Raiwaqa, Suva. Desmond Dutta was a Fiji-born Samoan who had left Fiji almost 20 years ago. His father was an Indo-Fijian and his mother a Samoan of Chinese ancestry. We first met in Fiji in the mid-1980s while I was doing fieldwork in Fiji's minority communities. Proud of his Samoan heritage, Dutta frequently discussed with me his desire to retrace his mother's family.[1] These topics were the focus of our regular Friday afternoon discussions at the Suva market where he earned a living selling the popular cumquat fruit juice. Soon after Fiji's two coups in 1987, Dutta made good on his word and left Fiji for Samoa.

When he returned to Fiji, he appeared fragile, ageing prematurely, his body bent and face drawn with signs of affliction by diabetes. But now he was looking forward to returning to Samoa again:

> Our side of the *'aiga* has just won a major court case over the [Manuleleua] family title. It took us six years to fight this case, and lots of money went into it. Boy, I took a lot of hammering. But, the title has finally returned to the right side of the family.

'What do you mean by hammering?' I asked.

> During the court case, the other family parties called me by all sorts of names. *Fai mai o a'u o le Fiki. Ga lau lo'u Igikia. Fai mai o a'u o le Saiga oga o le kiga o le Saiga. Fai mai o a'u o le Fiki ua sau fia pule i le aiga.* [They called me an *Igikia* (Indian), a *Saiga* (Chinese) because my mother is Chinese and they said that I was a Fijian who was coming to take over the family.] It was very painful. But you know what our fa'a Samoa is like, eh? That is part of our culture. One minute we're stabbing each other and the next we're crying and making the *lotu* [church] to forgive each other. And we forget everything that was thrown at each [other] until the next court case. Oh, I tell you, our fa'a Samoa, it's funny, eh?

We both laughed knowingly and then parted. Dutta had not only retraced his roots but was revelling in the consequences of that knowledge.

Modern Samoa is a nation that is a product of all the forces of globalisation. The legacy of the wave emanating from the west 3,000 to 3,500 years ago is apparent in the way the island nation is governed largely through family and village titles. As ancestral names, titles are passed down in families and are ceremonially conferred on chosen individuals who then represent the family in public life. Without a title, an individual has no right to speak in family and village councils. A title secures membership and rights within a family to land and common village property. Conferral ceremonies can range from elaborate gift exchanges for high titles to tea

---

1   His mother, Mali Dutta, is a descendant of the Manuleleua family clan, titular orator of Vaimoso village (see Tuimaleali'ifano 1990:45–46).

parties for minor ones. The normal practice is for the family to consult the village council on a date for their candidate's installation in a *saofa'iga* (an installation ceremony) and thereupon, formal admission into the village council. Titles are also significant because, as the sole decision-makers in the village, councillors collectively control about 80 per cent of the land.[2] From the west, the second wave, beginning in 1492 and finally reaching Samoa in the 19th century, introduced the apparatus of a modern state. When titles are disputed, virtually every development effort under the state apparatus is threatened, including land rights, homes and livelihoods. There is little incentive to develop. Under the laws of the first wave of colonisers, when families could not agree, war decided the disputes, but wars had a habit of lingering. These forms of conflict resolution and settlement were inefficient and disruptive to second-wave settlers and eventually led to colonial takeover.

When Germany took over in 1900, the German administration effectively circumvented local conflicts by establishing a Land and Titles Commission (later a court) to arbitrate disputes. It did not stop the conflicts, but it stopped the wars. The Germans managed to successfully channel local disputes through the court system. Since independence in 1962, title disputes have become so numerous that resolution of conflict can take years. And this is what I would like to consider. In Samoa, as elsewhere in the Pacific, the problem of resource ownership such as land is tied inextricably to family titles. In Fiji, the land issue is tied to leases controlled by the Native Land Trust Board, and the relationship between it and the landowner and tenants. In Samoa, when families are locked into a title succession dispute as they often are, production invariably is restricted (Tuimaleali'ifano 2006).

How are these titles appointed and their titleholders installed, and what are the consequences for the social and state apparatus? What is the place of cash in the title installation process? Is cash, much of it generated in the global economy beyond Samoa's shores, corrupting that process? More broadly, in what ways is Samoan tradition adapting to, and being corrupted by, the forces of globalisation?

---

2   The balance comprises 16 per cent government land and 4 per cent freehold. This control, it has been argued, is more theoretical than actual and much Samoan land is de facto under individual tenure.

My case study is the Samoan village of Salelologa, on the island of Savai'i, fabled home of Hawaiki. In early 2001, my mother's 64-year-old cousin and holder of the Luamanuvae title, Kirika Fiso, approached me with his wish to install new family titleholders, including one of my mother's children. Appointed in 1970 as a co-titleholder, Fiso had outlived many of his peers and had held the senior elder position in the Sa Luamanuvae clan of the Li'aga branch for some time. Though many appointments had been made, many titleholders chose to live outside the village. The title Luamanuvae was one of two titular titles of Salelologa village.[3] Like many of his generation, Fiso had moved between subsistence and the cash economy having been a clerical officer with various merchandising companies and government departments. He had also served in managerial positions with the Congregational Christian Church in Samoa and overseas and with the Seventh-Day Adventists. In inviting us to assume the title, he made it clear that he could not guarantee another opportunity during this lifetime. When he finished his story, I thanked him and accepted the offer, and told him that it was largely out of respect for the memory of my mother's longstanding desire to honour her ancestors. During her lifetime, her children were all young and more immediate needs assumed higher priority.

Fiso had an ulterior motive, which he hinted at but which I did not comprehend fully until after the installation. In the mid-1980s, Salelologa, Tafua and Fa'ala, located along the south-eastern coast of Savai'i, entered into an agreement with a Swedish environmental non-government organisation (NGO) in which the villages were to be paid several thousand dollars in aid not to develop or log their land for at least 50 years, and to use the forest only for customary uses, such as the occasional harvesting of timber for local needs and of plants for medicines. The arrangement worked well with regular payments and minimal pressure on the land. But after most of the money had been paid, in 1999, the Salelologa Council was induced by the Tofilau Eti Alesana–led Human Rights Protection Party (HRPP) government to sell 1,162 hectares of its conserved rainforest land for a politically motivated township scheme. The council saw nothing wrong with selling the land it had already agreed

---

3   The other was Muagututi'a (Methodist Board of Trustees 1985:142–45). The Sa Luamanuvae clan is split in two branches, Pouseilala and Li'aga, each with sub-branches.

and been paid to preserve.[4] In early 2002, the government paid $4 million to Salelologa. Instead of using some of this money to repay the Swedish NGO for violating the agreement, the village council was instead incensed at the NGO for not paying the final 10 per cent instalment of the money due (Whistler 2002:150–51; similar compromises are also appearing in Fa'ala)! After the $4 million was paid, another faction of the Salelologa Council, led by Pauli Elisara, petitioned the Supreme Court, claiming that they should have been paid $45 million based on 'unfair evaluation' by the government valuer (*Samoa Observer* 2002). This case continues with many senior *matai* creating new titleholders in a bid to cash in on the likelihood of more handouts.

My family's acceptance of the title implied expenses for the ceremonial gifting. The next question for the installation was costs: Fiso said the total outlay would be $35,000. In order to defray the costs, there would be six to seven titleholders, thus reducing the individual outlay to about $5,000 a person.

Who Gave What and Where Did it Come From?

On the evening before the title installation, the extended family and their candidates met to take stock of their contributions. Immediately, a problem arose. Two of the seven expected candidates failed to attend and that meant the five candidates had to come up with an additional $2,000 to meet the $35,000 outlay. This was clearly impossible with less than 12 hours left before installation. Who were the five candidates and what were their contributions?

1. Tovia, son of late Luamanuvae Lokeni and Poufitu: 40 years old, a gas stove manufacturing company employee in Mangere, South Auckland, New Zealand: $5,000, seven cartons of mackerels and 11 large fine mats.

2. Mokeni (Morgan), son of Ta'alefili, the granddaughter of Luamanuvae Pae'e: 47 years old, university lecturer, Fiji: $3,500, two cartons of chickens and six fine mats.

---

4   The late prime minister, Tofilau Eti Alesana, had earlier represented Fa'asaleleaga No. 1 in which Salelologa was included under his tenure of the Luamanuvae title. His Luamanuvae connection was to the Pouseilala branch.

3. Tofu, son of Tia'itupe Luamanuvae Tofu and Leatigaga Fa'aafu of Lauli'i village, 'Upolu: 34 years old, Apia-based employee (after the installation, he and his young family migrated to live in Salelologa in February 2002): $3,000, five *'ie toga*, seven cartons of mackerels and five large fine mats.

4. Punivalu, son of Luamanuvae Pule: 43 years old, a village farmer from Fatusi, Savai'i: $3,000, 10 large fine mats.

5. Keli, grandson of Luamanuvae Tofu: 64 years old, casual worker for the Electricity Power Corporation and the only candidate who was a permanent resident of Salelologa. He donated $1,000 consisting of $300 cash and $700 worth of groceries, five cartons of mackerels and five large fine mats. He had also undertaken extensive repairs to the family house in which the installation ceremony was conducted.

At the meeting, an elderly female family member, Mateai, attended and contributed $280. Mateai and her son, Fonoia, lived 1 kilometre away and were gifted $20 for the bus fare and were driven home. The total amount collected was $15,780, 19 cartons of mackerels[5] and two cartons of chicken.[6] Although the 38 fine mats were considered a small number, they were all high-grade mats, as attested by those present. The immediate problem was the cash. Though short by $20,000, it covered the cash payments and fine mats for religious ministers, the speech-maker, clan heads and lesser titleholders in attendance at the *'ava* ceremony, who received less than at previous installations.

Where Did This Cash Come From?

It was considered bad taste to seek details of sources of income from the other four co-titleholders, and this paper is limited to my own sources. In Suva, my wife and I took the view, one common to many, that since I was the recipient, we should take the initiative and provide at least half the cash. As we did not have spare cash, we raised funds by selling *umu* packs, organising cake drives and making monthly cash deductions from salary and allowances. Our Suva *umu* packs were sold for $20 each (two *luau*, one *taro*, one bowl of raw fish, one No. 12 chicken and a bowl of fruit salad). Our dollar target was $4,000, with the expectation that my

---

5   A carton of mackerel retailed at $71 and a carton of chicken for $81.
6   In addition to the Luamanuvae title, the Le Atigaga title was also on offer for $400–500.

siblings would make up the $1,000 balance. Despite our ambitious plans, our efforts raised the modest sum of $700, barely enough for one return airfare. In the end, the bulk of the money came from two sisters and a brother living in the US,[7] two of whom were awaiting green cards from the Department of Immigration and Naturalization Services. What were their sources of livelihood? My oldest sister worked as a primary school teacher and the other worked at a pharmaceutical plant and was studying part time. My 39-year-old brother had only recently begun working as a part-time primary school teacher after being an unpaid volunteer for almost 10 years. They contributed $3,000. The only one who could travel from the US, my oldest sister, attended the installation at her own expense and bought more food. In addition to her airfare, she paid $1,000 for hotel accommodation and a rental car, and another $100 contribution to the first Sunday *to'ona'i*, a lunch following the installation. In addition, my three siblings contributed to other installations. One thousand tala ($1,000) was given to another sister's husband whose uncle was installed in Satupa'itea;[8] $2,000 for a New Zealand-based brother, a recipient of two titles;[9] and $2,000 for a Samoan-based brother for taking a title from Iva village.[10] At the last moment, more titles were on offer for cash and, for another $1,000, my oldest sister was persuaded to take one from the same village.[11] The total amount for installations came to $8,500 (about A$4,000), in addition to about $100 customary contributions for each new titleholder for the Sunday lunches. Almost all of this money was derived from the modest wages of primary school teachers and factory workers.

The Installation Ceremony and the Political Agenda

At installation ceremonies, there are two main events. After the introduction and exchange of pleasantries and collection of *'ava* stems from the assembled *matais*, the first major item is the *fa'atau*— the selection of the speech-maker through an open contest among the orators. The second is the *lauga*—the act of making the speech, during which reference is made to the genealogy of the title and the title is

---

7   Pinelo Laura (45), Suatipatipa Tuimaleali'ifano (39) and Vaivase Maualaivao (37).
8   Falani and Vaosa Asiata for the Gasu title.
9   Wellington Fiso for Le Atigaga in Salelologa and Fiso in Vaito'omuli, Palauli.
10   Lilomaiava Rev. Nerony Fiapia Tuimaleali'ifano for the Tofilau title in Iva village.
11   Laura was conferred as the Tagaloasa orator title at the same ceremony in Iva.

situated within existing village and district hierarchies. When strong and powerful speakers take the stage, the contest is the most thrilling part of the ceremony, with seasoned orators eager to display their political wares. The contest provides a window of opportunity for newly installed titleholders to witness firsthand the power structure and those behind it. The higher the title, the higher the rewards are likely to be.

Salelologa, like most other villages, operates under a dual system of authority exercised by titular family heads and orator clan heads, in oppositional relationship to each other. While the two titular titles stand at the apex of the hierarchy, their power is largely ceremonial. Effective power is wielded by two bands of orators, the *falefia* and *falesalafai*, numbering seven clans.[12] In the speech contest, everyone waited expectantly for the customary rivalry between the two groups. Pipi Lavilavi, the head of the Pipi clan and leader of the *falefia* on that day, initiated the contest. He began by acknowledging clan heads and stated firmly and clearly his wish to speak on behalf of their band, and each clan head of the *falefia* conceded their right in favour of him. Pipi then turned to the three clan heads of the *falesalafai* and repeated his wish. The head of the Seumanu clan, Seumanu Tupea, responded on their behalf and obtained Pipi's concurrence to allow their band to negotiate a consensus. After about 30 minutes of protracted negotiations with the *falefasalafi*, Seumanu obtained their vote to represent them against the *falefia*. Seumanu then turned to Pipi and thus began a two-way contest.

For the next 45 minutes, the two clan heads dug deep into their political repertoire of emotional blackmail and vanity, to outmanoeuvre the other. Both stood their ground and there was considerable entertainment value as they parleyed and toyed with each other's apparent foibles. Those new to the contest feared physical violence.[13] In the contest, the two men showed no sign of yielding and eventually Pipi resorted to higher authority. In front of a captive audience, he told Seumanu that their absent leader, Matamua (Pua'atoga), on account of ill health, had appointed him as his

---

12   Falefia aka To'afia and comprises the titles Taotua (represented by Ioane), Pipi (represented by Lavilavi), Matamua (unidentified), and Fonoia (absent). Falesalafai comprises Seumanu (represented by Tupea), Pauli (represented by Afele) and Fiu (represented by Loimata II). See Methodist Board of Trustees 1985:142.

13   I was later informed of earlier contests between Seumanu Tupea and Matamua Pua'atoga, the head of the Matamua clan and highest-ranking orator. At an earlier contest, the rivalry over the speech led to physical blows. The two elders rolled about the centre of the house hurling abuse at each. It ended as both quickly ran out of breath. No one lifted a finger to stop them. Scores were settled for the time being until the next round of *saofa'i*.

representative. Pipi explained that before the installation, the *falefia* had assembled at Matamua's residence and waited for the *falesalafai*. When the latter failed to attend this preliminary meeting, Matamua extended his blessing and anointed Pipi as spokesperson. As proof, Pipi lifted Matamua's flywhisk as the badge of office. Seumanu at this point became visibly angry and reaffirmed his allegiance to Matamua as leader and, in regretful tones, turned to his *falesalafai* colleagues and asked them to accept Pipi as their spokesman. Pipi returned the compliments and proceeded with his speech, first acknowledging the assembled dignataries, then outlining the procedure for *'ava* distribution and enunciating the family genealogy. Before he could continue with the genealogy, he was stopped by the head of the Muagututi'a clan, Muagututi'a Ami, who politely interjected and asked Pipi to skip this aspect, and beckoned him to go straight to the blessing of the titleholders and distribution of *'ava*. Pipi concurred and, as he concluded his speech, the master of the *'ava* ceremony, from the back of the house, began the chant and enunciated each titleholder's *'ava* cup title. It began with the new titleholders followed by the clan heads according to a predetermined order of precedence, with the older peers first.

As the clan heads received their *'ava* cup, each took the opportunity to give words of advice to the new titleholders. In wishing them well, they also emphasised the importance of commitment to family, the village council (by implication, its constituent women and non-titled men and women elements), the church and the government, in that order. They spoke of the customary relationship between the orator groups and the titular clans as represented by senior holders of Muagututi'a and Luamanuvae titles. Others emphasised the courtesies expected of us as younger and newer titleholders towards older and more senior titleholders. Others were more blunt in their expectations, as graphically illustrated by the head of Fiu Loimata II, representing the Fiu clan. A former member of parliament and a forceful speaker, his advice was a stinging reminder of the paradoxical relationship between titular and orator chiefs. Pointing to senior Luamanuvae and Muagututi'a titleholders sitting at the opposite end of the house, Fiu spelt out to us the relationship in dollar terms. He said:

> *E uma le ola o kama la ia makou. O le lakou masagi a fekaui ma I makou i le makeki, e ke'i a ua fai mai, ku'u aku le selau kala I lau kaga. Pe o'o i se isi kaeao, fagu fagu mai, kago mai I lau afe kala lea e ku'u I lau kaga'.*

The lives of those men [pointing to senior Luamanuvae and Muagututi'a] end with us. They make it their habit, whenever we meet, to give us money. They will say to us, 'Here, take this $200 and put it in your pocket.' Or early one morning, they would wake us up and say, 'Here, take this $1,000 and put it in your pocket.'[14]

In other words, it was his view that the orators' role was to support and speak on behalf of titular titleholders and it was the role of the titular titleholder to pay the orators, which in Fiu's terms was best done not by fine mats and pigs but in cash.

The Gifting

Although I had been to other title installation ceremonies, the Salelologa ceremony was different. The one-way gifting without immediate return was of serious concern. Moreover, nothing had prepared me for what was to happen that day. I would not have believed the shameless public demands if I had not seen them myself. After the speech and drinking of *'ava*, the assembly of clan heads moved to the open space outside for refreshments and in anticipation of receiving customary gifts. The sponsors also moved outside ready to distribute what had been planned the night before. As they received their gifts of cash and fine mats, some orators shamelessly demanded more and publicly stated, '*Fa'aatoa mai le fia …tala o la'u lafo*' ('Give me some more dollars to make up the rest of my entitlement'). One threatened to recommend deregistering the newly installed titleholders. When our party, the sponsoring party, tried to appease them, some begrudgingly sat down only after being promised more cash.

Pipi Lavilavi, the speaker at the ceremony, as expected, got the lion's share. But having receiving $1,000 in cash plus the largest and choicest fine mats, he then made an extraordinary plea on behalf of the 70-year-old sickly and absent Matamua Pua'atoga. In the lead-up to the gifting, it was expected that whatever gifts the speaker received would be shared with the absent orator. Instead, Pipi demanded a similar donation be given on the basis that the absent orator was sickly and might not live to see another

---

14   From DVDs of the ceremony (Laura 2002).

installation. In other words, so it seemed, we were asked, on behalf of the village, to provide a parting gift. The stunned sponsors took a full minute to recover and renegotiate amid muffled terse epithets.

Seeds of Corruption

These gifting events have a life of their own and have significant consequences. As remembered events, they are transmitted and re-lived at the next crisis such as a title installation or funeral. If the payback is not matched or bettered, the sponsoring family is stigmatised. The consequences are transmitted to a future generation of *matai* titleholders and their families. As opportunity arises, they will demand no less than what was demanded of them as their 'just due'.

When expectations of titleholders and families are not matched by return gifts, conflict is apt to spiral into other arenas, including places of employment, churches and schools as part of loyalty to family and village. Customary gifts derived from a subsistence economy are less likely, these days, to satisfy the needs of a family and clan structure accustomed to cash and remittances. While there is always money, there are not enough fine mats, pigs and foodstuffs.[15] When food was gifted instead of cash, tropical climatic conditions required efficient redistribution. But when cash infiltrates gifting, whether in the form of remittances or otherwise, redistribution is not required and gifting is taken out of the public into the private and individualised arena. As reciprocal exchanges increasingly take the form of cash payments, they enter a world of capitalism never intended for this type of family-oriented activity. In the past, installations encouraged family gatherings and redistribution of gifts. The cash installation in Salelologa did not elicit redistribution of any sort among the candidates and their families. They dispersed knowing they had debts to return to and there was little else to discuss or take home to celebrate. It seemed, at least for those remaining behind, that the focus was on payback at the next life crisis.

---

15   I am grateful for Dr William Clarke's interest in and pertinent comments on this paper on 28 October 2005.

References

Laura, P. 2002. Family DVDs of *Saofa'is* in Foua, Salelologa, Samoa (copy on file with author).

Methodist Board of Trustees 1985. *Ole Tusi Fa'alupega o Samoa Atoa.* Compiled by the Tusi Fa'alupega Committee. Apia: Methodist Printing Press.

Samoa Observer 2002. Salelologa wants $45m, 21 December.

Tuimaleali'ifano, A.M. 2006. *O Tama a 'Aiga: The Politics of Succession to Samoa's Paramount Titles.* Suva: University of the South Pacific.

Tuimaleali'ifano, M. 1990. *Samoans in Fiji: Migration, Identity and Communication.* Institute of Pacific Studies, Fiji, Tonga and Western Samoa Extension Centres, University of the South Pacific, Star Printery.

Whistler, W.A. 2002. *The Samoan Rainforest, A Guide to the Vegetation of the Samoan Archipelago.* Honolulu, Hawai'i: Isle Botanica.

6

Making Room for Magic in Intellectual Property Policy

Miranda Forsyth

Miranda Forsyth: Personal Journey

I first went to Vanuatu in 2001 as a volunteer legal officer and worked in the Office of the Public Prosecutor for a year. During this time, I became fascinated with the non-state system of justice (*kastom*), with its emphasis on dialogue and relationships, and the way in which it interacted with the state criminal justice system. After returning to Melbourne, I successfully applied for a position at the School of Law at the University of the South Pacific (USP) and returned to Vanuatu as soon as I could to take up the position. It was a fantastically vibrant time at the School of Law, with considerable interest in bringing the state and non-state justice systems in the region meaningfully into the curriculum as much as possible. This was helped by the enormous work that went into establishing and running Pacific Islands Legal Information Institute (PacLII), the Pacific electronic database for case law and legislation, housed at the Emalus campus of USP in Port Vila.

During my time at USP, I pursued my PhD in law as a distance student through The Australian National University (ANU). My subject was the relationship between the *kastom* and state justice systems in Vanuatu and I did my fieldwork around Vanuatu during semester breaks. As a lecturer, I learnt an incredible amount from the students and their insights into how law operated in practice in the region and its complex entanglement with custom and Christianity. I thoroughly enjoyed the challenge of teaching across multiple jurisdictions and learning with the students about the similarities and differences to approaches to legal questions across the region.

Introduction

Although the global intellectual property regime[1] is often positioned as being the only intellectual property regime across the globe, there are currently many different regimes regulating the production of, and access to, a range of intangible resources. These alternative intellectual property regimes—such as customary systems, informal contracts, trade secrets and other informal normative systems—are often highly relational and deeply embedded in the social, cultural and political matrix of the group they regulate. Today many of these systems operate in pockets where the global intellectual property system has not as yet spread, but these areas are quickly diminishing as the global system continues to colonise both new geographical regions and also new types of subject matter.

This paper argues that local knowledge and innovation systems are often rendered invisible by the dominance of the global intellectual property system. This is largely due to the state-centric, positivistic paradigm within which the global system, and the institutions that manage it, operate. This in turn means that when new types of intangible resources or innovation start to be recognised as valuable by the global North, such as traditional knowledge, there is a tendency to fail to see the existing regulatory structures that surround them as these structures rarely operate at the level of the state. This type of myopia has been referred to as the 'blank slate fallacy' (Twining 2009:285–86) by legal pluralists who reveal a repeated pattern of marginalisation of non-state regulatory

---

1   The term global intellectual property regime is used to refer to the international regulatory system established by the Agreement on Trade Related Aspects of Intellectual Property (TRIPS) and subsequently supplemented by a range of multilateral intellectual property agreements.

orders by state-based legal systems (see, for example, Griffiths 1986; von Benda-Beckmann 1985:187). As a result, the global intellectual property system often colonises these 'new' regulatory spaces through imposing transplanted regulatory regimes. The existing systems are often changed in fundamental ways as a result of the new rules, ideologies and categories of winners and losers, introduced by the new system.

This paper explores these issues through a discussion of the role of magic or spirits in Melanesian intellectual property systems, first identifying their importance in local intellectual property systems and then asking what happens when this dimension is left out by the introduction and dominance of the global intellectual property system. We see how the global system approaches the regulatory challenge of protecting traditional knowledge by separating the 'object' of protection (traditional knowledge) from the system that formed the necessary environment for its production. I then discuss two problematic consequences of failing to take local intellectual property systems into account when extending the global intellectual property regime into new areas. First, the creation of new forms of property rights is likely to interfere with the existing systems in potentially corrosive ways. This is linked in part to what Drahos has referred to as the 'tragedy of commodification' (Drahos 2014:203) as it involves the introduction of new forms of property rights geared towards facilitating exchange in a market system. The second problem is that it means the true value of these knowledge and innovation systems is missed by the global North, particularly the ways in which they suggest the need to expand our epistemic and metaphysical horizons. These lessons are particularly important in relation to climate change, where the value of seeing the earth as a balanced system, a central tenet of many local knowledge systems, has particular resonance (ibid.:206–07).[2] The final

---

2   Indeed the most recent calls for paradigm shifts are heavily based upon a revaluing of small-scale, sustainable agriculture that is underpinned by local knowledge and innovation systems. The UNCTAD Trade and Environment Review (2013) argues that small-scale organic farming is the only viable and sustainable way to feed the world and advocates 'a rapid and significant shift from conventional, monoculture-based and high-external-input-dependent industrial production toward mosaics of sustainable, regenerative production systems that also considerably improve the productivity of small-scale farmers'. A similar approach is urged by the final report of the Special Rapporteur on the Right to Food, Oliver de Schutter (2014), who stresses the need for a 'new paradigm focused on well-being, resilience and sustainability' to 'replace the productivist paradigm'. He dismisses the idea that the problem of food security can be addressed through a technological fix, such as by increasing yields, and instead argues that it is essential to change unsustainable consumption habits and to shift towards sustainable production through the adoption of agroecology. This refers to a range of agronomic techniques that reduce the use of external inputs and rely heavily on local farmer knowledge, and are often the techniques being used by the rural poor in the poorest countries of the world today.

part of the paper then explores one possible approach that could be used in order to make room for these local systems in intellectual property regulation, namely intercultural legal pluralism.

As a preliminary point, it is necessary to discuss a problem of terminology. The term traditional knowledge is widely used to refer to the knowledge held by indigenous peoples that has been transmitted from generation to generation.[3] However, this definition sets up problematic binaries between traditional and modern knowledge that do not take into account the continually evolving nature of knowledge. It also ignores the importance of local innovation in contributing to developing bodies of knowledge. This paper therefore uses the terms traditional and local knowledge and innovation as an imperfect way of taking account of these difficulties. The final section of the paper argues that the focus should not be on the knowledge or innovations themselves per se anyway, but rather on the knowledge systems of which they are an integral part, thereby also solving this terminological problem.

Local Melanesian Intellectual Property Regulatory Systems

This section sketches out four local systems that regulate a variety of intangible resources in different parts of Melanesia. These brief descriptions are intended to challenge the hegemonic tendencies of the global intellectual property system and to illustrate the fundamentally different ontological and epistemological frameworks in which they operate.[4] It should be stressed that these brief descriptions are themselves historically contingent, as systems for the production and use of knowledge are as dynamic and contested in this part of the world as everywhere

---

3   There is a wide variety of definitions of tradition knowledge (see, for example, Antons 2009:1–4). For example, the Pacific Islands Model Law 2002, discussed below, contains four criteria:

        traditional knowledge includes any knowledge that generally (a) is or has been created, acquired or inspired for traditional economic, spiritual, ritual, narrative, decorative or recreational purposes; and (b) is or has been transmitted from generation to generation; and (c) is regarded as pertaining to a particular traditional group, clan or community of people; and (d) is collectively originated and held.

4   Of course such systems exist in many other parts of the world as well. See the excellent literature review by Tom Griffiths (1993) that was kindly photocopied for me by G. Dutfield.

else. As Simet observes, 'Increasing globalisation threatens the ability of communities in Papua New Guinea to control access to and use of their traditional knowledge' (Simet 2000:78).[5]

The first is a description of part of the intellectual property system of the Tolai people from the Gazelle Peninsula in Papua New Guinea. Jacob Simet, the Executive Director at the PNG National Cultural Commission observes:

> Ownership of knowledge among the Tolai is highly regulated, and the ways of acquiring it are clearly defined. Knowledge is owned either by an individual, group or the wider public and may be protected by means of *pidik* (secrecy). A particular class of spirits known as *turangan* are present in the creation, transfer and use of knowledge (ibid.:64–65).

He explains that the Tolai recognise five ways of acquiring knowledge: dream, school, gift, purchase and inheritance. The level of ownership is moreover determined by the manner in which the knowledge is acquired. Different spirits are also associated with the different ways in which knowledge is imparted. Even in the case of knowledge gained through attending school, 'the person merely acquires the ability to be associated with spirits that later begin to deliver knowledge to him' (ibid.:65). The rights to knowledge are clearly differentiated from mere access to it:

> anyone may know which plant materials are used for healing or other kind of knowledge and may observe the various ritual actions and procedures involved in the performance of healing, knowledge, magic or dance. But they cannot claim ownership of the knowledge these plants and rituals are associated with nor can they practice this knowledge. Rights to knowledge are determined by possession of the *wanvul* [chant]. At all times the owner of the knowledge keeps this *wanvul* as *pidik* (secret) from everyone (Simet 2000:65).

Simet also explains that the Tolai have types of knowledge that is owned by groups, in particular by clans. These clans own *tubuan* (a type of spirit) designs, magic, songs, dance headdress, necklace designs and the oral history of the clan. In addition, there is also public knowledge that everyone in that society knows or has a right to access, including marriage

---

5   The section that follows is extremely indebted to the project led by anthropologist Marilyn Strathern in the late 1990s to early 2000s that investigated issues of cultural property in PNG. Their scholarship, as well as other anthropological works, reveals complex and varied intellectual property regimes. See Hirsch and Strathern 2005; Kalinoe and Leach 2004.

procedures, gardening and fishing techniques, some songs, dances and rhymes. This knowledge is, however, only public in the limited sense that everyone in the village has access to it and can utilise it. There are complex rules regarding the rights of those in neighbouring villages and those who are related to those from the village, but now live in distant villages, to use the knowledge. Tolai society also recognises that there are 'others' beyond this defined public who may use their public knowledge. However, in such a case 'the worst that can happen to them is that they will be ridiculed or made fun of. The normal rules of ownership, rights and claims are not applied here' (ibid.:76).

A second description comes from Stern, an ethnomusicologist, who describes the way in which the production and use of music occurs in North Vanuatu as follows:

> In Vanuatu some people are recognised as song specialists, a kind of composer … Maurice, an elderly composer … explained to me that, if someone commissions a song from him, he composes it and gives it to the person in exchange for a payment. The composer himself must forget the song, because, henceforth, it belongs to the person who commissioned it. The explanation of the 'forgetting' composer is very explicit concerning the existence of rights to music … There is a close connection between spirit entities and composition. Most of the time, people believe that a song or a dance was brought to the living ancestors' spirits in dreams while asleep or walking alone in the bush … This super-natural origin of songs is an important part in the conception of rights because it plays a large part in the protections of songs … Magic ensures that [the rule over payment and transfer of rights] is respected (Stern 2013:59, 64–65).

However, she also notes that there are some categories of music that are inalienable and can only be transmitted within a specific group of people. Two examples of these are magic songs that influence the weather and tides, and songs that testify to ownership of a particular piece of land. In both cases these songs can only be transmitted inside a group along specific kinship relations and it is kept secret. She observes, 'Knowledge belonging to one group of people—genealogies, family histories, artistic knowledge, magic learning etc.—gives this group a common identity and, as it were, a certain prestige over others who do not share this knowledge' (ibid.:66–67). Finally she describes particular types of music exchanges that can only take place within a particular hierarchical grade system that is based upon political and economic competition. To move up through this grade requires the initiate to acquire a certain amount of cultural wealth, and once the grade is achieved the holder is entitled to rights to 'a certain reserved musical repertoire' (ibid.:68). Stern comments that:

> Knowledge—music, names, dances etc.— is prestigious and requisite to access a social and political rank … the exchanges of which music is part, are also an important way of consolidating social relationships. An individual relies on his/her relationships to directly access different kinds of knowledge and hierarchical grades implying them (ibid.:71).

Once the knowledge is acquired it is kept secret, and this creates a special bond between the initiates. It also means that the right to publicly perform a secret song confers greater prestige.[6]

The third example comes from the Rai Coast of Papua New Guinea. Anthropologist James Leach describes some of the intellectual property and cultural property questions that arose at the local launch of a book he co-wrote with Porer Nombo, a man from the area, about local plants and their uses:

> Porer was meticulous throughout our collaboration to include only plants that he had direct understanding of and for which he could trace the route (people, kinship connection) through which he knew them. For example, during the collecting work for the first edition of the book in 1995, we stumbled across a plant (used for love magic) in the bush, photographed and discussed it, but then removed it from our records because as we talked Porer realised that it is central in a myth told by people from the neighbouring village of Serieng. While everyone who knows the myth knows the possibilities for its use, the myth named ancestors of other people. Porer was not in a position to use the names of those people (Leach 2012:258).

> Porer told us that he had been given recognition as a person (a person who was in a position to receive and utilise these names and plants) by the acceptance of pigs, shells and other things by his mother's brothers and wife's kin during the course of many ceremonies. That what we were calling 'knowledge of plants' was a part of his relation to them, and thus part of his position, his very constitution (ibid.:260).

---

6   The song is kept secret even though publicly performed because 'the initiates dance to the rhythms of rattles worn on their feet and beat bamboo drums, but the inaudible songs arc performed only in their heads so as not to reveal them' (Stern 2013:67).

Leach also describes how a decision was made in the creation of the book to leave out certain parts of the knowledge about the various plants described. The parts left out were the names of characters in myths and tunes from those myths that are 'a crucial part of the effect of many of the plants in our book' (ibid.:259). This was done consciously both to protect the secrecy of the knowledge and to require those searching for that knowledge to go to Porer and to be given access through the right channels. Leach paraphrases Porer as saying:

> If you want these things to work for you, come and talk to me or to others who have received them through the right channels. Come and ask respectfully and I will give them. But they are not simple keys. There is 'hard work' involved (ibid.:259–60).

A final example concerns taro (a staple root crop) and taro production, in Solomon Islands and comes from a study by the Solomon Islands Planting Material Network and Kastom Gaden Association. The report states:

> Cultivation and ownership of taro landraces and knowledge takes place in the context of mutual kinship obligations and competition for control of important resources, which are central components of Melanesian culture … Some farmers maintain landraces of taro that they do not share easily with others. These may be traditional landraces that have been grown by their clan or line for generations. They may be special landraces acquired by a farmer that he/she does not want others to have in order to have an economic or social advantage. Farmers expressed feelings of advantage, respect, power and prestige in having landraces of taro that other people did not have. Such taro can be used to advantage during feasts, sharing through social obligations, and sometimes in marketing. Hidden taro landraces were often associated with hidden taro 'kastom' or knowledge that allowed successful taro farmers to produce good taro crops and hence gain social status and respect (Jansen 2002:20).

The report also describes three different ways of naming taro cultivars. The first is to name the taro after the place it came from, this could be the name of a village or another island. Second is to name taro after the person who 'discovered' them in a garden (new landraces of vegetatively propagated crops such as taro appear sporadically amongst crops of other cultivars as a result of random mutation and must be identified as new by the farmer), or the person who introduced them to the area. The third is to name cultivars after a situation or circumstance that led to the acquisition of the taro landrace. The author states:

For example a commonly planted cultivar in Temotu is named *'selfis'* (selfish) because one farmer who grew it refused to share it with others. It was presumably eventually stolen from her garden (ibid.:19).

These brief descriptions of some of the systems of regulation over intangible resources in Melanesia reflect a number of important features. First, the systems of regulation are embedded within the social, cultural and political context of the societies they regulate. As such, they resonate with the observation of Curry, a human geographer, that one cannot separate the economy and society from each other in Melanesia because 'the economy is intensely social and the social is intensely economic' (Curry 2003:419). Second, the systems of regulation both reflect, and are bound up with, questions of relationships between different groups and between individuals and the group. In this respect they reflect a relational ontology, by which I mean a world view or basic assumptions about the kinds of entities thought to exist in the world (Escobar 2010:4). Escobar has observed that relational ontologies:

> can be differentiated from the dualist ontologies of liberal modernity in that they are not built upon the divides between nature and culture, us and them, individual and community; the cultural, political and ecological consequences of taking relationality seriously are significant; relationality refers to a different way of imaging life (ibid.).

This point about a different ontological framework is also clear from the frequent references to spirits and magic, which are viewed as essential elements and part of the complex networks of relationships and power structures that bind society together. This is still a widely held viewpoint in many parts of the region. For example, in the archipelago nation of Vanuatu, a joint project was recently established between a range of government departments, academic institutions and donors to deal with the meteorological implications of climate change.[7] In a meeting to discuss the project on one of the islands in 2013, it was reported that the chiefs highlighted a number of contributions that could be made, including traditional cropping calendars and practices and traditional climate change adaptation processes. The chiefs also stressed as 'essential', however, the acknowledgement and valuing of the contribution of local

---

7   A similar project was developed in Africa (see Ziervogel and Opere 2010).

weathermen, called *tupunas*, who have an important and widely recognised role in enhancing agricultural production and enabling food security for communities on Tanna Island (Government of Vanuatu 2013).

The references to spirits and magic in the descriptions also draw attention to the very different conceptualisation of creativity and innovation that are at play in these societies. In particular, inspiration and new ideas are said to come from spirits and dreams, and not to be attributable to the individuals who first voice them, rendering the notion of authorship in copyright rather meaningless. Lindstrom observes:

> Islanders do not explain their production of songs or other new knowledge in terms of a knower's individual talent, genius or creativity. Local epistemology seeks authorities and not individual authors ... the Tannese intimate that they are repeating truths told by their fathers, whispered by spirits when intoxicated by kava, or revealed by ancestors in dreams (Lindstrom 1990:316).

Further, in many Melanesian societies, the value of creativity is located in productive relationships, and not in things (Leach 2005; Lindstrom n.d.). Brazilian anthropologist Viveiros de Castro similarly argues that among the Amerindian of Amazonia, culture is not seen as a product of invention, but of transference, a borrowing of prototypes already possessed by animals, spirits or enemies. 'The idea of transformation/transfer belongs to the paradigm of exchange' (de Castro 2004:477). The difference between the creation paradigm (*poiesis*) and the transformation paradigm (*praxis*) is said to be:

> In the creation paradigm, production is causally primary; and exchange, its encompassed consequence. Exchange is a 'moment' of production (it 'realizes' value) and the means of reproduction. In the transformation paradigm, exchange is the condition for production since, without the proper social relations with nonhumans, no production is possible (ibid.).

Thus the magical dimensions of these intellectual property systems once again point us back to the fundamental importance of social relationships. Third, these regulatory systems operate at a non-state level and are administered by local leaders and based on customary norms, thus demonstrating that the state centralist orientation of the global intellectual property system is not the only regulatory possibility. This alerts us to the opportunity for regulatory agency at a variety of different levels: local as well as state and international. Finally, these regulatory frameworks demonstrate a very different epistemological framework to the dominant one used in the global North where knowledge can be, and often is, objectified. In Melanesian societies, in contrast, 'all knowledge is subjective knowledge … there can be no detachment of the knower from the known as in mainstream Anglo-European epistemology' (Gegeo and Watson-Gegeo 2001:62). This point is developed further below.

In concluding this section, it is important once again to acknowledge that today the societies within which these intellectual property systems are situated are changing fast, and new claims of ownership and registers of creativity arc becoming more prevalent (see Dalsgaard 2009; Geismar 2013). However, before too hastily discounting these existing systems and replacing them with shiny new TRIPS-compliant regimes, it is important to reflect on what is lost in so doing, and whether there are benefits in preserving at least elements of them.

Two Sites of Colonisation?

Having established the existence of a range of alternative intellectual property systems in one small region of the world, I now turn to consider two ways in which these systems and others like them are being, or risk being, marginalised and undermined. The first is through the increasing web of regulation of traditional knowledge by national and international bodies, and the second is through the identification of the informal economy as a new domain in which global intellectual property rights are required.

The Regulation of Traditional Knowledge

Traditional and local knowledge is currently the subject of, or impacted by, multiple actual and proposed new regulatory regimes. This attention has been occasioned over the last decade by a range of concerns, including bio-prospecting, misappropriation, ensuring equity in the global intellectual property regime, the possibilities of traditional knowledge and local or grassroots innovation for development in the global South and amongst indigenous communities, and finally as part of claims of indigenous communities across the globe for recognition of their human rights and rights to their cultural heritage. The current international framework comprises the Convention on Biodiversity, TRIPS, the International Union for the Protection of New Varieties of

Plants Convention, the Nagoya Protocol, the International Treaty of Plant Genetic Resources for Food and Agriculture, the United Nations Declaration on the Rights of Indigenous Peoples, the UNESCO Convention for the Safeguarding of Intangible Cultural Heritage 2003, and the International Labour Organization Convention 169 on Indigenous and Tribal Peoples in Independent Countries. There are also ongoing negotiations over the formulation of international instruments being carried out under the auspices of the World Intellectual Property Organization (WIPO) Intergovernmental Committee on Intellectual Property, Genetic Resources, Traditional Knowledge and Folklore (the IGC). These various different frameworks are beyond the scope of this paper to describe in detail, and indeed this has been done expertly elsewhere (see, for example, Tobin 2013:142).

At a regional Pacific Islands level, there are also a number of relevant legal frameworks, including the Melanesian Spearhead Group Treaty on Traditional Knowledge (still not ratified in 2015), the Pacific Model Law for the Protection of Traditional Knowledge and Expressions of Culture 2002, and the *Pacific Model Traditional Biological Knowledge, Innovations and Practices Act 2001* and associated guidelines. At a national level in the Pacific Islands region, there is draft legislation in a range of countries (Fiji, Vanuatu, Samoa, Solomon Islands), and the Cook Islands recently enacted its *Traditional Knowledge Act 2013*. There are also specific provisions relating to traditional or indigenous knowledge in a range of existing pieces of intellectual property regulation.[8]

Whilst there is a good deal of variation in the approaches of these different regulatory regimes, most of them focus on drafting new legislation, centralising the state as the regulator of traditional knowledge and creating exclusive property rights in traditional knowledge that are vested in communities or groups (see Forsyth 2011, 2012, 2013a). In general, the international treaties and legislation actually in force or in development deal with traditional knowledge by conceptualising it as another subject-matter for the global intellectual property regime to regulate. This is entirely consistent with the dominant, economics based, Anglo-American approach to intellectual property that views intellectual property rights essentially as commodities, in which their fundamental value is to produce revenue. Thus, although these approaches are often

---

8   For example, Part 7 of Vanuatu's *Copyright and Related Act 2000* and Section 30 of Samoa's *Copyright Act 1998*.

referred to as *sui generis,* in many respects they are simply extending the global intellectual property system, rather than trying to regulate traditional knowledge in a truly original way. This can be seen by the way in which the IGC has divided traditional knowledge up into separate categories of traditional knowledge associated with genetic resources, traditional knowledge and traditional cultural expression, thus following western intellectual property categories and undermining indigenous understandings of the three areas as intrinsically linked. Traditional knowledge is seen as being able to be abstracted from the social context in which it has been developed, and turned into a form in which it can be traded in the global market. This economic focus is reinforced in the area of genetic resources and their associated traditional knowledge by an emphasis on benefit-sharing agreements (see Kariyawasam 2008:84; WIPO 2013). As pointed out by an increasing number of scholars, however, this is problematic because the focus on compensation and justice has led to the sidelining of the need for nurturing traditional and local knowledge and innovation (Robinson 2008), and has also led to numerous cases of community conflict (see, for example, Peteru 2008; Vermeylen 2013).

Whilst these new developments are certainly preferable to ignoring the intellectual property issues surrounding the global North's recent appreciation of the value of traditional knowledge, it is an extremely limited approach. It fails to take into account the ontological and epistemological context from which the knowledge and innovation arise; instead embedding them within global normative frameworks that operate according to a very different register of value. This follows the same fallacies that were tried, and failed, with regard to transforming customary land and marine tenure into exclusionary and restrictive Western legal categories (Vierros et al. 2010). Bragdon makes similar observations in the context of discussions about genetic resources and local knowledge:

> Currently, the focus of discussions in intergovernmental fora, including the IGC, is on traditional knowledge over traditional resources and not on this dynamic technology development process by farmers where all gennplasm—modern or traditional—is treated as potential input for direct use or further improvement. In international fora the emphasis is on genetic resources per se and the role of farmers in conserving local and traditional landraces, rather than on the innovative process by which genetic resources are continually refined and developed (Bragdon 2013).

Related problems can be identified in the tendency to value traditional cultural expressions purely for their aesthetic and commercial purposes in the development of new economic opportunities amongst indigenous populations. For example, in referring to the regulatory strategy over sand drawings, an important part of Vanuatu's cultural heritage, the Director of the Vanuatu Cultural Centre stated:

> the drawings are often showcased as a form of decorative folklore for the tourist industry and other commercial purposes. If left unchecked, this tendency to appreciate sand drawings on a purely aesthetical level may result in the loss of the tradition's deeper symbolic significance and original social function. Sand drawing is a fundamental form of traditional communication and conceptualization, which has the potential to play a central role in developing cultural identity and maintaining cultural continuity for communities in Vanuatu through the promotion of creativity and the preservation of diversity (Vanuatu Cultural Centre 2010).

The economic focus that is being adopted in regard to the regulation of traditional knowledge can also be demonstrated by the virtual exclusion of customary law from the treaties being developed, and its marginalisation in much existing and draft traditional knowledge statutes. Thus Tobin has observed that the IGC draft treaties have been increasingly 'shorn' of their references to customary law, and that the European Union's 2012 draft treaty for the implementation of the Nagoya protocol makes no reference at all to customary law and restricts protection to a small fraction of traditional knowledge (Tobin 2013:161). Customary law is seen as being too uncertain to be used within a market-based system in which the concern is to ensure ease of use for the 'buyers'.[9]

Intellectual Property and the Informal Economy

This concern with the way in which traditional knowledge is becoming another site for the expansion of the global intellectual property regime, and its reductionist economic focus, is mirrored by parallel developments in regard to local innovation. There are a number of current projects and scholars seeking to find ways to make intellectual property work for the

---

9   For a discussion (and refutation) of the perception of customary law as 'uncertain', see Forsyth 2013b.

world's poor.[10] For example, Madhavi Sunder argues that 'intellectual property rights in poor people's knowledge are increasingly considered a key to third-world development' (Sunder 2007:111). She observes:

> after a decade of resisting the Western imposition of intellectual property, now many in India— from the intellectual property professors and lawyers in the cities to the farmers and artisans in the villages—were beginning to ask: how can intellectual property rights work for them? TRIPs protected the knowledge and economic interests of the developed world, the rich corporations of the West. Can intellectual property be a tool for protecting poor people's knowledge as well? Many seem to think so (ibid.:98).

As part of this new interest there is an emerging focus on the way in which intellectual property rights can be used as a stimulus for innovation in the informal economy. For example, following recommendation 34 of the 2007 WIPO Development Agenda 'to conduct a study on constraints to intellectual property protection in the informal economy', a study was carried out on the link between informal economy and intellectual property through three country studies in Africa (De Beer at al. 2013). At a presentation of the findings at the WIPO Committee on Development and Intellectual Property meeting in May 2014, a number of panellists observed that the project revealed the extent of innovation occurring in the informal sector that had hitherto been overlooked. Sacha Wunsch-Vincent, senior economic officer in the WIPO Economics and Statistics Division, characterised it as 'constraintbased innovation' that mostly consists of adapting, applying and improving existing knowledge' (Astruc 2014).

This WIPO project is complemented by a growing body of research into what is sometimes referred to as grassroots innovation (De Beer et al. 2013:18). Emerging research shows that grassroots innovation occurs in the context of particular social and cultural understandings about the use and transmission of knowledge, and is often subject to non-state systems of intellectual property regulation, such as informal contracts, codes of access and customary norms. For example, wind turbine development can originally be traced to a culture of collaborative craft production and

---

10   For example, the World Bank published a report that presented a range of case studies demonstrating the importance of 'promoting the innovation, knowledge, and creative skills of poor people in poor countries, and particularly about improving the earnings of poor people from such knowledge and skills' through the use of global intellectual property rights (IPR) (Finger and Schuler 2003).

a tradition of cooperative organisation in Denmark. Ely et al. observe that 'Social networks built up shared knowledge, experience and ideas about turbine construction and use' (Ely et al. 2013:107).

While WIPO's informal economy project is extremely valuable in starting to chip away at the notion that innovation only occurs within the formal economy, it raises the question about whether the project may lead to a colonisation of this new space by the global intellectual property regime, rather than being used as a springboard to explore fresh approaches about the regulation of innovation and creativity in the informal economy. There are suggestions that this project may be used to develop policies to move people from using 'alternative knowledge appropriation strategies' to formal intellectual property. For example, Herman Ntchatcho, senior director of the Department for Africa and Special Projects of the WIPO Development Sector, stated that, 'recognising interactions between formal and informal economics, at some stage of the journey many of the entrepreneurs need to move to the more formal spheres of activity, particularly where IP and innovation are concerned' (Astruc 2014). This reflects the same type of 'imperial narrative of progress and advancement, a narrative which posits some societies as having achieved its promise and as other still en route towards it' that has proved so problematic in development to date (Pahuja 2011:212). Further evidence of the potential for colonisation comes in a policy recommendation at the end of the central study paper that 'an important policy challenge will be to make IE [informal economy] actors aware of the possibilities that formal IPRs offer' (De Beer et al. 2013:48). This informal economy example is just one of many components of the current expansion of the global intellectual property system into the developing world on the uncertain premise that it promotes 'development' and is necessary in the absence of existing regulatory structures.[11]

---

11 This argument is developed at length in Forsyth and Farran 2015.

What are the Problems with Overlooking Local Intellectual Property Systems?

We have just seen that two areas of local knowledge and local innovation are being increasingly threatened with being enclosed within an intellectual property regime that focuses purely on economic considerations at the expense of the social and the cultural. This gives rise to a range of potential problems, but here I focus on just two.

First, the creation of new forms of property rights is likely to interfere with the operation of the existing local systems in a variety of problematic ways. The narrow economic focus that the global intellectual property regime brings to bear on the regulation of traditional knowledge creates the risk that the real benefits of local knowledge and innovation for development may fail to eventuate for the same reasons that the economic focus of the development project itself has not resulted in the anticipated benefits for the global South (see Collier 2007; Easterly 2006; Escobar 1995). In particular, it glosses over key issues about distribution of benefits and ensuring equitable access to resources. The establishment of new market-based regulatory systems over tangible resources, such as land, has a history of enabling resources that were once of broad benefit to large numbers of people to be effectively captured by a small and closed group of people. This small group is often comprised of male elites and then of foreign corporate interests at the last stage of the commodification process.[12] Similar consequences are likely to flow from a market-based approach to traditional knowledge regulation.

In this respect, there are real lessons to be learnt from the work of those who have investigated the problems created by the transformation of customary tenure into western-style property regimes (Fitzpatrick et al. 2012; Platteau 1996, 2000) and also the breakdown in social relationships caused by the transformation of labour into a market-based paradigm in Melanesia (see, for example, Curry and Koczberski 2012). The expanding bodies of literature in these fields demonstrate that the social tensions caused by disputes over how to calculate and distribute resource rents have led to the phenomena known as the 'resource curse', whereby developing countries that are resource rich often struggle to translate their wealth

---

12   Economist Thomas Piketty predicts that the upper 10 per cent will have about 60 per cent of all income by 2030 (Piketty 2014).

into broad-based development and social conflict eventuates (see Bainton 2010; Filer and Macintyre 2006; Regan 1998). However, although generally pessimistic, there are a number of hopeful directions emerging from this literature—for example, the diverse economics approach that rejects what J.K. Gibson-Graham has termed 'capitalocentricism' and explores alternative economic models that coexist with capitalism in a variety of contexts (Gibson-Graham 1996, 2006). These demonstrate the possibilities and benefits of experimenting with ways to adapt global or western regulatory schemes in ways that are more congruent with existing regulatory structures, and which take into account a relational perspective, as developed below.

These observations lead me to suggest that attempting to regulate local knowledge and innovation through a purely economic, positivistic framework risks creating significant harm through the disruption of the social relationships upon which this knowledge and innovation is currently produced. Disregarding existing relationships jeopardises valuable knowledge-exchange networks, social capital and trust that are not only essential to meeting economic objectives, but also social, cultural and political needs, and also are an important incubator for future knowledge and innovation generation. As Leach and Davis note:

> different registers of value locate knowledge in relation to something else and this can create hierarchies, appropriation, replacement or elision of pre-existing values. While knowledge may create value, new value does not always supersede previous value, sometimes an entity carries more than one value, more than one set of relationships (2012:221).

Reducing the way in which knowledge is viewed to an economic perspective thus risks prioritising one set of values over others, and in turn reordering existing relationships. This is certainly not to say that existing systems need to be kept unchanged, or that without support or adaptation they can meet all the new demands that regulation of intangible resources involves today. However, in creating regulatory frameworks in this area, cognisance does need to be had of the existence of such systems and the various social, political and economic roles they play.

The second main problem with overlooking existing intellectual property systems is that their value is missed by the global North, particularly the ways in which they suggest the need to expand our epistemic and metaphysical horizons. As suggested in the introduction, the tendency to overlook existing non-state regulatory systems comes from a western epistemic tradition of objectifying knowledge. This can be illustrated by the way in which traditional ecological knowledge is starting to be used by climate change projects in Pacific Island countries. Over the past decade, attention at both global and domestic levels has started to be paid to the potential of traditional knowledge and local or grassroots innovation in a range of developmental contexts, and particularly in the context of climate change adaptation.[13] Both are seen as possessing great potential utility for assisting the global South to manage the various crises associated with climate change, such as problems of food security and coping with extreme weather events. For example, attention has been drawn to the value of traditional navigation systems, traditional resource management, traditional fisheries systems, and vernacular architecture (UNESCO 2013). At the Pacific Climate Change Roundtable in Nadi, Fiji in 2013, the importance of combining science and traditional knowledge was stressed. The Director General of the Pacific Regional Environmental program highlighted the importance of the practical application and blending of modern science with traditional knowledge, stating, 'The value of good science must be blended with traditional knowledge to address related climate change issues affecting the region today'.

Many of these traditional ecological knowledge projects, however, adopt a very narrow view of the benefits of traditional knowledge, seeing it essentially as an object that can be extracted from its social context and applied within a western scientific framework. For example, there are currently a number of organisations compiling databases of various aspects of traditional knowledge in the Pacific Islands region, and also a number of projects that seek to collect traditional knowledge and then validate it against scientific knowledge (see Chand et al. 2014; Narsey Lal et al. 2009). Typically such projects compile such knowledge in a way that emphasises the instrumental value of the knowledge from a western scientific perspective, isolating it and decontextualizing it from its cultural context. Margaret Jolly comments on such processes, noting:

> typically such processes have been leached of their cultural or spiritual significance, flattened and reduced to secular techniques which can hopefully be remembered and recreated in the face of future catastrophe … Selectively collecting such indigenous knowledge and practice and corralling it under the acronym TEK [Traditional Ecological Knowledge] seems to demean both the immensity of the problem, the indigenous

---

13 See the literature review in McNamara and Prasad (2013).

knowledge itself and Pacific peoples' creative capacities for survival in drastically changed circumstances, including their appropriation of western science (2014).

Such projects are certainly not concerned with the spiritual and magical dimensions of traditional and local knowledge. In one way this is a good thing, as it means that attempts are not made to trespass on areas of knowledge that are considered highly secret and restricted by local populations. It can also be argued that it is not strictly necessary as epistemic cooperation/convergence between two cultures operating with radically different metaphysical schemes is possible—for example, at the level of sharing observations about the properties of plants (Claudie et al. 2012). However, the relative invisibility of this dimension to Western scientists, and its ready dismissal, is symptomatic of a blindness to the different world views in which traditional and local knowledge is produced. This *is* problematic because it limits the ability of climate scientists and others in the global North to be challenged by the possibilities of reframing the types of research problems they are investigating. As Drahos argues, juxtapositions of people from different cosmologies is more likely to lead to de-routinisation, a 'process in which actors begin to question their adherence to conventional routines of thought and behaviour' (Drahos 2014:209). This in turn creates the types of conditions necessary for the bold conjectures that Popper argues are necessary for the advancement of science (Popper quoted in ibid.:205–07). These insights are, however, not likely to arise if merely instrumentalist use is made of local knowledge by outsiders: it is necessary to at least be aware of the different ontology within which the knowledge is situated, to respect it, and preferably to be prepared to walk around a little inside it. As Quijano, the renowned Peruvian sociologist, points out, intercultural communication can only occur if each party to the dialogue recognises the partiality of their perspective (Quijano 2007:177).

Exploring a new ontology may, for example, allow us to see important connections between different phenomena that our own ontology does not perceive a relationship between.[14] For example, anthropologist James Leach describes how the Rai Coast people of PNG have certain magic procedures that are necessary to make plant medicinal knowledge effective for them. Yet he observes that these are left out of descriptions of the processes in order for those processes to appear as 'knowledge' to

---

14 For an excellent example of such an intellectual endeavour, see Wen-yuan Lin and Law 2013.

outside observers (Leach 2012). He argues that taking the magic out of the definition of this knowledge means overlooking the key role that the magic performs—namely, 'the effective positioning of persons in relation to one another' (Leach and Davis 2012:214). Similarly, Cruikshank demonstrates how certain narratives about glaciers as 'knowledge' for climate scientists and government agencies means leaving out what makes them actually effective for the native people in the Yukon (Cruikshank 2012). Leach and Davis thus observe:

> The effect of the recognition of these practices as knowledge in both cases is to make them less effective, or render them incomprehensible and useless, as the definition of knowledge employed by those in a position to make the recognition is not only narrow, but colonising in the sense of only admitting certain sources of effect [i.e. rational and scientific and not magical] (2012:213).

Creating awareness of the local intellectual property systems within which local knowledge and innovation are embedded is one way of making the different ontological and epistemic perspectives at work apparent. This in turn is more likely to promote the type of profound questioning likely to occasion much-needed scientific paradigm shifts, particularly those related to climate change. For example, going back to the Vanuatu meteorological example raised before, what might happen if, rather than focusing on integrating traditional weather indicators into a western knowledge framework, the *tupunas* (weathermen) and their powers, *were* seen as a pivotal part of the study as the local chiefs suggested? This may lead to truly transformative ways of thinking about the natural world and relationships between man and nature, rather than merely thinking about local knowledge in purely utilitarian ways (Cruikshank 2012:240; Vermeylan 2010). For example, they may help to break up many of the binaries within which western science is currently constrained (nature vs culture, mind vs matter), which some leading indigenous scholars, such as Vivieros de Castro, argue have impoverished 'modern thought' (de Castro 2004). He shows how engaging with different ontological frameworks, and thereby taking seriously their different divisions between nature and human, is absolutely essential if we are *really* interested in learning from indigenous knowledge.

Making Room for Magic: A Pluralist and Intercultural Approach

One way to engage with alternative perspectives to the dominant intellectual property paradigm is to adopt a pluralistic and intercultural approach. This approach is based upon a recognition that there are many different models of intellectual property regulation both possible and currently in existence, of which the global system is just one. These alternative systems include indigenous knowledge systems, informal norms built up among group members over time, trade secrets, codes of conduct and informal contracts. Further, these different systems are culturally, historically and politically contingent, and are in a continual process of contestation and transformation as a result of their interaction with each other, and with other forces such as colonisation and globalisation. A pluralist approach is one that recognises the need to make space for consideration of these different systems, and an assessment of their respective merits and capacities for change in meeting new challenges and regulatory requirements.

A pluralist approach thus rejects the pretences to universalism that are apparent in the dominant intellectual property system, whereby it is positioned as being the only valid system to deal with all aspects of the regulation of intangible resources, even traditional and local knowledge and innovation. It requires a commitment to a pluralistic process along similar lines to that advocated by Berman:

> We might deliberately seek to create or preserve spaces for productive interaction among multiple, overlapping legal systems by developing procedural mechanisms, institutions. and practices that aim to manage, without eliminating, the legal pluralism we see around us (2012:10).

A pluralistic approach does not necessarily prioritise any system, nor does it reify or romanticise non-state systems, or overlook their need and capacity for change.[15] Simply it means that that due attention should also be paid to them by the international community, donors, nation states and local communities as a possible focus for protecting traditional knowledge.

15　These are some common but misguided criticisms made of legal pluralism. See, for example, Porter 2012.

Such a pluralistic approach should be complemented by commitment to interculturality, which recognises the need for dialogue and real communication between those who represent different systems, from a position of mutual respect. Walsh explains this concept as follows:

> It allows imagining and opening of pathways towards a different society based on respect, mutual legitimacy, equity, symmetry and equality where difference is the constitutive element and not merely a simple addition. Interculturality also requires an understanding that behind the relations to be constructed—among groups and between the structures, institutions and rights that the state might propose—are distinct logics, rationalities, customs and knowledges (2009:79–80).

Applying this notion to a legal context as an illustration, Tobin describes intercultural legal pluralism as 'a world of legal interfaces that cannot be imposed but must be negotiated, tested and modulated in response to the realities of differing worldviews, value systems and legal visions' (2013:161). In relation to intellectual property, the concept of interculturality is important because it highlights that attention must always be paid to the social and cultural context of intellectual property regulation. It also requires us to explore, rather than assume, local understandings about the value of knowledge, the meaning of innovation and the stimulus for creativity. The development of regulatory frameworks at local, national and international levels for local knowledge and innovation therefore require engaging with the different ontological and epistemological perspectives involved, and making spaces for the differences in opinion and values that these entail to be articulated and discussed.

Some mechanisms that may be usefully considered to advance both a pluralistic and an intercultural approach to intellectual property are as follows.

Reconceptualise Traditional Knowledge as Being about Local Knowledge Systems

As discussed above, local knowledge is currently conceptualised in international and national regulatory frameworks as a static, ' traditional' object that exists independently of the social, political and economic structures that have in many ways produced it. Very similar assumptions are often made about customary law, as demonstrated by a continuous string of failed attempts since colonial times to codify customary norms (Engle Merry 1991:867). However, as I have argued elsewhere, both customary norms and traditional knowledge are deeply embedded within their social and cultural context (Forsyth 2011). Although indeed one particular item of knowledge can be separated and treated as an object, this would ignore the processes that led to its production in the first place, the continuation of which is far more important than ensuring the preservation of particular items of knowledge at a particular moment in time. Further, these practices have not stopped, but are ongoing, as existing knowledge is adapted and blended with new knowledge in innovative ways.

I therefore suggest that we start to think of local knowledge and innovation as being part of living, changing and adapting *systems*. This approach sees knowledge and innovation as based on cycles of knowledge creation, use, dissemination and more creation. It rejects the current binary between traditional and modem knowledge and requires us to pay attention to the conditions of the social structures, including their regulatory mechanisms, within which they operate. These knowledge systems furthermore reflect the priorities of particular societies, and demonstrate their underlying cultural values, such as respect for the wisdom of elders, connections with the spirit world, the primacy of social relationships, connections with place and land, and so forth. This approach also garners support from the suggestions recently made by Drahos and Frankel that, rather than focusing on the knowledge itself, it is more useful to focus on the system of indigenous innovation:

> The generation of useful knowledge and techniques implies a set of institutions working in convergent ways to produce innovation. A systems perspective on innovation requires one to look more broadly at the institutions that contribute to innovative performance, as well as the distinctive linkages and interactions amongst institutional actors that characterise an innovation system (Drahos and Frankel 2012:4).

As they observe, adopting this perspective then suggests a variety of different questions to the usual one of 'how do we protect traditional knowledge?' such as 'how indigenous innovation might be supported?' How collaboration may be encouraged 'between cosmologically anchored indigenous networks and scientific networks?' and 'how can we turn indigenous networks into development networks?'(ibid.)

Use Vernacular Languages

Another mechanism that furthers a pluralistic and intercultural perspective is the use in state legislation of vernacular terminology. The use of vernacular language in state laws can destabilise assumptions that terms are read and understood by those from different cultural backgrounds in the same way. This is of particular importance in countries where there are indigenous minorities. For example, the revised *New Zealand Patent Act 2013* creates a Māori Advisory Committee similar to that existent for trademarks. Members must, 'in the opinion of the Commissioner', have knowledge of *te ao Māori* and *tikanga Māori* (Lai 2013). The use of these vernacular terms signify that there are different epistemological frameworks at play that need to be considered. Another example is the use of *uBuntu,* an indigenous South African value, by the Constitutional Court and by other levels of the judiciary in South Africa (Cornell and Muvangua 2012).

Use Indigenous and Local Institutions

A further very important mechanism is the use of indigenous or local institutions in the regulation of local knowledge and innovation systems. As found in a 2003 report of a Consultancy for the Capacity Needs Assessment on Access and Benefit Sharing and the Protection of Traditional Knowledge, Practices and Innovations for Samoa:

> Traditional knowledge in particular is inextricably woven with the *fa'a Samoa* [the Samoan way]. Any access and benefit sharing scheme needs to incorporate the *fa'a Samoa* and build upon that sense of ownership in order to be successful. The consultation outcomes also demonstrated that any scheme to regulate access and benefit sharing must be undertaken as a partnership between central government and villages (Urwin Consulting 2003:31).

I have discussed elsewhere the importance and the difficulties in engaging in this type of pluralist endeavour, and the need to avoid the mere referencing of customary law or customary institutions while at the same time effectively disempowering them (Forsyth 2011). A recent example of national legislation that recognises meaningful roles and responsibilities for indigenous customary institutions is the Cook Islands' *Traditional Knowledge Act 2013.* This centralises the Are Korero, which is the traditional meeting house in the Cook Islands (Buse and Taringa 1995), in both the process of the registration of traditional knowledge and decisions about entitlements to rights over traditional knowledge.

Take Account of the Values and Principles Underlying the Existing Systems

A final mechanism is to extract and reference the values and principles that underlie local intellectual property systems in the creation of new regulatory regimes. This follows Drahos' suggestion that 'simple rules and principles offer the beginnings of a regulatory system that engages seriously with indigenous peoples' knowledge systems' (Drahos 2014:101). Principles are able to 'permeate and orient' a regulatory system (ibid.), and are particularly important when establishing *new* regulatory systems, as they offer important guidance for the future development of the system. Pacific Islands peoples have engaged in a similar exercise in their ongoing development of local research methodologies. These new methodologies fundamentally challenge the dominant Eurocentric approaches and involve new approaches based on indigenous epistemic practices and codes of ethics (see, for example, Smith 1999; Vaioleti 2006).

Conclusion

In conclusion, I wish to briefly reflect on what the above exegesis of local Melanesian intellectual property systems can offer for critical intellectual property discussion more broadly. There are two broad observations that emerge. The first is the value of plurality in this field that is currently so heavily dominated by standardisation and a quest for uniformity. The preceding discussion suggests that there are serious side effects of a uniform approach to intellectual property regulation, and that it can even undermine the conditions that are most likely to lead to innovation and creativity in all its wondrous diversity. In other words, although seeking to incentivise further creativity and innovation, the global intellectual property system is actually gradually homogenising the conditions in which creativity and innovation is produced. Ironically, and almost certainly, this is likely in the long run to lead to less creativity and innovation, or at least less radical and heterogeneous creativity and innovation. The examples from Melanesia illustrate that it is a mistake to try to separate the systems that regulate intellectual property from the resources themselves. Therefore, if as a matter of global policy we really do value innovation, in its real sense of offering true alternatives and new directions, we should also recognise and value alternative intellectual property mechanisms to the dominant global model. Although these systems are more apparent in places such as Melanesia where the global intellectual property system has not as yet established a strong hold, they exist throughout the world in areas such as the informal economy and elsewhere there are intangible resources not currently regulated by the global system. I suggest that rather than merely accepting as inevitable their ultimate domination by the global system, there is exploration of ways in which this can be resisted and a plural regulatory approach adopted. The ways in which this will occur will need to be worked out on a case-by-case basis depending upon the particular circumstances and opportunities, but can only occur if there is first of all a change of mindset towards an embracing of pluralism and an awareness of the undesirability of the global system's current claims of universality.

The second observation emerging from the investigation of Melanesian intellectual property systems is that the current neoliberal or market-based focus of the global intellectual property system is a narrow one. Problematically, it largely renders invisible a whole range of factors that have powerful impacts upon both the creation of new intangible resources and their distribution. These include social relationships and cultural and cosmological understandings. A market-based focus can also obscure the fact that there may be values associated with particular intangible resources that are unable to be factored into a purely neoliberal economic framework—for example, values associated with particular aspects of cultural heritage or even genetic resources. One response is to seek to carve out certain areas as being explicitly inalienable and available to all, such as the Italian public cultural public domain (see articles 822.2, 826.2 and 3. of the Italian civil code). An alternative approach is to work towards gradually imbuing intellectual property mechanisms with more non-economic considerations, such as, for example including questions of culture as relevant (or even central) to intellectual property policy design.

References

Antons, C. (ed.) 2009. *Traditional Knowledge, Traditional Cultural Expressions and Intellectual Property Law in the Asia-Pacific Region*. The Netherlands: Kluwer Law International.

Astruc, M. 2014. Innovation Occurs in Informal Economy, Needs Policy Framework, Panellists Say. *Intellectual Property Watch*, 3 June. www.ip-watch. org/2014/06/03/innovation-occurs-in-informal-economy-needs-policy-framework-panellists-say/

Bainton, N. 2010. *The Lihir Destiny: Cultural Responses to Mining in Melanesia.* Canberra: ANU E Press. doi.org/10.22459/LD.10.2010

Berman, P. 2012. *Global Legal Pluralism: A Jurisprudence of Law beyond Borders.* Cambridge University Press. doi.org/10.1017/CBO9781139028615

Bragdon, S. 2013. *Small Scale Farmers: The Missing Element in the WIPO–IGC Draft Articles on Genetic Resources.* Briefing Paper No. 1. New York: Quaker United Nations Office. www.quno.org/resource/2013/7/small-scale-farmers-missing-element-wipo-igc-draft-articles-genetic-resources

Buse, J. and R. Taringa 1995. *Cook Island Maori Dictionary.* Cook Islands: Ministry of Education, Government of the Cook Islands and The Australian National University.

Chand, S.S., L.E. Chambers, M. Waiwai, P. Malsale and E. Thompson 2014. Indigenous Knowledge for Environmental Prediction in the Pacific Island Countries. *Weather, Climate. and Society* 6(4):445–50. doi.org/10.1175/WCAS-D-13-00053.1

Claudie, D.J., S.J. Semple, N.M. Smith and B.S. Simpson 2012. Ancient but New: Developing Locally Driven Enterprises Based on Traditional Medicines in Kuuku I'yu Northern Homelands, Cape York, Queensland, Australia. In P. Drahos and S. Frankel (eds), *Indigenous Peoples' Innovation: Intellectual Property Pathways to Development.* Canberra: ANU E Press. doi.org/10.22459/IPI.08.2012.02

Collier P. 2007. *The Bottom Billion: Why the Poorest Countries are Failing and What Can Be Done About It.* Oxford: Oxford University Press.

Cornell, D. and N. Muvangua (eds) 2012. *uBuntu and the Law: African Ideals and Postapartheid Jurisprudence.* New York: Fordham University Press.

Cruikshank, J. 2012. Are Glaciers 'Good to Think With'? Recognising Indigenous Environmental Knowledge. *Anthropological Forum* 22(3):239–50. doi.org/10.1111/j.1944-8287.2003.tb00221.x

Curry, G. 2003. Moving Beyond Post development: Facilitating Indigenous Alternatives for 'Development'. *Economic Geography* 79(4):405–23. doi.org/10.1111/j.1745-5871.2011.00733.x

Curry, G. and G. Koczberski 2012. Relational Economies, Social Embeddedness and Valuing Labour in Agrarian Change: An Example from the Developing World. *Geographical Research* 50(4):377–92.

Dalsgaard, S. 2009. Claiming Culture: New Definitions and Ownership of Cultural Practices in Manus Province, Papua New Guinea. *The Asia Pacific Journal of Anthropology* 10(1):20–32. doi.org/10.1080/14442210802706889

De Beer, J., K. Fu and S. Wunsch-Vincent 2013. Economic Research Working Paper No. 10: The informal economy, innovation and intellectual property— Concepts, metrics and policy considerations. Geneva: WIPO. www.wipo.int/edocs/pubdocs/en/wipo_pub_econstat_wp_10.pdf

de Castro, E.V. 2004. Exchanging Perspectives: The Transformation of Objects into Subjects in Amerindian Ontologies. *Common Knowledge* 10(3):463–84. doi.org/10.1215/0961754X-10-3-463

de Schutter, O. 2014. Final Report of Special Rapporteur on the Right to Food to the UN Human Rights Council: *The Transformative Potential of the Right to Food*. www.srfood.org/en/final-report-to-un-human-rights-council

Drahos, P. 2014. *Intellectual Property, Indigenous People and their Knowledge*. Cambridge: Cambridge University Press. doi.org/10.1017/CBO9781107295230

Drahos, P. and S. Frankel 2012. *Indigenous Peoples' Innovation and Intellectual Property: The Issues*. In P. Drahos and S. Frankel (eds), *Indigenous Peoples' Innovation: Intellectual Property Pathways to Development*. Canberra: ANU E Press. doi.org/10.22459/IPI.08.2012.01

Easterly, W. 2006. *The White Man's Burden: Why the West's Efforts to Aid the Rest Have Done So Much Ill and So Little Good*. Oxford: Oxford University Press.

Ely, A., A. Smith, A. Stirling, M. Leach and I. Scoones 2013. Innovation Politics Post-Rio 20+: Hybrid Pathways to Sustainability? *Environment and Planning C: Government and Policy* 31. doi.org/10.1068/c12285j

Engle Merry, S. 1991. Law and Colonialism. *Law & Society Review* 25:889–922. doi.org/10.2307/3053874

Escobar, A. 1995. *Encountering Development. The Making and Unmaking of the Third World*. Princeton: Princeton University Press.

Escobar, A. 2010. Latin America at a Crossroads. *Cultural Studies* 24(1):1–65. doi.org/10.1080/09502380903424208

Filer, C. and M. Macintyre 2006. Grass Roots and Deep Holes: Community Responses to Mining in Melanesia. *Contemporary Pacific* 18(2):215–31. doi.org/10.1353/cp.2006.0012

Finger, J.M. and P. Schuler 2003. *Poor People's Knowledge: Promoting Intellectual Property in Developing Countries*. Washington, DC: World Bank.

Fitzpatrick, D., A. McWilliam and S. Barnes 2012. *Property and Social Resilience in Times of Conflict: Land, Custom and Law in East Timor*. Farnham, UK: Ashgate.

Forsyth, M. 2011. The Traditional Knowledge Movement in the Pacific Island Countries: The Challenges of Localism. *Prometheus* 29(3): 269–86. doi.org/10.1080/08109028.2011.629869

Forsyth, M. 2012. Lifting the Lid on 'The Community': Who Has the Right to Control Access to Traditional Knowledge and Expressions of Culture? *International Journal of Cultural Property* 19:1–31. doi.org/10.1017/S0940739112000021

Forsyth, M. 2013a. How Can Traditional Knowledge Best be Regulated? Comparing a Proprietary Rights Approach with a Regulatory Toolbox Approach. *The Contemporary Pacific* 25(1):1–31. doi.org/10.1353/cp.2013.0004

Forsyth, M. 2013b. How Can the Theory of Legal Pluralism Assist the Traditional Knowledge Debate? *Intersections: Gender and Sexuality in Asia and the Pacific* 33(December). intersections.anu.edu.au/issue33/forsyth.htm

Forsyth, M. and S. Farran 2015. *Weaving Intellectual Property Policy in Pacific Island Countries*. Cambridge: Intersentia.

Gegeo, D. and K. Watson-Gegeo 2001. How We Know: Kwara'ae Rural Villagers Doing Indigenous Epistemology. *The Contemporary Pacific* 31(1):55–88.

Geismar, H. 2013. *Treasured Possessions: Indigenous Interventions into Cultural and Intellectual Property*. Durham: Duke University Press. doi.org/10.1215/9780822399704

Gibson-Graham, J.K. 1996. *The End of Capitalism (As We Knew It)*. Minnesota: University of Minnesota Press.

Gibson-Graham, J.K. 2006. *A Postcapitalist Politics*. Minnesota: University of Minnesota Press.

Government of Vanuatu 2013. Nikoletan Chiefs Declaration on Climate Change in Vanuatu. Press release, 17 December. Vanuatu: National Advisory Board on Climate Change and Disaster Risk Reduction.

Griffiths, J. 1986. What is Legal Pluralism? *Journal of Legal Pluralism* 18(24): 1–55. doi.org/10.1080/07329113.1986.10756387

Griffiths, T. 1993. *Indigenous Knowledge and Intellectual Property: A Preliminary Review of the Anthropological Literature.* Report prepared for the Foundation of Ethnobiology at the University of Oxford (copy on file with author).

Hirsch, E. and M. Strathern (eds) 2005. *Transactions and Creations: Property Debates and the Stimulus of Melanesia.* New York: Berghahn Books.

Jansen, T. 2002. *Hidden Taro, Hidden Talents: A Study of On-farm Conservation of colocasia esculenta (taro) in Solomon Islands.* Solomon Islands Planting Material Network and Kastom Gaden Association. Formerly available at issuu.com/terracircle (site discontinued).

Jolly, M. 2014. Futures, Past or Foregone? Horizons and Rifts in Conversations about Climate Change in Oceania. Paper for Workshop on Pacific Futures: Past and Present. University of Otago, Dunedin, 18–21 June.

Kalinoe, L. and J. Leach (eds) 2004. *Rationales of Ownership: Transactions and Claims to Ownership in Contemporary Papua New Guinea.* Wantage: Sean Kingston Publishing.

Kariyawasam, K. 2008. Protecting Biodiversity, Traditional Knowledge and Intellectual Property in the Pacific: Issues and Challenges. *Asia Pacific Law Review* 16(1):73–89. doi.org/10.1080/10192557.2008.11788179

Lai, J. 2013. Maori Traditional Knowledge and New Zealand Patent Law: The 2013 Act and the Dawn of a New Era? atrip.org/wp-content/uploads/2016/12/2013-2Jessica-Lai.pdf

Leach J. 2005. Modes of Creativity and the Register of Ownership. In R. Ghosh (ed.), *CODE: Collaborative Ownership and the Digital Economy.* Cambridge MA: Massachusetts Institute of Technology Press.

Leach, J. 2012. Leaving the Magic Out: Knowledge and Effect in Different Places. *Anthropological Forum* 22(3):251–70, 258.

Leach, J. and R. Davis 2012. Recognising and Translating Knowledge: Navigating the Political, Epistemological, Legal and Ontological. *Anthropological Forum* 22(3). doi.org/10.1080/00664677.2012.724007

Lin, W.-y. and J. Law 2013. A Correlative STS? Lessons from a Chinese Medical Practice. CRESC Working Paper Series, Working Paper No. 128. hummedia.manchester.ac.uk/institutes/cresc/workingpapers/wp128.pdf

Lindstrom, L. 1990. Big Men As Ancestors: Inspiration and Copyrights on Tanna (Vanuatu). *Ethnology* 29:313–26. doi.org/10.2307/3773601

Lindstrom, L. n.d. A Genealogy of Creativity. Unpublished paper (copy on file with author).

Narsey Lal, P., J. Kinch and F. Wickham 2009. *Review of Livelihood Impact, Assessments of, and Adaptation to, Climate Change in Melanesia.* Secretariat of the Pacific Regional Environment Programme.

McNamara, K.E. and S.S. Prasad 2013. Valuing Indigenous Knowledge for Climate Change Adaptation Planning in Fiji and Vanuatu. Guest Article for UNU-IAS Traditional Knowledge Initiative. www.unutki.org/news.php?news_id=l 82&doc_id=39 (site discontinued).

Pahuja, S. 2011. *Decolonising International Law: Development, Economic Growth and the Politics of Universality.* Cambridge: Cambridge University Press. doi.org/10.1017/CBO9781139048200

Peteru, C. 2008. Access and Benefit Sharing issues in the Pacific: The Fable of the Mamala Tree. Presentation. gfbr9.hrc.govt.nz/presentations/Clark%20Peteru.doc (site discontinued).

Piketty, T. 2014. *Capital in the Twenty-First Century.* Boston: Harvard University Press. doi.org/10.4159/9780674369542

Platteau, J.P. 1996. The Evolutionary Theory of Land Rights as Applied to Sub-Saharan Africa: A Critical Assessment. *Development and Change* 27(1):29–86. doi.org/10.1111/j.1467-7660.1996.tb00578.x

Platteau, J.P. 2000. Does Africa Need Land Reform? In C. Toulmin and J. Quan (eds), *Evolving Land Rights, Policy and Tenure in Africa.* London: DFID Issues Series, IIED and Natural Resources Institute, 51–74.

Porter, D. 2012. Some Implications of the Application of Legal Pluralism to Development Practice. In B. Tamanaha, C. Sage and M. Woolcock (eds), *Legal Pluralism and Development: Scholars and Practitioners in Dialogue.* Cambridge: Cambridge University Press, 162–76. doi.org/10.1017/CBO9781139094597.014

Quijano, A. 2007. Coloniality and Modernity/Rationality. *Cultural Studies* 21(2–3):177.

Regan, A. 1998. Causes and Course of the Bougainville Conflict. *Journal of Pacific History* 33(3):269–85. doi.org/10.1080/00223349808572878

Robinson, D. 2008. Beyond 'Protection': Promoting Traditional Knowledge Systems in Thailand. In J. Gibson (ed.), *Patenting Lives: Development and Culture.* London: Routledge, 121–38.

Simet, J. 2000. Copyrighting Traditional Tolai Knowledge? In K. Whimp and M. Busse (eds), *Protection of Intellectual, Biological and Cultural Property in Papua New Guinea*. Canberra: Asia-Pacific Press, 62–80.

Smith, L.T. 1999. *Decolonizing Methodologies: Research and Indigenous Peoples*. London: St Martin's Press.

Stern, M. 2013. Music in Traditional Exchanges in North Vanuatu. *Pacific Studies* 36(1–2): 59–76.

Sunder, M. 2007. The Invention of Traditional Knowledge. *Law and Contemporary Problems* 70:97–124.

Tobin, B.M. 2013. Bridging the Nagoya Compliance Gap: The Fundamental Role of Customary Law in Protection of Indigenous Peoples' Resource and Knowledge Rights. *Law, Environment and Development Journal* 9(2):142–62. www.lead-journal.org/content/13142.pdf

Twining, W. 2009. *General Jurisprudence: Understanding Law from a Global Perspective*. Cambridge: Cambridge University Press.

UNCTAD 2013. *Trade and Environment Review 2013*: *Wake Up Before It Is Too Late*. unctad.or g/en/PublicationsLibrary/ditcted2012d3_en.pdf

UNESCO Office for the Pacific States 2013. Traditional Knowledge for Adapting to Climate Change: Safeguarding Intangible Cultural Heritage in the Pacific. Apia, Samoa and Republic of Korea. unesdoc.unesco.org/images/0022/002253/225313E.pdf

Urwin Consulting 2003. Consultancy for the Capacity Needs Assessment on Access and Benefit Sharing and the Protection of Traditional Knowledge, Practices and Innovations: Final report. www.mnre.gov.ws/documents/reports/CapacityNeedsAssessmentABSandTKJune2003.pdf (site discontinued).

Vaioleti, T.M. 2006. Talanoa Research Methodologies: A Developing Position on Pacific Research. *Waikato Journal of Education* (12):12, 21–34.

Vanuatu Cultural Centre 2010. The National Action Plan for the Safeguarding of Sand Drawing, a UNESCO Masterpiece of the Oral and Intangible Heritage of Humanity. archive.is/PwCLj

Vermeylen, S. 2010. Law as a Narrative: Legal Pluralism and Resisting Euro-American (Intellectual) Property Law Through Stories. *Journal of Legal Pluralism* 61:53–78. doi.org/10.1080/07329113.2010.10756642

Vermeylen, S. 2013. The Nagoya Protocol and Customary Law: The Paradox of Narratives in the Law. *Law, Environment and Development Journal* 9(2): 187–201.

Vierros, M., A. Tawake, F. Hickey, A. Tiraa and R. Noa 2010. *Traditional Marine Management Areas of the Pacific in the Context of National and International Law and Policy*. Darwin: United Nations University–Traditional Knowledge Initiative. archive.ias.unu.edu/resource_centre/Traditional_ Marine_Management_Areas_Sept_2010_single_page_webversion_v2.pdf

von Benda-Beckmann, F. 1985. Some Comparative Generalizations about the Differential Use of State and Folk Institutions of Dispute Settlement. In A. Allott and G.R. Woodman (eds), *People's Law and State Law: The Bellagio Papers*. The Netherlands: Foris Publications. doi.org/10.1515/ 9783110866285.187

Walsh, C. 2009. The Plurinational and Intercultural State: Decolonization and State Re-founding in Ecuador. Kult—Special Issue 6. Epistemologies of Transformation: The Latin American Decolonial Option and its Ramifications. Postkolonial.dk/artikler/kult_6/WALSH.pdf

World Intellectual Property Organization (WIPO) 2013. *Intellectual Property, Traditional Knowledge and Traditional Cultural Expressions/Folklore: A Guide for Countries in Transition*. Geneva.

Ziervogel, G. and A. Opere (eds) 2010. *Integrating Meteorological and Indigenous Knowledge-Based Seasonal Climate Forecasts in the Agricultural Sector*. Climate Change Adaptation in Africa learning paper series. International Development Research Centre, Ottawa, Canada.

PART 2: POLITICS AND POLITICAL ECONOMY

7

Postcolonial Political Institutions in the South Pacific Islands: A Survey

Jon Fraenkel

Jon Fraenkel: Personal Journey

I arrived at the University of the South Pacific (USP) in December 1995, straight out of the English winter into Fiji's baking summer, and completed a PhD thesis on the British economy while being chewed by mosquitoes on the balcony at Knolly Street. After several years as a joint appointee of the economics and history/politics departments, I helped set up the new Pacific Institute of Advanced Studies in Governance and Development (PIAS-DG). Teaching mature professional students from around the Pacific Islands in the master's program of PIAS-DG was one of the most interesting and rewarding teaching jobs I've ever had. I'm still in contact with many of those students. I moved to The Australian National University in March 2007, just after the military coup, but retain many links and friendships with those at USP. In 2012, I moved again to Victoria University of Wellington, another regional university with close links to USP. Visiting Fiji in January 2019, I took my 13-year-old son onto the USP Laucala campus. Upon seeing the elegant *vavai* (rain trees), *sekoula* (flame trees) and towering royal palms he said, 'Dad, this is way cooler than your other workplaces'.

Fraenkel, J. 2013. Post-Colonial Political Institutions in the South Pacific Islands: A Survey. In D. Hegarty and D. Tryon (eds), *Politics, Development and Security in Oceania*. Canberra: ANU Press, 29–49.

Republished with the kind permission of ANU Press.

Vue d'ensemble des Institutions politiques postcoloniales dans le Pacifique Sud insulaire

A partir du milieu des années 80 et jusqu'à la fin des années 90, les nouveaux pays du Pacifique sortaient d'une période postcoloniale marquée au début par l'optimisme et dominée par une génération de dirigeants nationaux à la tête d'un régime autoritaire pour connaître par la suite une période marquée par les difficultés et l'instabilité et qui a connu le coup d'Etat de Fidji de 1987, la guerre civile à Bougainville, le conflit néo-calédonien et l'instabilité gouvernementale au Vanuatu et ailleurs. Dans les pays de la Mélanésie occidentale, cette instabilité a été exacerbée par des pressions exercées par des sociétés minières et des sociétés forestières étrangères. Cette étude retrace l'évolution et explore les complexités des diverses institutions politiques postcoloniales dans le Pacifique Sud à la fois au sein de ces institutions et dans leurs relations entre elles ; elle montre que les questions de science politique classique ont été abordées de façons extrêmement différentes dans la région. On y trouve une gamme de systèmes électoraux comprenant à la fois des régimes présidentiels et des régimes parlementaires ainsi que des situations de forte intégration d'un certain nombre de territoires au sein de puissances métropolitaines. Entre les deux extrêmes de l'indépendance totale et de l'intégration, les îles du Pacifique sont le lieu où l'on trouve un éventail d'arrangements politiques hybrides entre les territoires insulaires et les anciennes puissances coloniales. Cet article examine l'absence de partis politiques disposant d'une base populaire dans le Pacifique, les faibles taux de représentation des femmes et l'expérience acquise par le Pacifique en matière d'accords de partage du pouvoir ; il pose également la question de savoir si la fin de la période de l'état de grâce qui a suivi l'indépendance représente un glissement vers une instabilité permanente ou simplement un intermède précédant une certaine consolidation du pouvoir.

After decolonisation, the new Pacific nations mostly experienced a brief honeymoon period, presided over by a generation of relatively strong national leaders: Fiji's Ratu Sir Kamisese Mara, Papua New Guinea's Michael Somare, Vanuatu's Walter Lini, Amata Kabua in Marshall Islands, Ieremai Tabai in Kiribati, and Nauru's Hammer de Roburt. The late 1980s and 1990s saw the demise of that initial postcolonial optimism. Fiji witnessed its first coup in 1987, and a year later the Bougainville civil war began in earnest. New Caledonia erupted into conflict in the mid-1980s until tensions were calmed by the 1988 Matignon and then 1998 Noumea Accords. Vanuatu's bipolar party system began to fracture in the late 1980s, and intense government instability reigned across the 1990s. For later decolonisers, like Tuvalu, the watershed was also later;

the two elections of 1993 proved the catalyst for an end to the early era of stability, after which the fall of governments became more frequent (Panapa and Fraenkel 2008). In the Marshall Islands, it was the death of Amata Kabua in 1996 that ended a hitherto unipolar style of government with no genuine opposition, and precipitated the opening of a period of sharper rivalry between the deceased president's successor, Imata Kabua, and the opposition United Democratic Party (UDP) led by a commoner, Kessai Note.

In the western Melanesian countries, heightened instability during the 1990s was encouraged by increasing interest from foreign companies in the natural resource extractive sectors. The Solomon Islands Government remained reasonably stable until Solomon Mamaloni's second government, when most ministers acquired strong links with logging companies (Frazer 1997:41). The political links of mining and forestry companies became increasingly important in PNG politics, particularly around election time. Growing popular discontent with parliamentary processes was indicated by high turnover rates among elected members of parliament (MPs). Issues of corruption became a focal point for the assembly of loose opposition coalitions; the reformist governments that took power in the Solomon Islands under Francis Billy Hilly in 1993 and under Bartholomew Ulufa'alu in 1997 both tried to define themselves through opposition to the 'Mamaloni men' (a reference to backers of the governments of Solomon Mamaloni, 1981–84, 1989–93, 1994–97, which were closely associated with Asian logging companies). Even in Tonga, where the monarchy remained in control, in the 1990s, 'Akilisi Pohiva and the other pro-democracy activists turned from agitation against abuses of office to radical demands for a shift away from royal control over government. Only Samoa remained reasonably stable, as the Human Rights Protection Party (HRPP) saw off challenges from the Tūmua and Pule movement in 1994 and consolidated its grip on state power.

The Pacific Islands region includes entities closely incorporated with the metropolitan powers located around the Pacific Rim, such as Guam (US), Rapa Nui (Chile) and Tokelau (New Zealand), as well as independent states like Papua New Guinea, Fiji and Kiribati. The region includes countries that achieved independence less than 30 years ago, as well as those that are still in the process of adjustment to the postcolonial order. It includes resource-rich territories with strong potential for integration into the world economy alongside chronically resource-poor countries with limited avenues for export-driven economic growth. It includes territories with open access to metropolitan labour markets, and countries without. It includes an extraordinary ethnolinguistic diversity, mostly in Melanesia, which alone accounts for one fifth of the world's documented living languages.[1] It includes relatively big nations like Papua New Guinea (6.6 million) alongside tiny micro-states like Niue, which has a population of only 1,500, and minute dependent territories like Pitcairn Island with only 45 inhabitants. Of the 9.7 million people that inhabit the 551.5 thousand square kilometre land area of Oceania, just over two-thirds are in Papua New Guinea.

Classical political science questions have been addressed in strikingly different ways across the region—whether to accommodate ethnic diversity through unitary, devolved or federal systems; whether to handle conflict through majoritarian or proportional electoral systems and/or through power-sharing arrangements and whether to adopt parliamentary or presidential systems; or, as in Kiribati and in the autonomous region of Bougainville, some hybrid between the two. Other important questions for the region have been how to meld traditional forms of governance with imported institutions; how to respond to exceptionally low levels of women's representation; and how to build states in countries where—for many who live in rural areas and engage largely in subsistence cultivation—the state matters little.

Electoral Systems

Oceania has a history of electoral experimentation. Enthusiasm for preferential voting in the Pacific has been encouraged by Australia's adoption of the alternative vote (AV) for the federal parliament in 1918. Colonially inherited first-past-the-post systems have been ditched in favour of single-member preferential systems in Fiji and Papua New Guinea, although in both cases without the expected results (Fraenkel and Grofman 2006; May 2008). In Fiji, the alleged 'unfairness' of outcomes under the AV system was used to justify coups both in 2000 and 2006. When it was adopted in the mid-1990s, AV was intended to boost the chances of the moderate centrists, and to disadvantage ethnic extremists. Instead, it triggered a sharpening of electoral polarisation.

---

1   Based on data from the US Summer Institute of Linguistics, www.ethnologue.com/ethno_docs/distribution.asp?by=area.

Nauru has a unique simultaneously tallied preferential voting system, which oddly resembles the arrangements invented by 19th-century French mathematician Jean-Charles de Borda (Reilly 2001). Kiribati uses a two-round system similar to that in mainland France, although unusually in multi-member constituencies. That system permits voters to express preferences, although over two rounds rather than in a single round of AV voting.[2] It is also considerably simpler to administer and count than the AV system, even if the need for two elections inevitably raises administrative costs.

List proportional representation (PR) systems are used only in the French territories. Unlike majoritarian systems, list PR systems aim to make the share of seats won by each party roughly equivalent to its share of votes, although there is a 5 per cent threshold below which parties gain no seats at all. By definition, list PR requires multi-member constituencies. New Caledonia, for example, is divided into three constituencies, the south (with 32 seats), the north (with 15) and the Loyalty Islands (with seven) for elections to the 54 member territorial congress. Voters simply tick the ballot paper next to their favoured political party and the parties submit lists of their candidates in order of preference. After the votes are tallied, electoral officials calculate which members are elected according to each party's share of the vote. In 2004, President Gaston Flosse modified French Polynesia's list PR voting system so as to give a 30 per cent seat bonus to the winning party, thus deliberately removing the system's proportionality. His aim was to give his Tahoeraa Huiraatira Party a stable working majority and to end many years of dependence on coalition government. The result was a crashing defeat for Tahoeraa Huiraatira, and the election instead of pro-independence leader Oscar Temaru. Instead of opening an era of stability, French Polynesia entered a politically chaotic period, with the presidency switching back and forth between the various factions. Paris stepped in to squash Flosse's failed reform in 2007.

Vanuatu is one of the few countries in the world to still use the single non-transferable vote (SNTV) system, alongside Jordan and Afghanistan. In an effort to bind francophone secessionists into the emerging Vanuatu state, British and French colonial authorities agreed on SNTV in the hope of avoiding a clean sweep for Walter Lini's anglophone Vanua'aku Pati (VP). Under SNTV, voters have a single vote, but constituencies have multiple members. Thus, if there is a 40 per cent francophone minority

---

2   AV is often called 'instant runoff voting' in the US due to this characteristic.

in a three-seat constituency, and if francophones avoid splitting their votes, they should be able to pick up at least one of the three seats. The system achieved its objective reasonably well in the initial elections after independence, when the parties were reasonably disciplined and the contest was a bipolar one between the VP and the francophone Union of Moderate Parties. From the late 1980s, however, the francophone/anglophone cleavage faded in significance, and parties splintered (Van Trease 2005). As political parties multiplied, SNTV became less predictable, victor's majorities reduced in size, and an increasing number of independent candidates contested.

Principles of universal suffrage and voter equality have, in some parts of the Pacific, sat awkwardly alongside traditional systems of authority. In Tonga, the king has not been—as often characterised—an absolutist monarch. Tonga's kings have been bound by the 1875 Constitution. It is the weak powers of parliament that have set Tonga apart from its neighbours. The prime minister and cabinet have been selected directly by the king, and sat in the legislature alongside nine nobles and nine people's representatives. Although there has been universal adult suffrage, there has been no effort to achieve voter equality: the holders of 33 noble titles selected nine noble representatives, while the rest of Tonga's 100,000 people chose nine people's representatives. Commitment to change has been in the air since 2005, oddly preceding the riots that destroyed much of Nuku'alofa in late 2006. In 2005, for the first time one of the people's representatives, Dr Feleti Sevele, became prime minister. The king subsequently declined to over-rule Dr Sevele's choice of cabinet ministers.

Upon his coronation in 2008, the new king, George Tupou V, committed to a majority popularly elected parliament. Parliament settled upon a first-past-the-post system and elections to the country's first-ever majority popularly elected assembly took place in November 2010. Under the new arrangements, the nine nobles' seats remain, but now together with 17 elected 'people's representatives'. Contrary to expectations that pro-democracy campaigner 'Akilisi Pohiva would assume control, his party gained only 12 of the 17 popularly elected seats. The remaining five independents aligned themselves with the nine nobles to select Noble Tui'vakano as prime minister. Although no longer responsible to the king, Tonga retains its tradition of strong centralised government: the prime minister is entitled to nominate an additional four members of parliament, and cannot be ousted by a 'no confidence' vote for 18 months after an election.

The principle of universal suffrage was not accepted by the architects of Samoa's 1962 constitution. Initially, both voters and candidates had to be holders of *matai* titles (a term often misleadingly translated as 'chief', but possibly better translated as 'family head'). A visiting United Nations team in 1959 argued that since there was an internal family decision-making process prior to the awarding of *matai* titles, the Samoan system could be regarded as one of 'election at two stages' (So'o and Fraenkel 2005:335). During the 1980s, that system was widely perceived—within Samoa—to have led to a proliferation of matai titles, triggered by rival parties exploiting the constitution's incentives to expand their voter bases by awarding titles. In 1990, there were 21,649 such titles, almost double the level a decade earlier. In that same year, the country voted to shift to a universal suffrage, although retaining the *matai*-only qualification for candidates. The change had several important repercussions for Samoan politics, but it did not halt the multiplication in the number of *matai* titles. In 1999, over 35,000 *matai* titles were on the books of the Land and Titles Court (So'o and Fraenkel 2005:342).

Presidential or Parliamentary Systems

The Pacific's presidential systems are mostly in the north where the US influence exerts greatest sway. Freely associated Palau most closely resembles the US model, with a president and congress and even a miniature replica of Washington's Capitol Building. The Commonwealth of the Northern Marianas, Guam and American Samoa have governors, rather than presidents, but are faithful to the American model of having direct popular elections for the head of government. The Marshall Islands and Nauru depart from the pattern in having 'presidents' that are more like prime ministers in the Westminster system; they are elected by parliaments. Kiribati is a unique hybrid since, although it has a directly elected president, (i) the nominees for the presidential election are selected through a complex parliamentary ballot, (ii) the president must form his cabinet from within parliament, and (iii) the president, despite being directly elected, can be ousted by a no-confidence vote within parliament, but doing this precipitates a general dissolution of parliament. Those choices are aimed at lessening the possibility of gridlock between an unpopular president and a hostile parliament, diminishing the likelihood of mid-term removal of the head of state and giving the head of government a direct popular mandate. As a result, Kiribati has experienced much less political instability than neighbours like Tuvalu and Nauru.

In the Pacific parliamentary systems, government formation can entail a delicate balancing act. In Solomon Islands, forming a cabinet has always entailed a careful harmonising of representation from the most populous island of Malaita with that from Guadalcanal and the Western Province. Oddly, this has at times benefited politicians from none of those three provinces, such as three-time prime minister Solomon Mamaloni (from Makira) or 2001–06 prime minister Sir Allen Kemakeza (from tiny Savo Island), who could appear to stand above the fray. In Papua New Guinea, it is inconceivable that a cabinet should exclude representatives from the highlands, or Papua, or the Islands. Even Fiji, which in many respects departs from Melanesian political norms owing to its bipolar indigene-Indian cleavage, cautious inclusion of powerful regions becomes politically astute. When Laisenia Qarase sought to forge a power-sharing government with the Fiji Labour Party in May 2006, he was careful to secure his indigenous Fijian base by drawing in paramount chiefs from the Kubuna, Burebasaga, and Tovata confederacies. The neglect of the Tongan-influenced Lau Islands, already suffering from a fading of the former glory associated with the deceased Ratu Mara's years as prime minister and then president, proved to be that government's Achilles' heel. The revenge of Mara's descendants, or rather the husbands of his daughters, was to become an important aspect of the coup of December 2006.[3]

Romantics often criticise the colonial imposition of 'Westminster' and see this as having disturbed traditional styles of political organisation, which were, it is claimed, characterised by consensus and the 'Pacific way'.[4] Yet the cleavages that prevail across the Pacific between government and opposition are not mere reflections of inherited institutions. In the small close-knit micro-states, hostility between the government faction and the opposition leadership can on occasions become far more bitter than in the industrialised mass democracies (even though alliances can also, in other circumstances, become fluid and personality-based, and many opposition leaders will, at some point, have served as ministers together in cabinet with those who are now adversaries). Opposition leaders may

---

3   Ratu Epeli Ganilau was not reappointed as a government nominee to the Great Council of Chiefs in 2004, consequently also losing his position as chair. Ratu Epeli Nailatikau lost his position as speaker after the May 2006 election and was to become ambassador to Malaysia until the 2006 coup intervened. Both men joined the post-2006 coup interim cabinet.
4   A term coined by Fiji's Ratu Sir Kamisese Mara (although it has other claimants) and used to convey a familiar set of contrasts, such as relaxed timekeeping, a preference for leisure over work and consensus over confrontation, felt to distinguish the Pacific from industrialised societies. Similar ideas are found in the Caribbean and Indian Ocean islands.

find themselves out of government for consecutive parliamentary terms, rendering them vulnerable in their home constituencies. Government victories are carried beyond the floor of the parliamentary chamber, affecting, for example, opposition leaders' private business interests or the promotion prospects of those in their kin groups. When a chance presents itself to dislodge such governments (either through a no-confidence vote or a prime ministerial election), opposition leaders can become desperate and willing to make deals they would otherwise prefer not to make with wavering opportunists. That sharp rivalry amongst Pacific leaders is not, as often imagined, a mere reflection of colonially inherited institutions and can be seen by the regular legal contestation of imposed limits on prime ministerial power (for example, Billy Hilly, Solomon Islands, 1993; Saufatu Sopoanga, Tuvalu, 2002; and Serge Vohor, Vanuatu, 2004, to name but a few).

Absence of major ideological cleavages or political parties with a substantial extra-parliamentary membership can give Pacific parliamentarians considerable freedom for manoeuvre. Occupying a ministerial portfolio not only provides a salary and status that is often impossible for a local to equal in the private sector, it also provides access to state funds and state leverage over foreign-controlled resource-extractive industries. Particularly in Melanesia, MPs have been known to engage in spectacular changes in affinity as they cross the floor to join government, often justifying this by claiming—probably accurately—that they were not elected to government in order to remain on the opposition benches. Many outside cabinet in PNG have preferred to sit on the 'middle benches', poised between government and opposition, so as to be open to offers of ministerial portfolios but equally accessible to being courted by opposition schemers planning assembly of a new government. Regular no-confidence votes in Solomon Islands are popularly believed to be money-making schemes: even if they do not succeed, the MPs all round earn large sums of cash as recipients of rival factions' bids for political support. After Vanuatu's 2008 prime ministerial election, two MPs were inadvertently heard live on national radio talking about the amounts of cash that had exchanged hands, unaware that the microphone was still turned on (Van Trease 2009).

Pacific parliamentarians, although not constrained by powerful party machines, may nevertheless be pressured by local constituents, *wantoks* or urban networks. The threat of electoral annihilation haunts Western Melanesian incumbents, who generally experience turnover rates well above 50 per cent. Politicians in Kiribati are intensely sensitive to home island opinion: while debate on government tabled legislation commands slender interest, question time (when MPs can be heard live on national radio interrogating ministers about matters of local significance) attracts intense interest. Popular engagement in parliamentary processes may be weak, but public interest is strong. When the Marshall Islands Nitijela is in session, most shared taxis running down Majuro's main street will be tuned into the debates. During the 1998–99 struggles between the Kessai Note's UDP and former president Imata Kabua, the public gallery of the Nitijela was packed with onlookers. Jousts between government and opposition leaders in Samoa can likewise grip public attention. Voter turnout is far higher in the Pacific Islands than in North America or Western Europe, and would be higher still if duplicate or deceased voter registrations were deleted from the rolls. Popular engagement with politics is greater than often recognised in the Pacific Islands, even if popular participation in decision-making (e.g. through select committees) is weak and accountability mechanisms work only through the crude three to five yearly ditching of incumbents at each general election.

Decolonisation

Close integration of territories with metropolitan powers is a legacy of the colonial experience. Hawai'i became the 50th Pacific state in 1959, while other American Pacific territories—Guam, American Samoa and the Commonwealth of the Northern Marianas—are described by the US Supreme Court as having become 'appurtenant to but not a part of the United States' (Underwood 2006:7). Rapa Nui was annexed in 1888 but only legally absorbed into Chile's Valparaiso Province in 1966. Residence on the island by Chileans is still restricted, as is acquisition of property by those not of Rapa Nui descent. By contrast, after West Papua was absorbed into Indonesia with United Nations approval after the Act of Free Choice in 1969, a mixture of spontaneous and sponsored transmigration brought in three-quarters of a million people, mainly from the islands of Java and Sulawesi. Integration with a powerful neighbour tends to open the floodgates to settlement, as on Saipan (Commonwealth of the Northern Marianas) where the majority were non-indigenes in 2000, mostly from the Philippines or China.

New Caledonia, French Polynesia, and Wallis and Futuna are in law part of the French nation state; all participate in elections for the national assembly and the presidency. The CFP franc, the currency in all three territories, is pegged to the euro. In 1958, French president General Charles de Gaulle insisted on the doctrine of the 'one and indivisible republic', and forced voters in French Polynesia to choose between colonial integration or abrupt secession. Sixty-four per cent voted in favour of staying with France. The pro-independence movement was defeated, and after disturbances in Papeete, its leader, Pouvanaa a Oopa, was imprisoned (Henningham 1992:123–26). The peoples of the French Pacific remain confronted with those stark options, although in modified forms: since 2003 they may opt to become 'territorial collectivities', with considerable autonomy. French Polynesia went a step further by adopting its own autonomy statute. New Caledonia is unique: as a result of the 1998 Noumea Accord, the territory has special legislative powers and a schedule for phased expansion of domestic political control ahead of a referendum on independence between 2014 and 2019. To agree to that accord entailed such a rupture with the doctrine of indivisibility of the Republic that France had to hold a nationwide referendum, the result of which earned New Caledonia a special provision in the constitution (Maclellan 2005:397).

Of the 16 territories in the world that remain on the United Nations list of non-decolonised territories, the Pacific accounts for five: American Samoa, Guam, New Caledonia, Pitcairn Island and Tokelau. Neither of Tokelau's two referenda (2006 and 2007) on whether to become self-governing achieved the required two-thirds majority, and Pitcairn Island's links with Britain have, if anything, been reinforced by adjudication of child abuses cases by the British Privy Council. American military build-up on Guam in the new millennium makes independence less likely, despite longstanding Chamorro disquiet about existing arrangements. Inclusion on, or exclusion from, the UN list can prove highly controversial, with behind-the-scenes manoeuvring at the UN headquarters in New York or Geneva being used to exert leverage towards independence back home. The incentives are clear. In 2008, UN Secretary General Ban Ki-moon urged the world 'to complete the decolonisation process in every one of the remaining 16 Non-Self-Governing Territories'.[5] Pro-independence leader

---

5   Message to Decolonisation Seminar, Indonesia, 14 May 2008.

Oscar Temaru, after his initial election as French Polynesia's president in 2004, sought to get his country onto the UN list following the precedent set by New Caledonia in the wake of the 1980s Kanak uprising.

Samoa was the first of the Pacific Island states to secure independence in 1962, and the unique constitutional arrangements chosen at that time (discussed later) have probably contributed to that country's postcolonial stability. Tonga formally became independent in 1970, but here the colonial hand was, for the most part, light. Financial irregularities under King George Tupou II (1893–1918) led the British colonists to demand closer control (Fusitu'a and Rutherford 1977:180). Britain became preoccupied with Europe during the 1914–18 war, and on its heels the Great Depression enabled Tupou II's more capable successor Queen Salote to preserve Tonga's political autonomy. Fiji's independence was inevitably problematic because of the need to reconcile the competing aspirations of the majority Fiji Indian and minority indigenous Fijian leaders (Norton 2004). Ethnic Fijian claims that since the country had been ceded to Queen Victoria by their chiefs in 1874, it should now be returned to those indigenous chiefs were to become a rallying cry of the ethno-nationalists who overthrew elected governments in 1987 and 2000. Fiji Indian claims that the communally based electoral system left as a compromise by the British at independence perpetuated race-based voting were to become a prominent theme of the military-backed interim government that emerged in the wake of Fiji's third coup in December 2006.

Constitutional choices made at independence also had enduring implications elsewhere in the region, in contrast to Africa where initial legal frameworks bequeathed by colonial powers were often torn up and new arrangements adopted (Chazan et al. 1992). Depth of consultation made a difference to the political authority of whatever structures were chosen. Papua New Guinea (1975) and Kiribati (1979) used constitutional conventions for deliberation, which left recommendations that had lasting political legitimacy (Macdonald 1982). By contrast, although there was more local consultation than is often appreciated in Solomon Islands, the 1978 Independence Order dealt with issues of citizenship in ways that pleased the British Colonial Office and swelled the size of the golden handshake, but provided no durable answer to what was to become a perennial issue in Solomon Islands politics: how to balance the powers of the central government against those of the separate islands.[6] The western breakaway movement that emerged in 1978 was echoed by demands for devolution during a constitutional review a decade later, and then again in the wake of the June 2000 coup when many provinces threatened to secede from the nation (Premdas et al. 1984; Mamaloni 1988; Fraenkel 2004:182). In Vanuatu, the Santo rebellion in 1980 was the most severe of the secessionist crises accompanying independence anywhere in the Pacific region; Jimmy Stevens' Vemerana Provisional Government on Santo threatened to break up the emerging state, until the rebellion was halted by the deployment of British, French and Papua New Guinean troops. The only actual case of secession in Oceania was exceptionally peaceful: in 1976, the British Gilbert and Ellice Islands decided to go their separate ways and a few years later became independent as Kiribati (1979) and Tuvalu (1978).[7] Bougainville's decade-long conflict first with Papua New Guinea and then internally is the most severe of the modern-day secessionist disputes. Its peace settlement, like that of the New Caledonian crisis of the 1980s, included a central provision that delayed the decision on independence for at least a decade.[8]

In between the extremes of independence and incorporation, the Pacific Islands are host to a range of hybrid political arrangements between island territories and former colonial rulers. New Zealand experimented with Compacts of Free Association with Niue and the Cook Islands. Palau, the Federated States of Micronesia and the Republic of the Marshall Islands entered Compacts of Free Association with the US that gave them considerable autonomy (allowing them, unlike the Cook Islands and Niue, to join the United Nations), but left the US with 'strategic denial' rights, enabling the exclusion of other rival superpowers from establishing military bases in that American sphere of influence. As a result of an associated deal, missiles can be fired from Vandenberg air base in California across a 6,760 kilometres arc through the Pacific sky before plunging into the lagoon of Kwajalein Atoll in the Marshall Islands. From there, they can be retrieved and studied by US scientists working

6   For background on the constitution-making process, see Ghai 1983.
7   The Congress of Micronesia also broke up into Commonwealth of the Northern Marianas, Republic of the Marshall Islands, Palau and Federated States of Micronesia, but the former was always a US-controlled Trust Territory, not an independent state.
8   New Caledonia's 1988 Matignon Accord put off the scheduled independence vote for a decade. However, in 1998, parties signed the Noumea Accord, which put the scheduled independence vote back further, to some point between 2014 and 2019. Bougainville's peace agreement provides that there will be a vote on independence at some point between 2015 and 2020.

at the nearby Ronald Reagan Ballistic Missile Defense Test Site. For this, Kwajalein's chiefs—including former president Imata Kabua—receive substantial rental payments, only a fraction of which trickles down to the Ebeye indigenous settlement adjacent to the American base. Negotiations around a new land use agreement for Kwajalein remain an issue of contention between Kwajalein chiefs and the Majuro-based Marshallese government. Washington pragmatically extended its 17 December 2008 deadline for achieving agreement over Kwajalein for a further five years.

For the Marshall Islands and the Federated States of Micronesia, the 1986 Compacts of Free Association expired in 2001. They were extended two years before being renewed for a further 20-year period in 2003, although now with greater scrutiny by the US Department of the Interior. Palau commenced its 15-year compact later than its neighbours in 1994, and so the arrangement expired only in 2009. US secretary of state Hillary Clinton agreed to a one-year extension, and 'compact review' talks commenced in May 2009. Renewed compacts provide the US-associated states with sizeable additions to government revenue—US$3.2 billion over the 20 years for the Federated States of Micronesia and the Marshall Islands. They also give access to costly federal programs, for example in health, education and the US mainland postal service.

Atomic rents kept French Polynesia prosperous for many years. Between 1966 and 1975, 41 atmospheric tests were conducted on the remote atolls of Mururoa and Fangataufa, followed by 137 underground tests ending in 1996, when France signed the Comprehensive Nuclear Test Ban Treaty. French aid then declined, but it still accounts for 35 per cent of the French Polynesian GDP. Due to French finance, New Caledonia and French Polynesia easily have the highest income per capita in the Pacific. For the American nuclear-affected islands, independence comes at a price. The Marshall Islands earned global notoriety because of the Bravo nuclear test on Bikini Atoll in 1954. In total, 67 tests were carried out on Bikini and neighbouring Enewetak between 1946 and 1958, the effects of which spread eastwards to Rongelap and Utrik. Washington insists that the US$250 million paid to the Marshallese Nuclear Claims Tribunal under the first compact, and the similar amount paid for federal programs to affected victims, was 'full and final' compensation. The Marshallese government disagrees. MPs representing the nuclear-affected islands have at times made common cause with Kwajalein's chiefs to urge a more belligerent negotiating stance over the new compact and the land use agreement for the Ronald Reagan Ballistic Missile Defense Test Site.

The economic advantages of close integration with a wealthy metropolitan power are everywhere apparent; the independent states are, on average, poorer than those which have been incorporated by powerful neighbours around the Pacific Rim or those that have retained close ties with former colonial powers (Bertram 1999:114). For many in the French territories, 'free association' arrangements such as those that connect Pacific states to America and New Zealand would be preferable to the controls from Paris, but the conventional French government position, echoing the Gaullist doctrine of 1958, is to insist that postcolonial linkages can only be decided after the territory settles upon independence. Financial incentives thus act as strong deterrents to loosening ties, even if such marked internal inequalities exist that indigenous groups still back political parties that push for independence.

Political Parties and Integrity Legislation

Nowhere in the Pacific Islands have the popularly based political parties that are so central to conventional western political thinking emerged. Nowhere do left–right ideological cleavages shape the divide between government and opposition. The only Pacific Island territories with fairly robust political parties are Fiji and New Caledonia, although Vanuatu and French Polynesia have some history of political party organisation.[9] Ever since independence in Fiji, there has been one party that appeals to the vast majority of ethnic Fijians[10] and another that represents the Fiji Indians.[11] The Fijian party has stood little chance in the Indian-dominated constituencies and vice versa. In 1997, when Fiji abandoned the first-past-the-post system in favour of the AV system, politicians were persuaded that adopting this modified majoritarian system would be most likely to encourage multi-ethnic government. That proved false. Over the three elections under AV, the party system polarised, so that by the third election under the system in 2006 one party claimed 80 per cent of the ethnic Fijian vote while the other had over 80 per cent of the Indian vote. Despondency as a result of the failure of the AV system to generate

---

9   For a survey of political parties across the region, see Fraenkel 2006a.
10   From the 1966 election until the 1987 polls, the Alliance Party, in 1992 and 1994 the Soqosoqo Vakavulewa ni Taukei (SVT) and from the 2001 polls Laisenia Qarase's Soqosoqo Duavata ni Lewenivanua. The exception was the 1999 elections, when the SVT managed only 38 per cent of the Fijian vote, with the remainder split among four other parties.
11   First the National Federation Party and then the Fiji Labour Party.

anticipated pro-moderation outcomes helps to explain why former centrist politicians and associated civil society activists sympathised with the military coup of December 2006, even if their choice to do so only legitimised Bainimarama's power grab.

In New Caledonia, issue-based political polarisation has also proved sharp, but not on the ethnic pattern of Fiji. Rivalry in the 1980s between the Front de Libération Nationale Kanak et Socialiste (FLNKS) and the French loyalist Rassemblement pour la Calédonie dans la Republique (RPCR) was intense, but ethnicity was not coterminous with political allegiance. Some indigenous Kanaks backed the RPCR, while the pro-independence parties always obtained at least some support outside their core Melanesian voter base. The Noumea Accord process in New Caledonia may also have served to erode the bipolar divide, in the sense that parties on both sides have fractured politically. Institutional incentives took the heat off the bipolar conflict and permitted the political emergence of alternative currents of opinion. The territory had long used a closed list proportional representation system, but in the 1998 Noumea Accord supplemented that proportionality in the formation of cabinet through mandatory power-sharing rules. The 1998 deal also devolved power to the provincial assemblies. The contrast between the experience of Fiji and New Caledonia illustrates the perils of using majoritarian systems in bipolar societies with race-based voting.

Few Pacific states have witnessed a strengthening of political party-style organisation. In the Marshall Islands, Kessai Note's UDP administration was elected in 1999 on a 'good governance', accountability and transparency platform ousting Imata Kabua's government. The UDP government survived the 2003 election, but by 2007 was confronted by a rival party that was backed by Imata Kabua and other leading chiefly families in the Ralik chain, the Aelon Kein Ad (AKA). The AKA struck a deal with Nitijela speaker and Ratak chief Litokwa Tomeing, and won the 2007 election. Despite the appearance of an 'evolution' towards political party-style organisation, allegiances remain fluid in the Marshall Islands. The triumph of the 'visionaries' against the 'old guard' in Nauru in 2004 was not accompanied by development of political parties; the reformist's access to political power always depended on courting wavering opportunists with offers of the presidency. In the smaller Pacific states, a hardening of the opposition often entails the formation of a political party, but, if successful in obtaining office, the new government will usually prefer to decry political party-style organisation and claim instead to be ruling in the general interest.

Towards the western Pacific, the absence of robust political parties has become a major issue, leading in some countries to ambitious legislation aimed at encouraging the construction of party-based systems. Papua New Guinea's 2001–02 Organic Law on Political Parties and Candidates aimed to fast-track the development of strong parties by requiring those who back a prime minister after a general election to stick with that choice in any votes of confidence, budgetary votes and votes on constitutional amendments. In an effort to avoid the horse-trading that follows each general election, the party with the largest share of votes is to be given the first opportunity to form a government.

That legislation is widely believed to have ushered in a period of greater stability in PNG; Sir Michael Somare's National Alliance government survived a full 2002–07 term in office, the first government since independence to have achieved this. Somare also succeeded in getting re-elected for a further term after the general election in 2007, and survived beyond the 18-month grace period that ended in February 2009. Yet there are doubts about this simplistic assessment of the stabilising merits of OLIPPAC. While the prime minister remained Somare, deputy prime ministers changed repeatedly over 2002–07, and ministers were regularly reshuffled. Contrary to the rules against floor-crossing, 11 MPs switched sides from government to opposition during the 2002–07 parliament, but none lost their seats as the law said they should do. The Ombudsman—who was in law empowered to act in such cases, if necessary to recommend a forfeit of seats—wisely preferred not to do so. The law proved a toothless tiger, even if in practice floor-crossing did diminish due to the perception of the threat of dismissal. Opposition inside parliament became subdued not so much because of OLIPPAC but because of the presence of a partisan speaker who closed down hostile debate and ruled out of order questions that might embarrass the government. In July 2010, PNG's Supreme Court ruled that key elements of the OLIPPAC violated the freedom of movement provisions in the constitution.[12]

---

12   Special Reference by Fly River Provincial Executive Council; Re Organic Law on Integrity of Political Parties and Candidates, Supreme Court of Papua New Guinea, 7 July 2010.

Despite this, the myth of OLIPPAC-engineered stability obtained considerable currency, for there could be little doubt that the political order was more stable than during the chaotic turn-of-the-millennium years (Standish 2000). The more plausible explanation was better handling of the country's second resources boom (Baton et al 2009), and the availability of a good deal more money to grease the political wheels. Other Melanesian countries have been inspired by the PNG experiment, hoping also to discipline their allegedly feckless and unruly backbenchers. Serge Vohor's short-lived 2004 government in Vanuatu wanted to introduce PNG-like 'grace periods', but the court ruled the attempt unconstitutional, and Vohor's government fell to a no-confidence challenge. In Solomon Islands, the post-2007 Sikua-led government was assisted by Australian think tanks in deliberations aimed at adopting legislation inspired by OLIPPAC in PNG (Haywood-Jones 2008). However, several ministers in Dr Sikua's cabinet conspired against the proposed constitutional amendment, which failed to obtain the required two-thirds majority. Those ministers were sacked by Dr Sikua for this act of rebellion, but they re-emerged, holding key portfolios, in the government led by new prime minister Danny Philip after the August 2010 election.

In PNG, Solomon Islands, and Vanuatu, bills and laws have been ostensibly aimed at beefing up political parties, but in practice at strengthening governments and weakening the opposition. Grace periods during which governments cannot be voted out of office tend to be much more popular than financing a costly political party registration apparatus. Although popular concern centres on the horse-trading prior to prime ministerial elections, the rule giving the largest party the first crack at forming a government—by making this a one shot game—generates even greater potential for corruption and instability than the previous arrangements. The risk with 'grace periods', and other forms of restriction on 'no-confidence' motions, is that they allow a deeply unpopular government to retain office, and/or that they require the law courts to intervene to control the minutiae of parliamentary conduct.

Women's Representation

Of the nine countries worldwide that have zero women members of parliament, Oceania accounts for five (Solomon Islands, Federated States of Micronesia, Nauru, Palau and Tuvalu).[13] Papua New Guinea and the Marshall Islands have only a single female MP. Fiji had eight until Bainimarama dissolved parliament in December 2006. Samoa and Niue have four; Guam, Cook Islands and Kiribati have three; and Vanuatu two women MPs. Male dominance of the political stage occurs not only in the national parliaments, but also in local-level assemblies. Traditional male preponderance in the political sphere, and the conservatism of island societies, are the most frequently heard explanations for inequality in political representation. Yet change is in the air, at least in some parts of the Pacific. In western Melanesia, a growing number of women are now contesting elections. By contrast, in some of the smaller and more remote islands, few women contest and those that do are subjected to extraordinary pressures. In some Pacific Island polities, female leaders prefer to keep out of the male-dominated political world, and to concentrate instead on influencing decisions behind-the-scenes or through civil society activism (McCloud 2002). Increasingly aggressive electoral contests have also diminished women's chances on the campaign trail: in the PNG highlands, for example, candidates need access to large sums of cash to win, and they need large numbers of male campaign backers in order to sustain control over the polling booths and coordinate the process of 'assisted voting' (i.e. the completion of ballot papers en masse by sympathisers).

Temporary special measures have been used to increase the number of women in parliament in the French territories and on Bougainville. The French law on parity has given New Caledonia and French Polynesia close to 50 per cent female members of territorial assemblies. That law has not yielded similar results in the third largest French territory, Wallis and Futuna, where constituencies are smaller and where numerous parties enter the contest. Although the parity law requires parties to lodge lists that alternate men and women, since most 'parties' in Wallis and Futuna obtain only a single member, the law does not have the intended effect. Adopting parity laws would have similar results in the other party-less

---

13   Data from Inter-Parliamentary Union (IPU) website, www.ipu.org/wmn-e/classif.htm. The other states with zero women members are Saudi Arabia, Oman, Qatar and Belize. The IPU dataset records only states that are members of the United Nations, not territories like American Samoa and Commonwealth of the Northern Marianas that also have zero female MPs.

Pacific microstates (Fraenkel 2006b). Where political parties are absent or weak, reserved seats are the only legal measure likely to increase the number of women in parliament. The autonomous region of Bougainville is the sole entity in Oceania to have adopted reserved seats for women. Three of Bougainville's 41 seats are reserved for women. In both Papua New Guinea and Solomon Islands, increasing numbers of female candidates are contesting elections, and in both countries there are pressures for reserved seats to increase the number of women in parliament.

Although women are poorly represented in Pacific parliaments, they tend to be better represented at the top levels of the civil service, where appointments are more likely to be on merit. For example, as of late 2009, Kiribati women accounted for only three MPs in its 46 member parliament (6.5 per cent), but seven of the 15 top positions in the I-Kiribati civil service (46 per cent). In Solomon Islands, Nauru, and Samoa, the percentage of women in top positions in the ministries is also markedly higher than the share in parliament. The secretaries in the I-Kiribati ministries are, probably uniquely in the Pacific, paid considerably more than parliamentarians. Much of the consultation around new legislation occurs through the ministries, prior to agreement in cabinet and before bills are tabled in parliament. In Kiribati, as in many other Pacific countries, highly qualified women prefer to take positions formulating and implementing policy, rather than going on the election campaign trail or joining male-dominated legislative assemblies. The Kiribati parliament is an assembly open to those over the civil service retirement age of 55, and it is a place where MPs focus largely on constituency matters rather than law-making.

Power-sharing Accords

The Pacific has an interesting but little internationally known experience with mandatory power-sharing accords. Nowhere in the world has witnessed such extensive litigation about mandatory power-sharing rules as Fiji. In the 1997 Fiji constitution, a power-sharing provision required that all parties with 10 per cent or more of seats be proportionally represented in cabinet. The provision was modelled on that in South Africa during the transition from apartheid, and similar rules were adopted in Northern Ireland as part of the Good Friday Agreement in 1998. When Mahendra Chaudhry formed his Labour-led People's

Coalition cabinet after the 1999 Fiji election, he proved able to exclude the largest Fijian party, Rabuka's Soqosoqo Vakavulewa ni Taukei, on the grounds that its leaders imposed conditions on cabinet entry that amounted to a decline of the invitation. When Chaudhry's arch-adversary Laisenia Qarase tried to follow that legal precedent after the elections of 2001, the Court of Appeal rejected his efforts as contrary to the 1997 constitution. Qarase appealed and the cases dragged on until 2004 before the Supreme Court left Qarase's Soqosoqo Duavata ni Lewenivanua party with no option other than to invite Chaudhry's Fiji Labour Party (FLP) into cabinet. Qarase reluctantly complied by offering the FLP a series of token minor portfolios in a cabinet so swollen that his former ministers also retained their portfolios. It was, unsurprisingly after so much legal action, a compromise with the letter but not the spirit of the law. The FLP condemned the expansion in cabinet size as a costly imposition on Fiji's people and criticised the portfolios as trivial. Since a fresh election was anyway looming on the horizon, Chaudhry chose instead to occupy the opposition benches.

After the 2006 election, Qarase complied more wholeheartedly with Fiji's multi-party cabinet rules, drawing nine senior FLP parliamentarians into cabinet, and giving them major portfolios. It proved an enormously popular decision, but Fiji's political leaders again failed to make the arrangements work. Chaudhry stayed out of cabinet, and eventually expelled two of the participating FLP ministers. The short-lived 2006 power-sharing cabinet was the first government since independence to have brought members from the country's two largest parties—one representing the Fijians and the other the Fiji Indians—into cabinet (Green 2009). It lasted just seven months before being overthrown by military commander Frank Bainimarama.

In New Caledonia, by contrast, power-sharing provisions agreed as part of the 1998 Noumea Accord worked more smoothly, even if they left the pro-independence parties in a minority. In all post-accord cabinets, the loyalist parties dominated, based on their ascendancy in the more densely populated Southern Province and their ability to gain a minority of seats in the majority Kanak Northern Province. During the initial post–Noumea Accord government, the pro-independence groups regularly took legal action regarding the composition of government. However, after the 2001 assumption of the presidency by the RPCR's Pierre Frogier, Kanak activist Déwé Gorodé was selected as vice president, thus meeting one of the major FLNKS demands. The 2004 election saw a fracturing amongst the loyalist parties, with the emergence of Avenir Ensemble, a trend continued at the 2009 election, with further splits this time affecting Avenir Ensemble. Pro-independence parties have also been prone to schisms. The other Noumea Accord provisions of devolution of powers from Paris to Noumea, and a re-balancing of income towards the predominantly Kanak Northern and Loyalty Islands Provinces have helped to encourage the emergence of new alignments also among the Kanak parties.

New Caledonia's arrangements had a more solid foundation than those in Fiji. Provisions for the proportional distribution of ministerial appointments fitted better with New Caledonia's list PR electoral system than with Fiji's majoritarian AV system. Fiji's Westminster-based 1997 constitution was not sufficiently redrafted after the belated inclusion of the 10 per cent rule, and drafters did not fully consider the likely difficulties of a prime minister needing to form a coalition government to 'command a majority' on the floor of the house while at the same time being required to form a power-sharing cabinet that includes all the qualifying parties. Whereas Fiji's power-sharing rule generated bipolar incentives for each ethnic group to avoid splits that might entail parties falling below the 10 per cent threshold required for cabinet participation, New Caledonia's rules allowed smaller parties to combine with larger parties to boost cabinet entitlements. New Caledonia's arrangements were considerably assisted by French aid subventions, and by a growing flexibility emanating from Paris as regards which institutions might prove acceptable. Fiji had to tackle its problems alone, with little in the way of helpful advice from supranational institutions or powerful neighbours.

Conclusion: Postcolonial Trends

Does the closing of the post-independence honeymoon era represent a shift to permanent volatility, or merely a hiatus before some new leadership consolidation? Efforts by elites to stabilise and regiment the political order have been most ambitious in Papua New Guinea, with OLIPPAC and 'grace periods', but, as we have seen, similar devices are being experimented with in Solomon Islands and have been tried, unsuccessfully, in Vanuatu. Samoa's HRPP is the only political party across the region that has remained in office for close to a quarter of a century, consolidating its control by expanding cabinet size, increasing the parliamentary term to five years, outlawing party switching and creating new sub-ministerial positions for pro-government backbenchers. Solomon Islands and Tuvalu have sought to increase cabinet size, so as to render the executive more resilient to parliamentary challenge. Whether those efforts prove successful, whether they prove harbingers of emergence of more authoritarian political elites, or whether the post-independence era's highly contested and fluid styles of politics reassert their influence remains to be seen.

References

Bertram, G. 1999. The MIRAB Model Twelve Years On. *The Contemporary Pacific* 11(1):105–38.

Chazan, N., R. Mortimer, J. Ravenhill and D. Rothchild 1992. *Politics and Society in Contemporary West Africa*, 2nd ed. Boulder: Lynne Rienner. doi.org/10.1007/978-1-349-12976-8

Fraenkel, J. 2004. *The Manipulation of Custom: From Uprising to Intervention in the Solomon Islands*. Wellington: Victoria University Press.

Fraenkel, J. 2006a. The Political Consequences of Pacific Island Electoral Laws. In R. Rich, L. Hambly and M. Morgan (eds), *Political Parties in the Pacific Islands*. Canberra: Pandanus.

Fraenkel, J. 2006b. The Impact of Electoral Systems on Women's Representation in Pacific Parliaments. In *A Woman's Place is in the House—the House of Parliament: Research to Advance Women's Political Representation in Forum Island Countries*. Suva: Pacific Islands Forum Secretariat.

Fraenkel, J. and B. Grofman 2006. Does the Alternative Vote Foster Moderation in Ethnically Divided Societies? The Case of Fiji. *Comparative Political Studies* 39(5):623–51. doi.org/10.1177/0010414005285032

Frazer, I. 1997. The Struggle for Control of Solomon Islands Forests. *The Contemporary Pacific* 9(1):39–72.

Fusitu'a, E. and N. Rutherford 1977. George Tupou II and the British Protectorate. In N. Rutherford (ed.), *Friendly Islands: A History of Tonga*. Melbourne: Oxford University Press.

Ghai, Y. 1983. The Making of the Independence Constitution. In P. Larmour (ed.), *Solomon Islands Politics*. Suva: University of the South Pacific.

Green, M. 2009. Fiji's Short-lived Experiment in Executive Power-Sharing, May–December 2006. State, Society and Governance in Melanesia Discussion Paper 2009/2. Canberra: The Australian National University.

Hayward-Jones, J. 2008. *Engineering Political Stability in Solomon Islands: Outcomes Report*. Sydney: Lowy Institute.

Henningham, S. 1992. *France and the South Pacific; A Contemporary History*. Sydney: Allen and Unwin.

Macdonald, B. 1982. *Cinderellas of Empire; Towards a History of Kiribati and Tuvalu*. Canberra: Australian National University Press.

Maclellan, N. 2005. From Eloi to Europe: Interactions with the Ballot Box in New Caledonia. *Commonwealth & Comparative Politics* 43(3):394–417. doi.org/10.1080/14662040500304890

Mamaloni, S. 1988. *1987 Constitutional Review Committee Report, Vol. 2*. Honiara: Government Printer.

May, R. 2008. The 2007 Election in Papua New Guinea, State Society and Governance in Melanesia Briefing Note 7, Canberra: The Australian National University.

McCloud, A. 2002. Where Are the Women in Simbu Politics? *Development Bulletin* 59:43–46.

Norton, R. 2004. Seldom a Transition with Such Aplomb: From Confrontation to Conciliation on Fiji's Path to Independence. *Journal of Pacific History* 39(2):147–62. doi.org/10.1080/0022334042000250715

Panapa, P. and J. Fraenkel 2008. The Loneliness of the Pro-Government Backbencher and the Precariousness of Simple Majority Rule in Tuvalu. State, Society and Governance in Melanesia Discussion Paper 2008/2. Canberra: The Australian National University.

Premdas, R., J. Steeves and P. Larmour 1984. The Western Breakaway Movement in Solomon Islands. *Pacific Studies* 7(2):34–67.

Reilly, B. 2001. *The Borda Count in the Real World: The Electoral System in the Republic of Nauru*. Macmillan Brown Centre for Pacific Studies Working Paper 8. Christchurch: University of Canterbury.

So'o, A. and J. Fraenkel 2005. The Role of Ballot Chiefs and Political parties in Samoa's Shift to Universal Suffrage. *Commonwealth & Comparative Politics* 43(3):333–61. doi.org/10.1080/14662040500304973

Standish, B. 2000. *Papua New Guinea 1999: Crisis of Governance*. Australian Parliamentary Library, Research Paper 4. Canberra: Parliamentary Library, Parliament of Australia.

Underwood, R. 2006. Micronesian Political Structures and American Models: Lessons Taught and Lessons Learned. *Journal of Pacific Studies* 29(1):4–24.

Van Trease, H. 2005. The Operation of the Single Non-Transferable Vote System. *Commonwealth & Comparative Politics* 43(3):296–332. doi.org/10.1080/14662040500304833

Van Trease, H. 2009. Vanuatu's 2008 Election—Difficulties of Government Formation in a Fractionalized Setting. State, Society and Governance in Melanesia Briefing Note 2009/1. Canberra: The Australian National University.

8

Neo-Liberalism and the Disciplining of Pacific Island States—the Dual Challenges of a Global Economic Creed and a Changed Geopolitical Order

Claire Slatter

Claire Slatter: Personal Journey

I graduated from the University of the South Pacific (USP) in 1973, then spent a year at the University of Papua New Guinea doing a master's qualifying course and tutoring part-time in political studies. I was inspired by many academics I met there, including Sione Latukefu, Ruth Latukefu, John Ballard and David Hegarty, all of whom subsequently joined The Australian National University (ANU). In 1984, I applied for and was offered a scholarship to do an MA in politics at ANU and was privileged to have John Ballard as my principal supervisor. I returned to Fiji in late 1986 and joined the Department of History/Politics, where I began an academic career teaching politics. In 1997, I commenced PhD studies at Massey University under a USP staff training award. I retained informal links with ANU over the years, mostly through Greg Fry, who became and remains a close friend; William Sutherland, a fellow Fijian and close friend who joined Department of Political and Social Change at ANU; and, after 2004, Stewart Firth, whom I was fortunate to have as Head of Department at USP for six years. Largely through these connections, I was invited to ANU conferences now and again, including a workshop organised by Jan Jindy Pettman in 2001.

My research on externally driven economic and governance reforms in the Pacific region, which formed the subject of my PhD thesis, engaged me in critiquing some of the research emanating from ANU in the early 1990s, specifically the Pacific 2010 doomsday reports from the National Centre for Development Studies and polemical papers by the late Professor Helen Hughes.

Slatter, C. 2006. Neo-Liberalism and the Disciplining of Pacific Island States — the Dual Challenges of a Global Economic Creed and a Changed Geopolitical Order. In M. Powles (ed.), *Pacific Futures*. Canberra: Pandanus Books, 91–110.

Republished with the kind permission of ANU Press.

Introduction

Post–Cold War development and aid discourses on Pacific Island states reflect an ideological struggle for the hearts and minds of political leaders and policymakers in Pacific Island states and their traditional benefactors in Australasia by free-market policy advocates based in or linked to academia. A pronounced feature of these discourses, which advocate structural adjustment policies, or what is euphemistically termed 'reform' in the Pacific region, has been their employment of positive and negative imagery, ridicule and praise in analysing Pacific Island states, economies and societies. Seemingly complimentary references to Pacific Islander 'risk-loving, enterprising, seafaring forebears, whose voyages opened the vast South Pacific, and who developed a distinct material culture and civilization in remote, resource poor islands', like praise for how well Islanders who have more recently ventured into the outside world have adapted to 'an extended individualistic order', encourage enterprise and risk-taking in the unchartered economic seas of a deregulated global economy and a journeying away from all that Pacific Islanders have known, and held dear (Kasper et al.1991:70).[1] At the same time, derogatory references in the discourses to Pacific Island states' economic dependency on aid, and ridicule of their standing as micro-political entities in the world of larger nation-states, deter smaller island governments from questioning, much less resisting, the new economic wisdom of 'reform',

---

1   References to voyages and voyaging appear in Kasper et al. 1991; Hughes 1998; and the World Bank 2002.

while eroding the notion and value of national sovereignty (Kasper et al. 1988, 1991; Hughes 2003). In these discourses, enterprising citizens—as individuals or as owners/shareholders of corporate bodies—rather than states, are presented as the primary agents of economic development, and the growth prospects of islands, as opposed to the viability of nation-states and national economies, appear as the principal concern.

Consensus among multilateral and bilateral donors in the region on what the Pacific Island states' best economic policy options are has seen the prioritisation of reform in donor aid programming since the mid-1990s. The ideological foundation on which structural adjustment policies are based is neoliberalism, a philosophy that hinges on beliefs in free enterprise, deregulated economies and labour markets, private ownership, individual property rights, small government, reduced taxes, a market-friendly state, and global trade liberalisation, or the opening up of the world's markets, labour pools and resource bases to all economic competitors on theoretically equal terms. Many of the most ardent advocates of neoliberalism are linked to economic policy think tanks that exist for the primary purpose of influencing political leaders and policymakers through strategic dissemination of their publications. The one-size-fits-all economic model that they advocate is the same as that promoted by multilateral lending institutions and bilateral donors through structural adjustment policies, and there are indeed close interconnections between the advocacy work of neoliberal think tanks and the policies of multilateral agencies and bilateral donors.

In the past 15 years, free-market advocates within Australian and New Zealand academia have been producing analyses of Pacific Island economies and states, some of them commissioned or otherwise supported by their governments, or written for multilateral institutions such as the World Bank and the Asian Development Bank (ADB). The use of ridicule and praise in several of these reports reflects the evident ideological project in which their authors are engaged and the far from value-free scientific basis on which their analyses and prescriptions rest. Selling market fundamentalism, like other variants of extremism, entails securing conversions through the combined strategies of castigation and shaming for wrongdoing on the one hand, and promising a better life after repentance and return to the right path on the other. The subjection of Pacific Island states to neoliberal demagoguery and donor-driven economic and trade liberalisation constitutes what might be called a disciplining of island states in the post–Cold War, unipolar world of corporate-driven globalisation where free-market ideas appear to reign supreme. With the justification and cover for new forms of economic and political domination provided by the United States' 'war against terrorism', and the continuing influence of neoliberal thinking, so-called 'failed' and 'non-viable' Pacific Island states could find themselves even more deprived of their sovereignty in the years ahead.

This chapter focuses on the fostering of neoliberal economic ideas in the Pacific from the 1990s, the routes through which they have gained entry to and acquired credence in the region, the economic policy changes that derive from them, and the changed geopolitical context, global compacts and treaties that are the hallmarks of the new global economic order underpinned by neoliberalism. Attention is drawn to how neoliberal ideas and their proponents have been shaping thinking within the Pacific, and about the Pacific and its future, especially since the 1990s, and to some of the implications of fully embracing these ideas and the policies they inspire.

Academic Pushers of Neoliberalism in the Pacific

Neoliberal economic policies were first advocated in the Pacific region by Australian economists based at The Australian National University (ANU). In 1988, barely a year after the first military coup in Fiji, a book entitled *Fiji—Opportunity from Adversity* (Kasper et al. 1988) proposed a three-part reform that seemed designed to make Fiji a Hong Kong in the middle of the Pacific. Published by the Centre for Independent Studies (CIS), a think tank promoting free markets, individual liberty, 'democratic government under the rule of law', and a 'free civil society', the research on which it was based was initiated by the National Centre for Development Studies (NCDS) at ANU and was funded by the Australian International Development Assistance Bureau (AIDAB), now known as AusAID. It was a collaboration that illustrated well the close links between neoliberal think tanks, universities, and government aid bureaus.[2] The book's chief recommendations were: constitutional guarantee of civic and economic

---

2   The CIS then had offices in New South Wales and Auckland. From the mid-1980s to the early 1990s, many of its members were also members of the powerful New Zealand Business Roundtable, whose proposals, according to Kelsey (1993:135–36), were indistinguishable from those of Labor and National governments from 1984, when New Zealand's economic reform program began to be implemented.

rights to all Fijian citizens to restore confidence and security; rapid deregulation of labour, capital and produce markets; and comprehensive privatisation to reduce the size of the government and invigorate activities stifled by bureaucratic and union controls. The authors viewed the break in Australia–Fiji aid relations, as a consequence of the 1987 coups, as a timely opportunity for Australia to re-evaluate its aid strategy given changes in general thinking on economic and development policy around the world and the new 'hard-nosed philosophy' that was spreading in donor countries (Kasper et al. 1988:xii). They advised the Australian Government against providing unconditional aid to post-coup Fiji, saying it would be tantamount to 'an outright subsidy to a growing class of politicians, military and bureaucrats', who were accountable to neither Australian nor Fijian taxpayers. The key requirements for economic growth, they argued, were not aid but 'economic and social policies and the attitude of the population to work, learning, and capital formation'. They proposed the introduction of conditionality in Australian aid and advocated directing more aid through 'private channels' (specifically, voluntary agencies and private companies), and a more openly self-interested approach to using Australian aid.[3] This was the first clearly articulated neoliberal economic policy guide proposed to a Pacific state.

A second CIS publication on aid and development policy in the Pacific blamed aid for inhibiting economic advance and judged it unnecessary, since capital required for development could be secured through foreign direct (private) investment (Kasper et al. 1991).[4] Transfers of wealth from Pacific Islanders living and working abroad to their families in the Islands were seen as inducing increases in public sector wages and salaries, exerting upward pressure on national wages and exacerbating difficulties in a number of Pacific Island countries (e.g. by raising agricultural wages

---

3   For example, inducing (private) Australian health clinics and hospitals to set up branches in Fiji and encouraging pre-retirement Australian health personnel to undertake two- or three-year contracts there; reducing assistance to the University of the South Pacific and providing a larger number of scholarships to Fijian citizens to study in Australia; using aid to provide Australian supervision and technical advisors in private schools and training schemes; and supporting the establishment of 'cheap community colleges' to help improve racial balance in economic life (Kasper et al. 1988:146).

4   The volume brought together papers presented at a session on development in the South Pacific from a Pacific Regional Meeting in Christchurch in November 1989 sponsored by the Mont Pelerin Society, a highly influential, private think tank founded in Switzerland in 1947 by European and American intellectuals strongly opposed to socialism, central planning and the regulatory state, and dedicated to promoting the ideas of economic liberalism. The moving force behind the formation of the society was Austrian-born British economist Fredrich Von Hayek, and one of its 39 original founders was Milton Friedman. Kasper and other members of the CIS were members of the society in 1997, as was Ruth Richardson, former National Government Finance Minister of New Zealand.

in Tonga, Samoa and Cook Islands and making it increasingly difficult to secure agricultural labour). Traditional systems (such as the absence of a tradition of genuine private property), favourable natural endowments (which provide basic necessities with little effort, encouraging a work ethic that does not link work effort with survival), a benign or non-traumatic colonial experience, and continuing postcolonial patronage through aid (which subsidised Pacific economies and maintained a level of 'subsistence affluence' and inappropriately large national governments modelled on those of larger states and run as personal fiefdoms by traditional or new elites) were together seen as inherent constraints to economic development.

Pacific Island states were said to be 'unfamiliar with genuine poverty' and were enjoying middle-income status by World Bank definition (with French Polynesia and New Caledonia 'exceeding New Zealand's modest living standards'), which could not be maintained by local production and productivity without perpetual aid. Fundamental problems were predicted and 'peaceful social evolution, cohesion, prosperity and stability' were seen as attainable only through the 'openness, vertical mobility, and scope for individual rivalry and self-realisation' that markets, civil rights and equality before the law could provide (Kasper et al. 1991:64). Changes in Pacific ways were considered necessary, namely 'more work, more systematic work, more savings, and a longer-term planning horizon', and the costs to cherished culture and values in embracing the 'growth and performance-oriented economic lifestyle' would be minimal.

In the first instance of deriding Pacific Island states, Kiribati was ridiculed for seeking to 'play a grand international role' by hosting a regional ministerial meeting in 1989 at enormous cost to Australian taxpayers, who footed the bill for a navy ship, which was dispatched to provide accommodation for participants. And 'most of the best-educated Pacific Islanders' were disparaged as 'professional aid seekers who increasingly regard foreign aid as a right and threaten to make political mischief if they don't get it' (Kasper et al. 1991:79). Pacific leaders were evidently expected to be shamed by these deprecatory remarks into accepting the 'wisdom' of economic restructuring, and to trust that Western technology, management and economic modes of behaviour could be adopted in the Pacific, as they had been in Asia 'without giving up one's Chinese, Malay, Korean, Japanese or Indian identity' (ibid.).

The CIS's analyses of Pacific economies predated the World Bank's Pacific reports of 1991 and 1993, which together provided donors with authoritative texts for pushing 'reform' in Pacific Island states. Yet, there were obvious echoes of the CIS authors' perspectives and arguments in the World Bank reports.

Making Structural Adjustment Policies the New Development Framework in the Pacific

In its first report on the state of Pacific Island economies, the World Bank highlighted the 'sluggish' economic growth performance of Pacific Island states compared with the 'more dynamic island economies of the Caribbean (5 per cent) and the Indian Ocean (7 per cent)', and despite their receipt of 'some of the highest inflows of per capita development assistance' (World Bank 1991:1, 3). Inward-looking economic strategies, such as protection of local industries, state enterprises and over-regulation, were blamed for this. A number of trade-centred 'dynamic growth strategies' were proposed as remedies: abandoning inward-looking, import-substitution policies and promoting private sector investment and export production; shifting away from producing primary commodities toward production of processed products for export; concentrating on a few specialised areas in which they had 'a clear comparative advantage'; and introducing greater flexibility in wages. Developing entrepreneurial capacity and expanding private sector participation in investment and economic activity were especially emphasised as the key to economic growth, and the primary challenge for Pacific Island economies in the 1990s, according to the World Bank, was providing a policy environment to facilitate private investment (World Bank 1991:iv).

Among the recommended macroeconomic policies were fiscal adjustment to reduce fiscal deficits to more manageable levels, appropriate wage and exchange rate policies to maintain external competitiveness and keep wages in line with economy-wide productivity, restructuring the tax system to broaden the tax base, lower direct taxes, eliminate trade-inhibiting taxes, and a shift towards an indirect tax system that 'does not discriminate across productive sectors' (World Bank 1991:iii). Tariff reform, to reduce high tariff levels and remove protective arrangements, was recommended as an essential part of tax reform. Corporate taxes were recommended 'at rates conducive to private investment and growth' (World Bank 1991:iv).

Recommended public sector management policies included reducing the administrative budget (particularly public sector wages and salaries, which were considered to have grown excessively and had inflated wages throughout the economy), improvement of physical infrastructure and introduction of a program of privatisation, particularly for commodity marketing boards and other enterprises that 'crowd out private investment' or that 'could be more efficiently managed by the private sector'. Additionally, the report proposed the abandonment of five-year planning and the adoption of a new approach to national planning—one that 'emphasises macro-economic assessment and the preparation of broad development strategies' (World Bank 1991:viii).

With expanded export production, economic and labour market deregulation, privatisation or corporatisation of state-owned enterprises, and a strengthened private sector as its main policy prescriptions for Pacific Island economies, the World Bank showed little consideration for the peculiar limitations of small economies suffering distinct disadvantages in respect of resource bases, physical infrastructure, human resources and geographical location. The policy package offered to its Pacific member countries was little different from those offered by the bank to other countries, with vastly different economies.

The second World Bank report on Pacific economies appeared more mindful of the peculiar specificities of its Pacific member countries and even claimed that its objective was 'not to impose some model derived elsewhere, but to adapt approaches' (World Bank 1993). While more holistic in its coverage, with comprehensive chapters on human resource development and environmental issues, its economic analysis and policy prescriptions differed little in substance from those advanced in the earlier report. Public sector reform, efficiency in the use of foreign aid and the crucial role of the private sector were reiterated as the keys to attaining sustainable economic growth, with high-growth economies of East Asia, the Maldives and Barbados cited as models for Pacific emulation. The 'Pacific Paradox' was coined to describe the conundrum posed by the absence of growth in average real per capita income in the past decade despite favourable natural and human resource endowment, high levels of aid and reasonably prudent economic management (World Bank 1993:ix, 1). A 'development partnership' between the state and the private sector was advocated as the key to achieving economic growth (World Bank 1993:37). The bank recommended more effective economic engagement with the rest of the world, enhancing international competitiveness, broadening trade and investment links, especially with the East Asian growth centres, and reforming the public sector by restructuring, consolidating, privatising, downsizing and lowering public sector wages, which were deemed to be 'well in excess of average national incomes' (World Bank 1993:ix–x).

Neoliberal Development Studies

One of the first agencies to draw on the World Bank's first Pacific report as an authoritative text was NCDS. This was not surprising, as its director in the early 1990s, Professor Helen Hughes, had worked for many years at the World Bank. In a series of research papers funded by AIDAB and published under the theme Pacific 2010, the NCDS aimed to alert Pacific governments and those who delivered aid to the Pacific region of a doomsday scenario that, in the opinion of the project's lead scholars, awaited the Pacific states unless they met the challenge of facing up to their looming economic and social problems. In assuming this role in the 2010 project, the NCDS revealed itself as an institution committed to advocacy in support of neoliberal economic policies, a project to which its postgraduate training program targeting future policymakers in developing countries, especially in the Asia-Pacific region, was also geared.

The first Pacific 2010 publication was introduced by comments from NCDS's Islands/Australia Programme Director and former Fiji colonial government officer Rodney Cole, who called Pacific Island states 'adroit players of the aid game', which had ensured for themselves 'a strong and regular flow of largesse, first from former colonial powers, but now, at the beginning of the '90s, from the world at large' (Cole 1993:vi). According to Cole, the inhabitants of South Pacific Island states now 'want[ed] more out of life than subsistence affluence', and Pacific Island leaders 'and their financial mentors' faced enormous difficulties in meeting the wants and needs of their 'rapidly expanding populations'. The publication's lead article provided a futuristic portrayal by *The Australian Financial Review* journalist Rowan Callick.[5] Intended by the project's leaders to present 'a more colourful picture, a grim and challenging picture, but one that is nevertheless disturbingly close to the drier portrait available from the data', Callick's 'doomsday scenario' of the Pacific in the year 2010

---

5   See Rowan Callick's 'A Doomsday Scenario' in Cole 1993.

was based on population projections of NCDS's demographers, who predicted a doubling of the region's population to 9 million in just more than 15 years (Callick 1993:1). Callick's wild imagining of the Pacific in 2010 was evidently calculated to shock Pacific leaders (who might not have found the picture painted by the demographers 'easy to read') into taking steps to avoid what he portrayed as an otherwise inevitable nightmare: beggars on the streets of every South Pacific town, endemic malnutrition, a rising incidence of AIDS deaths, lagoons declared unfit for human activity and public water supplies unsafe for drinking, labour a major export from the region, modern and traditional narcotics major sources of foreign currency, gangs of youth extorting their own form of 'tax', and (an evident horror for Callick) 'a greater number of Asian workers arriving … [with] mosques … now found in almost every island capital' (Callick 1993:5). Underlining the need for reform, Callick wrote:

> Pacific Islanders lack sufficient savings to develop their region in pace with their aspirations and dreams, as opposed to their nightmares. Most forecasts assume a static or declining level of direct aid, concessional loans and even commercial capital available to the region, as other priorities take precedence. The South Pacific, it is said in such quarters, has had a good enough run, and now is its chance to stand on its own two feet (1993:7).

In Callick's view, regional policymakers needed to accelerate the

> conceptual shift … from a traditional emphasis on the importance of *distribution* of wealth (where a chief or big man gains stature from his gifts and from the generosity of his feasts) to an emphasis on *production*, on building (amassing), managing, and re-investing that wealth (ibid.).

He wrote:

> A new type of generosity is thus required—*one that may mean standing by to make room for people with special talents, especially to do business profitably*. This shift can only take place through an example being set by the South Pacific leaders themselves—politicians, senior officials and traditional chiefs (ibid.).

Assuring Pacific leaders that 'the appropriate domestic policies, implemented wholeheartedly by island nations—not just governments, but communities as a whole … with the support of a friendly external environment [could] turn the grim trends around', Callick highlighted policies that he said were required urgently to be put in place: population policies to reduce national growth rates, national environmental policies based on national audits of existing environmental problems confronting each nation, and economic adjustment (Callick 1993:8–9). He then itemised the required economic reforms: tighter budgetary discipline; measures to enhance competitiveness; corporatisation and privatisation; reform of the financial sector; adjustment of exchange rates; altering the way wages are determined; and reorganisation of government priorities so that a greater proportion of the budget is spent on education, health and infrastructure (Callick 1993:10–11).

> [A] greater sense of international interdependence will have to emerge, perhaps starting within the South Pacific Forum. The success stories, economically and politically, will be those emphasizing openness and links—trade, investment, even the movement of skilled workers, foreigners and nationals, in and out of the country—rather than those emphasizing a defiant independence. A greater focus within the region on free trade would help to frame the right mentality (ibid.).

In the only substantive analysis in the book, education professor and economist Ken Gannicott discussed the likely higher costs of education within the seven countries in the next 20 years, showing three different scenarios of the financial burden for each country of providing primary and secondary education under conditions of moderate enrolment increases and 'low GDP', more rapid enrolment increases and low GDP, and more rapid increases in enrolment and 'high GDP' (Cole 1993:18–24).[6] Gannicott went on to prescribe 'what needs to be done': a population policy, a lowering of school unit costs by World Bank recommended strategies such as cost recovery in higher education, reallocation of expenditure within the education sector and decentralised management, and higher economic growth through structural economic reforms (Cole 1993:26–27). Accepting without question the bank's projections 'of the faster [economic] growth that would be possible from structural and policy reform in the region', Gannicott's tables aimed to show that 'if the economy grows at the much faster rates considered feasible if structural economic reforms are carried out … [educational objectives] can be achieved [at a lower] per cent of GDP' (Cole 1993:21, 27).

Gannicott also addressed labour force growth and employment, highlighting the particularly difficult times that lay ahead for Kiribati, Papua New Guinea, Solomon Islands and Vanuatu, with high rates of

---

6   See Ken Gannicot's 'Population, Development and Growth' in Cole 1993.

increase of the labour force, the generally 'poor record' of Pacific Island countries in creating employment and the fact that much of the wage employment in the Pacific region (about 40 per cent) had been in the public sector (Cole 1993:30–31). He reiterated the exaggerated employment projections of the World Bank's high GDP scenario (with structural reforms) for Papua New Guinea—'formal sector employment could grow from 214,000 in 1990 to 327,000 in 2000' (World Bank 1991a:30, cited by Gannicott in Cole 1993:32)—and cited extensively from the World Bank's 1991 report, *Towards Higher Growth in the Pacific Islands Economies*, reproducing its arguments that incomes were too high in the Pacific, that they were sustained not by domestic savings but by remittances and official transfers, that the large inflows of aid had fostered growth in the government sector at the expense of the private sector, and that high wages in the government had 'disincentive effects' on other sectors in the labour market, notably agriculture (Cole 1993:39).

Gannicott's concluding proposals could have been lifted verbatim from the World Bank report: develop policies to promote a climate for private investment by removing 'distortions in exchange rates, wages, and tax and trade policies' as well as 'regulatory hurdles to private activity'; channel more aid to the private sector to support the development of private sector employment opportunities; improve efficiency in the public service and improve its capacity 'to support private sector development' through public expenditure restructuring, tax reform, public pricing policy and reduced public sector involvement in services that the private sector can provide more efficiently; and provide cost-effective education.

Intervening in Pacific Islands States through the South Pacific Forum

Greg Fry (1997) has written of how the Pacific 2010 publication gave 'intellectual authority' to the then newly elected Australian Labor Government's new aid policy for the South Pacific, enunciated later in the same year by Gordon Bilney, minister for the newly established portfolio of Pacific Island Affairs. According to Fry, Bilney's address signalled that Australia's new Pacific policy would be focused not on the earlier Cold War preoccupation with 'regional security', but on 'radically transform[ing] the regional economic order' to bring it into line with Australia's own reform agenda and generally prevailing policy trends (Fry 1997). Fry's prophetic assessment was that the new policy approach would involve 'an intended level of intervention in Pacific Island societies and states not contemplated since the colonial period', and that its purpose would be 'to transform not only the development model and to reform government procedures, but also to effect change in cultural structures and traditional practices such as customary land tenure' (Fry 1997:292).

The selected target for the launch of this new policy thrust towards a regional agenda of economic restructuring, informed by World Bank and NCDS thinking, was the South Pacific Forum (now called the Pacific Islands Forum), which met in Brisbane that year. In the words of Sutherland, the Brisbane meeting of the forum marked a 'turning point' in its history (2000:465). Three decisions directly relating to a regional agenda of economic restructuring were made by Pacific leaders at that forum. First, after agreement that the private sector 'had an important role to play in the reforms now being undertaken in the region and needed to be strengthened to enable it to lead the next stage of growth', the Forum Secretariat was directed 'to undertake a greater facilitating role in providing policy advice to member governments in these areas' (South Pacific Forum Secretariat 1994). Second, it was agreed that annual Forum Finance Ministers' Meetings be held to consider appropriate aspects of economic reform and Australia's offer to fund the first such meeting at the Forum Secretariat the next year was accepted. Third, it was agreed to encourage the participation in Forum Economic Ministers' Meetings of representatives from the international financial institutions—that is, the World Bank, the International Monetary Fund, and the ADB. Two further decisions made at the Leaders' Retreat that followed the Brisbane forum, from proposals put by the Australian Government, were to 'reform the [Pacific Islands] Forum process to ensure greater effectiveness' and to restructure its Secretariat (Sutherland 2000:465).[7] The latter process, according to Sutherland, was already under way, but clarification of its purpose would not have gone astray. The decisions were aimed at creating optimum conditions for achieving focused discussion on specific issues (highlighted by a theme), securing prior political agreement on specific reforms and on a program for implementation, and narrowing the responsibilities of the Forum Secretariat to the core business of supporting and facilitating the agenda of economic restructuring.

---

7   The Pacific Islands Forum was then known as the South Pacific Forum.

The forum has been an effective avenue for the transmission of neoliberal economic ideas and thinking to Pacific Island leaders by external agents, and, as the members of the forum with the most resources and the considerable leverage of their donor status, the Australian and New Zealand governments have been in a strong position to influence agendas, frame debates and propose policy decisions. By 1994, when the broad outlines of a regional restructuring agenda began to emerge with distinct coherence within the South Pacific Forum, Australia and New Zealand were themselves heavily committed to economic restructuring within their own countries, and were intent on exporting their economic policies to the Pacific region.[8] The proposed restructuring of the Forum Secretariat was a crucial step in a multilateral, donor-driven process aimed at achieving the twin objectives of economic restructuring and governance reform, and the administrative and program restructuring that occurred between 1994 and 1995 effectively narrowed the Forum Secretariat's functions to providing technical and administrative support for the region-wide implementation of economic policy reforms.[9] Indeed, after 1995, the facilitation and oversight of economic, financial and trade reforms in the region became the core business of the Forum Secretariat. From convening and servicing annual meetings of Pacific Island finance and trade ministers, attaining collective, time-bound commitments from them to implement reform targets, and establishing monitoring mechanisms to ensure these commitments were met, to advancing trade liberalisation through the mechanisms of regional trade agreements, the Forum Secretariat's role has been central to implementing the externally driven program of economic, financial and trade reforms aimed at achieving region-wide economic, financial and trade liberalisation.

---

8   Neoliberal ideas, termed 'economic rationalism' in Australia, began to take hold under Bob Hawke's Labor Government in the 1980s and early 1990s; more radical commitment to structural adjustment emerged under the government of Paul Keating from 1993–95 (Fry 1997:317). New Zealand's experiment with structural adjustment began in 1984, with the application of 'Rogernomics' (the neoliberal economic policies of Treasurer Roger Douglas) under the Labour governments of David Lange and Mike Moore. It was continued, with even greater vigour, by successive National Party governments.

9   The restructuring of the Forum Secretariat followed a review and regional consultation exercise by three consultants: Savenaca Siwatibau, then Director of the ESCAP-Pacific Operations Centre based in Vanuatu and a strong advocate of economic restructuring in the Pacific Island states; Bruce Davis, an Australian national, former Deputy Secretary-General of the Forum Secretariat, and, at this time, a senior officer within AusAID; and Makarita Baaro, a sociology graduate of the University of the South Pacific and then Secretary for Foreign Affairs in Kiribati. Their report is not a public document, but the reorganised Forum Secretariat that resulted from their review indicates the evident intention to streamline the Secretariat's functions and narrow its scope and program to support reform.

At the 26th South Pacific Forum meeting in Madang in 1995, and at the Leaders' Retreat that followed it, discussions were guided by the theme Securing Development Beyond 2000, and a plan of action and a vision statement were adopted (South Pacific Forum 1995). A comprehensive list of national economic policy measures and regionally based activities were endorsed by the Pacific leaders as key to securing development beyond 2000, and, not surprisingly, it read like a checklist for neoliberal policy measures:

- securing the potential benefits of globalisation by enhancing competitiveness through promoting price stability (low inflation)
- avoiding artificial distortions to the prices of domestic resources (land, labour, and capital)
- reducing trade taxes and import duties, which adversely affect export competitiveness
- removing implicit and explicit barriers to foreign direct investment
- adopting and implementing the investment principles agreed to by APEC members as a signal to potential investors of the region's serious intentions to promote and encourage foreign direct investment
- working towards implementation of trade reform measures as requested by GATT/WTO, including by replacing non-tariff barriers with tariffs and setting timeframes for minimising tariff levels
- promoting trade within and outside the region by standardising administrative procedures in areas of customs and quarantine, labelling and packaging, export and import controls, exchange controls and technical standards
- improving public sector efficiency and cost effectiveness through the rationalisation of public services, policy coherence and commitment to the principle of good governance (South Pacific Forum 1995:16).

By 1995, there was an evident convergence in World Bank and South Pacific Forum thinking. Sutherland reported that by the time the World Bank published its third report on its Pacific member countries in 1995, 'the task of convincing the islands to undertake reforms had been achieved' and the 'pleadings and urgings' of its earlier reports had given way to 'specific, sector-focused advice and even a statement of "Priorities for Regional Actions" in the 1995 report' (Sutherland 2000:462). By the second half of 1998, he said the regional reform agenda was reportedly 'well and truly in place' (Sutherland 2000:468).

Between 1995 and 1998, program lending by the ADB in support of 'economic, public sector and governance reforms' assumed a significant proportion of the bank's lending in the Pacific (Knapman and Saldanha 1999:1), a change in 'operational focus' that saw the ADB funding policy reform implementation in six Pacific Island states—Cook Islands, Federated States of Micronesia (FSM), Marshall Islands, Samoa, Solomon Islands and Vanuatu. By 1998, no less than 11 other donor agencies were funding or had assisted public sector reform projects in one or more of the following seven countries of the region—Cook Islands, FSM, Fiji, Marshall Islands, Vanuatu, Samoa and Tonga (AusAID and NZMFAT 1998:1).[10]

From 1995 onwards, regular meetings of forum finance ministers— from 1997, Forum Economic Ministers' Meetings—effectively charted the course for the systematic implementation of structural adjustment in the region. Pacific Islands Forum meetings from 1995 were clearly being provided with direction and leadership by this grouping of finance (and, after 1997, economic) ministers. The institution of this strategic political mechanism involving the political heads of national treasuries was an effective mechanism in advancing the regional reform agenda. Meetings of finance ministers functioned as a sub-council of the forum, carrying out advance planning of national economic and trade policies for implementation across the region. Later, through reporting mechanisms that were adopted, they monitored policy implementation. The institution of Finance Ministers Meetings effectively moved national economic planning and decision-making beyond the domain and purview of national constituencies. And the inclusion of representatives of international financial institutions in the annual meetings of Forum Finance (and Economic) Ministers from 1995, at the suggestion of the Australian Government, placed donor agencies and international financial institutions in a strategically advantageous position to influence economic policy decisions and to follow up policy advice with financial and technical assistance to facilitate national implementation of policy reform. More importantly, it facilitated the development of an integrated, multilateral approach to restructuring Pacific economies and states. The high level of coordination and collaboration in designing and implementing economic

---

10   These included the IMF, the Pacific Financial Technical Advisory Centre, WHO, UNDP, the European Union, AusAID, the New Zealand Ministry of Foreign Affairs and Trade, the Japanese Development Agency, French Aid Agencies, USAID and other US agencies, and ESCAP-Pacific Operations Centre.

restructuring in the Pacific Island states achieved between 1995 and 1998 was grounded in what the ADB described as a consensus among donors in respect to development assistance to the Pacific Island states (Knapman and Saldanha 1999:9).

Ensuring Participation and Ownership — the ADB Approach to Reform

The political neutrality and considerable financial and technical resources of the ADB favoured it as the lead designer/coordinator and financier of economic restructuring within the island states of the Pacific, as evinced in the following explanatory note provided in the report of a joint Australian and New Zealand government review of the ADB's role in regional reform, undertaken in 1998:

> Bilateral donors are unable to respond in the same way [as the ADB] because of historical links with Pacific Governments or inability to mobilise sufficient resources and the broad range of expertise required to address financial management, macro economic policies, public service restructuring, debt, legislative and governance issues as well as the social impact of reforms (AusAID and NZMFAT 1998:1).

A shift in the ADB's strategic focus for October 1995 to accommodate the lead role it was to assume for macroeconomic policy reform in the Pacific Islands states appears to be the outcome of Australian and New Zealand government intervention. Both governments, out of a concern to 'foster a high level of coordination and collaboration', had commissioned a joint review of the ADB's technical assistance programs in 11 Pacific Island countries in 1995 (ibid.). This followed the creation of an Office of Pacific Operations within ADB's Manila headquarters in January 1995. The subsequent shift from 'sector and project lending' to 'support for macro-economic stabilisation and structural adjustment, and public sector and governance reform' (Knapman and Saldanha 1999:1) saw the ADB take on the role of supporting government policy reform efforts through the provision of Public Sector Reform Programme loans and chairing new consultative group processes in the Marshall Islands, the FSM and Cook Islands (AusAID and NZMFAT 1998:38). By 1999, the ADB was designing and underwriting restructuring programs in no less than seven Pacific Island states with the support of bilateral donors—

namely, New Zealand (in Cook Islands and Samoa), the United States (in FSM and Marshall Islands), Australia (Solomon Islands), France and the EU (Vanuatu and Solomon Islands).

The ADB's view of what it has been doing appears disinterested and technocratic, its interventions presented as necessary responses to restore macroeconomic stability in Pacific Developing Member Countries facing fiscal crises. In the words of Knapman and Saldanha, the response to crisis by Pacific Island states and donors usually followed a pattern:

> The first step of government has been to appeal to external funding agencies for initial and urgent fiscal support to tide over the crisis. Such agencies, including the Bank, have taken the opportunity to engage the government in examining the root causes of the fiscal crisis, viz. economic policy and management, poor governance and an out of control public sector. In most cases this process has culminated in the preparation of a reform framework that includes a conditionality matrix covering the key factors that need to be addressed (in the case of Cook Islands, RMI, FSM, Vanuatu) or a more informal meeting (as in the case of the Solomon Islands) at which the government and external funding agencies have agreed on the framework for reform and related external support (1999:6).

The ADB puts an emphasis on achieving what it calls 'participation and ownership', usually through national summit meetings (Cook Islands, Vanuatu, FSM and Fiji). These have played a critical role, according to Knapman and Saldanha, in engendering national consensus on the need for reform, thereby enabling governments to 'proceed with reform agendas that would otherwise have been unpalatable to the general population'. Summits, they said, presented opportunities (in Cook Islands, FSM and Vanuatu) for representatives of the people to not only 'express their unhappiness with the state of governance', but to 'vent their frustrations with continued misgovernment' (Knapman and Saldanha 1999:13). These exercises of setting governments up to receive strong public criticism and of giving 'representatives of the people' an understanding that they were being consulted and listened to helped soften up governments and national constituencies for reform. In Knapman and Saldanha's words, 'the messages offered were accepted and provided a strong basis for developing and ensuring public acceptability of the reform programmes' (1999:13). Equally as significant as summit meetings for engendering ownership and participation is having a 'champion or group of champions of the reform process'. In all six Pacific countries, they reported, 'the top political leadership' championed the reform, thereby engendering 'strong political and public commitment' (Knapman and Saldanha 1999:9).

The Forum Secretariat and the Push for Regional Trade Liberalisation

Structural adjustment policies are now widely recognised as paving the way for a global regime of free trade, a 'borderless world' in which free access to the resources and markets of the globe will theoretically be enjoyed equally by all competitors, irrespective of where they are located. As Gita Sen of feminist network DAWN[11] has put it, structural adjustment policies were evidently the 'battering ram' for trade liberalisation. The strategy of achieving global trade liberalisation incrementally through the imposition of structural adjustment policies and bilateral and multilateral treaty processes or social contracts between or among states, with resulting agreements emerging as enforceable global trade laws under the multilateral trading system of the World Trade Organization (WTO) reflects the current geopolitical order, dominated by advanced capitalist states and the transnational corporations that run their economies. As the growing conflict between developed and developing states within the WTO at the past three Ministerial Conferences amply signals, the global architecture of free trade is being framed in the interests of the economies of developed states and the corporate interests that dominate them, to the detriment of developing countries. In this context, what Pacific Island states have to gain from the end point of reform or structural adjustment, which is to say global free trade, is open to contention. Yet, Pacific Island states continue to pursue liberalisation policies as if there were no alternative, a response that has resulted from the apparent conversion of key political leaders and policymakers in the region to neoliberal economic ideas, and from the role played by the Forum Secretariat in advancing the agenda of trade liberalisation.

From 1999, the Forum Secretariat worked to secure Pacific Island states' compliance with WTO trade principles and rules through the modality of two regional free trade agreements. One of these, the Pacific Island

---

11   Development Alternatives with Women for a New Era, a global feminist network that analyses global policies and issues that impact poor women in the developing world.

Countries Trade Agreement (PICTA), was portrayed as the realisation of a regional dream and the answer to the Pacific's economic woes; the other, the Pacific Agreement on Closer Economic Relations (PACER), as a benign 'umbrella agreement' aimed at 'keep[ing] the Forum family together'. Region-wide political support for PICTA was mustered on the basis of the idea that regional (as opposed to external) interests underlay the agreement and would be served by it. The bullying by Australia and New Zealand within the Pacific Islands Forum that led to the establishment of PACER, and its implications for the Pacific Island economies, remained a closely guarded secret until a study of the origins, content and implications of the PACER, commissioned by the Pacific Network on Globalisation, exposed them (Kelsey 2004). The Forum Secretariat's fast-tracking of the free trade agreements from conceptualisation to ratification was a feat accomplished by skilful marketing of PICTA, engagement of free trade advocates as consultants/advisors, speedy drafting of the agreements by New Zealand consultants, and successful lobbying of Pacific Island governments for their signature and ratification.

Although PACER was not supposed to come on stream until after PICTA had been in force for eight years, PACER was more speedily ratified than PICTA (by the requisite six Pacific Island states plus Australia and New Zealand), and so came into force in October 2002, ahead of PICTA.[12] This development, which was anticipated by the Pacific Network on Globalisation (PANG) in its critique of the Forsyth and Plange social impact study, threw into question the 'stepping stone' that PICTA was supposed to represent and the two consultants' blithe assurances that PICTA's impacts would be minimal (PANG 2002).[13] As a member of PANG wrote in February 2002:

12   Moreover, an in-built provision in PACER (Article 6) triggers 'mandatory consultations or free trade negotiations with Australia and New Zealand' if any forum island country that is a party to PACER enters into negotiations for a new free trade arrangement with either 'an outside developed country' or a developing country with 'a per capita GDP higher than that of New Zealand'. If the forum island countries as a group begin free trade negotiations with any outside country, consultations with Australia and New Zealand have to be held. The provisions of Article 6 were expected to trigger negotiations on PACER as early as September 2002, when EU–ACP (Africa, Caribbean, Pacific group) negotiations for Economic Partnership Agreements under the Cotonou Agreement were expected to begin (PANG 2002:10–11).

13   The Forsyth and Plange study, commissioned by the Forum Secretariat, relied on the findings of Scollay (1998) that the impacts of PICTA would be minimal, and that the benefits would outweigh the costs.

The Social Impact Assessment on PICTA is being cleverly used to give the impression that since PICTA will have minimal impact on Pacific Island countries, PACER will also have minimal impact. A used car salesman could not have done a better job … the money spent on … the PICTA study is money down the drain … what Pacific Island countries need to see is a Social Impact Study on PACER.

In July 2003, University of the South Pacific economist Dr Wadan Narsey confirmed that once the free trade pact with Australia and New Zealand came into effect it would be 'catastrophic for local businesses'. 'I would estimate that over 80 per cent of local businesses here in Fiji would fold,' he was quoted as saying, adding:

I think governments have not thought through the consequences of joining a free trade area … We hear all this talk of … efficiency and economies of scale. But the reality is, small companies will be forced out once the big players come to town … Governments have not worked out an alternative plan on how to re-employ people if factories close and people are left without jobs (Narsey, cited in Tavita 2003).

Narsey's study on the implications of including alcohol and tobacco in PICTA, commissioned by the Forum Secretariat, concluded that once PACER was operational and duties against Australian and New Zealand exports were removed, British American Tobacco, which owned all tobacco production in the Pacific, would likely concentrate production in just one forum island country.[14] Parent companies of foreign-owned beer factories in the smaller Pacific Island countries will likely also take advantage of economies of scale and market access to concentrate on marketing their highest-selling products, with Fiji, Papua New Guinea and possibly Samoa benefiting at the expense of Vanuatu, Tonga, Palau and Cook Islands in the short term. Once Australia and New Zealand are included in the free trade area, all Pacific beer consumption is likely to be supplied from Australia. Narsey suggested that this could be the scenario for other manufacturing industries and cautioned Pacific Island governments against encouraging firms to expand to take advantage of PICTA if the benefits to be derived from doing so are to be lost once PACER kicks in.

---

14 The forum study has not been released but its findings are summarised in Narsey (2004).

The negative implications of trade liberalisation for the Pacific Island states go beyond expected contractions and closures in the manufacturing sector. Aside from the loss of revenue from tariff cuts, and the increased indirect tax that will likely be imposed to compensate governments for this revenue loss, the push to open up services under the General Agreement on Trade in Services (GATS) has seen formal requests being made by the EU for the opening of land for purchase by non-citizens in Melanesia and the elimination of work permit restrictions on foreign companies. The GATS holds serious implications for public health and education systems in the Pacific (reduced subsidy, lowered quality and lower access), as do any future WTO agreements on the so-called 'Singapore issues' of government procurement, investment and competition policy.

The Challenges of Neoliberalism

Despite growing doubts about the benefits to be derived by Pacific Island economies from trade liberalisation, advocacy for trade liberalisation continues unabated in the region. And neoliberal analyses of Pacific states and societies continue to influence the way the Pacific and its future are perceived by donor governments, and the interventionist strategies being pursued in the region.

A recent article offering a 'roadmap for rapid growth and development in the Pacific' argues that 'the best way to support the Pacific is through continuing trade liberalisation to reward the steps necessary to increase exports from the Pacific and thus create incomes and growth' (Hughes 2004b:1). Published by the CIS and titled *The Pacific is Viable!*, the paper is the second on the Pacific written by former NCDS Director Helen Hughes and published by the CIS in the past two years. In addition to restating her arguments on the negative effects of aid and resource rents, and the absolute necessity of abandoning communal land ownership in favour of individual property rights, Hughes continues her ridicule of smaller island states and advocacy for their integration into a federation to avoid costly national and bureaucratic structures and 'inappropriately elevated international representation' (Hughes 2003).[15] Not surprisingly, given Prime Minister John Howard's known support for the work of the

---

15   Hughes's earlier article, published in 2003 and titled *Aid Has Failed the Pacific*, elicited much criticism within the region and in Australia and New Zealand, and many of the critical responses to the paper are available on the Internet.

CIS, the federation idea has found favour with the Australian Government, which has advanced a proposal for a pacific economic community with a single (Australian) currency and a regional central bank, together with a regional legal and administrative structure to respond to law and order breakdowns.[16] The prospects for the Pacific Island states joining such a community, dominated politically and economically (under PACER) by Australia, are hardly advantageous. Australia's recent intervention in the Solomon Islands, justified by the Australian Strategic Policy Institute (ASPI), another neoliberal think tank, on the grounds of the 'failed state' thesis, has already been shown to be about more than restoring law and order and security. And the presence of Regional Assistance Mission to Solomon Islands (RAMSI) has ensured an orderly return to the implementation of structural adjustment policies in the Solomon Islands. Many speculate that direct intervention by Australia in Papua New Guinea will follow. In July 2004, the CIS published a report on Papua New Guinea by Hughes that offered a free-market blueprint for more aggressive Australian intervention in that country (Hughes 2004a). The report was released as 230 Australian officials and police were preparing to take over key posts in the PNG police force, courts, finance and planning ministries, customs, and civil aviation. In other Pacific countries, large numbers of Australian and New Zealand consultants on contracts financed by bilateral aid programs already occupy positions within key ministries and state agencies, advising, supervising or drafting legislation for reform implementation.

In an evident downplaying of sovereignty, Hughes's argument that Norfolk Island, which without aid has a per capita income nearly twice that of Australia, is a model for emulation (Hughes 2003:4) is restated in her more recent article. The inclusion of Norfolk Island in a comparative table on Pacific Island states and territories, and the use of the term 'islands' as referents, rather than states or countries (as in 'All Pacific islands could be viable at high standards of living within a generation if they adopted policies that matched their endowments' and, 'The policy measures needed to make every Pacific island viable are well known') reflect the neoliberal bias against states as political entities with regulatory and other powers that can be used against the interests of free enterprise. The conceptualisation instead of islands as economic entities, presumably run

---

16 Howard paid tribute to the CIS at its 20th anniversary dinner in 1996 in Sydney, as recorded on the CIS's website, www.cis.org.au.

by free market technocrats, suggests island populations not of citizens with rights, but simply of producers and consumers, or buyers and sellers—in other words, societies defined and governed by the market. This raises a number of fundamental questions about the future being envisaged for us by neoliberals such as Hughes. First, is the emphasis on islands as opposed to states in Hughes's neoliberal discourse calculated to prepare Pacific Island states for an even more reduced role in future years? If so, how will Pacific citizens in such societies exact accountability from those who make economic and social policies that severely impact their lives? And what meaning will we attach to elections, or to the implicit social contract between democratic states and citizens, that oblige states to protect the interests of all their citizens, and that assure them of a broad range of rights and entitlements, not least those enshrined in longstanding protective laws? And how are Pacific Islanders, dispossessed of the communally held land that is the basis of their semi-subsistence livelihoods, expected to respond to a rash of land sales to wealthy foreigners and corporations? The aggressive marketing of neoliberalism and its core values of individual advancement, private wealth accumulation and open access to resources strikes at the heart of things that have long been enshrined in law, cultural value systems and social practice in the Pacific Islands. The time is long overdue for critical investigation and public debate on the long-term implications of following a course set by outside navigators whose final destination is not of our choosing.

References

AusAID and NZMFAT (Development Cooperation Division, New Zealand Ministry of Foreign Affairs and Trade) 1998. Joint Australian and New Zealand Review of the Asian Development Bank's Role in Public Sector Reform in Selected Pacific Island Countries.

Callick, R. 1993. A doomsday scenario. In R.V. Cole (ed.), *Pacific 2010: Challenging the Future*. Canberra: National Centre for Development Studies, Research School of Pacific Studies, The Australian National University.

Cole, R.V. (ed.) 1993. *Pacific 2010: Challenging the Future*. Canberra: National Centre for Development Studies, Research School of Pacific Studies, The Australian National University.

Fry, G. 1997. Australia and the South Pacific: the Rationalist Ascendancy. In J. Ravenhill and J. Cotton (eds), *Seeking Asian Engagement: Australia in World Affairs 1991–95*. Melbourne: Oxford University Press, 314–34.

Hughes, A.V. 1998. *A Different Kind of Voyage*. Manila: Asian Development Bank.

Hughes, H. 2003. *Aid has Failed the Pacific*. St Leonards: The Centre for Independent Studies.

Hughes, H. 2004a. *Can Papua New Guinea Come Back from the Brink?* St Leonards: The Centre for Independent Studies.

Hughes, H. 2004b. *The Pacific is Viable!* St Leonards: The Centre for Independent Studies.

Kasper, W., J. Bennett and R. Blandy 1988. *Fiji—Opportunity from Adversity*. St Leonards: The Centre for Independent Studies.

Kasper, W., P. Bauer and S. Siwatibau 1991. *Aid and Development in the South Pacific*. St Leonards: The Centre for Independent Studies.

Kelsey, J. 1993. *Rolling Back the State: Privatisation of Power in Aotearoa/New Zealand*. Wellington: Bridget Williams Books.

Kelsey, J. 2004. *Big Brothers Behaving Badly: The Implications for the Pacific Islands of the Pacific Agreement on Closer Economic Relations (PACER)*. Suva: Pacific Network on Globalisation (PANG). doi.org/10.7810/9780908912421

Knapman, B. and C. Saldanha 1999. *Reforms in the Pacific: An Assessment of the Asian Development Bank's Assistance for Reform Programs in the Pacific*. Manila: Asian Development Bank.

Narsey, W 2004. PICTA, PACER and EPAs: Odd Detours in PIC Development. Paper presented at Beyond MIRAB: The Political Economy of Small Islands in the 21st Century, Victoria University, Wellington, 23–25 February.

Pacific Network on Globalisation (PANG) 2002. What's in it for the Pacific? A critical response to PICTA, PACER and the Pacific Islands Forum's Social Impact Assessment. *The Fiji Sun*, 18 February.

Scollay, R 1998. *Free Trade Options for the Forum Island Countries*. Suva: Forum Secretariat.

South Pacific Forum 1995. *Forum Communiqué: Annexes 1 and 2*. Suva: South Pacific Forum.

South Pacific Forum Secretariat 1994. *Forum Secretariat News*. December.

Sutherland, W. 2000. Global Imperatives and Economic Reform in the Pacific Island States. *Development and Change*, 31(2):459–80. doi.org/10.1111/1467-7660.00162

Tavita, T. 2003. Free Trade Worries at Nadi Meeting. *Samoa Observer*, 2 July.

World Bank 1991. *Towards Higher Growth in the Pacific Island Economies: Lessons from the 1980s*. Vol. 1: Regional Overview; Vol. 2: Country Surveys. Washington, DC: World Bank Group.

World Bank 1993. *Pacific Island Economies: Toward Efficient and Sustainable Growth*. Vol. 1: Overview, Report No. 11351-EAP. Washington, DC: World Bank Group.

World Bank 1995. *Pacific Island Economies: Building a Resilient Economic Base for the Twenty-First Century*. Report No. 13803-EAP. Washington, DC: World Bank Group.

World Bank 2002. *Embarking on a Global Voyage: Trade Liberalisation and Complementary Reforms in the Pacific*. Report No. 24417-EAP. Washington, DC: World Bank Group.

9

Defending the Inheritance: The SDL and the 2006 Election

Alumita Durutalo

Durutalo, A. 2007. Defending the Inheritance: The SDL and the 2006 Election. In J. Fraenkel and S. Firth (eds), *From Election to Coup in Fiji: The 2006 Campaign and Its Aftermath*. Canberra and Suva: ANU E Press and Asia Pacific Press, IPS Publications, 78–88.

Republished with the kind permission of ANU Press.

Only five years after its birth, the Soqosoqo Duavata ni Lewenivanua (SDL) won a second general election on the basis of a promise to unify indigenous Fijians. The SDL's victory in Fiji's 2006 election signified an extraordinary achievement. The party showed that it had successfully inherited the mantle of its mainstream Fijian precursors, in the process renewing and reviving an ideological orthodoxy inherited from the Alliance Party and the Soqosoqo ni Vakavulewa ni Taukei (SVT). All three parties proved able to capture the majority of Fijians' votes. In each case, ascendancy has been founded on successfully upholding platforms based on the trinity of vanua, lotu and matanitu (defined and discussed below). This chapter explores the emergence of the SDL after the crisis of 2000, the party's election strategies, its merger with the Conservative Alliance–Matanitu Vanua (CAMV), the role of the Methodist Church, and the way in which the party is influenced by the traditional politics of the *vanua*.

It concludes that, in 2006, the ideology of *vanua*, *lotu* and *matanitu* once again unified indigenous Fijian support behind the party most Fijians identify as being on their side.

The Formation of the SDL

The SDL party was formed after a period of severe division amongst Fijian leaders occasioned by the coup of 19 May 2000. It was intended to fill a power vacuum within Fijian society and within mainstream Fijian politics. Although the newly emergent Fijian party differed in some respects from its predecessors, in its core philosophy it continued a long journey that was started by the Fijian Association in 1956. The Alliance Party had advanced an orthodoxy of *vanua*, *lotu* and *matanitu* between 1967 and 1987, and a similar fundamental ideological framework became the bedrock of the SVT from 1992 to 1999.[1] Like its predecessors, the SDL emerged as an eastern Viti Levu–based and Vanua Levu–based Fijian political party. As with its predecessors, the link with the all-Fijian provincial councils provided the critical organisational underpinning for the party, and the backing of the Methodist Church proved of fundamental importance to the party's success.

The formation of the SDL was inspired by the need to unify indigenous Fijians once again under a single political umbrella, after the decimation of the SVT at the 1999 poll. That fracturing of the Fijian vote had ensured victory for the Fiji Labour Party (FLP)–led coalition in 1999, although that government lasted only a year. In the wake of its overthrow in May 2000, the Republic of Fiji Military Forces installed an all-Fijian 'interim' administration. Led by prime minister Laisenia Qarase, that interim government reconstituted itself as the SDL in the run-up to fresh elections held in August 2001, in the process reviving the staple orthodoxies of Fijian rule. The 2001 organisational structure of the SDL is shown in Figure 1.

---

1   The Alliance Party was not a Fijian party in quite the same sense as were its successors. While it relied primarily on the Fijian Association and on the votes of Fijians, it was nonetheless a coalition of different groups, and had substantial Indian support during the 1970s.

General Assembly

Management Board
Constituency council

Village/Tikina Branches   Settlement Branches   Urban Branches

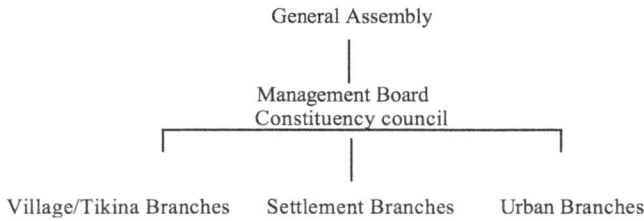

Figure 1. Organisational Structure of the SDL party.
Source: Constitution of the Soqosoqo Duavata ni Lewenivanua (SDL) United Fiji Party
(UFP): 2–3.

The SDL proved a well-organised and well-funded Fijian political party
from its inception. It was dominated by educated middle-class Fijians,
of whom current prime minister Laisenia Qarase is an outstanding
example. Qarase and other ministers in the 2000–01 interim government
might instead have joined or taken over one of the already existent Fijian
parties, such as the SVT or the Fijian Association Party or, most likely, the
Veitokani ni Lewenivanua Vakarisito party. But these were all parties in
decline, and Qarase eventually chose instead to forge a new party. From
the start, the party faced a new rival, the CAMV, which was formed before
the SDL. Perhaps the CAMV's close association with supporters of the
Speight coup was a reason that Qarase preferred to form a different and
seemingly neutral Fijian party to unite indigenous Fijians. However, the
CAMV became successful in its own right, especially in Vanua Levu and
in Tailevu North, Speight's power base.

Due to the similarities in political vision between the SDL and CAMV,
after the 2001 election, the two parties coalesced and formed government
between 2001 and 2006. Both parties stressed the need to address longstanding Fijian development problems, which they believed contributed
to political instabilities in Fiji. The CAMV believed that Rabuka, as
SVT government leader between 1992 and 1999, had not delivered on
his 1987 coup promises to indigenous Fijians. Initial support for the
formation of the CAMV was concentrated in the various *vanua* of the
provinces of Cakaudrove, Bua and Macuata on Vanua Levu. Later, an
invitation to join the party was extended to George Speight's supporters
on Viti Levu. The CAMV was formed: (i) to ensure that Fiji would always
be controlled by indigenous Fijians, and to incorporate that requirement

into the constitution; (ii) to strengthen affirmative action for indigenous Fijians; and (iii) to introduce legislation to enable indigenous Fijians to be in full control of the development of their resources (Durutalo 2005).

The SDL had similar goals, but its early advantage was a more practical strategy for accomplishing these and a greater respectability (at least insofar as the link with the coup instigators was less clear). The SDL attempted to address Fijian issues through what it termed the Blueprint for Affirmative Action for Indigenous Fijians and Rotumans, which became a major plank of the party's 2001 manifesto. The 2001 SDL party manifesto explains affirmative action as:

> Special programmes of assistance to help remove the economic differences between the Fijians and other communities ... these are ... provided for in the constitution ... At the moment the Fijians are falling behind in education, the professions, business and income ... the affirmative action blueprint is about our vision of a country where different ethnic communities live in peace, harmony and prosperity. It is about creating a foundation for a stable and prosperous Fiji. It affirms our commitment to securing basic economic rights and a fairer division of wealth ... inequities and inequalities ... pose a threat to our social stability. Failure to address these would put society at peril and deny social justice to a large section of the population (Manifesto Summary 2001).

The point of convergence between the SDL and CAMV that led to their coalition between 2001 and 2006, and their merger prior to the election in 2006, was their common vision that addressing Fijian economic underdevelopment was a prerequisite for Fiji's future political stability. The overall SDL vision of a Fiji of 'peace, harmony and prosperity' could only be achieved by first finding solutions to critical Fijian under-development problems.

Background

Many Fijian political parties were formed between 1960 and 2006, reflecting regional cleavages and the sociopolitical diversity of Fijian society. However, the three most powerful ones, which emerged and were consolidated mostly in eastern and northern Fiji, but were usually weaker in western Viti Levu, were the Fijian-dominated but multi-ethnic Alliance Party, formed in 1965; the SVT, formed in 1991; and the SDL, formed in 2001. After the two military coups in 1987, the SVT emerged to replace the Alliance and, subsequently, in 2001, the SDL emerged to replace the SVT. The parties have all given expression to a political ideology that proclaims the virtues of Fijian political paramountcy and unity.[2]

The three Fijian political parties sustained the dominance and ideological orthodoxy of the eastern and northern chiefdoms. The concepts of *vanua*, *lotu* and *matanitu*, upon which the orthodoxy was founded, have to be understood in terms of Fijian political evolution since the 19th century. *Vanua* identifies and demarcates a geopolitical boundary within which Fijian cultural practices and chiefly rule prevail. *Lotu*, meaning the new post-1835 Christian religion, replaced various forms of traditional Fijian religion and became grounded in the *vanua*. Matanitu is a Fijian word that denotes traditional government, and is associated with the country's three confederacies: Kubuna, Burebasaga and Tovata. Linkages between the *vanua* and paramount confederacy chiefs give political parties traditional sources of authority for indigenous Fijians. Legitimacy and recognition were enhanced by the employment of some eastern and northern chiefs in the colonial native administrative system of indirect rule. *Matanitu* became a symbol of the respect for authority and the new rule of law.

The dominance of the eastern chiefs was evident in appointments to the Legislative Council between 1904 and 1960. These were also the leaders behind the formation of the Fijian Association in 1956. This organisation, which obtained around 75 per cent of Fijian support in its 30 years of existence, was formed to counter Indian demands for a common roll.[3] In the 1950s and 1960s, the divergent political demands of Fiji's three largest communities shaped the process of decolonisation. On one hand, Fijians demanded the paramountcy of their interests. On the other, Indians wanted political rights that emphasised equality and were non-discriminating. In the middle, Europeans were adamant that their privileges be preserved and their special position be maintained (Ali 1986:9).

While other Fijian parties have tried to embody these three pillars in their party identity in one way or another, the Alliance Party, the SVT and the SDL have successfully maintained the orthodoxy as a common rallying

---

2   I argue that the Alliance, the SVT and the SDL parties depict a version of Fijian paramountcy in order to unite the diverse sociopolitical groups of Fijian society. The chiefdoms in eastern and northeastern Fiji are similar to the hierarchical Polynesian types of chiefdoms, while those in western Fiji, where chiefs are regarded as 'first amongst equals', are more egalitarian.
3   The common roll would have allowed for a one-person-one-vote electoral system.

point for their Fijian supporters. During the era of the Alliance (1967–87) and in the first half of SVT leadership (1991–94), political unity under the *vanua*, *lotu* and *matanitu* were accepted as givens within Fijian society. Challenges by Western-based political parties in the early 1960s were not extensive enough to pose a threat to chiefs in the Alliance Party.

The formation of the FLP in 1985 and then the defeat of the Alliance Party in 1987 posed the first direct challenge to the orthodoxy. After the post-1987 coup formation of the SVT—another party intended to unify all indigenous Fijians under one umbrella—other Fijian parties, like the Fijian Association and the Veitokani ni Lewenivanua Vakarisito (VLV), emerged to pose a further challenge to the orthodoxy. The challenge intensified after George Speight's attempted civilian coup in 2000, in the sense that the coup leader did not readily accept the pronouncements of the Great Council of Chiefs. Rabuka's SVT had ushered in a new era in Fijian politics. In the process, the ideology of *vanua*, *lotu* and *matanitu* was modified.

Although the Council of Chiefs did not directly back the SDL party in the way that it had explicitly backed the Alliance Party and the SVT, support for the party emerged through the co-option of *vanua* chiefs as well as through the Methodist church—as part of the *lotu ni vanua*— and through individual support. The party continued to express the collective political aspirations of the majority of indigenous Fijians as their representative in modern politics.

SDL Strategy for the 2006 Election

The SDL's principal objective of achieving 'Fijian unity' was, perhaps inevitably, not achieved. But the party's biggest achievement in this direction was its ability to persuade its coalition partner, CAMV, to join the SDL. The merger occurred on 17 February 2006, although a number of CAMV members and supporters did not sanction the move. Some supporters on Viti Levu complained that they were being marginalised by the Lau islanders in the SDL party. [4] Yet, the newly combined party

---

4   In my discussion with some of the disgruntled members on the day of the merger, they voiced their concern about the way those in the top management of both parties forced the unity on grassroots supporters. There were quite a number of members from Tailevu North, for example, who voiced their concern about the future of their demands, such as the release of George Speight, in the new SDL party.

proved successful in retaining under the new umbrella all six of the seats won by the CAMV in 2001. With 80 per cent of the overall Fijian votes, and 36 out of the 71 seats, the strategic readjustment of indigenous Fijian politics proved successful.

Strategic Methodist Church Alliance

Central to the structure of the SDL was the use of *lotu* as a powerful uniting force amongst indigenous Fijians. The SDL emphasised the *lotu* and Christian morality as political virtues in its 2006 candidate line-up. Candidates seeking SDL nominations were required to show evidence of adherence to family values. Additionally, as seen in the curriculum vitae of a number of candidates, a number were Methodist lay preachers in their own churches.[5] While direct chiefly leadership in Fijian party politics has declined since 1987, the emphasis on the *lotu*, uniting both chiefs and commoners, was a most important factor in SDL victory at the 2006 election. The same strategy was attempted by the VLV in 1999, but it was able to secure only around 20 per cent of the overall 1999 Fijian vote. The key difference was that, in the intervening years, the SVT had collapsed, leaving space for a new Fijian party to emerge.

In the SDL primary elections for the 2006 election, Methodist Church membership was considered an important yardstick by which to measure a candidate's sense of morality and commitment to societal development. In large urban centres like Suva, where Fijians from the rural areas have relocated to work, and where the influence of the *vanua* is not as strong, the church was used to identify SDL candidates for the 2006 election. For example, within the Samabula Tamavua Open constituency, leaders of the local Methodist churches in the area—including Vunivau, Samabula East, Raiwai and Raiwaqa—were in charge of local applications for the primary elections. After the primary elections in each constituency,

---

5   For example, Ratu Peni Volavola, one of the two SDL candidates in the Suva City Urban constituency, stated that he had been a lay preacher since 1980; church steward in the Samabula East Methodist Church since 1999; representative to the 2006 Methodist Bose ko Viti conference; and member of the Methodist Church of Fiji Working Committee. Likewise, the curriculum vitae for Misaele Weleilakeba stated that he was a confirmed lay preacher in the Methodist church and chairman of the Raiwai Methodist Church Financial Committee. See also the curriculum vitae for Ratu Mosese Volavola and Misaele Yadraca Weleilakeba, also SDL candidates in the 2006 election (in the personal collection of the author).

the winning candidate's name was submitted to the management board, which had the final decision on SDL candidates for each constituency (Baba 2006).

In some cases, those who had won the primary elections were not ultimately selected. Instead, more prominent candidates were chosen by the management board. The party used customary methods of reconciliation to appease those who were eliminated. Conflicts were, in some cases, resolved amicably.[6] This political strategy by the SDL highlights the use of both modern and customary institutions of society to not only win elections, but also to maintain internal party peace in the process of electioneering.

Strategic *Vanua* Alliance

In 2006, the SDL considered the support of chiefs as fundamental to the success of the party, even if they did not compete as candidates. Chiefs, as traditional political leaders, are often nominated as office bearers in Fijian political parties. President of the SDL Ratu Kalokalo Loki, for example, is Tamavua high chief, who, through his chiefly influence, is able to attract people from the *vanua* in Naitasiri to the party.[7]

Furthermore, an addition to the new cabinet, appointed through the Senate, was Bau and Kubuna high chief Adi Samanunu Talakuli Cakobau. She became minister without portfolio in the prime minister's office. The absence in government of any high-ranking Kubuna chief from Bau made Adi Samanunu's appointment a strategic one for maintaining the traditional balance of power and Kubuna support for the new SDL government. In addition, Adi Samanunu had been a strong rival to Qarase for the prime ministership back in July 2000, and one backed by the Speight group against the military's chosen candidate. Bringing her into the prime minister's office was designed to heal that rift, and to quash a potential source of ethno-nationalist opposition to the new multi-party cabinet arrangements.

---

6   In Dr Tupeni Baba's Samabula/Tamavua constituency, the second SDL candidate, Pita Nacuva, responded to his party listing him as second preference by urging supporters to vote below-the-line, much to the frustration of SDL campaign manager, Jale Baba. In the event, neither candidate was able to take this highly marginal seat, but Dr Baba was given an SDL Senate position, while Pita Nacuva became speaker of the house.

7   Tamavua is a *vanua* in the province of Naitasiri. The *vanua* owns much of the land at the northern end of Suva city.

The Burebasaga fort has been maintained by the Minister for Education, Youth and Sports, Ro Teimumu Kepa, Roko Tui Dreketi (the leading title of the Burebasaga Confederacy). Her re-election, although hotly contested by her nephew, Ro Filipe Tuisawau, maintains some form of unity in Rewa (Saumaki 2007). The Tui Cakau, Ratu Naiqama Lalabalavu, head of the Matanitu Tovata or Tovata Confederacy, won in the Cakaudrove West Fijian Provincial Communal constituency. His cousin and traditional competitor to the Tui Cakau title, leader of the New Alliance Party of Fiji (NAPF), Ratu Epeli Ganilau lost in the Suva City Open constituency. The Tui Cakau's inclusion in cabinet is intended to ensure the support of the Cakaudrove Confederacy.

On Viti Levu, Tui Namosi Ratu Suliano Matanitobua's re-election highlighted the support of the Namosi people for the SDL government. The SDL's hold on Fijians in western Viti Levu was strengthened by the inclusion of chiefs like Ratu Meli Saukuru of Nadi, who was formerly vice president of the Methodist Church of Fiji, as well as Nadroga chief Ratu Isikeli Tasere and Navosa chief Ratu Jone Navakamocea.

The SDL managed to win all of the 17 Fijian provincial communal seats and all six of the urban Fijian communal seats in the 2006 election. The party secured 80 per cent of indigenous Fijian votes. In some constituencies, chiefly leadership contests were exacerbated by modern leadership competition in party politics, as seen in the Rewa Provincial Fijian Communal constituency. The SDL won a smaller proportion of Fijian votes (56 per cent) in this constituency than in any other Fijian constituency. Ro Filipe Tuisawau, who stood as an independent candidate after failing to secure the SDL nomination, obtained 41 per cent of the Rewa vote, perhaps also indicating continuing political dissent in Rewa. Since 1974, when the Fijian Nationalist Party was formed by Sakeasi Butadroka, the province of Rewa has been the power base of the Fijian Nationalist Party. Both Ro Teimumu Kepa and Ro Filipe Tuisawau were from the same chiefly household (Durutalo 2000:87–88). Within Fijian society, political parties are more than institutions for democratic representation; they also serve as vehicles for continuing subtle yet powerful ancient rivalries.

The SDL faced sterner competition in the open constituencies, where eligible citizens from all communities vote together. Ethnic voting was still observable in the open constituencies. For example, SDL won in the constituencies where Fijians predominated, such as the Lomaivuna-

Namosi-Kadavu Open constituency. The FLP, on the other hand, won in constituencies like Labasa Open, where Indians predominated. Where an Indo-Fijian was fielded as an SDL candidate in a constituency with a strong SDL power base, the Indo-Fijian candidate won. The two Indo-Fijian SDL candidates in the Ra Open constituency and the Cunningham Open constituency both won their seats. Likewise, Fijians standing for the FLP in areas with a strong FLP power base also won their seats. This was the case for Fijian candidates in the Macuata East Open and the Yasawa Nawaka Open constituencies.

Neither the SDL nor the FLP had the unchallenged ascendancy in the open constituencies that they enjoyed in the communal constituencies. The open constituencies were shared almost equally between the SDL and FLP parties. The SDL won 13 of the 25 seats, and the FLP won the rest. Competition in some marginal constituencies was intense. For example, in the Laucala Open constituency, the SDL won with a margin of only 11 votes (7,856) over the FLP (7,845) (Fiji Election Results 2006).

Conclusion

The SDL's victory demonstrated the continuing political importance of the Fijian orthodoxy of *vanua*, *lotu* and *matanitu* as a unifying ideology for indigenous voters. In this context, any attempt by the party to concurrently promote Fijian political paramountcy with multi-racial politics is a real challenge, unless non-Fijians readily accept the promotion of policies such as '50/50 by 2020: the blueprint for affirmative action for indigenous Fijians and Rotumans' (Fiji Government 2002). As we have seen, the SDL attempted to present a multi-ethnic front in 2006 by including Indo-Fijians in its election line-up, and is likely to do so in future elections.[8] The SDL's strategy of facilitating policies for Fijian development has been a reaction to the long-term demands by some Fijian resource owners for greater government support in the development of indigenous resources.

---

8   There were 19 Indo-Fijian SDL candidates in the Indian Communal constituencies and six in the open constituencies. Two of these candidates, Rajesh Singh, who stood in the Cunningham Open constituency, and George Shiu Raj, who stood in the Ra Open constituency, were successful in the election.

The 2006 election reminds us that party politics for many indigenous Fijians is a means of expressing two sets of rights and demands—democratic and indigenous. Indigenous demands are being expressed through the electoral system against non-Fijian groups and as a means of extending ancient internal Fijian rivalries. In the long term, however, these indigenous demands may become problematic in a society of diverse sociopolitical and cultural realities, and the SDL's policies may, in the long term, be seen as offering solutions to some groups of indigenous Fijians only.

References

Ali, A. 1986. Political Change: 1874–1960. In B.V. Lal (ed.), *Politics in Fiji*. Sydney: Allen & Unwin.

Baba, T. 2006. Interview with SDL candidate in the Samabula Tamavua Open constituency in the 2006 election. Suva, Fiji, 16 June.

Durutalo, A. 2000. Elections and the Dilemma of Indigenous Fijian Political Unity. In B.V. Lal (ed.), *Fiji Before the Storm: Elections and the Politics of Development*. Canberra: Asia Pacific Press, The Australian National University.

Durutalo, A.L. 2005. Of Roots and Offshoots: Fijian Political Thinking, Dissent and the Formation of Political Parties (1960–1999). PhD thesis, The Australian National University.

Fiji Election Results 2006. www.elections.gov.fj/results2006/constituencies/47.html

Fiji Government 2002. *50/50 By Year 2020: 20 Year Development Plan (2001–2020) For the Enhancement of Participation of Indigenous Fijians and Rotumans in the Socio-Economic Development of Fiji*. Parliamentary Paper No. 73/2002. Suva: Government of Fiji.

Manifesto Summary 2001. Good Leadership for a Secure and Stable Fiji: Soqosoqo Duavata ni Lewenivanua, the SDL's Plan for Prosperous Fiji. Manifesto Summary, 8.

Saumaki, B. 2007. Bose Ni Vanua and Democratic Politics in Rewa. In J. Fraenkel and S. Firth (eds), *From Election to Coup in Fiji: The 2006 Campaign and Its Aftermath*. Canberra: ANU E Press, 213–24.

PART 3: REIMAGINING

10

Re-Presenting Melanesia: Ignoble Savages and Melanesian Alter-Natives

Tarcisius Kabutaulaka

Kabutaulaka, T. 2015. Re-Presenting Melanesia: Ignoble Savages and Melanesian Alter-Natives. *The Contemporary Pacific* 27(1):110–46.

Republished with the kind permission of the University of Hawai'i Press.

In his statement to the 19th Melanesian Spearhead Group (MSG) Leaders Summit in Noumea, New Caledonia, on 21 June 2013, Solomon Islands Prime Minister Gordon Darcy Lilo couched his speech around the theme 'MSG: Our Place in the Sun in Oceania' and called on 'Melanesians to rise up to the challenges facing their region and find their place amongst the nations of the world' (Lilo 2013). This was a bold statement, especially given the enormity of the social, political, and economic challenges that Melanesian countries face. Further, it is daring, given over two centuries of generally negative representations of Melanesian peoples and societies in Western discourses—negative representations that have over time been internalised by Pacific Islanders, including Melanesians, and used to perpetuate relationships with Melanesia that have racist, essentialist, and social evolutionary elements. The challenges for representing Melanesia are therefore not just socioeconomic but also epistemological. But Prime

Minister Lilo's call illustrates the fact that Melanesians have now appropriated the term Melanesia and are using it to challenge the negative representations—to represent and alter the images of Melanesia as it vies for its 'place in the sun'. Lilo's statement therefore acknowledges both the potential for economic developments in Melanesia due to its comparatively large population and land area and rich terrestrial and marine resources as well as the opportunity for people from this southwestern corner of Oceania to carve their place in the region and beyond.

In this essay, I examine the dominant representations of Melanesia as a place and Melanesians as a peoples and how these have influenced understandings of and responses to contemporary developments in this subregion.[1] I begin with an overview of the discourses that influenced the mapping of Oceania and the negative representations of Melanesians. These have, in turn, framed and influenced discourses about and relationships with Melanesia and Melanesians, including Melanesian perceptions of themselves and their relationships with others.

Against this background, my focus is on how Melanesians have recently appropriated the term Melanesia and are using it in positive, empowering and progressive ways to mobilise, redefine and represent themselves. In the process, they have constructed a pan-Melanesian identity (or identities) that embraces and celebrates the subregion's ethnolinguistic and cultural diversities. This is manifested through the concepts of the 'Melanesian Way' and 'wantokism', intergovernmental organisations such as the MSG, the arts and popular culture.[2] Through all of these, Melanesians are altering the native and re-presenting what might be called the ignoble savage. This process and discourse constitute Melanesianism.

The Black Islands

The mapping and naming of Oceania as Polynesia, Melanesia and Micronesia has been extensively discussed and critiqued elsewhere (see, e.g., Campbell 2010; Douglas 1998, 2010, 2011; Tcherkézoff 2003;

---

1   Here, the term 'Melanesia' is used to refer to the islands in the southwestern Pacific Ocean, consisting of the island of New Guinea (Papua New Guinea and West Papua) and its outlying islands, Solomon Islands, Vanuatu, Kanaky/New Caledonia and Fiji.

2   'Wantokism' is derived from the term *wantok*, which is pidgin for 'one talk', meaning people who speak the same language. It is also about relationships and looking after each other as people who are related through kinship, language, island and region.

Thomas 1989). Here, I provide a brief overview of how the division and naming of Oceania was influenced not only by Europeans' search for Terra Australis or Zuytlandt (South land) but also by ideas of race that were dominant in Europe from the mid-18th century or earlier (Douglas 2010; Tcherkézoff 2003).

French botanist and explorer Rear Admiral Jules-Sébastien-César Dumont d'Urville is the person most often credited for the tripartite division of Oceania. His 1832 paper 'Sur les isles du Grand Océan' (On the Islands of the Great Ocean) popularised the terms and the divisions (d'Urville 2003). However, variations of these terms and the meanings attached to them existed among many Europeans—especially aristocrats, scholars, navigators, explorers and natural scientists—prior to the presentation and publication of Dumont d'Urville's paper. He was, therefore, popularising and reiterating terms and ideas that were prevalent in Europe at that time (Tcherkézoff 2003).

This was not just a geographical mapping of the region; it was also a racialist mapping that reflected long-held ideas about race and social evolution (Tcherkézoff 2003; Douglas 2010). Bronwen Douglas discussed how the 'science of race' influenced how places in Oceania (and elsewhere) were named and how people were categorised. She pointed to the 'systematic efforts made in various branches of natural history—particularly comparative anatomy, physiology, and zoology—to theorise physical difference between human groups as innate, morally, and intellectually determinant, and possibly original' (Douglas 2008:5). She clarified, however, that:

> the word 'race' (then a concrete genealogical term connoting a nation or people of common ancestry) was hardly used before the mid-eighteenth century, while the modern biological sense of a race (denoting permanent, innate, collective physical and mental differences) did not emerge until the 1770s (Douglas 2010:198).

Serge Tcherkézoff, on the other hand, proposed a much longer history of European essentialist and negative representations of other races, especially black people, dating back to the 15th- and 16th-century enslaving of Africans by Spanish and Portuguese traders (2003). This was reinforced by the 18th- and 19-century slave trade to America.

In mapping Oceania, Melanesia was the only subregion named after the skin colour of its inhabitants: the 'black-skinned people' or 'black islands'. The names Polynesia and Micronesia describe the geography of the islands.[3] The term Melanesia was deployed to invoke blackness, reflecting discourses about race in Europe that categorised human beings worldwide within a racial hierarchy that placed 'white' or Caucasian people at the top and 'black' people at the bottom (Douglas 2008, 2010). Tcherkézoff stated that the tripartite division of Oceania

> was not a simple matter of geography and map-making, but of race … long before Dumont d'Urville's invention, the 'black' races were already labelled in the most disparaging terms … The history of the contrast between Polynesia and Melanesia is not the story of a 19th-century French navigator, but the history of European ideas about 'skin colours', between the 16th and the 19th centuries (2003:175, 195, 196).

In Oceania, d'Urville identified two broad 'varieties' of people:

> Among the many varieties of the human species that live on the various islands of Oceania, all travellers, without exception, have reported two that differ very markedly from one another. Their many peculiar moral and physical features no doubt require us to regard them as two separate races (2003:164).

He described Polynesians as

> people of average height, with relatively pale olive-yellow complexions, sleek hair usually brown or black, a fairly regular build and well-proportioned limbs … Moreover, this race displays almost as much variety as the white race of Europe, that Duméril called Caucasian and Bory de Saint-Vincent, Japhetic (ibid.).

The group that he called Melanesians, on the other hand,

> comprises people with very dark, often sooty, skins, sometimes almost as black as that of the Kaffirs, and curly, fuzzy, fluffy but seldom woolly hair. Their features are disagreeable, their build is uneven and their limbs are often frail and deformed … Nevertheless, there is as much variety in skin colour, build, and features among the black people of Oceania as among the numerous nations who live on the African continent and make up the race that most authors have referred to as Ethiopian (ibid.).

---

3   The terms Polynesia, Micronesia and Melanesia are derivatives of the Greek words *poly* (many), *micro* (tiny or small) and *melos* (meaning black). 'Nesia' comes from the Greek word *nesos*, which means islands.

Europeans—as demonstrated in d'Urville's writings—drew a parallel between the physical features, morality and social organisations of Melanesians and Africans, implying that the dark-skinned people of Oceania were similar to, and therefore should be treated in the same way as, dark-skinned people elsewhere.

To illustrate this point, let me turn to our neighbour Australia, a place where race relations were of great concern by the mid-18th century and continue to be an issue today (see Wolfe 2006; Anderson 2003). Writing about people of mixed descent in Australia, historian Henry Reynolds argued that racial categories that had already taken root in Europe and North America were transmitted to Australia and helped define race relations there. Reynolds described how, at the first Commonwealth Parliament meeting in 1901, 'members and Senators agreed about the centrality of race. They agreed that there was a demonstrable hierarchy of races with the northwest Europeans, the Nordics or Caucasians at the top and the Africans, Melanesians, and Aborigines at the bottom' (2005:85).

In this racialist mapping, the 'Oceanic Negroes', which included Australian Aborigines and those from the southwestern Pacific, were placed in the same category as black people from Africa, who by then had long been subjected to European-perpetrated slavery in the New World. This categorisation reflected discourses that influenced European interactions with the rest of the world. Notions of racial hierarchy and references to 'black-skinned people' as the most primitive of human races were, its proponents argued, supported by science (Douglas 2008; Ballard 2008). One popular pseudo-scientific approach was phrenology, which involved the measuring of human skulls and brains to determine the place of their owners in the racial hierarchy. In these studies, the Oceanic Negroes, like their African 'relatives', were placed low in the hierarchy (Rochette 2003). In a lecture in 1819, the British biologist Sir William Lawrence asserted that the distinction of colour between white and black was not more striking

> than the pre-eminence of the former in moral feelings and mental endowments … The later … indulge, almost universally, in disgusting debauchery and sensuality, and display gross selfishness, indifference to the pains and pleasures of others, insensibility to beauty of form, order and harmony, and an almost entire want of what we comprehend altogether under the expression of elevated sentiments, manly virtues, and moral feeling. The hideous savages of Van Diemen's Land [Tasmania], of

> New Holland [Australia], New Guinea, and some neighbouring islands, the Negroes of Congo and some other parts exhibit the most disgusting moral as well as physical portrait of man (quoted in Reynolds 2005:86).

Reynolds quoted French aristocrat and novelist Joseph Arthur De Gobineau as saying that the Oceanic Negroes 'had the special privilege of providing the "most ugly, and degraded and repulsive specimens of the race" that seemed to have been created to provide a link between man and the brute' (Reynolds 2005:68). Similarly, in dividing Oceania into Polynesia, Melanesia and Micronesia, d'Urville, like his predecessors, emphasised skin colour. He identified Melanesians—which included the inhabitants of New Holland (Australia) and Van Diemen's Land (Tasmania)—as

> more or less black in colour, with curly, fuzzy or sometimes nearly woolly hair, flat noses, wide mouths and unpleasant features, and their limbs are often very frail and seldom well shaped. The women are even more hideous than the men, especially those who have suckled children, as their breasts immediately become flaccid and droopy, and the little freshness that they owed to youth vanishes at once (d'Urville 2003:169).

The racialist mapping of Oceania was also influenced by pseudo-evolutionary ideas about cultures and sociopolitical organisations. d'Urville, for example, stated that Polynesians 'are often organised into nations and sometimes powerful monarchies' (2003:164). This was in contrast to Melanesians, who

> are organised into tribes or clans of varying size, but very seldom into nations, and their institutions are far from attaining the degree of refinement that can sometimes be found among people of the copper-skinned race (ibid.).

The measure of the development of a society—and therefore race—was according to how similar to or different from European forms of government it was. Consequently, the absence of centralised authority and the relative egalitarian nature of societies in the southwestern Pacific and among indigenous Australians implied social deficiencies and therefore inferiority. Indigenous Australians were seen as the lowest in the social and racial hierarchy because of their nomadic hunter-gatherer societies (Ballard 2008; Reynolds 2005).

Another important aspect of this discussion is the link between race and gender. The difference between Polynesia and Melanesia was based not only on the colour of people's skin or the relative development of their sociopolitical organisations but also on how women were viewed and how they were seen to relate to both indigenous men and European strangers. Margaret Jolly (2012) suggested that, long before d'Urville's 1832 paper, Europeans made strongly contrasting judgements between the women of Polynesia and Melanesia in terms of beauty, sexual allure and access, work and status vis-à-vis indigenous men. While Polynesian women were often portrayed as 'dusky maidens' (Tamaira 2010), Melanesian women were portrayed in derogatory terms. This 'gendering of race' affects perception of Melanesian women and their place in contemporary societies (Jolly 2012).

Given European attitudes, it is therefore no surprise that the darkest of the Pacific Islanders were identified by the colour of their skin, rather than by the geographical characteristics of the places where they lived. Right from the beginning, the term Melanesia was impregnated with racialist overtones. Papua New Guinean scholar Regis Tove Stella discussed how race was used in European colonial discourse to describe and represent Papua New Guineans as inferior to Europeans and other Pacific Islanders, partly because of their darker skin. He stated:

> Colonial discourse produced and circulated knowledge and imagery that regularly depicted Papua New Guineans as inferior and subordinate, portraying them in positions of subjection, savagery, and powerlessness in accordance with the widespread operation of the discourse (Stella 2007:21).

This is true of the depiction of the rest of Melanesia, as discussed above. This essentialist and racialist view of Melanesia set the tone for how the peoples and cultures from Melanesia were represented in the centuries that followed colonisation.

Islands of Ignoble Savages

European images of Oceania were also influenced by the concept of the 'noble savage', which glorified a 'natural life' that was seen as uncorrupted by civilisation and therefore represented humans' innate goodness (Ellingston 2001). The portrayal of Pacific Islanders as noble savages was influenced largely by the accounts of European explorers like James Cook and Louis Antoine de Bougainville, who had documented and shared their encounters with South Seas peoples and places, especially Tahitian and Marquesan peoples and landscapes (Jolly 1997). I have often wondered how the view of Pacific Islanders as noble savages would have developed had it been based on European encounters with my ancestors from the Solomon Islands or with those from other parts of Melanesia. Perhaps the descriptor of the savage would have shifted from noble to ignoble.

Scholarly enterprises that developed with European and North American higher education also contributed to the construction and perpetuation of the negative representations of Melanesia. Central to this was cultural anthropology, a discipline that pioneered scholarly descriptions of Melanesian places, peoples and cultures. While this field of study has contributed to knowledge about Melanesia, it also added to distortions and misunderstandings and perpetuated the racialised division of Oceania. Epeli Hauʻofa commented on the role of anthropology in perpetuating what he called 'distorted' images of Melanesia:

> After decades of anthropological field research in Melanesia we have come up only with pictures of people who fight, compete, trade, pay bride prices, engage in rituals, invent cargo cults, copulate, and sorcerise each other. There is hardly anything in our literature to indicate whether these people have any such sentiments as love, kindness, consideration, altruism, and so on. We cannot tell from our ethnographic writings whether they have a sense of humour. We know little about their systems of morality, specifically their ideas of the good and the bad, and their philosophies (2008:6).

Hauʻofa took issue with the tendency to describe Melanesian polities as underdeveloped and backward compared to 'advanced' Polynesia. He argued that anthropological description 'denies that traditional Melanesian leaders have any genuine interest in the welfare of their people and insists that their public actions are all motivated purely by selfishness' (ibid.). He went on to say that this kind of ethnographic work is 'erroneous' and 'an invidious pseudo-evolutionary comparison between the "developed" Polynesian polities and the "underdeveloped" Melanesian ones' (ibid.). He decried the fact that Europeans have long romanticised Polynesians and denigrated Melanesians, and he warned that this kind of anthropology 'has the potential of bolstering the longstanding Polynesian racism against Melanesians' (ibid.).

Hau'ofa was referring, in particular, to the work of social anthropologists who often describe Melanesian polities as comparatively smaller and ethnolinguistically diverse with no centralised authority. In discussing the difference between Melanesia and Polynesia, Marshall Sahlins, for example, stated that 'the Polynesians were to become famous for elaborate forms of rank and chieftainship, whereas most Melanesian societies broke off advance on this front at more rudimentary levels' (1963:286). He went on to say that 'measurable along several dimensions, the contrast between developed Polynesian and underdeveloped Melanesian polities is immediately striking for differences in scale' (Sahlins 1963:289). Such descriptions resonate with early European writings and invoke pseudo-evolutionary comparisons. They are based on the fact that Melanesian polities did not resemble the models of the centralised state that were established in Europe and exported to the rest of the world through colonialism. Polynesian societies, on the other hand, had hierarchical chiefly systems that resembled the feudal systems in Europe. Furthermore, by the 1800s, centralised governments had been created in parts of Polynesia. The establishment of monarchs in Hawai'i, Tahiti and Tonga was often pointed to as a sign of development in Polynesian social organisation (see, e.g., discussion in Howe 1984:59–65). In Fiji, the rise and establishment of Bau as the central power was never complete because Ratu Seru Epenisa Cakobau did not have control over all of Fiji (Lal 1992). The perception that having large centralised institutions (in the form of states) was the best way of organising societies contributed to the denigration of Melanesian sociopolitical organisations.

The descriptions of Melanesian sociopolitical organisations as underdeveloped and backward were also due to Europeans' inability to relate to and understand the complexities of Melanesian societies. For instance, the Kula Ring in Papua New Guinea entailed complex interactions among peoples from different language groups involving trade, politics, ceremonial exchanges and social relationships that held these societies together and survived for thousands of years (Malinowski 1920; Ziegler 1990). Another example is the shell-money trade between the people of Langalanga Lagoon on Malaita in Solomon Islands and Bougainville, as well as other parts of island Papua New Guinea. This continues today, largely outside of the purview of the state and despite the trade and immigration regulations that the governments of Solomon Islands and Papua New Guinea impose (Guo 2006; Connell 1977). Perhaps Melanesian societies baffled early European visitors because they were vastly different and unfamiliar. Europeans therefore employed pseudo-evolutionary ideas that placed European social organisation at the top along with those that resembled them and those unfamiliar and dissimilar at the bottom.

Such attitudes are often reflected, albeit implicitly, in contemporary discussions of social, political and economic developments in Melanesia. In the last three decades, Melanesia has been portrayed predominantly as a place of conflicts, political instabilities and poor social and economic development. The diversity of cultures and languages is often presented as a problem rather than as a rich cultural heritage. Ethnolinguistic diversity, it seems, does not fit into the idea of a homogenising world, where collective 'imagined communities', to reference Benedict Anderson (1991), and national identities are normative and regarded as more civilised. Political scientists often describe Melanesian states as weak and failing and as part of an 'arc of instability' that stretches from Indonesia to Fiji (May 2003; Duncan and Chand 2002). Furthermore, these states are often referenced as the primary contributors to what some called the 'Africanisation of the Pacific' (Reilly 2000). This viewpoint invokes a perceived connection between Africa and Oceania, especially Melanesia, that was made in early European writings. It implies that these connections were natural and the same challenges were expected of black people whether they were in Africa or Oceania. Jon Fraenkel (2004) and David Chappell (2005) have challenged Ben Reilly's Africanisation of the South Pacific thesis, arguing that it made broad and erroneous generalisations and did not fully consider the colonial histories and experiences that have contributed to Oceania's contemporary challenges.

Political scientists explain contemporary issues and developments in Melanesia almost exclusively vis-à-vis Western ideas and models of governance. They measure the failures and successes of Melanesian societies by using Western criteria, often in the guise of universalising theories of governance. This is usually done without reference to the ways that Melanesians organised themselves in their own terms and how these strategies have kept their societies surviving for thousands of years. Terence Wesley-Smith (2008) pointed to this problem in his discussion of how the concept of the state is exported and promoted as if it were the most natural and appropriate institution for organising all human societies, including those in Melanesia. The state is often presented as unproblematic, or at least taken as given, in ways that ignore the violent history of the development of the Western states.

The negative representation of Melanesians—and hence the construction of the ignoble savage—is found not only in academic research and writings but in visual images as well. I am often troubled by images of Melanesians that are framed and hung on the walls of university buildings. To me they look uncomfortable, trapped in time for the entertainment, curiosity and amusement of those who walk the corridors. When I first went to The Australian National University (ANU), I found that the only picture of bare-breasted women on the walls of the Coombs Building was one of Solomon Islanders. I have written about that elsewhere (Kabutaulaka 1997). When I joined the East-West Center in Honolulu, I noticed that the only pictures of half-naked people on the walls of Burns Hall were those of people from Tanna in Vanuatu. These images were on the third floor, where the Pacific Islands Development Program, where I once worked, is located. As I walked along the corridor, I passed the half-naked Tanna people and then came to pictures of Micronesians who were dressed and represented in studio poses, as though they had been liberated from savagery, unlike the Melanesians at the other end of the hallway. I often wondered what those people in the pictures might have been thinking as they stared at me from their framed existence. They probably wondered why I was walking along the corridor and not framed and hung on the wall with the rest of them. Perhaps I am framed in a different way—still stuck in the racialised map of Oceania constructed by early Europeans and sustained by contemporary discourses.

This kind of stasis is what Homi Bhabha, in his discussion of representation in colonial discourses, referred to as the 'dependence on the concept of "fixity" in the ideological construction of otherness' (1994:66). The display of colonial subjects, or 'others', as naturally and permanently fixed in a particular time and state of being in turn naturalises and justifies their domination (see Hall 1997; Spurr 1993). The constant representation of Melanesians in books and in paintings on the walls of academic buildings as well as museums as naked or half-naked posing in jungles or villages portrays them as naturally trapped in a particular state of being and unchanging. These ignoble savages are therefore backward compared to the West (and the rest of Oceania), which is constantly changing and 'progressing'.

Negative representations of Melanesia are also found in popular writings. For example, in writing about his travels through Solomon Islands in 1911, Jack London had little good to say about the island group. In fact, he stated, 'If I were a king, the worst punishment I could inflict on my enemies would be to banish them to the Solomons. On second thought, king or no king, I don't think I'd have the heart to do it (London 2003:178). Travel writer Paul Theroux, writing in the 1990s, said that he found the Solomons to be 'the most savage islands in the Pacific' (1992:155). In his book *The Happy Isles of Oceania,* Theroux had a go at nearly all the Pacific Islands, but he reserved his most horrendous comments for Melanesians, describing Solomon Islanders in Honiara as 'among the scariest-looking people I had ever seen in my life' (ibid.). For Fiji, Theroux made a distinction between the people of eastern Fiji and those that he referred to as Melanesian Fijians. He wrote that 'the Lau Group is one of the pretty little star clusters in the universe of Oceania. Melanesian Fiji is another story. Fiji is like the world you thought you left behind—full of political perversity, racial fear, economic woes, and Australian tourists looking for inexpensive salad bowls' (Theroux 1992:219). While such descriptions may raise eyebrows, they also appeal to European curiosity about the savage Melanesians. It is no surprise that Theroux's book became a *New York Times* bestseller—it fed the Western imagination about Melanesian backwardness and savagery.

The media also contribute to the ignoble savage representation of Melanesia. In 2007, a British television company produced a three-part documentary series titled *Meet the Natives.* The producers promoted this as 'reverse anthropology', in which 'natives' would be taken to metropolitan cities and their interactions with the peoples and cultures of the West would be filmed. The first task was to find the native—and, of course, where did they look but Melanesia. In the first part of the series, five men from Tanna in Vanuatu were taken to London and filmed as they interacted with English peoples and cultures. Although I have not watched the series, I found the idea of reverse anthropology troubling.[4] On 8 September 2007, the British newspaper *The Independent* carried a story titled 'Strange Island: Pacific Tribesmen Come to Study Britain' (Adams 2007). In this article, the five men from Tanna had no voice; they were merely the exotic objects of media commentary.

After the London episode of *Meet the Natives* was aired, I received an email from the producers asking me to facilitate the production of a sequel to the documentary. This time they wanted to take men from the Weather Coast of Guadalcanal in Solomon Islands (where I come from), and

---

4   I am sure that if I had watched the documentary series *Meet the Natives*, it would have provided a close and useful reading and deconstruction of contemporary European visions of Melanesia.

especially the followers of the Moro Movement, to New York. I seriously considered their request, knowing that many of my *wantok* would love to go to New York, even if they had no clue where it was or what they were required to do. However, after careful consideration, I refused to facilitate the project and emailed the producers saying that I was unable to help. I saw the project not as reverse anthropology but as simply a relocation of the native or the ignoble savage who continues to be an object of Western curiosity. This time, however, the native was being placed in an unfamiliar environment and gazed at through television cameras and screens. I could imagine English families in their living rooms, gazing at the television and commenting on the natives, the faraway places they came from, how they must be fascinated by English culture, and I thought about how all of this would contribute yet again to the production of denigrating knowledge about Melanesians. It made my intellectual spirit quiver.

When I was approached, the mischievous side of me—which makes up quite a bit of me—was tempted to facilitate the project. I thought that since they didn't know what I looked like, it would be fun if I could fly home, dress up in *kabilato* (bark cloth) like the native they wanted to see and get myself recruited as part of the delegation to New York. I thought that it would be amusing if, in the middle of filming, I would start discussions about the politics of representation, demand to be taken to Broadway or to the United Nations headquarters, and ask to be wined and dined at the most expensive restaurants. I would suddenly break out of the native binary and run amok in New York. Perhaps that part of the series could be titled, 'Native Runs Amok in New York'. However, in the end, the sensible side of me prevailed and I dropped the idea.

While my focus in this essay thus far has been on European representations, it is important to note that the ignoble savage images of Melanesia have spread beyond the European imagination and become entrenched among non-Europeans as well. To illustrate this, let me recount an event that occurred in Canberra in the late 1990s when I was a PhD student at ANU. One afternoon, I was on a bus with John Naitoro, another Solomon Islander who was also working on his PhD at the university, on our way to ANU housing at Hughes, a suburb of Canberra where we lived. We sat at the back of the bus chattering away in Solomon Islands *pijin*. Next to us was a black man, whom we later learned was from Somalia. After listening to us for a while, he asked, 'Are you from Papua New Guinea?'

'Yes, we are from Papua New Guinea,' John quickly responded before I could say anything.

The man was quiet for a while and then asked, 'Do you eat people in Papua New Guinea?' I was shocked.

'Yes, we eat people,' John quickly responded.

'But that was long time ago, right?' the man asked after a moment of silence.

'No, we still eat people,' John quickly answered with a serious expression on his face. I looked at him and then at the man, wondering where this conversation was going.

After a while, and as though to assure himself of his safety, the man asked, 'But you only eat white people, right?'

'No, we eat black people as well,' John said looking straight at him and more seriously than before. The man stood up and went to the front of the bus.

That incident set me thinking about where and how an African had gotten the idea that Papua New Guineans in Canberra in the late 1990s could be cannibals. Perhaps he thought that you could take the man out of cannibal land, but not cannibalism out of the man. I also wondered what he would have asked if we had told him that we were from Tahiti. Perhaps he would have asked if in Tahiti we danced *tamure* all day, ate from abundant breadfruit trees and made love under coconut trees. I also wondered why John responded to him in the way he did. John said to me afterward, '*Hem na wat fo talem long pipol karage olsem* (That's what you say to people who are ignorant like that)'.

The ignoble Melanesian savage exists not only in European and African minds but also in Pacific Islander minds. The negative representation of Melanesians, and darker-skinned people more generally, has, to some extent, been internalised by Pacific Islanders, including Melanesians. This is reflected in the languages, perceptions and relationships among Pacific Islanders. This topic is not usually discussed openly because it is sensitive and people fear being labelled racist or causing unsettling waves in our *wan solwara*.[5]

---

5   *Wan solwara* is a Papua New Guinea *tok pisin* (pidgin) term that literally means 'one salt water' or 'one ocean'. It is also the name of the newspaper published by the journalism program at the University of the South Pacific (USP), Suva, Fiji. The name is an attempt to create a sense of Oceanic identity among USP students and faculty.

Let me take the risk and raise some of these languages and perceptions commonly referred to as *mea uli*. *Uli* is the word for black, and one of the most common meanings of *mea* is 'thing'. Hence, one could argue that the use of the term *mea uli* (either consciously or unconsciously) strips the black person of his or her humanity and reduces him or her to a thing—*mea uli*. In March 2009, there was a debate in the *Samoa Observer* following the use of the term *mea uli* to refer to the then newly elected first black president in the United States, Barack Obama. One of the contributors suggested the use of the term *tagata uli,* which literally means 'black man', and *taine uli* as appropriate for 'black woman (*Samoa Observer* 23 March 2009).[6] In Tongan, a black person may be referred to as *'uli'uli* (black) or, more rudely, *me'a 'uli* (black thing). As *'uli* is also the word for 'dirty', one wonders whether black people are considered dirty. In June 2010, I presented a version of this paper at the University of the South Pacific (USP) as a way of starting conversations about the perceptions associated with the divisions of Oceania and how Melanesians are represented. The USP student newspaper, *Wan Solwara,* published a story about my presentation and comments from USP students and faculty. This was later reprinted in the Auckland University of Technology Pacific Media Centre's online publication, Pacific.Scoop. The comments by two prominent Pacific Islander scholars were insightful and important in this conversation. Education Professor Konai Helu Thaman was reported to have said that 'referring to black-skinned people as *'uli* or *'uli'uli* is purely for descriptive purposes and not meant to be offensive'. She said, 'When Tongans say *'uli'uli* it does not mean that they are superior, being a Tongan. They are just describing the person, but if there is a feeling that whoever is *'uli'uli* is black and is compared to white, then that is problematic'. Historian Morgan Tuimaleali'ifano explained that the expression *mea uli* in Samoan meant black people without negative connotations. But he added that there were people who put 'value' behind the term (Khan and Po'ese 2010).

Epeli Hau'ofa, who was born of Tongan missionary parents in Papua New Guinea and spent his early years in that country, provided a slightly different perspective. In an interview with Nicholas Thomas in 2006, Hau'ofa stated:

---

6   Malama Meleisea used the term *tama uli* to refer to the descendants of Melanesians who were taken to work in the plantations in Samoa in the late 1800s and early 1900s (Meleisea 1980). This is seen as a more respectful way to refer to black people.

My upbringing in Melanesia was very important. I am extremely sensitive to Polynesian cultures and the contemporary situation and modernization, but they are rather dominant. Always, when I went to Tonga, I found that the way Polynesians feel and think about Melanesians [is] rather appalling. It's racist. There is a feeling of superiority. Because part of me is Melanesian, I'm always trying to go beyond that divide (Thomas 2012:126).

Polynesian views of Melanesians were perhaps influenced also by the experiences of Polynesian missionaries. The eastern Pacific was the first to have extensive contact with Europeans and to convert to Christianity. Polynesian missionaries were subsequently recruited to work in Melanesia. Sione Latukefu provided an insightful discussion of Polynesian and Fijian missionaries' interactions with Papua New Guineans and Solomon Islanders, as well as with their European counterparts. In commenting on the relation between Polynesian missionaries and Melanesians, Latukefu wrote:

> The Tongans and Samoans had no doubt whatsoever of their physical, mental and cultural superiority to the Melanesians, an attitude that was reinforced by their role of 'bringing light to the darkness of Melanesia' (1978:98).

He noted that Samoan missionaries found it most difficult to adjust, attributing this to the fact 'that Samoans had (and still have) a tremendous pride in their culture, the *fa'a Samoa* (Samoan tradition). Believing themselves to be the cream of the Pacific, they tended to look down on others, particularly the Papua New Guineans and Solomon Islanders' (ibid.). This, Latukefu suggested, might also have been influenced by the fact that Samoan pastors were treated as special at home and therefore expected that treatment elsewhere. The situation was different with Fijian missionaries, whom Latukefu described as:

> closer to the local people. Since they were Melanesians themselves, there were few barriers between them and the people, either racially or culturally. Marriage between Fijian missionaries and local women was quite common, especially among missionaries who became widowers during their term of service, but marriage between Samoans and Tongans and local people was extremely rare (ibid.).

I raise this not to accuse Tongans and Samoans (and other Pacific Islanders) of being racist toward Melanesians, but rather to highlight and begin examinations and discussions about how we Pacific Islanders have internalised the racial divisions of Oceania and the prejudices associated with their European constructions. This signifies the extent of the impact of colonial discourses and its role in preventing us from achieving the Oceanic identity that Hauʻofa aspired to in his essay 'Our Sea of Islands' (2008).

It is important to note that prejudice toward darker-skinned people also exists among Melanesians. Relatively lighter-skinned Melanesians sometimes speak in disparaging ways about darker-skinned Melanesians and associate them with more 'savagery' because of the colour of their skin. In Solomon Islands, for example, a month prior to independence in July 1978, the government newspaper published a poem titled 'West Wind' written by a man from Malaita, in which he described those from the western Solomon Islands, who are generally darker than other Solomon Islanders, as 'Black and ugly, proud and lazy' (*News Drum* 9 June 1978).[7] The poem incited debates (*News Drum* 23 June 1978) and fuelled sentiments for the Western Solomons to secede from the rest of the country (Premdas et al. 1984). The issue was deemed so serious that the author of the poem was charged with sedition (*News Drum* 8 Sept 1978). Consequently, in order for the discussions, especially among Pacific Islanders, to transcend the colonial binaries and establish and reinforce the trans-Oceanic identities that Hauʻofa talked about, it is important that Pacific Islanders acknowledge how these binaries have influenced how we perceive and relate to each other. This is a discussion that might be uncomfortable, but it is one that is important and that we must not shy away from.

Some have proposed the need to shift beyond these geographical and racial binaries and to emphasise the interconnections between Islanders. This, it was envisaged, would foster the construction of identities and connections that had existed prior to European contact—or, if they hadn't existed, that should be established because we belong to *wan solwara*. The late Ratu Sir Kamisese Mara, prime minister and president of Fiji, for example, started this by proposing the concept of the 'Pacific Way'. He was credited for coining and first articulating the term at a United Nations General Assembly meeting in October 1970. In that address, Ratu Mara

---

7 The 'West Wind' poem was written to ridicule the demands for greater autonomy being made by the people of the Western Solomons, who believed they could achieve that through a federal system of government, or state government, as it was commonly known in Solomon Islands at that time. The poem was therefore not primarily about race, although it made reference to race.

used the term to refer specifically to Fiji's smooth transition from colonial rule to independence as reflecting a Pacific Way that was consensual and peaceful (Mara 1997:238). However, the term has since been used broadly as anticolonial and representing Oceania as a region with similar cultures that is politically united, can address issues through collective diplomacy and invokes a pan-Oceanic identity (Crocombe 1976). But, as Stephanie Lawson pointed out, the term also reflects Polynesian values, especially Ratu Mara's aristocratic background, more than those of Melanesia and Micronesia (Lawson 2010, 2013).

Epeli Hau'ofa was also a proponent of pan-Oceanic identities. He highlighted how pan-Oceanic connections transcend national and subregional boundaries, arguing that the ocean connects rather than divides the Pacific Islands. He described Oceania prior to European contact as:

> a large world in which peoples and cultures moved and mingled, unhindered by boundaries of the kind erected much later by imperial powers. From one island to another they sailed to trade and to marry, thereby expanding social networks for greater flows of wealth. They travelled to visit relatives in a wide variety of natural and cultural surroundings, to quench their thirst for adventure, and even to fight and dominate (Hau'ofa 2008:33).

While I agree with Hau'ofa's proposal to strengthen our trans-Oceanic connections and identities, it must be noted that national and subregional boundaries persist and have become realities for most Pacific Islanders. In fact, while scholars have been engaged in critical debate about and deconstructions of the tripartite divisions—conversations that are important and must be encouraged—there is relatively less discussion about how the terms Polynesia, Micronesia and Melanesia have taken on lives of their own, appropriated by Pacific Islanders and used to frame their identities and influence relationships among themselves and with others. Political and cultural organisations in the region have adopted these names, indicating that Pacific Islanders have taken on these terms and used them for their own purposes. Examples of these include the Melanesian Spearhead Group, the Micronesian Chief Executives Summit and the Polynesian Leaders Group. On one hand, these subregional organisations could be viewed as perpetuating the colonial and essentialist divisions of Oceania. Alternatively, they could be seen as appropriating these terms and using them to construct new, useful and empowering identities. Melanesians, as will be discussed in the next section, have certainly taken the term Melanesia and built an identity around it.

Melanesianism and Alter-Natives

While negative representations of Melanesia linger in the shadows of scholarly and popular discourses, Melanesians are proactively trying to shed the ignoble savage image and aspire for 'a place in the sun'. They have appropriated the term Melanesia for self-identification and are 'altering' the 'native', creating 'alter-natives'. They are showing that Melanesians have complex experiences and cultures that are rooted in centuries of traditions, while at the same time adapting to new and dynamic futures that draw from within Melanesia and beyond. As Lawson stated:

> Melanesia has acquired a positive meaning for many of those to whom it applies, providing a basis for the assertion of an identity that is confident and imbued with pride, thus clearly transcending its origins and establishing a new 'reality' (2013:21).

Since the 1970s, Melanesian political and intellectual leaders have attempted to construct and assert a collective Melanesian identity (or identities). Lawson provided a detailed discussion of the complex postcolonial histories and politics behind the idea of Melanesia and the construction of 'Melanesianism'. This was a reaction to the negative representations of Melanesia that started with the mapping of Oceania in the mid-18th century and persisted through scholarly and popular discourses with mainly Euro-American and Australian origins. It was also a reaction to Melanesians' perception that Fiji (under Ratu Mara) and the Polynesian countries that gained independence earlier were dominating regional organisations such as the Pacific Islands Forum (PIF) and discourses about and representations of Oceania (Lawson 2013).

But the idea of Melanesia and the process of Melanesianism were influenced not only by past experiences, but also by the awareness of future potentials. I will return to discussions of the future potentials later. Here, let me explain what I mean by Melanesianism. This is a concept and a discourse that creates an 'imagined community' (Anderson 1991) and invokes shared values—both imagined and real—that are fluid, dynamic and constantly reinvented through ongoing *tok stori* (conversations) and shared experiences. Melanesianism is therefore a process rather than an ideology or a state of being. It is a discourse about an imagined community that takes form and becomes real through pan-Melanesian connections that are manifested in the idea of Melanesia and in organisations that forge political, economic and cultural cooperation. A common pidgin language that is spoken in Papua New Guinea, Solomon Islands and Vanuatu reinforces Melanesianism.

Melanesianism is also manifested and expressed through parallel and overlapping concepts such as the 'Melanesian Way', Melanesian socialism and 'wantokism'. Stephanie Lawson (2013), Ralph Premdas (1987) and Michael Howard (1983) provided detailed examinations and analyses of the history and politics of the Melanesian Way and Melanesian socialism. I do not need to repeat those here except to point out that Bernard Narokobi, the Papua New Guinean intellectual and public servant who popularised the term Melanesian Way never provided a precise definition for the term. He argued that it would be futile to attempt to define 'a total cosmic vision of life' (Narokobi and Olela 1980:8). Since then, nobody that I know of has attempted to concisely define the Melanesian Way. Perhaps it is this ambiguity and the fact that it was never framed and confined by specific definitions that have enabled Melanesianism to evolve and adapt in the last four decades, encompassing new experiences and innovative and creative forms of expressions. Melanesianism is rooted in and draws strength from the past but is not confined by it. It exists and is real because it is talked about, lived and experienced, not because it is defined.

Furthermore, Melanesianism, as expressed through the Melanesian Way, embraces the subregion's ethnolinguistic and cultural diversities.[8] Narokobi and Olela suggested that the Melanesian Way does not necessarily imply a single Melanesian identity. Rather, it is a celebration of Melanesia's diversity and the fact that such diversity is a source of strength rather than of problem and weakness (Narokobi and Olela 1980). This view advocates harnessing and celebrating the common worldviews that one often finds woven amid the diversities. Western scholarship and popular representations of Melanesia have tended to focus on and emphasise the differences, rather than the similarities. But in an attempt to assert Melanesianism, emerging Melanesian elites often use slogans such as 'unity in diversity' to mobilise for decolonisation (Scheyvens 1988) and invoke an idea of a community founded on the basis of shared diversities.

---

8   Melanesia is one of the most ethnolinguistically diverse places in Oceania and the world. As Tom Dutton stated, 'Here, scattered across New Guinea, the Solomon Islands, Vanuatu, New Caledonia, the Loyalty Islands and Fiji are to be found over one thousand languages, or approximately one-quarter of those spoken in the world today' (2006:207). Papua New Guinea has about 800 languages, Solomon Islands 87, and Vanuatu 118.

Francis Saemala (1982), for example, discussed how the foundations of decolonisation and postcolonial nation building in Solomon Islands were built on 'uniting the diversity'.

But translating the idea of unity in diversity into reality is challenging, as we have seen in violent events such as the Bougainville Crisis and the Solomon Islands conflicts that emphasised the differences, rather than the unity. The causes of these conflicts, however, lie in a variety of socioeconomic and political issues that have more recent history, rather than primordial ethnolinguistic differences (Regan 1998; Moore 2004). The causes of the Fiji coups in 1987, 2000 and 2006 are also more complex than simply an expression of the differences between the iTaukei (indigenous Fijians) and the descendants of Indian migrants (Tarte 2009).

Melanesian Spearhead Group

The political manifestation of Melanesianism was the establishments of the Melanesian Spearhead Group (MSG) in 1986, following informal discussions by the heads of the governments of Papua New Guinea, Solomon Islands and Vanuatu, and a representative of the Kanak Socialist National Liberation Front (FLNKS) in Goroka, Papua New Guinea. The 'Agreed Principles of Cooperation Among the Independent States in Melanesia' was signed in March 1988. The formal 'Agreement Establishing the MSG' and the MSG Constitution were not signed until March 2007, followed by the opening of the MSG Secretariat headquarters in Port Vila, Vanuatu, in 2008. The reasons that are often given for the creation of the MSG were political, especially in relation to Melanesian leaders' frustrations over what they saw as the region's indecisiveness on issues such as the decolonisation of New Caledonia (Lawson 2013; Grynberg and Kabutaulaka 1995; MacQueen 1989). Ron May asserted that 'the MSG had its origins in a broad sense of Melanesian cultural solidarity and a desire to assert a Melanesian voice among the members of the Pacific Islands Forum, which some island countries perceived to be dominated by Australia and New Zealand' (2011:6).

However, beyond these publicly expressed views, another reason for the establishment of the MSG was Melanesian leaders' concerns about the sense of superiority and domination that Polynesian leaders exerted at the regional level in the years after independence (MacQueen 1989). There were feelings that in the early days of Pacific Islands regionalism, Melanesians were looked down on. At that time, as noted earlier, this included Fiji under Ratu Sir Kamisese Mara, who came from Lau and had close connections with Tonga and Samoa. This was demonstrated, among other incidents, by Ratu Mara's opposition to Papua New Guinea's inclusion in the South Pacific Forum (later renamed the Pacific Islands Forum) during its inaugural meeting in Wellington in 1971. He was also opposed to the nomination of a PNG national, Oala Rarua, for the position of secretary general of the South Pacific Commission (later renamed the Pacific Community) (Lawson 2013:10). Furthermore, there were perceptions among Melanesian leaders that the concept of the Pacific Way as articulated by Ratu Mara, while pretending to be inclusive of the region, actually marginalised Melanesia and privileged Polynesian values, especially aristocratic leadership systems (Lawson 2013:8–12).

Consequently, Fiji was not part of the initial discussions and did not become a member of the MSG until 1996. According to former Fiji Prime Minister Sitiveni Rabuka:

> Fiji was not part of the initial group that joined the MSG because at that time Ratu Sir Kamisese Mara was regarded as one of the founding members of the Pacific Islands Forum with Australia and New Zealand so it would have appeared like Fiji was deserting the rest of the Pacific and going with the rest of the Western group, or Melanesian group (Koroi 2013).

In spite of this, Fiji is now embraced as an important member of the MSG.

Today, the MSG has emerged as a political and economic force in the region. It has 'expanded its purview to include climate change and security and is leading the process of regional economic integration' (Tarte 2014:312). Fijian academic Wadan Narsey (2013) described the MSG as 'the Western Pacific Powerhouse':

> The MSG offers very real and significant economic benefits to the Melanesian countries, and especially Fiji, Vanuatu, and Solomon Islands, who can work linkages with the new found minerals, LNG [liquified natural gas] wealth and booming economic growth of PNG. The MSG may well expand to include West Papua and FLNKS (Kanaky New Caledonia) both also resource rich, and both of whom will at long last find the regional support for their independence struggles, long denied them by [the] Forum Secretariat. Should Timor-Leste also be included in the future, the MSG will be even further strengthened as the most powerful regional integration movement, totally overshadowing the

economic possibilities from the Pacific Plan [a strategy for Pacific-wide regional cooperation endorsed by leaders of the Pacific Islands Forum in 2005]. There is also every likelihood that the resource rich MSG has far more complementary benefits to offer the atoll countries (Kiribati, Tuvalu, FSM, etc.) than the Eastern Polynesian countries.[9]

In March 2013, USP, in collaboration with the government of Fiji, hosted a Melanesian Week to mark the 25th anniversary of the establishment of the Melanesian Spearhead Group. The celebrations were laced with the theme 'Celebrating Melanesian Solidarity and Growth'. In his address, USP Vice Chancellor and President Rajesh Chandra pointed to the fact that the three MSG countries that are USP members—Fiji, Vanuatu and Solomon Islands—accounted for 82 per cent of the university's enrolment in 2012 and that the subregion:

> represents most of the population of our region, and its largest economies. MSG has given a stronger voice to the 90 per cent of Pacific Islanders that it represents. It embodies the spirit of Pacific pride and honour, and is a positive, complementary organisation to the Pacific Islands Forum Secretariat (PIFS) framework, and contributes to maintaining the balance between metropolitan powers and smaller Pacific Island nations (MSG 2013).

The MSG countries' potential for economic development contributes to their rising political power in the region. As Ron May stated, 'In terms of population, land and resources, the Melanesian countries—particularly Papua New Guinea—are the dominant forces in Pacific Island politics and economics, and have been largely responsible over recent years for the growing Chinese and European interest in the Pacific' (May 2011:1).[10] As a block, the MSG is already beginning to make its weight felt in regional politics, especially in countering the influence of Australia and New Zealand. This was vividly demonstrated when the MSG continued to support Fiji following its suspension from the Pacific Islands Forum and the Commonwealth and received diplomatic 'cold shoulders' and sanctions from Australia, New Zealand and the European Union following the 2006

9   While there is widespread support in the Pacific Islands Forum and the Melanesian Spearhead Group for an independence referendum in New Caledonia, the case of West Papua has proven more complicated. In the past five years, Indonesia has increased its presence in the region and asserted pressure on the MSG countries not to support West Papua independence. Vanuatu is the only country that has offered unwavering support for West Papuan independence.

10   Papua New Guinea's growing power in the Pacific Islands region is evident through its increasing influence in the Pacific Islands Forum and its emergence as an aid donor to smaller Pacific Island countries, including those in Melanesia (see Hayward-Jones and Cain 2014).

coup. In 2011, defying pressure from Australia and New Zealand, the MSG elected Fiji's coup leader and interim prime minister, Commodore Frank Bainimarama, as chair of the subregional organisation. This poured cold water on Australian and New Zealand attempts to use the Pacific Islands Forum to turn up the heat on Fiji. Papua New Guinea's foreign affairs minister told the 18th MSG Summit held in Fiji in March 2011:

> We must never lose sight of the fact that the MSG is a regional organisation that consists of nations who are an integral part of the Pacific. We also have an international persona that cannot be subjected to the dictates of nor subjected by instructional decisions of anybody or entity whether they be regional or international, including the Pacific Islands Forum and the Commonwealth (Loanakadavu 2011).

The MSG is the political and economic manifestation of the idea of Melanesia and the assertion of Melanesianism. It is the body in which this imagined community becomes real.

Wantokism

Wantokism is reinforced by a common pidgin language. The Melanesian subregion has a high language density with about 1,319 languages (Landweer and Unseth 2012).[11] But Melanesia also constitutes the largest population in Oceania—a little over 8 million people—who speak a common language other than English. Although there are slight differences between PNG *tok pisin,* Vanuatu *bislama* and Solomon Islands *pijin,* the people of these countries can carry on conversations entirely in pidgin. This is empowering and marks the pidgin-speaking Melanesian countries as *wantok* countries. Although Fijians do not speak pidgin, their interactions with other Melanesian countries through the Melanesian Spearhead Group have made them increasingly part of the *wantok* community. New Caledonia has long been viewed as part of the *wantok* community, although the Kanaks speak French, rather than pidgin.

---

11 'Language density' here refers to the number of languages in relation to land area. Lynn Landweer and Peter Unseth (2012) reported that there is a proportion of about 716 square kilometres per language in Melanesia, giving it the densest rate of languages in relation to land area on earth. This is almost three times as dense as Nigeria, a country famous for the high number of languages per land area.

This raises the importance of the concept of the *wantok* system or wantokism. Some scholars have often identified this as a factor contributing to poor governance and economic mismanagement. Francis Fukuyama (2008), for example, in writing about post-conflict and development challenges in Solomon Islands, argued that wantokism is one of the major obstacles to post-conflict development in Solomon Islands. Morgan Brigg, however, argued in favour of 'the innovative possibility of drawing on wantokism as a culturally recognised and valuable resource for addressing the current challenges faced by Solomon Islands' (2009:148). Brigg suggested that wantokism could be used to mobilise locally emerging national identities, that it does not necessarily drive corruption and that it could be utilised to facilitate governance at the local level. Gordon Nanau (2011) also discussed how the *wantok* system could potentially be an important network that enhances relationships both within and between countries. Wantokism or the *wantok* system could therefore be the foundation on which Melanesianism thrives.

Melamusic

Traditional and popular cultures are often used to reaffirm the idea of Melanesia. This is best demonstrated through the Melanesian Festival of Arts and Culture, a biannual event that started in 1998 and includes traditional and contemporary cultural and artistic expressions that assert and celebrate the idea of Melanesia. The 5th Melanesian Festival of Arts and Culture was held in Port Moresby from 30 June to 31 July 2014 and had the theme 'Celebrating Cultural Diversity'. This reaffirmed the notion of 'unity in diversity' mentioned earlier.

Music is another medium through which Melanesianism is often expressed and reaffirmed. Contemporary Melanesian music combines elements of indigenous musical styles with popular musical genres like reggae, hip-hop, folk and rock that have their origins elsewhere. It is the Melanesianisation of global music genres, similar to what Kalissa Alexeyeff (2004) has observed in the Cook Islands.

To illustrate this, let me refer to a few songs from Melanesian bands. The PNG band Haos Boi has a song titled 'Melanesia', with lyrics about 'living in paradise on this land I'll never give away' and about going to other places and realising that there is no place like PNG in Melanesia. The lyrics also affirm the values of Melanesian cultures and *tubuna pasin* (ways of the elders) (Haus Boi 2009). Popular US-based PNG-American musician Oshen (Jason Hershey), in his song also titled 'Melanesia', sings about 'Melanesia my Pacific Islands paradise'.[12] The lyrics combine PNG *tok pisin* and English and reflect the musician's experiences growing up in Papua New Guinea and valuing his connections with Melanesia (Oshen 2009). Fijian musician Jale Maraeau also celebrates his Melanesian connections with his song 'Melanesia', which he sings in the Fijian language (Maraeau 2010). A Solomon Islands band called Onetox (which is a play on the term *wantok* and the concept of wantokism), popular in Melanesia and Micronesia, celebrates the idea of Melanesia and reaffirms Melanesianism. Melanesian musicians have popularised pidgin, creating awareness about Melanesia in ways that transcend the negative representations. They also reach out to younger people who might have never read academic papers. Nowadays, Melanesian musicians are also using audio-visual technology and the Internet—especially YouTube and websites such as Papua New Guinea's www.CHMSupersound.com—to promote their music and positive images of both Melanesia as a place and Melanesians as peoples.

Challenges

It would be remiss of me to leave the reader thinking that Melanesia and Melanesianism are unproblematic. Melanesian places face enormous social, political and economic challenges, and Melanesianism continues to be contested, discussed and changed.

In spite of their resource endowment, Melanesian countries (especially Papua New Guinea and Solomon Islands) lag behind in social and economic development and are unlikely to meet their commitments under the Millennium Development Goals. The countries suffer from economic mismanagement and weak governance. In the last three decades, Melanesia was the site of some of the most violent conflicts that the Pacific Islands region has seen since the Second World War. These include the violence associated with the demands for decolonisation in New Caledonia in the1980s (Chappell 2013); the Bougainville crisis (Regan 1998); the Fiji coups (Tarte 2006); the Solomon Islands conflicts (Moore 2004); and the ongoing violence associated with the demands for

---

12   Oshen is a US-based musician who was born of American missionary parents and grew up in Papua New Guinea. He regularly visits Papua New Guinea and other Melanesian countries to seek inspiration for his music. He writes, performs and records songs in *tok pisin* and English.

independence in West Papua (King 2004). The law and order problems in Papua New Guinea are real and affect social and economic development (Dinnen 2001).

Apart from that, Melanesian unity has, in recent years, been tested by disagreements between countries on various issues.[13] In late 2010, a row between Fiji and Vanuatu ensued after the then Vanuatu prime minister Edward Natapei refused to give up the MSG chairmanship to the Fiji prime minister and coup leader Commodore Frank Bainimarama, arguing that 'there are basic fundamental principles and values of democracy and good governance that our organisation is built on, and we must continue to uphold them' (Radio Australia 13 July 2010). The issue was resolved after a change of government in Vanuatu and the election of Sato Kilman as prime minister; reconciliation between Fiji and Vanuatu took place in December 2010, sponsored by Solomon Islands. Bainimarama subsequently became MSG chair (Solomon Times Online 2010). In another incident, Fiji expressed disappointment with Papua New Guinea after the election of a PNG national, Meg Taylor, as secretary general of the Pacific Islands Forum Secretariat during the forum meeting in Palau in late July to early August 2014. On 4 August 2014, the *Fiji Sun* published a front-page article titled 'Backstabbed: PNG Betrays Fiji, MSG, and Derails Agreement to Back Tavola for Top Regional Job' (Delaibatiki 2014). The article argues that Papua New Guinea had reneged on an MSG agreement to support a Fijian, Kaliopate Tavola, for the position. The three finalists for the position—Meg Taylor (PNG), Kaliopate Tavola (Fiji) and Jimmie Rodgers (Solomon Islands)—were all from MSG countries. The third incident was the civil aviation row between Fiji and Solomon Islands that saw the two countries suspending rights for each other's national carriers, Fiji Airways and Solomon Airlines, to land in their respective countries (Pareti 2014a).[14]

---

13   At the centre of this is Fiji, a country entangled in the Melanesia/Polynesia binary. More importantly, since 2009, Fiji's regional and international diplomacy has been influenced by its attempts to re-establish its legitimacy following its marginalisation from the Pacific Islands Forum as a result of the 2006 coup.

14   By September 2014, when this paper was submitted, the civil aviation row between Fiji and Solomon Islands had not yet been resolved. There were calls for the prime ministers of the two countries to be involved to help resolve the impasse (Radio New Zealand International 2014). This was, however, resolved in January 2015, allowing Fiji Airways and Solomon Airlines to resume flights to Honiara and Nadi (Radio New Zealand International 2015).

The issue of West Papua has been a difficult one for the MSG. While Vanuatu has been consistent in its support for West Papuan independence, the other MSG countries insisted that it is an issue for Indonesia to resolve and have expressed their respect for Indonesian sovereignty. In July 2014, a membership application by the West Papua pro-independence movement, the West Papua National Coalition for Liberation, to join the MSG was blocked because MSG leaders asked for a more representative bid from West Papua. The issue has also caused tension among the MSG members because of the increasing influence of Indonesia, which was admitted as an MSG observer during Fiji's tenure as MSG chair (Pareti 2014b).

Such incidents could be perceived as evidence of Melanesian disunity, suggesting therefore that Melanesianism is a social and political façade and that the imagined Melanesian community is simply that—imagined. I would argue, however, that such incidents do not necessarily imply disunity or the absence of Melanesianism. Rather, they demonstrate the continuing discourse (*tok stori*) that embodies the idea of Melanesia and are part of the process of appropriating and owning the term Melanesia and asserting Melanesianism.

Conclusions

The early European mapping of Oceania, especially the tripartite division into Polynesia, Micronesia and Melanesia, was fraught with essentialist, racist and social-evolutionary elements. For centuries, Melanesia and Melanesians were generally represented in negative and derogatory ways in scholarly and popular discourses. That perspective has, to some extent, been internalised by Pacific Islanders, including Melanesians. It has also influenced contemporary representations of and relationships with Melanesia and Melanesians.

However, since the 1970s, Melanesians have appropriated the term Melanesia and used it for self-identification, turning it from a derogatory term to a positive one: a source of pride and self-identification. They have appropriated a colonial concept and deployed it as an instrument of empowerment. Since the late 1980s, they have used it to mobilise through subregional organisations such as the Melanesian Spearhead Group and events such as the Melanesian Festival of Arts and Culture. This has enabled Melanesian countries to assert political and economic power in Oceania and to redefine and re-present themselves.

This has engendered Melanesianism, a process and a discourse (*tok stori*) that celebrates the idea of Melanesian. They have subsequently created 'alter-natives' who are clawing their way out of the ignoble savage cocoon where they have been encased for centuries. Melanesians, armed with diverse and rich cultures, have captured the ignoble savage, turned it on its head and used the term Melanesia to establish their place in Oceania and beyond, creating new and empowering images.

Melanesians are asserting their 'place in the sun in Oceania'.

References

Adams, G. 2007. Strange Island: Pacific Tribesmen Come to Study Britain. *The Independent*, 8 September. independent.co.uk/news/uk/this-britain/strange-island-pacific-tribesmen-come-to-study-britain-5329192.html

Alexeyeff, K. 2004. Sea Breeze: Globalisation and Cook Islands Popular Music. *The Asia Pacific Journal of Anthropology* 5(2):145–58. doi.org/10.1080/1444221042000247689

Anderson, B. 1991. *Imagined Communities: Reflections on the Origin and Spread of Nationalism*. New York: Verso.

Anderson, W. 2003. *The Cultivation of Whiteness: Science, Health, and Racial Destiny in Australia*. New York: Basic Books.

Ballard, C. 2008. 'Oceanic Negroes': British Anthropology of Papuans, 1820–1869. In B. Douglas and C. Ballard (eds), *Foreign Bodies: Oceania and the Science of Race 1750–1940*. Canberra: ANU E Press, 157–201.

Bhabha, H. 1994. *The Location of Culture*. London: Routledge.

Brigg, M. 2009. Wantokism and State Building in the Solomon Islands: A Response to Fukuyama. *Pacific Economic Bulletin* 24(3):148–61.

Campbell, I.C. 2010. On the Historical Reality of Cultural Distinctions in Oceania. In J. Faberon and A. Hage (eds), *Mondes Océaniens: Études en l'honneur de Paul de Deckker*. Paris: L'Harmattan, 305–13.

Chappell, D. 2005. 'Africanization' of the Pacific: Blaming 'Others' for Disorder in the Periphery? *Comparative Studies in Society and History* 47(2):286–317. doi.org/10.1017/S0010417505000149

Chappell, D. 2013. *The Kanak Awakening: The Rise of Nationalism in New Caledonia*. Honolulu: Center for Pacific Islands Studies and University of Hawai'i Press. doi.org/10.21313/hawaii/9780824838188.001.0001

Connell, J. 1977. The Bougainville Connection: Changes in the Economic Context of Shell Money Production in Malaita. *Oceania* 48:81–100. doi.org/10.1002/j.1834-4461.1977.tb01326.x

Crocombe, R. 1976. *The Pacific Way: An Emerging Identity*. Suva: Lotu Pacifika.

Delaibatiki, N. 2014. Backstabbed: PNG Betrays Fiji, MSG, and Derails Agreement to Back Tavola for Top Regional Job. *Fiji Sun*, 4 August. fijisun.com.fj/2014/08/04/backstabbed/ (accessed 6 August 2014).

Dinnen, S. 2001. *Law and Order in a Weak State: Crime and Politics in Papua New Guinea*. Honolulu: Center for Pacific Islands Studies and University of Hawai'i Press.

Douglas, B. 1998. *Across the Great Divide: Journeys in History and Anthropology*. Amsterdam: Harwood Academic Publishers.

Douglas, B. 2008. Climate to Crania: Science and the Racialization of Human Difference. In B. Douglas and C. Ballard (eds), *Foreign Bodies: Oceania and the Science of Race 1750–1940*. Canberra: ANU E Press, 33–96. doi.org/10.22459/FB.11.2008.02

Douglas, B. 2010. Terra Australis to Oceania: Racial Geography in the 'Fifth Part of the World'. *Journal of Pacific History* 45(2):179–210. doi.org/10.1080/00223344.2010.501696

Douglas, B. 2011. Geography, Raciology, and the Naming of Oceania. *The Globe: Journal of Australia and New Zealand Map Society* 69:1–28.

d'Urville, J. 2003. On the Islands of the Great Ocean. Translated by I. Ollivier, A. De Biran and G. Clark. *Journal of Pacific History* 38(2):163–74. doi.org/10.1080/0022334032000120512

Duncan, R. and S. Chand 2002. The Economics of the 'Arc of Instability'. *Asian-Pacific Economic Literature* 16:1–9. doi.org/10.1111/1467-8411.t01-1-00001

Dutton, T. 2006. Language Contact and Change in Melanesia. In P. Bellwood, J. Fox, and D. Tryon (eds), *The Austronesians: Historical and Comparative Perspectives*. Canberra: ANU E Press, 207–28.

Ellingston, T. 2001. *The Myth of the Noble Savage*. Berkeley: University of California Press. doi.org/10.1525/california/9780520222687.001.0001

Fraenkel, J. 2004. The Coming Anarchy in Oceania? A Critique of the 'Africanisation of the South Pacific' Thesis. *Commonwealth and Comparative Politics* 42(1):1–34. doi.org/10.1080/14662040408565567

Fukuyama, F. 2008. State Building in the Solomon Islands. *Pacific Economic Bulletin* 23(3):18–34.

Grynberg, R. and T. Kabutaulaka 1995. The Political Economy of Melanesian Trade Integration. *Pacific Economic Bulletin* 10(2):48–60.

Guo, P. 2006. From Currency to Agency: Shell Money in Contemporary Langalanga, Solomon Islands. *Asia-Pacific Forum* 31:17–38.

Hall, S. 1997. The Spectacle of the 'Other'. In S. Hall (ed.), *Representation: Cultural Representations and Signifying Practices*. London: The Open University, 223–79.

Hau'ofa, E. 2008. Our Sea of Islands. In *We Are the Ocean: Selected Works*. Honolulu: University of Hawai'i Press.

Haus Boi 27 August 2009. *Melanesia*. Music video. YouTube. youtube.com/watch?v=zqyk7t2LvJA (accessed 23 July 2013).

Hayward-Jones, J. and T. Newton Cain 2014. Pacific Island Leadership: PNG Steps Up. *The Interpreter*, 28 August. Lowy Institute for International Policy. lowyinterpreter.org/post/2014/08/28/Pacific-island-leadership-PNG-steps-up.aspx (accessed 15 September 2014).

Howard, M. C. 1983. Vanuatu: The Myth of Melanesian Socialism. *Labour, Capital and Society* 16(2):176–203.

Howe, K. 1984. *Where the Waves Fall: A New South Sea Islands History from First Settlement to Colonial Rule*. Honolulu: Center for Pacific Islands Studies and University of Hawai'i Press.

Hviding, E. and G.M. White 2015. *Pacific* Alternatives*: Cultural Politics in Contemporary Oceania*. Herefordshire: Sean Kingston Publishing.

Jolly, M. 1997. From Point Venus to Bali Ha'i: Eroticism and Exoticism in Representations of the Pacific. In L. Manderson and M. Jolly (eds), *Sites of Desire, Economics of Pleasure: Sexualities in Asia and the Pacific*. Chicago: University of Chicago Press, 99–122.

Jolly, M. 2012. Women of the East, Women of the West: Region and Race, Gender and Sexuality on Cook's Voyages. In K. Fullagar (ed.), *The Atlantic World in the Antipodes: Effects and Transformations since the Eighteenth Century*. Newcastle upon Tyne: Cambridge Scholars Publishing, 2–32.

Kabutaulaka, T. 1997. I Am Not a Stupid Native: Decolonising Images and Imagination in Solomon Islands. In D. Denoon (ed.), *Emerging from Empire? Decolonisation in the Pacific*. Canberra: Division of Pacific and Asian History, Research School of Pacific and Asian Studies, The Australian National University, 165–71.

Khan, Z. and E. Po'ese 2010. Wansolwara: Academic Rues Islander Racism against Melanesians. *Pacific.Scoop*, 19 June, edited by Auckland University of Technology, Pacific Media Centre. pacific.scoop.co.nz/2010/06/wansolwara-academic-rues-islander-racism-against-melanesians/ (accessed 27 July 2013).

King, P. 2004. *West Papua and Indonesia since Suharto: Independence, Autonomy or Chaos?* Sydney: University of New South Wales Press Ltd.

Koroi, R. 2013. MSG Membership Crucial for Fiji. *Fiji Broadcasting Corporation*, 20 March. fbc.com.fj/fiji/8939/msg-membership-crucial-for-fiji

Lal, B.V. 1992. *Broken Waves: A History of the Fiji Islands in the Twentieth Century*. Honolulu: Center for Pacific Islands Studies and University of Hawai'i Press.

Landweer, M.L. and P. Unseth 2012. An Introduction to Language Use in Melanesia. *International Journal of the Sociology of Language* 214:1–3. doi.org/10.1515/ijsl-2012-0017

Latukefu, S. 1978. The Impact of South Sea Islands Missionaries on Melanesia. In J.A. Boutilier, D.T. Hughes, and S.W. Tiffany (eds), *Mission, Church and Sect in Oceania*. Ann Arbor: University of Michigan Press, 91–108.

Lawson, S. 2010. 'The Pacific Way' as Postcolonial Discourse: Towards a Reassessment. *Journal of Pacific History* 45(3):297–314. doi.org/10.1080/00223344.2010.530810

Lawson, S. 2013. 'Melanesia': The History and Politics of an Idea. *Journal of Pacific History* 48(1):1–22. doi.org/10.1080/00223344.2012.760839

Lilo, G.D. 2013. MSG: Our Place in the Sun in Oceania. Statement by the Prime Minister, Honourable Gordon Darcy Lilo, for the 19th MSG Leaders Summit, Plenary Session, Leaders Retreat, SPC, Noumea, 21 June. msgsec.info/images/PDF/21%20june%202013%20%20si%20pm%20statement%20at%20msg%20leaders%20plenary%20noumea.pdf (accessed 27 July 2013, site discontinued).

Loanakadavu, N. 2011. Don't Bow to Outside Pressure. *Fiji Sun*, 1 April. fijisun.com.fj/2011/03/31/dont-bow-to-outside-pressure/

London, J. 2003. *The Cruise of the Snark*. Washington, DC: National Geographic Society.

MacQueen, N. 1989. Sharpening the Spearhead: Subregionalism in Melanesia. *Pacific Studies* 12(2):33–52.

Malinowski, B. 1920. Kula: The Circulating Exchange of Valuables in Archipelagoes of Eastern New Guinea. *Man* 20:97–105. doi.org/10.2307/2840430

Mara, R.S.K. 1997. *The Pacific Way: A Memoir*. Honolulu: University of Hawai'i Press.

Maraeau, J. 2010. *Melanesia*. Music video. YouTube, 31 December. youtube.com/watch?v=LLaEIcYT8is (accessed 23 July 2014).

May, R.J. 2003. *'Arc of Instability'? Melanesia in the Early 2000s*. Macmillan Brown Centre for Pacific Studies Occasional Paper 4. Canberra: State, Society and Governance in Melanesia Project, The Australian National University; Christchurch: Macmillan Brown Centre for Pacific Studies, University of Canterbury.

May, R. 2011. *The Melanesian Spearhead Group: Testing Pacific Islands Solidarity*. Canberra: Australian Strategic Policy Institute.

Melanesian Spearhead Group (MSG) 2013. Melanesian Week program. USP Laucala Campus, 18–20 March. usp.ac.fj/MSG2013 (accessed 13 September 2014).

Meleisea, M. 1980. *O Tama Uli: Melanesians in Western Samoa*. Suva: Institute of Pacific Studies, University of the South Pacific.

Moore, C. 2004. *Happy Isles in Crisis: The Historical Causes for a Failing State in Solomon Islands, 1998–2004*. Canberra: Asia Pacific Press, The Australian National University.

Nanau, G.L. 2011. The Wantok System as a Socio-economic and Political Network in Melanesia. *OMNES: The Journal of Multicultural Society* 2(1):31–35. doi.org/10.15685/omnes.2011.06.2.1.31

Narokobi, B. and H. Olela 1980. *The Melanesian Way*. Port Moresby: Institute of Papua New Guinea Studies.

Narsey, W. 2013. The Pacific Sorely Needs Someone of the Stature of the Late Ratu Sir Kamisese Mara. *Fiji Today* Open Forum blog, 27 February. fijitoday.wordpress.com/2013/02/27/the-pacific-sorely-needs-someone-of-the-stature-of-the-late-ratu-sir-kamisese-mara/ (accessed 13 September 2014).

Oshen 2009. *Melanesia*. Music video. YouTube, 9 March. youtube.com/watch?v=lYdUMPYiFSM (accessed 23 July 2013).

Pareti, S. 2014a. Melanesian Spearhead Group's West Papua Meeting in Doubt. *Islands Business*, 6 February.

Pareti, S. 2014b. Fiji, Solomon Air War Worsens. *Islands Business*, 29 July.

Premdas, R. 1987. Melanesian Socialism: Vanuatu's Quest for Self-definition and Problems of Implementation. *Pacific Studies* 11(1):107–29.

Premdas, R., J. Steeves and P. Larmour 1984. The Western Breakaway Movement in the Solomon Islands. *Pacific Studies* 7(2):34–67.

Radio Australia 2010. Melanesian Spearhead Group Chair Defers Fiji Meet, 13 July.

Radio New Zealand International 2014. PMs Enter Fiji-Solomons Airline Impasse, 5 September. radionz.co.nz/international/pacific-news/253818/pms-enter-fiji-solomons-airline-impasse (accessed 13 September 2014).

Radio New Zealand International 2015. Fiji and Solomon Islands Flight Ban Lifted, 12 January. radionz.co.nz/international/pacific-news/263515/fiji-and-solomon-islands-flight-ban-lifted (accessed 13 January 2015).

Regan, A.J. 1998. Causes and Course of the Bougainville Conflict. *Journal of Pacific History* 33(3):269–85. doi.org/10.1080/00223349808572878

Reilly, B. 2000. The Africanisation of the South Pacific. *Australian Journal of International Affairs* 54(3):261–68. doi.org/10.1080/00049910020012552

Reynolds, H. 2005. *Nowhere People*. Sydney: Penguin Books.

Rochette, M. 2003. Dumont d'Urville's Phrenologist: Dumoutier and the Aesthetics of Races. Translated from French by I. Ollivier. *Journal of Pacific History* 38(2):251–68. doi.org/10.1080/0022334032000120567

Saemala, F. 1982. Solomon Islands: Uniting the Diversity. In R. Crocombe and A. Ali (eds), *Politics in Melanesia*. Suva: Institute of Pacific Islands Studies, University of the South Pacific, 62–81.

Sahlins, M. 1963. Poor Man, Rich Man, Big-Man, Chief: Political Types in Melanesia and Polynesia. *Comparative Studies in Societies and History* 5:285–303. doi.org/10.1017/S0010417500001729

Samoa Observer 2009. Daily newspaper. Apia, 23 March.

Scheyvens, R.A. 1988. Unity in Diversity? The Politics of Regionalism in Western Melanesia. BA thesis, Massey University.

Secretariat of the Pacific Community (SPC) 2014. National Minimum Development Indicators. spc.int/nmdi/ (accessed 9 October 2014).

Solomon Times Online 2010. Fiji Handed MSG Chairmanship, 16 December. solomontimes.com/news/fiji-handed-msg-chairmanship/5762 (accessed 14 August 2014).

Spurr, D. 1993. *The Rhetoric of Empire: Colonial Discourse in Journalism, Travel Writing, and Imperial Administration.* Durham: Duke University Press.

Stella, R.T. 2007. *Imagining the Other: The Representation of the Papua New Guinean Subject.* Honolulu: Center for Pacific Islands Studies and University of Hawai'i Press.

Tamaira, M. 2010. From Full Dusk to Full Task: Reimagining the 'Dusky Maiden' through the Visual Arts. *The Contemporary Pacific* 22:1–35. doi.org/10.1353/cp.0.0087

Tarte, S. 2009. Reflections on Fiji's 'Coup Culture'. In J. Fraenkel, S. Firth and B.V. Lal (eds), *The 2006 Military Takeover in Fiji: A Coup to End All Coups?* Canberra: ANU E Press, 409–14.

Tarte, S. 2014. Regionalism and Changing Regional Order in the Pacific Islands. *Asia and the Pacific Policy Studies* 1(2):312–24. doi.org/10.1002/app5.27

Tcherkézoff, S. 2003. A Long and Unfortunate Voyage towards the 'Invention' of the Melanesia/Polynesia Distinction 1595–1832. *Journal of Pacific History* 38(2):175–96.

Theroux, P. 1992. *The Happy Isles of Oceania: Paddling the Pacific.* New York: Ballatine Books.

Thomas, N. 1989. The Force of Ethnology: Origins and Significance of the Melanesian/ Polynesia Division. *Current Anthropology* 30 (1):27–41. doi.org/10.1086/203707

Thomas, N. 2012. 'We Are Still Papuans': A 2006 Interview with Epeli Hau'ofa. *The Contemporary Pacific* 24:120–32. doi.org/10.1353/cp.2012.0015

Wesley-Smith, T. 2008. Altered States: Regional Intervention and the Politics of State Failure in Oceania. In G. Fry and T. Kabutaulaka (eds), *Intervention and State-Building in the Pacific: The Political Legitimacy of 'Co-operative Intervention'.* Manchester: Manchester University Press, 37–53.

Wolfe, P. 2006. Settler Colonialism and the Elimination of the Native. *Journal of Genocide and Research* 8(4):387–409. doi.org/10.1080/14623520601056240

Ziegler, R. 1990. The Kula: Social Order, Barter, and Ceremonial Exchange. In M. Hechter, K. Opp, and R. Wippler (eds), *Social Institutions: Their Emergence, Maintenance, and Effects.* New York: Gruyter, Inc., 141–70.

11

Man versus Myth: The Life and Times of Ratu Sukuna

Steven Ratuva

Steven Ratuva: Personal Journey

I took leave from the University of the South Pacific (USP) in 2002–03 to take up a fellowship position in the State, Society and Governance in Melanesia program (now the Department of Pacific Affairs) at The Australian National University (ANU). I returned to USP to join the Pacific Institute of Advanced Studies in Development and Governance. Since then, and even after leaving USP for New Zealand, I have maintained a close relationship with ANU.

Ratuva, S. 2017. Man vs Myth: The Life and Times of Ratu Sukuna. *Fijian Studies: A Journal of Contemporary Fiji* 13:3–15.

Republished with the kind permission of the Fiji Institute of Applied Studies.

For generations, mythology about Ratu Sir Lala Vanuayaliyali Sukuna's superhuman imagery dominated Taukei political discourse. He was classed as a demigod of celestial proportions, a larger-than-life intellectual virtuosi whose wisdom and *mana* far outshone the most extraordinary of Fijian mortals. In a community where cosmological appeal helped frame world views, Ratu Sukuna was the human embodiment of deific perspicacity and a precious gift of the ancestral world to the Taukei community.

Superlative-laden poems, songs and dances were composed to deify the man, and generations of school kids (like myself) were reminded daily of the need to emulate Ratu Sukuna's grandiose behavioural dispositions and righteous moral virtues. Ratu Sukuna was seen by Fijians as the moral, political and intellectual icon of his era and revered almost the same way as Nelson Mandela or Martin Luther King, although their ideological orientations were far from similar. In an era where there was no media scrutiny of leaders, where chiefly leadership was considered divine and where oral tradition was the most accessible form of communication, Sukuna's phenomenal reputation established him as the undisputed *turaga vuku ka rai yawa* (profoundly wise and prophetically visionary) whose quintessence bordered on the supernatural.[1] How much of the man was myth and how much was real?

This essay revolves around Ratu Sukuna's biography *Ratu Sukuna: Soldier, Statesman, Man of Two Worlds* (1980) written by Deryck Scarr, a distinguished Australian scholar. The essay extends the analysis to deconstruct some of the myths about the great man by looking at his professional achievements, chiefly background, political power and the future implications and impacts of these on the Taukei community as well as Fijian society as a whole. In an unpretentious way, it is an attempt to provide an alternative framing of Ratu Sukuna, often concealed by the fascia of political myth-making.

Background

Born into a high-ranking chiefly status, Ratu Sukuna was no doubt the leading Fijian intellectual, statesman and leader of his era. His father, Ratu Joni Madraiwiwi, was a Roko Tui, a government administrative position (often given to high chiefs) that oversaw the governance of the *yasana* (provinces). Madraiwiwi's father, Ratu Kamisese Mara, was a flamboyant chief, whose womanising and political adventures in Fiji and Tonga became the stuff of legends.[2] His differences with a close relative, Ratu Seru Cakobau, one of Fiji's paramount warrior chiefs, led to his execution by hanging on 6 August 1859.[3] Although it would be too simplistic to

---

1   Taken from a Fijian poem written about Ratu Sukuna.
2   Fiji's first prime minister, Ratu Sir Kamisese Mara, was named after Ratu Sukuna's grandfather.
3   Ratu Cakobau styled himself Tui Viti (King of Fiji). He led the leading Fijian chiefs in ceding Fiji to Great Britian on 10 October 1874. He was often at war with neighbouring chiefdoms such as Rewa and was intolerant of those like Mara who despised his rule (see Waterhouse 1866).

call it vengeance, this incident, to some extent, whether consciously or subconsciously, shaped Ratu Sukuna's future political views and tactical manoeuvres by ensuring that Cakobau's direct descendants did not pose any more threat to his political ambitions and dominance. An example of this was his choice of Lauan chief Ratu Mara, his nephew and namesake of his slain grandfather, as his successor, rather than someone from his Cakobau paternal line. Another was when he appointed Joeli Ravai, a commoner, as Roko Tui Tailevu, ahead of a Bauan chief, which protocol at that time would have demanded. Ironically, high chiefs like Ratu Edward Cakobau had to carry the humiliation of working under someone of much lower sociocultural status as Ravai. The politics of Bau, often referred to as *verevaka-Bau* (Bauan conspiracy), was both manifest and latent and Sukuna played it strategically in subtle but effective ways.

Ratu Sukuna was born in 1888 and died in 1959. He studied at Wadham College, Oxford, and later at Middle Temple in London, and in 1921 graduated with a BA and an LLB degree. He was the first Taukei to be awarded a university degree. He became a barrister-at-law at the Middle Temple in London and returned to Fiji for an illustrious career in the civil service and politics. His Oxford studies were disrupted by the First World War. He joined the French Foreign Legion after being rejected by the British army on racial grounds. He was wounded and was later awarded the *Médaille militaire* (military medal) for bravery. Ratu Sukuna had a meteoric rise through the ranks of the colonial service as District Commissioner, Provincial Commissioner, Chairman of the Native Lands Commission, Secretary for Fijian Affairs and first Speaker of the legislative council. He helped set up the Native Land Trust Board to administer Taukei land and also made changes to legislations and regulations on Taukei governance. At a time when infrastructure and communication was at an embryonic stage of development, Ratu Sukuna walked for days across Viti Levu and Vanua Levu, the two largest islands in the Fiji group, and sailed hundreds of kilometres, criss-crossing the archipelago, for consultation on land ownership and registration as well as to extend the state's influence and control to remote parts of the country. Visitation to remote villages was seen as a gesture of *veivakaturagataki* (chiefliness) and *veinanumi* (deep concern) by someone so highly respected and esteemed and this fed into the community-wide exaltation as man of the people.

The Biography

Ratu Sukuna: Soldier, Statesman, Man of Two Worlds attempts to pull together the multiplicity of social, cultural, political, class and personal factors and forces that shaped Ratu Sukuna's privileged life as a Taukei chief, intellectual, colonial bureaucrat, soldier, politician and statesman. It is an official biography[4] of a man who put Fiji on the regional and global map through his academic achievements, military service and professional demeanour. Scarr fuses together real life experiences of Ratu Sukuna as well as of others he came into contact with, either directly or indirectly, using the historical narrative method. Although this method has often been criticised as positivistic because of its tendency to be merely descriptive of surface manifestations of a social phenomenon, it nevertheless helps to provide a broad account that can inform us of the occurring sequence of events.

It is thus not surprising that while the book provides a commendable historical narrative of Ratu Sukuna's life, it does not fully explore the deeper thoughts and philosophies of the man as well as his influence in modern day postcolonial Fiji. There is also no discussion of Ratu Sukuna's Oxford experience and how this shaped his future philosophy and ideology. Most biographies or autobiographies of important people emphasise the impact and influence of their university education on their professional lives, vision and achievements. This is a major drawback of the book. Nevertheless, Scarr's role as official biographer also extended to editing *The Three-Legged Stool: Selected Writings of Ratu Sir Lala Sukuna* (1984), a collection of speeches by Sukuna over the span of a number of years since his experiences in the First World War trench warfare as a member of the French Foreign Legion.

Contrary to mainstream assumptions, historical narrative method is neither 'objective' nor empirically irrefutable, but is based on implicit or explicit political, cultural and ideological conceptualisation, framing and interpretations of events and issues, articulated in a variety of historiographic texts and analysis. Some of these are imperial historiography, which deals with stories of colonial conquest and glory; nationalist history, which

---

4   Ratu Sukuna's biography committee was established by the Government of Fiji and comprised Ratu Sir Kamisese Mara (then prime minister), S. B. Patel, Sir Joshua Rabukawaqa, J. Thomson, L. G. Usher and Dr I. Q. Lasaqa (then secretary to Cabinet).

attempts to provide a local narrative of a group's struggle against external forces; elite history, which focuses more on the ruling classes; and social history, which is the story of ordinary people in everyday life.

Scarr's biography of Ratu Sukuna is an interesting mixture of imperial and elite histories. Much of the book revolves around Sukuna's life as a chief and his colonial experience. Ratu Sukuna loyally relished his chiefly position and thoroughly fetishised British imperial culture. The book weaves together Taukei chiefly narrative and British imperial discourse, intertwined in a rather odd symbiotic embrace and does not really reflect Fiji's social history. In fact ordinary Fijians, the very people who helped create the Sukuna myth, only exist as near invisible players in a class-based chess game.

The Chieftocratic Narrative

Fiji's chiefly aristocracy, which I refer to here as 'chieftocracy', was co-opted by the British colonial regime into their fold and in turn acted faithfully as trusted compradors between the colonial state and the Taukeis. Ratu Sukuna's father and later Ratu Sukuna himself, were part of this chieftocratic class, whose members were mostly related by blood and were drawn from loyal tribal groups that were considered politically reliable by the colonial state.[5] While Sukuna himself was an intelligent and visionary individual, his chiefly background and his father's connections to the colonial state provided him with the privilege and means for upward social mobility within the British imperial system. He was sent with his brother to study in Wanganui in New Zealand, and he later studied at Oxford. Ratu Sukuna's chiefly position and the British patronage of the chiefly system gave Ratu Sukuna a head start and commoners who were more academically inclined but did not have similar opportunities could not make it far enough and many remained disgruntled proletariats.

Because of his education, he stood out from other chiefs and was constantly pushing for the virtue of hard work by chiefs as a means of asserting their legitimacy. One of his most famous adages was *ai tutu sa sega ni itekiteki* (rank is not an ornament) to inspire chieftocrats to work hard and prove their worth as chiefs (Scarr 1980:125).

---

5   Those who resisted colonial rule were subdued in a systematic nationwide process of 'pacification' (see Nicole 2010; Ravuvu 1991).

Two or Multiple Worlds

In his busy life, Ratu Sukuna had to deal with a complex world, not just 'two worlds' as Scarr's title deceptively suggests. The British world at the time of Sukuna was not a homogenous one but a conglomeration of multiple subworlds consisting of the vestiges of the feudal order in the form of the royalty, sub-royals and lords who maintained unquestioned hegemony in the British class structure; an expanding corporate and merchant class that controlled the economy; an educated and globalised professional class; and a large working class. Britain was also a growing multiethnic society with people from other parts of the world, including the colonies, making the country their home. These were multiple worlds, not a single world. Fiji, although much smaller geographically and demographically, was equally complex. The Taukei community, contrary to what Scarr assumed, was far from homogenous given its vertical divisions between chiefs and commoners and divisions between regional and tribal groups based on distinctive locally defined identities and loyalties, a situation which Frances Stewart (2008) referred to as 'horizontal inequality'. A number of chiefdoms in the western and central Viti Levu attempted to assert their political and sociocultural distinctiveness by rebelling against the colonial state and the comprador chiefly class. The punitive response by the colonial state, supported by the comprador chiefs, in repressing the rebellion was to redefine the future dynamics and configuration of the Taukei community as the comprador chiefs exerted their hegemony and became the 'legitimate' representatives of the Taukei people. In addition to these complexities was the multicultural, multireligious and multiethnic nature of the colony. All in all, Ratu Sukuna had to deal with these diverse groups living in multiple worlds, often 'separated' from each other.

Ratu Sukuna's professional life oscillated between these groups, but he made it clear where his loyalty and identity was. Although he was a chief and saw himself as man of the people, he remained aloof from the ordinary people who treated him with ultimate veneration. While he enjoyed the rare privilege of entering whites-only private clubs in Suva as well as the feudal luxury of Boron House mansion (lent to him by European plantation owner James Boron), ordinary Taukeis were not even allowed into public bars and lived in villages in semi-subsistence poverty. While he enjoyed the fruits of his Oxford training, ordinary Taukeis were denied higher education. In short, Ratu Sukuna lived in his unique world while his own people lived in another.

One of the ironies of Ratu Sukuna's life was that, although loyally immersed into British education and cultural life, he was never fully accepted by the British as an equal. At most he would have been accepted as simply a very good imitator of British high-class accent and English eccentricity. The treatment he received by the colonial regime confirms that he was regarded as an honorary European. The colonial discriminatory laws that discouraged the Taukei from fraternising with whites did not apply to him (Norton 2013). Thus, for Scarr to simply state that Sukuna was a man living in 'two worlds' (British and Fijian) was an understatement and a simplistic assessment of the multiple worlds Sukuna encountered and engaged with in various ways and degrees.

Sukuna lived a life of paradoxes. The first paradox was his unrestrained accommodation of British high-class culture through his Oxford education, Oxford accent, acceptance of British decorations including a knighthood and living a life closer to that of the British than to a Fijian. But he was not fully accepted by the British who still saw him as an inferior native. In one instance, it was said that he overhead Juxon Barton, the colonial secretary, referring to him in a Suva club as a 'nigger' (Snow 1997:66).

The second paradox was that while he tried to fit into the Taukei community, he really did not gel in well because he was too well-educated and thus culturally too close to the British and ordinary Taukeis found it hard to approach him. Although Sukuna was not the highest ranked chief in Fiji, his British education and status within the colonial hierarchy easily overshadowed those of higher rank, such as the Vunivalu.

In a way, this position of relative autonomy from both groups worked well to his advantage because it enabled him to oscillate between the two groups with ease and to his convenience. He was able to see the Taukei situation from the British vantage point as well as see the British world from the prism of the Taukei. No one else around his time, British or Taukei, was able to do this effectively. Sukuna's utilitarian and adaptive disposition enabled him to use multipronged approaches to the multiple worlds he engaged with.

The 'Other' History

Because Scarr's biography is too narrowly focused on Ratu Sukuna himself and his immediate circle of kinship and colonial political actors, it provides minimal illumination on the socioeconomic, sociopolitical, sociocultural and cosmological situation of the Taukei community. It would have been a great opportunity to shed light on the dynamics on the ground, but this chance slipped by mutely. A significant historical moment would have been the contestation between competing Taukei ideologies. Around Ratu Sukuna's as well as his father's time, political persecution of dissenters such as Apolosi Ranawai, a commoner entrepreneur who wanted to introduce his vision for an alternative development path for Fijians though his *Viti Kabani* (Fiji company), was common.

As Robert Nicole argues, there was a deliberate and systematic cleansing of grassroots expressions of autonomous views and organisations through a collaborative punitive campaign between the comprador chiefs and British colonial state (Nicole 2010). Despite the façade of his humanitarian imagery, Sukuna continued with this 'pacification' process to subdue unconventional Taukei views and impose the comprador chiefly views as universally representing indigenous interests. This arbitrary imposition of dominant values, under the ideology of *i tovo vakaturaga* (chiefly way) became the accepted norm. Anyone who acted and behaved in contrary ways was considered 'un-Fijian'. This process, referred to by Pierre Bourdieu and J.C. Passeron (1990) as 'cultural arbitrary' became the ideological cornerstone of the so-called native policy. [6] Fijian administration was used by the colonial state and the comprador chiefs as cultural leverage to invalidate and silent dissenting views as well as represent and impose chiefly 'cultural arbitrary' as universal. Power (in both the Bourdieuan and Foucauldian senses) was reconfigured and reinstitutionalised to serve the interests of the comprador chiefly class and their allies and annihilated the political capacity of those who dared to resist. It was in the context of this process of 'internal colonialism' that Ratu Sukuna emerged and thrived as the undisputed champion of the Fijian cause. He benefited immensely from the pacification process of which his father was a champion. He was

---

6   This term refers to the arbitrary imposition of values and power, while concealing their historical, institutional and ideological sources through construction of universalised discourses, to justify intent.

a person born into the right family, at the right place and at the right time, and that gave him the advantage which catapulted him to uncontested heights.

The failure of the book to highlight the 'other' history of Fiji serves to reinforce the myths about Ratu Sukuna and provides an imbalanced view of Taukei history. If Ranawai's *Viti Kabani* had been allowed to carry out its entrepreneurial endeavours freely, Fijian history would have taken a different trajectory because the Taukei groundswell of support would have shifted, thus changing the balance of power considerably.

As is common in imperial and elite history, the narrative is very male focused—there is little gendered narrative. The colonial world is portrayed as a world of tough frontier men overshadowing the significance of women who only exist as behind-the-scene associates to provide social accompaniment and supporting cast to the husband in public occasions (Knapman 1986). Ratu Sukuna's wife, Lady Maraia, as she was fondly known, is simply treated as a feminine shadowy figure in the shadow of Ratu Sukuna. In the biography, there is only one 'substantial' (one page) encounter with the commoner woman who acted as confidant, wife and servant (Scarr 1980:83). Ratu Sukuna's decision not to marry a woman of high rank, although raised eyebrows and sent tsunamis of gossip around Fijian villages, was because of his desire to have a woman to serve him in his busy schedules rather than a woman who, due to high rank, may not be in a position to carry out daily domestic duties.

Taukei Voice: Impact on Fijian Politics

The biography does little to situate Ratu Sukuna's protectionist policies in the context of the broader colonial development strategies. Through Ratu Sukuna's reform of the Fijian administration in 1940, the paternalistic communal control of the Taukei was strengthened further and more deeply entrenched under the tutelage of chiefly hegemony. At one level, it was a system of social control and at another, according to Nayacakalou, it was:

> a system empowered by law to organise some of the activities of the Fijian people for their own social, economic and political development as well as for the preservation of their traditional way of life (1975:85).

Although Ratu Sukuna saw it as a means of creating a more 'autonomous' governance system for the Taukei and simultaneously weakening direct British control, the latent impact on the Taukei collective psyche was nevertheless that of gullible dependency on colonial institutions such as the Great Council of Chiefs, Fijian Affairs Board and Native Land Trust Board, on which Ratu Sukuna had considerable influence. The amplification of indirect rule through reform bolstered Ratu Sukuna's hegemonic clout further as the undisputed Taukei voice.

The reification of the colonial institutions above had long-lasting impact on Taukei self-perception. Originally inspired by Sir Arthur Gordon's social Darwinian orthodoxy of a dying culture that needed to be saved, the Taukeis were for paternalistic reasons cocooned further into a rigid subsistence life with little opening for social mobility, whether it be in commerce, education or professional life. Although there were semicommercial ventures that Ratu Sukuna encouraged, these operated within the ambit of communalism under the tutelage of chiefs who held supervisory positions as development officers (Ratuva 2013). Some of these ventures included the setting up of the cooperative movement (*Soqosoqo Cokovata ni Veivoli*) under the Co-operative Ordinance of 1947; the Fijian Banana Venture in 1950; the Fijian Development Fund (*Lavo Musuki in Veivakatorocaketaki*) by Ordinance No. 14 of 1951; the creation of economic development officer positions in 1954 (following the incorporation of economic development agenda into the Fijian administration); and more rigid control of the *galala* (independent farming) system (Spate 1959).

Moreover, although he did not have any training in development the same way as Ratu Mara (who studied at the London School of Economics after Oxford), he was still keen on grassroots socioeconomic development, even if his ideas on this were rudimentary:

> the village community, more especially the large village community, being of native growth and an attempt to solve the local problems of life in its own way, is the most natural, the most convenient and cheapest unit of administration … The village system has failed economically not from any inherent weakness nor from maladministration. It has failed to improve materially the life of the people because of the lack of markets for its crops (Scarr 1980:140).

Education was only available to selected chiefs like Sukuna in the beginning, and to other chiefs later, while the majority of the Taukei were deprived of western education and were expected to be loyally subservient to the whims of the colonial and traditional masters. While Ratu Sukuna encouraged technical training for basic skills like carpentry, he was weary of those with higher educational qualification and warned against the potentially subversive influence of the commoner intelligentsia who would be bent on 'undermining and confusing authority to their own ends' (Scarr 1980:146). Commoner scholars such as Ravuama Vunivalu and later Dr Rusiate Nayacakalou did not get any government support and had to rely on private sponsorship by Morris Hedstroms for overseas university training.

Rather than nurturing Taukei potential for economic advancement and self-empowerment, the incubation and domesticating strategy by Ratu Sukuna undermined their social mobility at a time when other ethnic groups were making headway into commerce, education and professional positions. Subsequently, when the rigid system of control was lifted and opportunities began to open up after the 1960s reform recommended by Nayacakalou, the Taukeis found themselves lagging behind other ethnic groups in the areas of commerce, education and professional achievement. This bred grievances that were later articulated in more open ethnonationalist expressions and violence. Near desperate affirmative action measures were put in place to address some of the more overt manifestations of ethnic disparity but with mixed success (Ratuva 2013). One of the forgotten ironies of Ratu Sukuna's legacies was that his great visions and policies to 'protect' the Taukei had the effect of disempowering and undermining their potential for progress. The responsibility was left with Ratu Sir Kamisese Mara, whom Ratu Sukuna groomed as successor, to disentangle and address the multidimensional socioeconomic and sociopolitical problems nurtured under the Sukuna reign. The obsession with the mythical character of Ratu Sukuna has blinded us from seeing the implications of his social reforms and policies.

While it is unfair to blame Ratu Sukuna for later problems, the circumstances at the time, often invoked by fear of perceived Indo-Fijian political threat and compounded by the British paternalistic colonial designs of making natives politically and culturally submissive, may have provided impetus to his protectionist vision. Nevertheless, rather than emancipating the Taukei from the excesses of colonial domestication, Ratu Sukuna's ideas and policies simply reinforced colonial hegemony.

Colonial Fiji was an apartheid-type colonial state with Jim Crow–type laws that kept non-whites away from public spaces such as swimming pools, private clubs and other European-designated places; fraternisation with 'natives' was a social sin to be avoided.

Ratu Sukuna was no Gandhi to fight off the scourge of colonialism nor a Martin Luther King to clamour for civil rights; he was intent on assimilating the Taukei into the British legal and political regime while making himself their dominant voice within the rubric of the colonial political paradigm. This was reflected in his scorn for democratic elections and preference for the system of nomination of Taukei representatives for legislative council membership. Unlike the fully fledged democratic election that the Indo-Fijians had demanded and achieved by 1931, the system of nomination acted as a social control mechanism that ensured that no Taukei with unwanted political beliefs would emerge and thus pose potential threat to Sukuna's dominance. Scarr observed that in the legislative council:

> when Indian members formally pressed for political equality between three races, Ratu Sukuna, again claiming to speak for all Fijians, had emphasised that they felt they were well-treated under the present regime, and said they looked for the next two, three, even four generations to European leadership. He had no wish to see the communal division broken down, as Indian politicians claimed to want, though he would happily eat curry with anyone (1980:110).

In Sukuna's own words:

> We have come to the parting of ways and looking ahead in the light not only of our own interests but also of those to whom we handed over this country, we choose, with the full support of native conservative and liberal opinion, the system of nomination believing that along this road and along it alone, the principal of trusteeship for the Fijian race can be preserved and the paramountcy of native interests secured (Fiji Legislative Council 1935).

Sukuna had virtually uncontested control over the Taukei voice, Taukei aspiration and Taukei vision for the future. He favoured slow reforms and was always wary of Taukei nationalists whose ideologies ran counter to the dominant chiefly discourse of respectful and subservient engagement with the colonialists (see Norton 2013).

The denial of democratic rights by the colonial state and Ratu Sukuna had profound implications on Taukei future attitudes towards democracy in the context of Fiji's changing multiethnic society. Even after universal suffrage, which allowed Taukeis to vote for the first time in 1965, there was still a perception that Fiji's democratic system was only legitimate as long as it continued to serve the political aphorism of 'paramountcy of Taukei interest'. Although this view continued to be contested and evolved incessantly over the years, the suspicion of democracy being against Taukei interest prevailed in various degrees, as manifested publicly during the 1987 and 2000 ethnonationalist coups.

Furthermore, as Scarr suggested, Ratu Sukuna was not too keen on multiculturalism, perhaps a learnt behaviour from the British, and saw intercultural engagement in simplistic terms such as eating curry together with Indo-Fijians. This is despite the fact that he had Indo-Fijian friends such as Gujarati lawyer S. B. Patel, who had once worked with Mahatma Gandhi before migrating to Fiji where he became a significant player in politics. Ratu Sukuna's position relating to other ethnic groups may have also influenced ordinary Taukeis he came into contact with and possibly inspired some ethnonationalist feelings over the years in explicit or subtle ways. However, there were other forces shaping the lives of the Taukei and many pursued their daily lives with minimal influence by Ratu Sukuna. Amongst these were the emerging Taukei proletariat, such as the unionised dockworkers and mineworkers, whose bread-and-butter concerns and loyalty to their class interests outweighed Ratu Sukuna's cultural and political appeal.

Concluding Remarks

As far as the Taukei community was concerned, Ratu Sukuna was the lighthouse that illuminated history in an awe-inspiring way. He was the model personality to be emulated, the holder of immeasurable wisdom and guiding beacon for Fiji's future. Indeed, his concerns and deeds were beyond reproach at his time. But with historical hindsight, questions need to be asked about the wisdom and implications of some of his ideas and policies.

The protectionist policies he so religiously cherished worked well during his era to maintain a sense of communal solidarity and group security in the colonial environment. The future implications of these on the Taukei themselves and the country as a whole need serious scrutiny. Some of these policies shackled the Taukei further into colonial servitude and feeble reliance on colonial institutions such as the Great Council of Chiefs and Fijian Affairs Board. By the time of independence, the Taukeis continued to rely on these to determine their future trajectory. The strict communal system Ratu Sukuna cherished helped undermine Taukei innovation and empowerment and was partly responsible for their lack of progress in education, commerce and professional endeavours. The system of nomination Ratu Sukuna vehemently advocated also nurtured a distrust in democracy and modernity. These factors collectively fuelled Taukei grievances in the postcolonial era and contributed to public and violent expressions of ethnonationalism.

Despite these, Ratu Sukuna's legacy will continue to linger and his historical profile will not be easy to overshadow, not in the foreseeable future. The man may have passed on but the myth liveth!

References

Bourdieu, P. and J.-C. Passeron 1990. *Reproduction in Education, Society and Culture*. New Delhi: Sage Publications.

Fiji Legislative Council 1935. *Legislative Council Debates*, 6 November. Suva: Government Printer.

Knapman, C. 1986. *White Women of Fiji 1835–1930: The Ruin of Empire?* St Lucia: University of Queensland Press.

Nayacakalou, R.R. 1975. *Leadership in Fiji*. Melbourne: Oxford University Press.

Nicole, R. 2010. *Disturbing History: Resistance in Early Colonial Fiji*. Honolulu: University of Hawai'i Press.

Norton, R. 2013. Averting 'Irresponsible Nationalism': Political Origins of Ratu Sukuna's Fijian Administration. *Journal of Pacific History* 48(4):409–28. doi.org/10.1080/00223344.2013.852706

Ratuva, S. 2013. *Politics of Preferential Development: Trans-global Study of Affirmative Action and Ethnic Politics in Fiji, Malaysia and South Africa*. Canberra: ANU E Press. doi.org/10.22459/PPD.07.2013

Ravuvu, A. 1991. *The Façade of Democracy: Fijian Struggles for Political Control, 1830–1878*. Suva: Reader Publishing House.

Scarr, D. 1980. *Ratu Sukuna: Soldier, Statesman, Man of Two Worlds*. London: Macmillan Education.

Scarr, D. (ed.) 1984. *The Three-Legged Stool: Selected Writings of Ratu Sir Lala Sukuna*. London: Macmillan Education.

Snow, P. 1997. *Years of Hope: Cambridge, Colonial Administrator in the South Seas, and Cricket*. London: Radcliffe Press.

Spate, O.H.K. 1959. *The Fijian People: Economic Problems and Prospects*. A Report for the Legislative Council of Fiji, Council Paper No. 13. Suva: Government Press.

Stewart, F. 2008. Horizontal Inequalities and Conflict: An Introduction and Some Hypotheses. In F. Stewart (ed.), *Horizontal Inequalities and Conflict: Understanding Group Violence in Multiethnic Societies*. Hampshire: Palgrave Macmillan, 3–24. doi.org/10.1057/9780230582729

Waterhouse, J. 1866. *The King and People of Fiji*. London: Wesleyan Conference Office.

12

All Saints' Primary, Labasa

Christine Weir

Christine Weir: Personal Journey

I studied history at the University of Cambridge in the United Kingdom and then trained as a history teacher. In 1976, I accompanied my husband Tony to the University of the South Pacific (USP) in Fiji, where he was employed as a lecturer in physics, and for eight years I taught in Fiji schools, learned about Pacific history and did some tutoring at USP in social science and education. This experience started my interest in Pacific history and anthropology and, during the following years while resident in Canberra, I returned to study at The Australian National University (ANU), completing a master's degree in anthropology with a focus on the Pacific.

I then embarked on a PhD in Pacific history at ANU (2003) on missionary ideas about work in Fiji and Solomon Islands. During this time, I was supervised by Donald Denoon, Bronwen Douglas and Brij Lal, and worked alongside Morgan Tuimaleali'ifano and Kambati Uriam, who were to become colleagues at USP. In 2007 I returned to Fiji to take up the position of lecturer in history at USP, which I held for seven years, teaching a variety of courses in Pacific and world history, supervising several research students, and researching colonial and contemporary Christianity in the Pacific. Since returning to Canberra in 2014, I have continued my research as an honorary lecturer in the College of Asia and the Pacific at ANU, and am currently working on a biography of Bishop Jabez Bryce, the first indigenous bishop of Polynesia.

Weir, C. 2004. All Saints' Primary, Labasa. In B.V. Lal (ed.), *Bittersweet: The Indo-Fijian Experience*. Canberra: Pandanus Books, 225–37.

Republished with the kind permission of ANU Press.

In the middle of 1958, All Saints' Anglican School in Labasa welcomed a series of visitors, all of whom recorded their impressions in the school's logbook.[1] Bruce McCall, secretary of the Australian (Anglican) Board of Missions (the school's sponsors), described the school as 'very impressive'; Mr G. William of the Colonial Office commented on the 'opportunities for lively and creative activity'; and the Indian High Commissioner thought 'the discipline excellent and the girls and boys neatly dressed and well behaved … they looked intelligent'. At the end of the year, 18 boys were accepted from class eight into secondary schools and the headmaster, Reverend K. Appasamy, could reflect on a highly successful year.

And, indeed, the All Saints' School logbooks of the 1950s and 1960s, now filmed by the Pacific Manuscripts Bureau in Canberra and available to researchers, show a thriving school. With a constant enrolment of about 400 students in classes one to eight, All Saints' was one of the largest schools in the district. It had a boarding hostel for about 20 boys, but most of the students were from the town and immediate surrounds— the children of shopkeepers, tradesmen and civil servants. With fees of 30 shillings a term,[2] it was beyond the financial reach of most small agriculturalists. This was acknowledged by the governing board, but there was felt to be little alternative if the school was to stay afloat financially. Reverend Appasamy commented in 1956, 'What we lose in quantity may be balanced in quality'. He noted with approval that in July 1957, 75 per cent of the boys were wearing shoes, clearly a marker of affluence. While it had a majority of Indo-Fijian students, All Saints' School offered the relatively rare experience of a multiracial education, with about 50–60 Fijian and part-European students, according to the few figures available of the racial composition of the school. Hindi and Fijian were taught alongside English. The school was coeducational in the first three

---

1   The All Saints' School logbooks for 1924–39 and 1952–70 have been filmed by the Pacific Manuscripts Bureau (PMB), The Australian National University, and are to be found at PMB 430. The information in this chapter, unless otherwise indicated, comes from these logbooks.
2   This was the figure in 1956. Boarding fees were then £10 a term, or £7 plus 60 pounds (27.2 kg) of rice.

years, the girls (or at least those whose parents allowed them to continue, a proportion that grew over the period) then going mostly to St Mary's Anglican School, two miles away.

It was a lively school. The school's scout troop went on regular hikes and camps: in 1952, they climbed the peak of Bukalevu in March and went on a 'tramping and island camp' in June. In 1958, and in later years, the school troop won the local proficiency challenge. There was a Brownie pack for the young girls. The school regularly displayed produce at the Young Farmers' Club Shows, sometimes winning prizes. The grounds were planted with shrubs and trees, for beauty as well as an agricultural exercise. In 1957, the boys planted 500 sticks of cassava, 100 pineapple plants and a row of banana trees, and constructed a pergola with creepers to camouflage the septic tank, while the next year, under Augustine Sitaram's guidance, senior boys planted a row of trees for Arbor Day. Soccer and athletics were popular activities, All Saints' soccer team proving particularly successful in the early 1950s, when one of their teachers, Mohammed Yasim Khan, also played for the Labasa soccer team. The students were regularly reminded of the empire and their loyalties to it. Empire Day school gatherings were addressed by the District Officer. Students attended films entitled *The Funeral of George VI*, *Royal Destiny* and *A Queen is Crowned*. Year groups went on end-of-year picnics to Malau, Batiri or the Three Sisters. Nurses and doctors visited the school to inspect teeth—finding in the process a distressing number of dental caries—and to inoculate children against tuberculosis and typhoid, and, by the mid-1960s, against the scourge of polio. All in all, this was a thriving and successful school.

And it was a Christian school, following a long tradition of mission involvement in the education of children. When the Methodists, the first Christian missionaries in Fiji, started village education, it was primarily to make their converts literate and able to read the Bible. Alongside this was the aim of 'civilising' Fijians and introducing 'British values'. Christianity and literacy had been readily adopted by Fijians and the small schools started by the Methodists soon became part of the village scene. Most were taken over by village committees during the 1930s, while the Methodist missions maintained responsibility for teacher training at Davuilevu, and at some secondary and higher elementary schools, including Lelean Memorial School for boys, Ballantine Memorial School for girls, Lautoka Boys' School and Jasper Williams School for girls.

In relation to the Indo-Fijians, the situation was different. Until 1901, the Methodist Church paid little attention to the *girmitiyas*, the indentured Indians. Although the Indian catechist John Williams arrived in 1892, the Mission Board in Sydney saw evangelising *girmitiyas* as low on their list of priorities.[3] What concerned missionaries was the effect of Indians on their Fijian converts who had accepted Christianity at the hands of the Methodists, but who were as yet 'babes in the faith', had not reached Christian maturity and could be easily subverted by 'evil'. The proprietorial attitude of Methodist missions towards 'their' Fijian converts is clear in the 1910 comment of a Methodist visitor to Fiji, Mr Morley, 'If we do not Christianise these Indians, they will Paganise our Fijians'. While those who worked with Indians—particularly Hannah Dudley, John Burton and Richard Piper—saw their conversion as an end in itself, the view that it was merely a means to the end of preserving the faith of Fijian Christians was prevalent among Methodists.

Education among Indo-Fijians was initially, as among Fijians, an aid to conversion and to enable the reading of the scriptures. But few conversions took place and Indians showed little interest in Christianity. Evangelism proved fruitless and frustrating; indeed, so frustrating that in 1919 the Methodists handed over their Indian work on Vanua Levu to the Anglicans and concentrated their efforts on Viti Levu. This explains why the non-Catholic Christian schools for Indo-Fijians in Labasa were run by the Anglicans; All Saints' School was started in 1924 by Miss Irene Cobb, an Australian lay missionary. The *girmitiyas*, however, while resisting attempts to convert them to Christianity, showed great interest in the education missions were offering. This remained true throughout the 20th century. Although the *girmitiyas* recognised early that education was their best means of economic advancement, indeed, even of survival, the colonial government was not much interested in providing such education.

Until the 1918 establishment of the (government-run) Natabua Indian School, mission education was the only education available to Indians and it remained important, especially at the higher grades. In 1944, 63 per cent of those Indian children who were in education attended committee schools, 7 per cent government schools and 30 per cent

---

3   For details of the Methodist catechists, teachers and missionaries to the Indo-Fijians, see Sidal 1997; Thornley 1974; Wood 1978.

Christian mission schools (Stephens 1944:12).[4] While the absolute number of Indo-Fijian children in school was higher in the 1950s, the proportions in the various types of school remained fairly constant. Some writers have suggested that Indians resisted mission education; it seems rather that, though they might have preferred it to be run by groups other than Christian missions, they welcomed any high-quality education. As the Anglican priest C. W. Whonsbon-Aston put it: 'The Indian of today in Fiji … is healthy and eager for education and filled with the growing pains of emancipation'.[5]

Clearly, Indians worked hard to establish their committee schools in the 1920s and 1930s, they welcomed the Arya Samaj and Sanatan schools, and advocated the establishment of more government schools. Indian opinion welcomed the Stephens Report (1944), which suggested gradually abolishing the 'voluntary system' (whereby the colonial government gave grants-in-aid to mission and committee schools rather than establishing their own schools). This would have secularised education and, Stephens envisaged, would have encouraged multiracial schools (Stephens 1944:58–60).[6] But when the government rejected most of Stephens' recommendations, since it calculated the voluntary system was cheaper, there was little Indians could do about it. In practice, any high-quality education was accepted, and most mission education was academically good. The Christian schools, such as Marist Brothers High School, Suva, and other Catholic schools, the Methodist schools in Lautoka and Suva, and the Anglican schools on Vanua Levu, were always oversubscribed.

From the point of view of the missions—Methodist, Catholic and Anglican—church schools had a twofold purpose: they were a way to expose students to Christianity in the hope that they might convert, and they were in themselves a service to the community. The hope of conversion was always present, but the very low success rate meant that arguments were developed in justification of Christian schools that acknowledged that most students were—and remained—non-Christian. These centred on the 'moral uplift' that Christian education offered to all who were exposed to it. Few in Fiji expressed the issue as succinctly as the Education Committee of the World Missionary Conference (held in Edinburgh

---

4   For further discussion of Indo-Fijian educational demands and provision, see Lal 1992:83–86, 102–07, 158–63.

5   *ABM Review* 1953:151 (the monthly journal of the Australian Board of Missions).

6   The Stephens report is also discussed in Whitehead 1978: Chapters 4 and 5.

in 1910) when discussing Christian education in India, where the issues were similar. In India and Ceylon, Christian mission schools and colleges were maintained not just for the education of converts; indeed, it was a matter of concern that few Christian children were in school. Rather, there was a perceived need to change general attitudes in India—what was called the 'leavening' or diffusion principle. The report writers put it this way:

> So far as the ideals of 'the new India' are Christian or semi-Christian; so far as the conceptions of Divine Fatherhood and human brotherhood, and Christian moral ideals, have come to prevail; so far as caste distinctions have weakened and the true position of women recognised; so far as prejudice against Christ and Christianity has been broken down, it is to the education given in mission schools and colleges that a great part of this good result is attributed (World Missionary Conference 1910:11).

It was acknowledged that most pupils in Christian schools and colleges were not Christian, but missionaries hoped that increased 'spiritual influence' might lead to a greater moral awareness and concern for other people, which would lead to a better society.

The same ideas can be seen at All Saints'. In 1939, the headmaster of All Saints', Rev. R. L. Crampton, wrote in the logbook:

> As a teacher one is aware of the great responsibility involved in preparing young Indians to take their places in the community of this Colony. Firmly believing that our Lord's teaching is the best foundation in life, we endeavour to hand on this teaching.

Or, as Canon W. G. Thomas, in a general article on Fiji for an Australian audience, wrote:

> In [the Labasa Anglican schools] many hundreds of young men and women have been helped to become good and useful citizens and the influence and example of dedicated mission teachers have helped to shape their characters (1954:140).

But the argument for church schools could be developed beyond the 'leavening principle'. During the 1920s, influenced in part by the principles behind the Covenant of the League of Nations, Christian scholars began to argue that for moral and humanitarian reasons they should prepare 'less-developed peoples' for self-government and the end of colonialism, primarily through education. In other words, assisting the secular education of Pacific Island peoples could be seen as a Christian duty. In Fiji, there were two aspects of education in which the missions believed they possessed unique insights rooted in Christian ideals: in running multiracial institutions and in the education of girls. Most mission schools, on principle, at least attempted to attract students from varying ethnic backgrounds, though language difficulties could make this difficult at the primary level. Christian missions had long regarded the respectful treatment and advancement of women—in theory, at least— to be a marker of western Christian culture. Methodists and Catholics emphasised the importance of girls' education and the Methodists prided themselves on the success of Dudley House School, Suva, and Jasper Williams School, Lautoka, in attracting and educating Indian girls.

The Anglican mission felt it important that All Saints' remain a multiracial school, even with a large Indo-Fijian majority, and made considerable efforts to have one Fijian teacher on the staff, teaching the Fijian language, even though the turnover in such a position was high. While it was predominantly a boys' school, the acceptance of girls in All Saints' junior classes was an attempt to encourage girls' education, for it was believed that parents would be more likely to let their girls go to school if they could accompany their brothers while small. The Anglican mission took as much care and effort over staffing and equipping St Mary's Girls' School as it did for All Saints'. Indeed, missionary teachers were employed at St Mary's for considerably longer than at All Saints'.

It was, however, debatable just how effective schools were as evangelistic institutions. In the 1940s, the Methodists considered just this issue. A questionnaire was sent out from the Methodist office in Sydney to all involved in the Indian mission, attempting to ascertain why there were so few conversions among Indo-Fijians. Reasons suggested by missionaries for the lack of interest in Christianity included the growth of Indian nationalism, the arrogance of European missionaries, resulting in perceived discrimination against Indians, the growth of the Arya Samaj, and disunity and bickering among Indian Christians. Questions were also asked about the effectiveness in evangelism of the schools. Stanley Andrews suggested that 'the influence of Christian teaching and example is remarkable … no one leaves hostile to Christianity'.[7] Ivy Lapthorne commented on 'the educated, happy children in the schools' and especially noted the number of girls undertaking nursing courses after Christian

---

7 The questionnaire and the responses to it are in the Methodist Overseas Mission archives at the Mitchell Library, Sydney.

education. Norman Wright saw schools as having 'the advantage of systematic Christian teaching and the opportunity to show the poverty and inadequacy of the old thought'. But he also noted how rare conversions were: between 1922 and 1944, 1,021 boys had passed through Lautoka Boys' School, but only 24 were baptised as a result of their Christian education there.

In general, the missionaries advocated more direct evangelism—more use of public preaching, home visiting and systematic biblical study. Ramsay Deoki pointed out that most Indian Christians, certainly 'the most satisfactory and staunchest supporters of our work', had converted after direct evangelism rather than through schools. In general, direct evangelism was increased by the Methodists in the 1940s and 1950s. No new Indian schools were opened, though existing ones developed their secondary classes and two of the existing schools were handed over to committee control in the 1950s. Established schools seem to have accepted that while conversions were unlikely, in the words of A. Harold Wood, 'the schools were respected in the community for their integrity of purpose and the quality of their teaching' (1978 2:52). While the Methodists may have come to this conclusion by the 1950s, the Anglicans, later in the field, were still struggling to assess the effectiveness of church schools; in many ways, the story of the 1950s and 1960s at All Saints' is the story of the Anglicans coming to terms with the limitations of schools as evangelistic institutions.

The tension between church schools as tools for evangelism and as preparation for secular citizenship showed itself over two practical issues: Christian staff recruitment and religious holidays. Until 1960, the head teacher of All Saints' was a missionary, usually a European priest, though from 1953 to 1955 a New Zealand woman missionary, Margaret Young, was in charge, and, from 1956 to 1959, the head was Indian-born, US-educated Reverend K. Appasamy. He was a Fellow of the Royal Geographic Society with degrees from Hartford and Boston and it is not clear why he was in Labasa; the Indian High Commissioner certainly thought he was wasting his time in a provincial primary school. Head teachers aimed to have Christian staff, but scarcity made this difficult. In most years, only three or four members of staff were Christian, though others, such as R. Chellappa Gouden, were married to Christians (ABM 1956:76). As Reverend Wallace commented in 1952, 'The only way to get a Christian staff is to have our own Christian boys stay on as recognised teachers [i.e. as unqualified teachers]'. He readily took on

'Jairam, who has recently been baptised' and who had just left class eight. There was competition between Christian schools for the few qualified Christian teachers. Jagdish Ram Sahay, a new teacher at All Saints' in 1961, left after two years to gain wider experience with the Methodists and became head teacher of Dudley High School in the late 1970s.

Since most students and staff were non-Christians, their desire to celebrate their own religious holidays became a contentious issue. A pragmatic man, Wallace closed the school in 1952 for the Holi festival and for Ram Lila. When Muslim teachers and students asked for leave for Eid, they were told that 'they were free to join in the worship of the festival and should count that their duty instead of coming to school, but that those who did not attend the festival should go to school'. Miss Young found herself in conflict with her staff when she tried to enforce only Christian holidays. She disapproved of teachers taking a day off for Holi, and when they requested leave for Diwali she refused, telling them it was not a school holiday. Three members of staff took absence regardless and were reported to the Education Officer. Appasamy was more pragmatic; faced with the choice of making Diwali or All Saints' Day (1 November) a school holiday, he chose Diwali because, he wrote, if he chose All Saints' Day most of the school would be absent on Diwali anyway and more time would be wasted.

In 1960, the first local, Jwala Prasad Singh, was appointed as headmaster. A Christian, he was married to Ethel, daughter of Methodist minister Ishwari Prasad, and they had both taught at All Saints' since 1947. In 1953, Jwala Singh was sponsored by the Anglicans to go to Auckland University for a year's study at undergraduate level and, on return, he gained promotion to grade one teacher. As headmaster from 1960 to 1962, he appears to have run a successful school. The government inspectors praised his administration, and visiting teacher Moti Lal wrote, 'A very good start has been made by the present Head Master. Discipline has vastly improved'. Secondary entrance results improved from eight passes in 1960 to 13 in 1961 and 20 in 1962. In practice, places at the less prestigious secondary schools were available to some children who had completed class eight but who had failed to pass all subjects in the entrance examination, so the numbers continuing on to secondary schools were somewhat higher. No fewer than four visiting clerics wrote glowing reports of the school in the logbook between September and December 1962. Singh ran his school with moderation and pragmatism; there were few disputes over religious matters. Indeed, the school was conforming to the government's expectations of providing good education through grants to voluntary groups. Missions and school committees acted as suppliers of education to, and in close association with, the colonial government, with regular visits from government inspectors, agricultural advisors and health workers.

Jwala Prasad Singh's successor, Reverend Peter Thirlwell, aimed to change the focus of the school, apparently reacting against Singh's academic and secular emphasis. Thirlwell wrote in the logbook in January 1963, 'It is the hope of the mission staff that All Saints' will once again become an effective instrument in the evangelisation [underlined] of this island'. The school day was extended to allow for 15 minutes of divinity for all students daily, though this soon proved problematic since there were only three Christian teachers on staff. When students and teachers were absent for Holi, they were reprimanded with the comment that 'this school observes Christian holy days'. May Day was 'observed in the Christian tradition as a day of Our Lady', with a sermon from the vicar and a hymn singing competition, and Ascension Day was similarly marked. All Saints' Day became the school holiday of choice and, when Hindu teachers requested leave for Diwali, they were refused. Half the students were absent anyway and the Hindu teachers complained to the Education Officer (Northern), who was not inclined to become involved. The new regime did not last. Thirlwell left after less than a year, and his term can be seen as a last evangelical fling before the school settled down to being an academic school, without undue emphasis on religion.

During the 1950s and early 1960s, the Anglicans, like the Methodists, changed their policy to place more emphasis on the direct evangelism of the Indo-Fijian community, rather than relying on the indirect influence of schools. Mr Jivaratnam, who had been the woodwork and Hindi teacher at All Saints', left teaching to become a full-time evangelist with the Anglican Mission in 1955 and, by 1958, a woman evangelist was being sought from India (ABM 1958a). It was now recognised that concentrating on the children was not enough; adult evangelism, bible study, home worship and village meetings were critical (ABM 1958b:104). These years saw other Anglican initiatives with the development of the Bailey Clinic in Suva and Sister Betty Slader's evangelism and medical work around the Rewa Delta from 1960. These projects, rather than the schools, were seen as the future of Anglican evangelism to the Indo-

Fijians. The acceptance at St John's College, Suva, of Edward Armogam, the first Indo-Fijian Anglican ordination student, was a matter for great rejoicing (ABM 1960:74).

Back in Labasa, R. Kalyan Chandra, another Indian Christian, was appointed headmaster at the beginning of 1964. He ran a regime much like Jwala Singh's. Visitors again commented on the high standards of academic and agricultural work, comments that suggest such standards may have slipped under the previous regime. Nonetheless, Chandra's administration satisfied the religious authorities. Bishop John Vockler, visiting in late 1964, noted, 'I have been very impressed with the appearance of the grounds and the School, which I believe to be the outward appearance of a good spirit'. After only nine passes in the secondary entrance examination in 1963 under Thirlwell, results steadily improved again: 16 out of 17 students passed in 1964, and all 28 candidates were successful in 1966. The new South Pacific Commission Tate reading scheme was introduced. All Saints' students won essay and other national competitions. In short, by the mid-1960s, the Anglican mission seems to have accepted the inevitability of very limited evangelical success, and concentrated on academic excellence and the extension of the school to secondary level in the mid-1970s. Its main task was now seen as the preparation of its charges to be good citizens of the new, independent Fiji.

References

Australian Board of Missions (ABM) 1953. *ABM Review*. October. Sydney.

Australian Board of Missions (ABM) 1954. *ABM Review*. September. Sydney.

Australian Board of Missions (ABM) 1956. *ABM Review*. May. Sydney.

Australian Board of Missions (ABM) 1958a. *ABM Review*. June. Sydney.

Australian Board of Missions (ABM) 1958b. *ABM Review*. August. Sydney.

Australian Board of Missions (ABM) 1960. *ABM Review*. June. Sydney.

Lal, B.V. 1992. *Broken Waves: A History of the Fiji Islands in the Twentieth Century*. Honolulu: University of Hawai'i Press.

Methodist Church of Australasia. Department of Overseas Missions Records, 1855–1953, MOM 238. Sydney: Mitchell Library.

Sidal, M. 1997. *Hannah Dudley, Hamari Maa: Honoured Mother, Educator and Missioner to the Indentured Indians of Fiji, 1864–1931*. Suva: Pacific Theological College.

Stephens, F.B. 1944. *Report on Education in the Colony of Fiji*. Fiji Legislative Council Papers No. 18. Suva: Department of Education.

Thornley, A. 1974. The Methodist Mission and Fiji's Indians: 1879–1920. *New Zealand Journal of History* (8)2:137–53.

Whitehead, C. 1978. *Education in Fiji: Policy, Problems and Progress in Primary and Secondary Education, 1939–1973*. Canberra: Development Studies Centre, The Australian National University.

Wood, A.H. 1978. *Overseas Missions of the Australian Methodist Church: Fiji* (Vol. 2). Melbourne: Aldersgate Press.

Wood, A.H. 1978. *Overseas Missions of the Australian Methodist Church: Fiji-Indian and Rotuma* (Vol. 3). Melbourne: Aldersgate Press.

World Missionary Conference 1910. *Report of Commission III—Education in Relation to the Christianisation of National Life*. Edinburgh: Oliphant, Anderson & Ferrier.

PART 4: RETHINKING DEVELOPMENT

13

Development Assistance Challenges

Vijay Naidu

Vijay Naidu: Personal Journey

For the past four decades I have been an engaged Pacific scholar and, during this time, I have read and been influenced by the work of some pioneering scholars from The Australian National University (ANU), worked closely with ANU colleagues, and enjoyed longstanding friendships with several who were at ANU at some point in their working lives.

My undergraduate class of 1971 at the University of the South Pacific (USP) included Brij Lal and Kesaia Seniloli (both of whom later completed their PhD studies at ANU, and Brij would later become a distinguished professor at ANU), Rajesh Chandra (former vice chancellor of USP) and Justice Daniel Fatiaki (former chief justice of Fiji and currently judge of the Supreme Court in Vanuatu). Among our lecturers in subsequent years were Professor Ron Crocombe and Dr Ahmed Ali, both of whom had ANU connections. Studying Pacific history and societies, Pacific Islands development and migration, and ethnicity in Fiji meant that from my undergraduate days I was exposed to the scholarly writings of Jim Davidson, E. K. Fisk, Gerry Ward, Harold Brookfield, Ken Gillion, Neil Gunson, Deryck Scarr, Dorothy Shineberg and Oskar Spate.

I worked closely with Professor Ron Crocombe as his tutor in the Advanced Pacific History course he taught at the third-year level. I owe my fortuitous entry into academia to him and Professor John Harre especially.

In addition to Brij Lal, other ANU scholars past and present with whom I have enjoyed friendship over the years, and/or whose work I have read and been influenced by, are Ahmed Ali, Stewart Firth, Greg Fry, William Sutherland, Ron Duncan, Ropate Qalo, Sandra Tarte, Scott McWilliams, Stephanie Lawson, Katarina Teaiwa and Jon Fraenkel.

Research collaboration and attendance at seminars and conferences have resulted in a number of publications in books published by ANU. David Hegarty, the former director of the State, Society and Governance in Melanesia program became a close associate and friend.

Naidu, V. 2006. Development Assistance Challenges. In M. Powles (ed.), *Pacific Futures*. Canberra: Pandanus Books, 142–63.

Republished with the kind permission of ANU Press.

In the first decade of the 21st century, Pacific Island countries (PICs), with the exception of Samoa and Tonga, are still only a generation away from independence from direct colonialism. Indeed, there are still a number of vestiges of colonial rule present in the region.[1] In the past 20 to 30 years, these countries have sought to develop as peripheral capitalist societies with varying degrees of 'traditional' forms of societal organisation and cultures still in existence. Development has meant for their peoples improving material standards of living, greater participation in political processes and access to public utilities such as potable water, electricity, sanitation and educational and health services. Disadvantaged groups in society such as women, youth, ethnic minorities, the disabled, rural dwellers and the poor have been recognised as needing attention. Not infrequently some of the latter categories have been reluctantly put on the development agenda as a result of the insistence of external development partners, donor countries and agencies.[2] PICs' efforts at development can be described as having had mixed success and their place in global development, characterised by an unbridled thrust toward free trade, is disconcerting.

---

1   France continues to practice direct colonialism in Kanaky (New Caledonia), Tahiti Polynesia (French Polynesia and Wallis and Futuna). The 'Compact' ties the former US Trust Territories of Federated States of Micronesia (FSM), the Marshall Islands, and Palau to the United States. The Cook Islands and Niue are closely linked to New Zealand and Tokelau remains under New Zealand's control. Indonesia occupies West Papua.

2   Middle-aged and old men (*unimane* in Kiribati) dominate decision-making in the patriarchal systems that characterise much of the region.

This chapter will examine development assistance in a holistic way, situating it within the broader framework of development and development assistance to developing countries. International trends in overseas development assistance or aid will be outlined. Significant donor countries will be identified, as will the nature of aid provided. Donor countries tend to be most supportive of their former colonies and territories that continue to be politically integrated with them.[3]

Besides unravelling some of the complexities of development assistance, the chapter will challenge existing stereotypes about overseas aid and island country dependency. Issues such as geopolitical strategic rent and interdependence between island and Pacific Rim countries will be highlighted. Of significance in terms of overall development trajectory, it will be pointed out that some island countries do not have prospects for meaningful 'independent' development and that there are degrees of 'independence' feasible for others. However, it will also be pointed out that the trade imbalances against island countries signify an extent of interdependence between them and donor country interests. It is not all one-way traffic.

The Contradictory Pacific Reality

Pacific Island people appear to continue to enjoy relatively high standards of living in the context of numerous traits that they share with other postcolonial states. In the recent past, these have included exposure to a downward trend in commodity exports, natural disasters and the diminishing capacity of the state in managing externally induced social transformation.

In the absence of a strong capitalist class in most island countries, the state played a lead role as a facilitator of private enterprise and as an owner/operator of enterprises in its own right. Areas of non-subsistence economic activities, such as plantations, mines, tourist resorts, urban centres that were centres of administration, wholesaling and retailing outlets, as well as services such as central hospitals and elite schools, drew island people from all over the interior and outer-island hinterland.

---

3   A view has emerged that closer political and economic integration and the lack of sovereignty have contributed materially better standards of living and human rights in such countries compared with those that are politically independent (Bertram and Watters 1985; Crocombe 2004).

The use of local resources for 'national development' in a less than transparent and equitable manner, the presence of strangers in territories claimed by resident 'indigenous' groups, competition over land and jobs, the destruction of natural habitats for subsistence livelihoods, the lack of participation by local communities in decision-making about the use of their resources, and the use of repressive measures by state power-holders against those who protest their legitimate concerns, have caused conflicts in a number of island states.

As very small and non-competitive producers of raw materials, these island states are extremely vulnerable to fluctuations in commodity prices. Most are heavily dependent on one or two commodities. They are price takers rather than price makers. They are producers of much that they do not consume and consumers of much that they do not produce. Human capital loss is a major concern for some of them. They are variously subject to a full range of natural hazards such as cyclones, droughts, flooding and tidal surges, earthquakes and tsunamis as well as volcanic activity. Brindley discusses three different vulnerability indexes, which show that PICs are among the most vulnerable countries in the world. A composite vulnerability index, which takes account of a country's openness (export dependence), lack of economic diversification and susceptibility to natural disasters, places PICs and other small island states among the top 30 of the most vulnerable of 111 countries. 'Vanuatu is ranked the most vulnerable of any of the 111 states; Tonga comes in 3rd, Fiji 8th, the Solomon Islands 11th, Samoa 20th, Papua New Guinea 30th, and Kiribati 59th' (Brindley 2004:23).

As if economic vulnerability and natural hazards are not enough to deal with, 'manmade' disasters abound. These include lack of accountability by state power-holders, serious shortcomings in the rule of law, public finance mismanagement, outright corruption and military intervention in democratic processes. In a number of the largest countries, security forces have become the primary sources of insecurity.[4] Poor leadership, lack of vision and the processes of peripheral capitalism have led to growing social inequality and poverty. In the larger island countries, significant numbers of children do not attend schools as these are not accessible or affordable.

---

4 The ethnically exclusive Fijian military has engaged in three military coups undermining democratic electoral outcomes; Solomon Islands police were involved in the 2000 coup that overthrew Prime Minister Bart Ulufa'alu's government; the PNG and Vanuatu security forces have mutinied periodically.

The lack of opportunities for gainful employment and amenities for recreational activities have spawned countercultures of delinquency, crime and drug abuse among unemployed young men and women.[5] Sexually transmitted diseases and HIV/AIDS are becoming widespread. Idle young men have become the foot soldiers for unscrupulous leaders in Fiji, Papua New Guinea, Vanuatu and Solomon Islands.

The World Bank has pointed to the 'Pacific paradox' and a 'doughnut effect' in Oceania with respect to economic growth (World Bank 1993). PICs are perceived as the hollow of the doughnut, the rim of which is made up of the more vibrant Asia-Pacific Economic Cooperation (APEC) countries. For much of the past two decades, PICs have experienced stagnating, and even periodically declining, rates of economic growth (see Table 1), even though in per capita terms a number of countries and the region as a whole have the highest development assistance flows. Hence the paradox.

Despite the size of these aid flows, real per capita growth rates over the period have been disappointing. The average for the Pacific over the 20-year period to 2001 was 0.8 per cent per annum, compared to 1.1 per cent for the rest of the world. However, the last decade has been even worse, with the Pacific averaging a contraction of 0.1 (per cent) per year, compared to the world average of 1.4 per cent growth (Brindley 2004:4).[6]

PICs are perceived as dependent, especially on aid, have negligible economic growth and increasingly pose problems for the larger rim countries. The 'MIRAB' model (Bertram and Watters 1985) highlights PICs economies that are dependent on migration (MI), remittances (R), aid (A) and a large bureaucracy (B) or public sector for employment. The countries included were Cook Islands, Niue, Tokelau, Tuvalu and Kiribati. To these can be added the Micronesian countries of FSM, the Marshall Islands, and Palau.

---

5   Region-wide, there is only one job for every seven people looking for employment (Pacific ACP 2007:22).

6   The heavily remittance-dependent economies of Samoa and Tonga have experienced growth. Samoa has engaged in the reform process most consistently and has shown annual growth rates in the past five years. With the collapse of its squash exports, Tongan economic prospects are not positive.

Table 1. Pacific Islands: Summary of economic aggregates.

	Population (2001)	GNI* per capita (US$ 2001)	Aid per capita (US$, 1982–2001 average)	Average growth of real incoming per capita (1982–2001)
American Samoa	70,000	a	–	–
Cook Islands	18,000	4,272b	–	–
Federated States of Micronesia	120,000	2,150	802	–0.15%
Fiji	817,000	2,150	56	0.74%
French Polynesia	237,000	c	1,517	1.58%
Kiribati	93,000	830	223	0.05%
Marshall Islands	53,000	2,190	1,016	0.44%
Nauru	12,700	2,830b	–	–
New Caledonia	216,000	c	1,642	1.95%
Niue	1,900	–	–	–
Northern Mariana Islands	80,000	c	–	–
Palau	20,000	6,780	1,779	1.30%
Papua New Guinea	5,253,000	580	80	0.50%
Samoa	174,000	1,490	213	1.27%
Solomon Islands	431,000	590	129	–0.17%
Tokelau	1,500	–	–	–
Tonga	101,000	1,530	241	2.06%
Tuvalu	10,000	1,560b	–	–
Vanuatu	201,000	1,050	237	–0.01%

Note: a. Estimated to be upper-middle income ($2,976–9,205); b. GDP per capita; c. Estimated to be high income ($9,206 or more); *GNI = gross national income.
Source: Brindley 2004.

According to Bertram and Watters:

'Aid' to these communities, although usually described as 'development aid', has in fact tended to have the character of a straightforward supplement to local incomes and consumption, and accounts for a large proportion of both. Up to half the budget of local governments is financed from offshore donors and the share of government employment in total cash employment on the islands ranges from about half to over 90 per cent. In balance-of-payment terms, aid inflows finance between 40 per cent and over 100 per cent of imports. Aid is, clearly, crucial rather than peripheral in the determination of incomes and consumption levels. (1985:499)

An extent of 'MIRABleness' also afflicts other Pacific states that have large bureaucracies, high rates of emigration and are aid dependent. This might give the wrong impression that the model is widely applicable to Pacific people. This is not the case as migration, remittances, aid and even a large bureaucracy (relative to population size) have not been significant to the same degree in Melanesia, which has nearly 7 million of the 8 million Pacific Islanders resident in PICs. Table 1 shows the enormous variations in development assistance to individual PICs, with Fiji receiving on average $US56 per capita on the one hand and Palau averaging nearly $US1,800 per capita for the 1982–2001 period.

Despite this high level of capital inflow, it is anticipated that Oceania will lag behind sub-Saharan Africa in achieving the Millennium Development Goals by 2015. These include reducing by half the number of people in extreme poverty and hunger; universal education; gender equality in access to higher education, wage employment and the proportion of seats in parliament; reducing child mortality by two-thirds; reducing maternal mortality by 75 per cent; combating HIV/AIDS, malaria and other diseases; ensuring environmental sustainability (reversing loss of environmental resources); halving the number of people without access to safe drinking water; and improvement in the lives of slumdwellers. While PICs statistics with respect to these goals and indicators are distorted by the Melanesian countries in general, and Papua New Guinea in particular, with almost three-quarters of the population, it is nevertheless a sobering reminder of a paradise lost.[7]

Global warming is likely to have a disproportionate effect on atoll states such as Kiribati, the Marshall Islands and Tuvalu. It will have consequences for all island countries, further reducing the ability of their people to literally keep their heads above water. They will suffer from saltwater inundation with rising sea levels—the consequence of activities in the industrialised world. The question is, will the latter take responsibility?[8]

---

7   HIV/AIDS has spread through virtually all PICs, but the situation in Papua New Guinea is especially worrying, with an estimated 40,000 HIV-positive cases. Illnesses such as malaria, TB and respiratory and infectious diseases remain significant threats in Melanesia. Lifestyle diseases such as diabetes and cardiovascular problems have become rampant in Micronesia and Polynesia.
8   Australia sided with the United States in downplaying the environmental impacts of human activities and sought to dilute the Kyoto Protocol, much to the chagrin of PICs representatives.

However, Pacific Islanders themselves have been most resilient in dealing with the challenges their countries face. Islanders have sought education. They have migrated from the context of limited opportunities in their homelands to many parts of the world, but especially to New Zealand, the United States, Australia, France, Canada and Holland. Export earnings, remittances from relatives abroad, tourism-related income and aid have contributed to relatively high standards of living and per-capita income levels compared with other developing countries. This is another dimension of the Pacific paradox—being able to enjoy relative wellbeing without the necessary expansion in incountry productivity.

A sector that is regarded as posing considerable impediment to economic growth is agriculture, and especially subsistence agriculture. In virtually all PICs, customary forms of land tenure are intimately bound with small-holder production. Customary land tenure is perceived as a major fetter to increased productivity, as group ownership does not allow land to be used as collateral in securing bank loans for investment in equipment, fertiliser and pesticides. Moreover, investments in other areas, such as tourism, housing, renewable energy and waste disposal, are seen as being unnecessarily stalled by land not being a factor of production that can be bought and sold in the market. However, it is also widely recognised that without the access that most (not all) Islanders have to plots of cultivable land, guaranteed by their membership in landowning groups, poverty levels would be much higher.[9]

Aid Paradigms and Development Assistance Trends

In terms of the overarching conceptual paradigm of aid, there have been several shifts and changes. These paradigm changes have been determined by developed countries with minimum regard to developing countries' perspectives. Indeed, with little regard to their own commissions on overseas development assistance (ODA). Thus, just on the release of the report of the Independent Commission on International Development Issues (1980), also known as the Brandt Report, the United States and the United Kingdom substantially reduced ODA, contrary to the report's

---

9   Some Pacific experts continue to subscribe to the notion of 'subsistence affluence', which in my view is not present equally in all PICs and in any case raises the issue of what is defined as affluence.

core recommendations. Without immediate tangible returns to the donor country, international aid did not fit into the monetarist and market-centred policies of Reaganomics and Thatcherite economics (Gounder 1995).[10] OECD countries and the multilaterals that are largely their instruments have determined the modalities, ebb and flow of aid.

From aid as overseas development assistance for the purpose of addressing many of the 'gaps' left behind after the colonial experience of most developing countries, thereby ensuring the continuing influence of the former imperial powers, aid, in the current era of 'conditional aid', has become a significant instrument for compelling structural adjustments. The quantum of aid and the mode of delivery have never been adequate to bring about systemic people-centred changes in recipient countries. More broadly, after colonialism established patterns of raw material production in the Third World, the Bretton Woods institutions have pushed postcolonial states the world over to produce the same export commodities, thereby triggering an oversupply, reducing their foreign exchange earnings and leaving them in their current predicament of dependence. A good example of this is the current predicament of coffee producers. The 1980s debt crisis and the imposition of stabilisation and accompanying conditionalities have further aggravated their situation (Ould-Mey 1994; German et al. 2004).

In the past two decades, the ability of a postcolonial state to foster its national economy has been seriously undermined.[11] This is the bigger picture within which ODA is better understood.

In broad terms, ODA increased from the 1960s to the 1980s, but declined in the 1990s. In real terms (using 2001 prices), in 1992, ODA from all development assistance countries (DAC)[12] stood at close to $US58 billion, declining to $US44 billion in 1997, and increasing to $US58 billion in 2002. 'In fact aid fell in real terms by 24% between 1992 and 1997' (German et al. 2004:181). This dramatic decline did not mean that the need for ODA had diminished but that domestic policies of donor countries took overriding priority. It is apparent that even after the Financing for Development Conference in Monterrey, Mexico, in

---

10   From 1977 to the early 1990s, the British Government had an Aid and Trade Provision system that ensured that development assistance was to benefit the British economy.

11   International financial institutions have a powerful invasive role where a country has fallen into the debt trap as well as a missionary role in determining macro-economic policies.

12   Comprises 30 OECD member states.

2002, the pledges of donor countries of about $US16 billion will be far short of the $US50 billion per annum needed to achieve the Millennium Development Goals.

When one considers that the world's countries spend more than $US1,000 billion on armaments and militaries, $US350 billion on agricultural subsidies and only $US57 billion on ODA (Wolfensohn cited in UNANZ 2004), the huge gulf between rhetoric and reality is striking. The total aid figure is significantly reduced when tied aid and the 'boomerang effect' of aid is considered. Substantial proportions of Australian and New Zealand development assistance is tied aid. The amount of aid funds transferred offshore can be minute.

Very few OECD countries have achieved the UN's target of 0.07 per cent of GNI ODA. Holland, Denmark, Luxembourg, Norway and Sweden are the exceptions (German et al. 2004). During the Marshall Plan period, the United States provided up to 2 per cent of its GDP in aid for the reconstruction of Europe; this volume of ODA from one country was unprecedented. Despite the adoption of the Millennium Development Goals and the global consensus to increased ODA at the Financing for Development Conference in Monterrey, significant increased development aid is yet to be seen (Akiyama and Kondo 2003).[13] In the current period, the following excerpt provides a succinct picture of the context of ODA:

> [Developed–developing world] resource transfers are declining and [developed-world dominated]–global institutions are consolidating a system of highly unequal relations between countries.
>
> NGOs [non-government orgnisations] have been increasingly angered by the cynical exercise of power by [developed-world] governments promoting 'good governance' and 'aid effectiveness', while defending narrow political and economic self-interests. Industrialised countries devoted US$353 billion (seven times total ODA spending) to protecting agriculture in 1998, according to UNDP. At the same time, the policy choices available to poorer countries are narrowed by conditionalities imposed by international finance institutions and bilateral donors. As reports from NGOs in Asia illustrate, southern governments are forced to privatise and liberalise, while OECD restrictive practices, tariff and non-tariff barriers cost developing countries US$160 billion a year.

---

13 A recent OECD news release (14 May 2004) stated that aid volume had risen by 11 per cent in the past two years, after a decade of decline.

This translates into real human suffering which the World Bank recently quantified as welfare losses of US$19.8 billion (German et al. 2002:2; emphasis in the original).

Development Assistance Post–September 11

It is apparent that the terrorist attacks on the twin towers of the World Trade Centre on 11 September 2001 have changed significantly the context of international politics and international aid. September 11 has caused a sea change in the United States, which has replaced communism as public enemy number one with the more amorphous 'terrorism' as the biggest threat to its security. The United States has indicated its willingness to take unilateral action against perceived threats to its security without the endorsement of the UN. There are many ramifications of this superpower's approach to 'go-it-alone', with a number of hangers-on. The geopolitics of bigger powers have significantly influenced aid flows and it is likely that the United States will reward those countries that its leadership sees as being supportive and/or of strategic value. Oceania has been a beneficiary of the change. Prior to this tragic event, the Pacific Islands were no longer perceived as strategically important. This applied especially to northern Pacific Micronesian states, and also to the US territory of Guam; this perception has since been reversed drastically (Underwood 2004).

September 11 has also triggered the more interventionist phase in Australian foreign policy and development assistance. It appears that there is a process underway of re-marking the boundaries of its backyard with an emphasis placed on the national interests and stability of countries in the neighbourhood. According to Bruce Davis, the Director-General of AusAID:

> The aid program is a long-term tool to address long-term problems. In particular, we need to persist with support for stability and for economic and governance reform over the long haul—strengthening the hands of reforming governments and supporting reform champions within struggling governments (noting that generational change may be required before benefits are fully realised).

> We don't have the luxury of walking away. These states are on our doorstep and our engagement with them is core business for our development cooperation program. Our national interests are inextricably linked to stability and peaceful development in the region (Davis 2003).

Implied in this excerpt is a growing preoccupation with Australian security and proactive development assistance to ensure stability. This will have repercussions for the nature of aid and aid delivery to PICs.

The Pacific Context of Aid

ODA in the South Pacific has undergone a number of shifts in the fashion of aid worldwide (see Hjertholm and White 1998). Former colonial rulers in the region, such as Britain and the United States, began to shift their interests before September 11 to other areas where their strategic and economic interests were seen to be better served.[14] Japan, China and Taiwan have begun to play an increasingly important role as bilateral donor countries. For these countries and the ANZUS partners, aid to island countries has been and continues to be an important foreign policy instrument (Tarte 1998; Teaiwa et al. 2002). For the duration of the Cold War era, aid was one of the ways in which the white Pacific influenced and controlled the black Pacific. Regional organisations wittingly and unwittingly learned how to play the aid game, becoming conduits of such influence. On the economic front, aid has ensured the consolidation of the linkages forged during colonial rule and the patterns of economic subordination remain. Politically, room to manoeuvre existed insofar as some island countries could threaten that they would go to the Soviets if certain of their requests were not met. However, any real attempts to establish such relationships were strongly opposed by ANZUS, with the Australasian media going into bouts of hysterical frenzy. Kiribati's fishing agreement with the USSR is a case in point (Neemia 1988).[15] Vanuatu's ties with Libya received strong condemnation.

In the current period, aid in the South Pacific ranges from the competitive chequebook diplomacy practised by China and Taiwan to the marine resource–related ODA by Japan and the more conditional aid of Australia and New Zealand. International finance institutions—namely the World Bank, the International Monetary Fund and the Asian Development Bank—likewise continue to push for reform, entailing structural

---

14   While the British contribution is partly incorporated in EU aid to the region and the United States makes direct subventions to the Compact states, these donor countries have shifted their interest to the former Soviet Bloc countries in transition, which have bigger markets and natural resources.

15   Australia and New Zealand had agreements with the Soviet Union allowing the latter's fishing boats into certain ports. This raised the issue of the white man's burden and continuing paternalism towards black Islanders.

adjustment conducive to market-centred development (Teaiwa et al. 2002; Slatter 2004). These bilateral and multilateral agencies have now shifted to a common rhetoric of poverty reduction requiring a continuation of vigorous reforms. There is a concern that the efforts to harmonise ODA in the region will lead to the homogenisation of aid in line with the agenda of the international financial institutions. Numerous contradictions abound. The one-size-fits-all structural adjustment programs have contributed to political instability in the complex multiethnic states. The 'blame the victim' syndrome is manifested in terms such as 'failed states' and 'arc of instability' (Fry 1999).

Geopolitical interests continue to be the primary motivation among Pacific Rim donor countries for aid (see Table 1). An examination of aid flows from donor countries to recipient countries shows a clear preponderance of aid to current and former colonies and to areas of influence. French aid is provided largely to French Polynesia and New Caledonia; US aid to its former Trust Territories—the Marshall Islands, the FSM and Palau; Australian aid to Papua New Guinea, Indonesia and East Timor; New Zealand aid to Samoa, the Cook Islands, Niue and Tokelau; Japanese aid to other Asian countries.

In terms of what donor countries receive in return, Poirine (1993) has written about 'military rent' and 'atomic rent' with respect to American interests in Hawai'i and Guam and French interests in French Polynesia. He has identified the importance of military rent or geopolitics in ODA and aid as 'geopolitical rent'. ANZUS interest in much of the Pacific can be regarded in a broadly similar way. Moreover, the 8 million people in Pacific Island states, small by world standards, do provide an almost captive market for goods and services from Australia and New Zealand. There is a huge trade imbalance in favour of the latter countries. Pacific Island economies are also tied up with these larger economies because of labour migration and remittance flows.

Forms of Development Assistance and Donor Agencies

Development assistance to Pacific Island countries takes several forms and includes monetary grants, soft loans, technical assistance, technology transfer and other in-kind contributions. At the broadest level, it can be bilateral or multilateral, involving government-to-government transfers and transfers by donor governments to international and regional multilateral organisations, which then transfer aid to island governments. In the past, virtually all overseas development assistance was official, involving government-to-government transfers. More than 80 per cent of development assistance continues to be bilateral. Much of the remainder is transferred to PICs through multilateral agencies—international and regional. Prominent among the regional organisations in this regard are the Pacific Islands Forum and the Pacific Community.

The relative autonomy of island states also gives them some room to manoeuvre with respect to development assistance. This manoeuvrability can be used strategically for longer-term development or it can be abused. Contradictions emerge between those seeking 'good governance' and those engaged in old-style chequebook diplomacy. Taiwan's competition with China in gaining recognition among island states has meant that both these countries readily provide funds to unsavoury leaders. How the funds are used appears to be of little concern. Thus, much of the multimillion-dollar assistance given by Taiwan after the conflict in the Solomon Islands in 2000 was used to pay compensation to politicians and gang leaders. Recently, it was reported that Vanuatu was pledged AU$9 billion by Taiwan for granting it diplomatic recognition (*Mercury* 2004).[16] Australia meanwhile has warned the Vanuatu Government that it will reduce bilateral aid if good governance is not given priority.

These days, donor agencies also make aid transfers directly to non-government organisations (NGOs) in developing countries and/or through development, relief and humanitarian NGOs based in metropolitan countries. The latter often network and form umbrella organisations to better coordinate their activities, share resources and engage in advocacy and campaigns. Eighty Australian development NGOs are affiliated with the Australian Council for International Development and 64 such NGOs are affiliated with the Council for International Development in New Zealand.

---

16   The *Los Angeles Times*, in an article headlined 'China, Taiwan Court Tiny Group of Islands', reported that Vanuatu had 'become the belle of the cross-straits ball as China and Taiwan open their chequebooks and compete for its loyalty' (2004). Taiwan had promised AU$30 million against China's AU$10 million. The article further reported that 26 countries recognised Taiwan—'mostly impoverished nations in Latin America, Africa, and the Pacific. An additional 160 recognize Beijing' (ibid.).

Development Assistance Challenges

There are numerous challenges to development assistance in the contemporary period, which are likely to extend for at least the next 10 to 20 years. These include donor countries prioritising national interests over international concerns; their preoccupation with security matters and development-related conflicts; bilateral versus multilateral aid; structural adjustment programs to promote 'governance' denoting marketisation and democratisation; engagement with civil societies; and participatory development and long-term partnerships. The biggest challenge for PICs is to deal with the forces of globalisation pushing neoliberal reforms that will erode the preferential access they have to overseas markets. PICTA, PACER and Economic Partnership Agreements with the EU are designed to move PICs into the 'rules-based' free trade regime of the World Trade Organization (WTO). ODA will be required to provide support to PICs as they seek to engage competitively with the economic giants of the world on a supposedly level playing field.

Maintaining and Increasing Aid Flow

There are many challenges to international aid in the Pacific region. A number of these are shared with other developing countries of the world. Central to these concerns is whether the coming decades will see an increase in ODA and a genuine long-term movement towards achieving 0.7 per cent of GNI of OECD countries. The massive drop in aggregate ODA in the 1990s is a precedent that could be repeated. This was explained as aid fatigue. Since 2002, Japan and Italy have significantly reduced aid.

Sub-Saharan Africa and the Pacific Islands are severely constrained in their ability to attract foreign direct investment. These constraints are structural: limited resource endowments, small population size and therefore minute markets, human resource limitations and institutional constraints, including rule of law and capital market issues. To maintain and improve the quality of life of people in these regions, ODA needs to meet the savings-investment gap as well as address social development areas such as education, health, housing, safe water and public utilities, which are of no interest to private investors if user-pay principles cannot be applied.

On per capita regional terms, the Oceania region is the highest recipient of aid, with $US183 per person. Sub-Saharan Africa received $US27 by comparison in 2002 (OECD 2003: Chart 1, Figure 1). In aggregate terms, however, the region received only about 2 per cent of world development assistance funds (OECD 2003: Chart 2, Figure 2). The largest donors have been France, Australia, the United States, Japan, New Zealand, the United Kingdom and various UN agencies. As is to be expected, the biggest recipients of aid were the French colonies of Tahiti Polynesia and Kanaky (New Caledonia), followed by Papua New Guinea with development assistance from Australia. The US Compact countries of Micronesia and the Marshall Islands come third, with the French territory of Wallis and Futuna next. Sectoral allocation of aid included education, health and population programs, other social sectors, economic infrastructure and services, production, program assistance and emergency assistance.

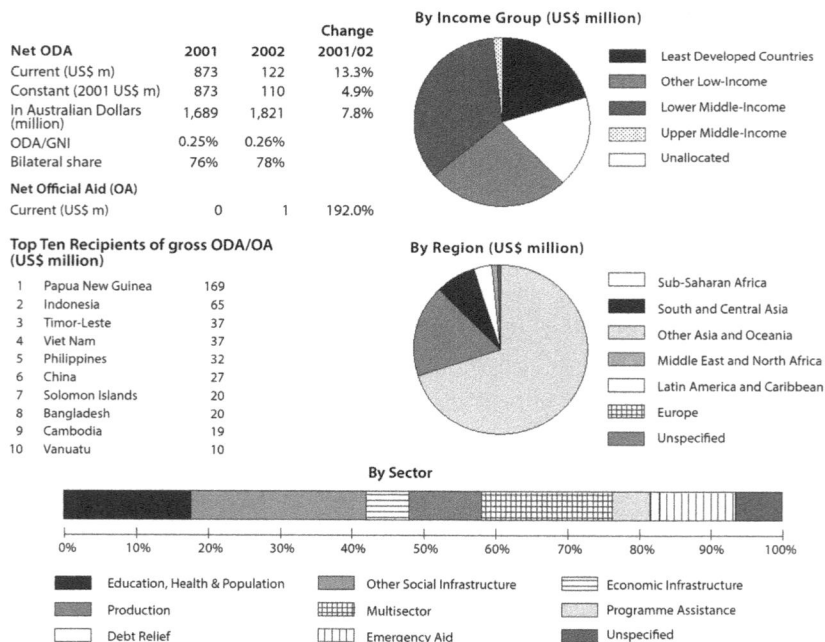

Net ODA	2001	2002	Change 2001/02
Current (US$ m)	873	122	13.3%
Constant (2001 US$ m)	873	110	4.9%
In Australian Dollars (million)	1,689	1,821	7.8%
ODA/GNI	0.25%	0.26%	
Bilateral share	76%	78%	

Net Official Aid (OA)			
Current (US$ m)	0	1	192.0%

By Income Group (US$ million)

- Least Developed Countries
- Other Low-Income
- Lower Middle-Income
- Upper Middle-Income
- Unallocated

Top Ten Recipients of gross ODA/OA (US$ million)

1	Papua New Guinea	169
2	Indonesia	65
3	Timor-Leste	37
4	Viet Nam	37
5	Philippines	32
6	China	27
7	Solomon Islands	20
8	Bangladesh	20
9	Cambodia	19
10	Vanuatu	10

By Region (US$ million)

- Sub-Saharan Africa
- South and Central Asia
- Other Asia and Oceania
- Middle East and North Africa
- Latin America and Caribbean
- Europe
- Unspecified

By Sector

0% 10% 20% 30% 40% 50% 60% 70% 80% 90% 100%

- Education, Health & Population
- Other Social Infrastructure
- Economic Infrastructure
- Production
- Multisector
- Programme Assistance
- Debt Relief
- Emergency Aid
- Unspecified

Figure 1. Gross Bilateral ODA, 2001–02 Australia.

Source: Adapted from Australia: Gross Bilateral ODA, 2001–2002, Aid Statistics, Donor Aid Charts, www.oecd.org/dac/stats/donorcharts, © OECD.

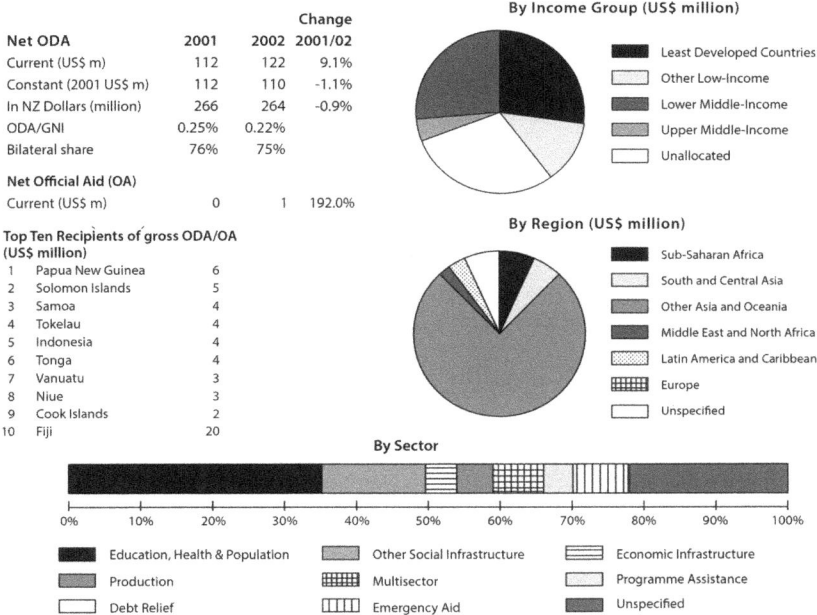

Net ODA	2001	2002	Change 2001/02
Current (US$ m)	112	122	9.1%
Constant (2001 US$ m)	112	110	-1.1%
In NZ Dollars (million)	266	264	-0.9%
ODA/GNI	0.25%	0.22%	
Bilateral share	76%	75%	
Net Official Aid (OA)			
Current (US$ m)	0	1	192.0%

Top Ten Recipients of gross ODA/OA (US$ million)

1	Papua New Guinea	6
2	Solomon Islands	5
3	Samoa	4
4	Tokelau	4
5	Indonesia	4
6	Tonga	4
7	Vanuatu	3
8	Niue	3
9	Cook Islands	2
10	Fiji	20

By Income Group (US$ million)

- Least Developed Countries
- Other Low-Income
- Lower Middle-Income
- Upper Middle-Income
- Unallocated

By Region (US$ million)

- Sub-Saharan Africa
- South and Central Asia
- Other Asia and Oceania
- Middle East and North Africa
- Latin America and Caribbean
- Europe
- Unspecified

By Sector

0% 10% 20% 30% 40% 50% 60% 70% 80% 90% 100%

- Education, Health & Population
- Production
- Debt Relief
- Other Social Infrastructure
- Multisector
- Emergency Aid
- Economic Infrastructure
- Programme Assistance
- Unspecified

Figure 2. Gross Bilateral ODA, 2001–02 New Zealand.

Source: Adapted from New Zealand: Gross Bilateral ODA, 2001–2002, Aid Statistics, Donor Aid Charts, www.oecd.org/dac/stats/donorcharts. © OECD.

With concerted efforts to halve poverty worldwide and to achieve other Millennium Development Goals, it is likely that donor interests will shift towards those countries and regions that are especially impoverished. A number of PICs classified as least-developed countries are hard pressed to justify their membership of this category of countries. Extreme poverty and hunger are emerging in the region but they are nowhere near comparable with sub-Saharan Africa and South Asia.

Ironically, issues less directly related to poverty reduction, such as the security concerns of Australia and New Zealand as well as the maintenance of their spheres of influence, will ensure that aid from these donor countries remains focused on Oceania. They currently direct 39 per cent and 44 per cent, respectively, of their total ODA to PICs (AusAID n.d.; NZAID n.d.). However, there are likely to be shifts in development assistance within the region towards Melanesia. Poverty reduction will also mean that aid funds will be targeted more to the poor. Already, NZAID has overhauled its education sector funding with very significant increases in the proportion allocated for basic education.

Securitisation of Aid

Oceania is perceived variously as an American lake and ANZUS's backyard. Besides the tensions on the Korean Peninsula and North Korea's supposed membership in the 'Axis of Evil', China is emerging as a major player in the region. This is coupled with the 'look north' foreign and trade policy change in a number of PICs. For instance, Fiji's political leadership has been positively inclined to Japan and China, as neither of these countries' governments opposed the military coups of 1987 and 2000 and do not take a position on human rights violations.

With the US-conceived and led war on terror, there has been a tendency to perceive all kinds of open violent conflict as being motivated by terrorism or at least providing fertile ground for terrorist organisations. Resources formerly used for humanitarian and developmental aid are now increasingly diverted to security matters. These include building security organisations and training and equipping military and police personnel. Legal and institutional frameworks might be established or modified using aid funding. There appears to be a significant reorientation of Australian development assistance to the region in this regard (Pacific Islands Trade and Investment Commission 2002).

Australia has adopted a more aggressive foreign policy approach, which includes how aid is used. The Regional Assistance Mission to Solomon Islands (RAMSI) from mid-2002 has marked a remarkable change from Australia's 'hands-off the internal affairs of its neighbours' position to one that seeks early intervention. Thus, with other regional countries, Australia is currently reforming Solomon Islands' political and economic institutions to address possible future problems of instability. The 'help 'em friend' approach has been extended to Papua New Guinea in the Enhanced Cooperation Programme (ECP). Australian public servants, including police personnel, have begun to hold ministerial and administrative positions. A regional police training facility and programmes, based in Fiji, are envisaged.[17] Australia and New Zealand have increased their funding of 'governance': Australia from 15 per cent in 1999–2000 to 33 per cent of its ODA in 2003–04 (AID/WATCH 2004a) and, in New Zealand, approximately 40 per cent of the aid budget to the Pacific was spent supporting governance-related activities (NZAID 2004).

Australia's more interventionist approach as the self-appointed regional sheriff has markedly affected its development assistance to the region. Although in aggregate terms it is reported that Australian aid has increased to the region in general and to Papua New Guinea and the Solomon Islands in particular, closer scrutiny reveals that additional funds are used to pay Australian public servants, police personnel and private companies (AID/WATCH 2004b). The current phase and style of Australian ODA to PICs raises the challenge of neocolonialism in the region.

Aid Actors

ODA in the earlier phase involved government-to-government transfers. International financial institutions also dealt with governments. While government-to-government interrelationships remain central, there have been changes in aid objectives and agencies. The reform agendas of OECD countries emphasise the promotion of the private sector and market. Human rights and the adoption of democratic institutions are also pushed. The role of the state as the lead actor in development and of state planning for development is de-emphasised and even openly criticised and ridiculed. International financial institutions have become leading advocates of private sector promotion and of minimising the economic role of the state.

---

17   A matter that is critical in development assistance, which can be the subject of a separate paper, is aid and ethnicity. With respect to training and equipping police and military forces, donor countries and agencies (such as the UN) must take cognisance of the ethnic composition of security forces. In Fiji, the Solomon Islands and Papua New Guinea, as well as in Vanuatu, ethnicity has been a factor in political destabilisation by and within security forces. In Fiji's case, it appears that in pursuit of their own interests, the UN and Australia are not prepared to reflect on the morality of arming one ethnic group in a multiethnic society. This in the context of a military that has a track record of three military coups and a mutiny in the past 17 years.

In the smallest Pacific countries, the private sector is miniscule because the domestic market is so small. The attempt to drive home the neoliberal dogma is not likely to produce any significant positive outcomes. Such countries might have difficulties in accessing aid because of conditionalities linked to marketisation.

Besides the emergence of private business as a development partner in the use of aid, there has emerged in the past two or three decades a new category of agencies in the development arena. NGOs, together with community-based organisations, constitute 'civil society' and have taken up various degrees of active work in advocacy, provision and implementation of development projects. Developed-country NGOs have become vocal critics of their governments, the international financial institutions and grossly unequal international economic and political structures. Globalisation and unfair trade rules pushed by the WTO have induced a global network of civil society organisations that share information, resources, and strategies to counter the policies of the G8, OECD and international financial institutions.

Developed-country NGOs have also become recipients of ODA funds as well as donations from citizens of OECD countries to engage in relief, humanitarian and development aid. In the Pacific, international NGOs such as OXFAM, the Red Cross, World Vision, Greenpeace, Save the Children Fund, World Wide Fund and DAWN are playing a number of roles. It is anticipated that autonomous organisations backed by governments and the private sector, such as the Pacific Cooperation Foundation, can facilitate greater understanding of the development challenges faced by island states.

As in most other developing regions of the world, Oceania has also seen a significant growth in NGOs. The older church-based groups have been supplemented by women's organisations and youth and environmental groups. Many of these groups are perceived as bringing support to their communities more effectively than government. Thus, domestic violence, which is widespread in the region, has been tackled largely by women's groups. Donor countries and agencies promote NGOs and seek partnership with them in some situations because government officials are seen to be corrupt and ineffectual.

Thus, the Australian Foreign Minister, Alexander Downer, in announcing new strategies for the delivery of aid, asserted that they included 'a plan to bypass failed governments. The breakdown and corruption of governments, particularly in Melanesia, means more of Australia's aid will go directly to community and church groups' (Pacific Islands Trade and Investment Commission 2002).

A challenge for donor countries and recipient country governments is how best to accommodate NGO participation in development. This is particularly so when NGOs have taken positions that are opposed to governments or when NGOs challenge government policies and actions.

Bilateral Versus Multilateral

As mentioned earlier, the bulk of ODA has hitherto been government-to-government transfers with aid to multilateral or regional organisations being relatively limited. However, it is likely that in the near future there will be a shift towards greater funding of regional-level initiatives and programs. There are several areas of common interest in the region, which include shipping, fisheries, transport and communication, higher education, environmental management and security, which benefit from a broader regional approach. The EU is already funding programs centred on the Pacific Islands Forum, the Pacific Community and the University of the South Pacific. These institutions also draw considerable support from some of the larger bilateral donors such as Australia, New Zealand, Japan and France.

Some intergovernmental regional organisations face difficult challenges. The Forum Fisheries Agency (FFA) in the past was hindered by distant water fishing nations (DWFNs) approaching PICs on a bilateral basis. Although PICs' exclusive economic zones have the most richly endowed tuna fisheries in the world and account for one-third of the world's tuna catch, the returns to island states are very small. Only 11 per cent of the total catch of 1 million metric tonnes each year is caught by PIC-owned vessels. While the value of the total catch is $US2 billion, the fees paid to island countries in the late 1990s amounted to $US54 million (Pacific ACP 2007:20). Without the efforts of FFA, many of the agreements with DWFNs would not have been possible, but in the negotiation process DWFNs have tried to weaken the regional approach.

All-of-Government Approach, Harmonisation, and Sector-wide Approach

Just as regional approaches to certain common problems faced by PICs are seen as the most appropriate, there is increasing discussion about an 'all-of-government approach' in evolving common strategies towards the region and to individual PICs. While such an approach is seen as being more effective, as it reduces duplication of efforts and wastage as well as minimising contradictory directions in development assistance, there is a danger that it will also contribute to a lead government agency overshadowing the legitimate concerns of other departments. Thus, the orientation and thrust of AusAID, NZAID and the Japanese International Cooperation Agency (JICA) might become even more closely tied up with foreign affairs and trade as well as security matters serving the donor country's national interest rather than meeting the development aspirations of aid-receiving countries.

Harmonisation has become a buzz word among donor countries and agencies. Again, there appears to be a commonsense rationale for all donors to engage with each other in deliberating on and sharing approaches, resources and programs. This reduces duplication and promotes a sharing of best practice in development assistance at macro and micro levels and sectorally. Thus, a common approach to achieving Millennium Development Goals among donors might result in a pooling of resources, a more efficient allocation of funds to areas of need and a sharing of the different tasks on the basis of expertise. However, there are a number of fundamental issues with harmonisation. First, donor agencies do not necessarily have identical agendas with respect to their overall development goals and methods of achieving them. The question is whose approach will prevail. Allowing the World Bank or the Asian Development Bank to get the lead role in poverty reduction might not be the best outcome of such efforts at harmonisation.

The sector-wide approach has also been in vogue in recent times and is likely to become important in the future. This entails minimising the time and effort spent by government personnel in recipient countries making numerous reports to several donor agencies. For instance, civil servants in the Ministry of Health do not continue to report back separately to WHO, AusAID, NZAID, JICA, the Food and Agriculture Organization, EU, etc., on how their funds were used. Instead, supporting programs in a sector of a recipient country would be on the basis of budgetary support for that sector. This would not only significantly reduce the time and effort of senior government personnel in the paperwork for reporting back, but would release them to do the policy and supervisory work that they are supposed to be engaged in.

The danger of the sector-wide approach is that it reverts to official channels as the primary conduits for development aid and in doing so provides support to government as against wider civil society. It also harkens back to the top-down approach to development. Given the politics of a government, it is likely that the consolidated support of donor countries and agencies might not be equitably used. It is not clear that the poorest of the poor will benefit or indeed that such an approach will help women and disadvantaged minorities. In this regard, the extent to which the sector-wide approach will ensure participatory development and empowerment is open to question. There is also the concern from smaller donors' points of view that in the pooling of resources their distinct contribution will not be given due recognition.

Local government in PICs has been a neglected area, which may or may not benefit from the sector-wide approach. In the aftermath of RAMSI, the discussion over a federal-type constitution for Solomon Islands has rekindled issues relating to local government in the region. Decentralisation of power away from the capital city is a major development challenge in most PICs that will draw on the support of donor countries and agencies.

Participatory Development and Partnerships

In the development community there is recognition that for development to be sustainable it requires the participation of people who are its beneficiaries. Considerable thought needs to be directed at how their knowledge, skills, views and aspirations are to be incorporated in activities designed for their benefit. Participatory Rural Appraisal and Participatory Learning and Analysis, and a range of other participatory approaches and techniques, have shown that people who are the grassroots recipients of aid can and do make a significant contribution to the analysis of their situation and the strategies that could improve their lot. With decisions being made about development assistance by donor countries and agencies thousands of kilometres away, and through governments that often have little to do with the poorest of their citizens, there is a huge challenge of nurturing participation. This in turn gives local ownership and ensures a greater degree of sustainability.

In this regard, NZAID's support for the Rethinking Pacific Education project is quite remarkable and might provide a good framework for ensuring a participatory approach to development assistance. This project, led by Dr Kabini Sanga, a Pacific educator and senior lecturer in education, with colleagues at the Institute of Education, University of the South Pacific, has been providing meeting grounds for discussion, research, critical evaluation and alternative policy formulation for educational development in PICs. Funded by NZAID, which does not interfere in the process, the project has generated new ways of conceptualising Pacific education, building capacity and confidence among island educators, bringing academics, policy-makers, and practitioners together in the task of creating more country and regionally relevant education. This type of donor-recipient relationship is a productive partnership.

Another significant point that emerges out of this project is the recognition of not only the existence of potential local partners in all projects, but of using the expertise that Pacific Islanders have acquired through years of research and reflection as well as by living in PICs on a continuing basis. It is vital that as part of generating local ownership more local people are used as expert consultants on matters that affect them and their societies.

From a situation of relative unequal standing between the giver and the receiver, there has been a trend towards an approach of 'we are in this together for the long haul' and that there are mutual benefits for both parties. This has engendered mutual respect and longer-term strengthening of relationships well beyond project or program cycles. As in all relationships, there will be ups and downs, but there is a willingness to keep channels open for dialogue and discussion.

Building national-level capacities in PICs so that there is leadership and the capacity to negotiate with donor agencies and in deliberations over international treaties on relatively equitable terms is critical to long-term partnerships. This means that human resource development is also a core issue in development assistance. Opportunities for tertiary and postgraduate education continue to be important in the emerging prioritisation of basic education.

Conclusion

PICs are relatively poor and powerless in the global community. As part of the developing world, Oceania will be subject to the outcomes of negotiations over international trade, environmental (especially marine), security and labour agreements. Individual countries have different prospects depending on their human resources, institutional capacities, natural resource endowments and the nature of their incorporation in the global system. Their relative poverty means that on many fronts, including managing their limited resources, they need development assistance.[18] Regional approaches have served a number of useful purposes in the past and will need to be consolidated to meet common challenges.

The current push for a free-trade regime will have serious repercussions for island economies and government revenues. Donor countries and agencies will need to work with PICs to provide buffers against the negative repercussions. Such support will have to be seen as assisting PICs as partners in development who need a 'leg up' in particularly difficult circumstances. The beneficiaries of such assistance will not only be Islanders but donor countries. Instability and out-migration would be minimised and PICs and traditional donor countries would benefit.

There is a need to ensure that beyond providing resources for policing and law and order institutions, the participation of Islanders is enhanced in the decision-making processes of their countries. Development assistance needs to address issues of human capacity in PICs as a core dimension of development.

References

AID/WATCH 2004a. *Downer Puts 'Governance' before Sustenance in Aid Budget*. Media Release, 11 May.

AID/WATCH 2004b. *Australians Query PNG Aid*. Media Release, 17 November.

18　This chapter has not addressed the use of ODA to meet the dangers posed by unsustainable exploitation of natural resources such as fisheries and forestry. Australia and New Zealand, together with the Global Environment Facility and the South Pacific Regional Environmental Programme, have made efforts to mitigate the destruction of natural resources and biodiversity in PICs.

Akiyama, T. and M. Kondo (eds) 2003. *Global ODA since the Monterrey Conference*. Trends in Development Assistance, Series Two. Tokyo: Foundation of Advanced Studies on International Development, International Development Research Institute. www.fasid.or.jp/_files/e_publication_trends/2/global.pdf

AusAID (n.d.). Australia's Aid Program. ausaid.gov.au (site discontinued).

Bertram, G. and R.F. Watters 1985. The MIRAB Economy in South Pacific Microstates. *Pacific Viewpoint* 26(3):497–519. doi.org/10.1111/apv.263002

Brindley, D. 2004. *Aid, Governance, and Economic Development in the Pacific*. PhD Seminar paper, presented at the University of New South Wales, School of Economics, Kensington, Australia.

Crocombe, R. 2004. *The Pacific Plan Among Larger and Smaller Regional Approaches*. Conference paper for Securing a Peaceful Pacific, University of Canterbury, Christchurch, 15–17 October. posc.canterbury.ac.nz/documents/Conference%20Programme%20A4%20v1.pdf (site discontinued).

Davis, B. 2003. Statement by the Director General of AusAID. Inquiry into PNG and the Island States of the Southwest Pacific, 1–10. www.ausaid.gov.au/hottopics/pacific/opening_statement.pdf (site discontinued).

Fry, G. 1999. *South Pacific Security and Global Change: The New Agenda*. Working Paper No. 1999/1. Canberra: The Australian National University.

German, T., J. Randel and D. Ewing (eds) 2002. *Reality of Aid: An Independent Review of Poverty Reduction and Development Assistance*. London: Earthscan. realityofaid.org/

Gounder, R. 1995. *Overseas Aid Motivations: The Economics of Australian Bilateral Aid*. Avebury: Aldershot.

Hjertholm, P. and H. White 1998. *Survey of Foreign Aid: History, Trends and Allocation*. Denmark: Institute of Economics, University of Copenhagen. econ.ku.dk/wpa/pink/2000/0004.pdf (site discontinued).

Independent Commission on International Development Issues 1980. *North-South, a programme for survival: report of the Independent Commission on International Development Issues*. London: Pan Books.

Los Angeles Times 2004. China, Taiwan court tiny group of islands, 13 November. indystar.com/articles/3/194417-3823-010.html (site discontinued).

Mercury (Hobart) 2004. Taiwan Gets an Official Pacific Partner, 9 November.

Neemia, U. 1988. Kiribati: Russophobia and Self Determination. In R. Walker and S. Sutherland (eds), *Peace, Security and the Nuclear Issue*. London: Zed Books.

NZAID (n.d.). Aid and Development. nzaid.govt.nz

NZAID 2004. *NewZAID No. 19*, September. nzaid.govt.nz/library/newsletters/0409-newzaid.html (site discontinued).

OECD 2003. *Donor Aid Charts: Australia and New Zealand*. oecd.org/country list/0,2578,en_2649_34447_1783495_1_1_1_1,00.html

OECD 2004. Aid Ministers Note Rise in Aid Volume and Push for Aid Reform and New Approaches to Security-Development Linkages. News release. oecd.org/document/51/0,2340,en_2649_33721_31505523_1_1_1_1,00.html

Ould-Mey, M. 1994. Global Adjustment: Implications for Peripheral States. *Third World Quarterly* 15(2):319–36. doi.org/10.1080/01436599408420382

Pacific ACP 2007. *European Community: Pacific Regional Strategy Paper and Regional Indicative Programme, 2002–2007*. ec.europa.eu/development/body/csp_rsp/print/r6_rsp_en.pdf

Pacific Islands Trade and Investment Commission 2002. Australia to shift aid focus to South Pacific. *Pacific Outlook*, September–October.

Poirine, B. 1993. Economic Development and Cultural Change in the Pacific Islands: A Case of Market Failure? *Three Essays from French Polynesia*. Sydney: Centre for South Pacific Studies, University of New South Wales, 40–59.

Slatter, C. 2004. The Politics of Economic Restructuring in the Pacific with a Case Study of Fiji. PhD thesis, School of Social Policy and Social Work, Massey University.

Tarte, S. 1998. *Japan's Aid Diplomacy and the Pacific Islands*. Canberra and Suva: National Centre for Development Studies, The Australian National University and Institute of Pacific Studies, University of the South Pacific.

Teaiwa, T., S. Tarte, N. Maclellan and M. Penjueli 2002. *Turning the Tide: Towards a Pacific Solution to Conditional Aid*. Sydney: Greenpeace.

UNANZ 2004. *UNA NZ News April 2004*. unanz.org.nz/Portals/0/Web%20Sept%20newsletter.PDF (site discontinued).

Underwood, R. 2004. Pacific Security—a Micronesian Perspective. Paper presented at Securing a Peaceful Pacific conference, University of Canterbury, Christchurch, 15–17 October.

World Bank 1993. *Pacific Island Economies: Toward Efficient and Sustainable Growth*. Washington, DC: World Bank.

14

Breaking Fiji's Coup Culture through Effective Rural Development

Joeli Veitayaki

Joeli Veitayaki: Personal Journey

I am currently an associate professor at the University of the South Pacific's (USP) School of Marine Studies. I am also Director for the International Ocean Institute Pacific Islands, based at the USP, as well as Co-Chair of the Korea-South Pacific Ocean Forum. I am a member of the High Level Panel of Experts for a Sustainable Ocean Economy that has been put together by the World Resource Institute in support of a high-level panel consisting of 13 heads of government. I am a trained teacher with a BA and MA from USP and a PhD in Environment Management and Development from the National Centre of Development Studies at The Australian National University (ANU).

At ANU, I was fortunate to work with some prominent Pacific Island scholars such as Elspeth Young, Padma Lal, Meg Keen, Gerry Ward, William Clarke, Brij Lal, Colin Filer, Stewart Firth, Ron Duncan and Greg Fry. Most of these scholars had worked at USP. ANU was also special in that many other young Pacific scholars congregated there to perfect their skills to allow them to best serve their people, countries and region. ANU is a great place to forge lasting friendships, contacts and networks.

I teach and conduct research in different parts of Fiji and the Pacific Island countries with partners from USP and abroad. I have worked with governments and development partners on the sustainable use and management of marine resources. I have written articles and books on the importance of subsistence and artisanal fisheries, indigenous knowledge and traditional resources management systems, culture, capacity building, climate change, disaster risk reduction, community-based resource management, sustainable development, the Law of the Sea, maritime transport and regional cooperation in the Pacific Islands. I have also worked as a trainer and researcher in most Pacific Island countries as well as in many other countries around the world.

Veitayaki, J. 2008. Breaking Fiji's Coup Culture through Effective Rural Development. In B. V. Lal, G. Chand and V. Naidu (eds), *1987: Fiji Twenty Years On*. Lautoka: Fiji Institute of Applied Studies, 39–156.

Republished with the kind permission of the Fiji Institute of Applied Studies.

The transition of Fiji's independent subsistence communities to a modern, interdependent economy has not proceeded as well as expected. The change in the last 20 years has been dominated by four coups, which were largely supported by the indigenous Fijian-dominated rural populace. The political shocks, which caused incalculable economic, social and cultural hardships, were seen by them as a means to a better future while the poor conditions in rural areas were used by the different coup leaders to convince the people that the change in government was necessary and in their own best interests. The reality is different from the expectations. People now understand that coups, despite all their justifications, are disruptive and damaging.

The six successive governments since independence have failed to improve conditions in rural areas. The nation has been transformed from a model developing country in the early 1980s that the world might emulate, to a typical developing country that has a coup culture, stagnant economy, ineffective rural development, inadequate infrastructure, poor governance and lack of ability to implement set plans and strategies.

I argue here that the coups were related to ineffective rural development, which was used by the coup leaders to gain support of the rural populace. The lack of development in rural areas divides the country into the main centres and the periphery, while the inability of each government to address the needs of the people and the lack of improvement to living conditions in rural areas made people dissatisfied with them. Consequently, the coup culture that has become established in Fiji can be broken only if rural development is more effective, so that the mass that live in rural areas support and trust their governments because they are provided living conditions similar to those enjoyed by their counterparts in the urban areas. Unfortunately, history made Fiji multiracial and tied the issue of backward rural areas to indigenous Fijians even though there are also poor Indians in rural areas. To end coups, rural development must improve the living conditions in rural areas and reduce the tension between the major races.

Fiji has gone through colonisation, political independence, military coups and a change of status from dominion to republic. In all of this time, the country has continued to search for a rural development strategy that provides people with the opportunities they require to improve their lot. The *Strategic Development Plan 2003–2005* (Government of Fiji 2002) listed the nation's priorities to be macroeconomic management, and economic, social and community development.

These priorities have been difficult to achieve given Fiji's highly scattered rural population. Six per cent of Fiji' s population is scattered over 95 of its 97 inhabited outlying islands. Like their counterparts in the rural parts of the two main islands, these rural dwellers have to be provided with the opportunities for involvement in the economic affairs of the nation. Strategies such as decentralisation have not worked well up to now because the concentration of population and economic activities in the centres in Fiji's two main islands presents a dichotomy of an urban-centred and economically important sector and a rural-based poor periphery. For this reason, the provision of infrastructure and support services is an important part of rural development.

Native land constitutes approximately 82.4 per cent of all the land and is surveyed, registered and administered on behalf of the indigenous owners by the Native Land Trust Board. Reserved land comprises over a third of native land but most of this is too marginal for agriculture. State land (9.4 per cent) and freehold land (8.2 per cent), both unreserved, comprise the remaining. Although both the reserved and unreserved land can be leased, the reserved land leases are for indigenous Fijians only. Land leases under the existing Agricultural Landlord and Tenant Act have been expiring since 1997 and have been a contentious issue, as the:

form of tenure under which land is owned and made available for use is a major determinant of how and by whom it is used, and the type of settlement people create on it (Ward 1998:92).

Involving people in rural development has been a continuous concern to policy-makers and governments alike. The majority of indigenous Fijians reside in their villages in the rural areas while Indians and other minority groups dominate the formal and business sectors and the urban population. In 1969, the then Chief Minister, Ratu K.K.T. Mara, in a memorandum on rural development, highlighted a concern that remains topical today:

> The notable economic advance in recent years has not spread evenly across the countryside. Growth tends to concentrate in particular points, and those living away from them are cut off from its immediate benefits. Yet there are increasing stirrings in the rural area for a greater share in progress (Kick 1998: Appendix F/2).

Although the indigenous Fijian-dominated Alliance Party governed the country from independence in 1970 to the time of the general election of 1987, the plight of indigenous Fijians in rural areas remained a major concern. During this time, Fiji enjoyed political stability and prided itself on being 'The Way the World Should Be'. However, the results of the general election that year saw a coalition of the two main Indian-dominated parties—the National Federation Party and the Fiji Labour Party (FLP)—come to power as the result of widespread dissatisfaction with the ruling Alliance party. The new government promised to better the record of the indigenous Fijian-dominated governments of the previous 17 years, but was vehemently opposed by indigenous Fijian nationalists who plotted its overthrow even though its policies aimed to improve the conditions of the rural masses. On 14 May 1987, Lieutenant Colonel Sitiveni Rabuka staged the first of his two military coups that year, ostensibly to protect indigenous Fijian interests. Race relations in the country were polarised and indigenous support for the coup was quickly secured.

In one of his first press conferences after the coup, Rabuka declared that indigenous Fijians had gained victory—implying that indigenous Fijian interests were under threat and would now be safeguarded. Given the protection of Fijian interests in the constitution, it is logical to argue that perhaps Rabuka was referring to the development aspirations of the indigenous Fijians who felt marginalised and disadvantaged. Consequently, Rabuka put in place policies to address indigenous Fijians' concerns and aspirations.

The 1990 constitution, decreed into existence after the 1987 coups, reflected what indigenous Fijians believed to be the remedy for their political and development predicament (Lal 1997:75). Government policies emphasised affirmative action (positive discrimination) aimed at improving the position of indigenous Fijians and Rotumans and ultimately securing their control of government. Parliamentary elections were contested subsequently along totally racial lines while the prime ministership and the presidency, amongst other senior positions, were reserved for indigenous Fijians. In education and employment within the civil service, indigenous Fijians and Rotumans were allocated 50 per cent of all the available places, even with inferior qualifications. The principle of merit was often disregarded. Financial assistance was offered by government-owned financial institutions to allow indigenous people to invest, buy homes and set up commercial enterprises (Denoon et al. 1997).

It has been argued that indigenous Fijians gained more under the 1990 constitution than during the 17 years under the 1970 constitution (Fisk 1995:260). The affirmative action policy was to make development equitable and give people in the rural areas the opportunity to improve their living conditions, or at least provide for their basic needs. The policy benefited many people, particularly middle- and upper-class indigenous Fijians, who were in a position to take advantage of the schemes that were mounted for their group. There were some dismal failures, however, which reflected the way these initiatives were hurriedly planned and implemented. There was little improvement in the rural areas where the people remained poor, grappling with the problems of lack of opportunities, infrastructure, support services and employment.

The affirmative action policy was judged discriminatory by the international community, and Fiji was pressured to make amendments. Opponents of the policy argued that equity for one group in society should not be addressed by discriminating against another. The critics questioned why race determined which group of poor was more deserving of assistance, and argued that a merit-based system was important if the resources of the country were to be productively utilised. In addition, they argued that the affirmative action policy would lower standards, foster dependency and restrict peoples' contributions to the development of the country.

Fiji held its first election under a revised and internationally accepted 1997 constitution in May 1999. Subsequently, it had its first prime minister of Indian descent. Fiji was readmitted into the British Commonwealth.

For a time afterwards, it seemed that Fiji was moving 'away from the cul-de-sac of communal politics and ethnic compartmentalisation' (Lal 1997:76). However, the political rumblings in 2000 and the takeover of government in May of that year showed that racial problems were still important in national affairs, that racial feelings could still be manipulated for political ends. Many Fijians in rural areas supported the coup, which they were led to believe would provide them with another chance to improve their position.

George Speight's reasons for overthrowing Mahendra Chaudhry's Labour Party-led People's Coalition government in 2000 were similar to those of Colonel Rabuka 13 years earlier. He promised to safeguard the interests of indigenous Fijians, which he claimed were being eroded. Many rural villagers and chiefs who saw the coup as a chance to get their concerns addressed supported George Speight. Indian farmers and settlers in rural Fiji were terrorised and robbed. Roadblocks were set up around the country, while the takeover of the military camp in Labasa, the police station in Korovou in Tailevu and the hydroelectric power station in Monasavu demonstrated the support of the rural communities for the coup. Indigenous Fijians were mistakenly convinced that the overthrow of government would improve their lot.

An interim administration, led by Laisenia Qarase, and made up of a new crop of national leaders, many from professional backgrounds, took the country to the general election in 2001, which they contested under the new Soqosoqo Duavata ni Lewenivanua (SDL) banner. The party broke away from the Great Council of Chiefs–sponsored Soqosoqo Vakavulewa ni Taukei (SVT) party and promised a new road map for the protection of indigenous Fijian interests. However, indigenous Fijians were deeply divided and only the favourably weighted political set-up and not their dominant numbers assured them political leadership.

The SDL won the election and put in place strategies to appease indigenous Fijian aspirations, which they argued was the only way to achieve peace and prosperity in Fiji. Qarase reintroduced the affirmative action under the *Blueprint for the Protection of Fijian and Rotuman Rights and Interests and the Advancement of their Development* (Government of Fiji 2000; Denoon et al. 1997; Samisoni 2008). Indigenous Fijians and Rotumans were given government assistance, which included access to former Crown land (Schedule A and 8), ownership of customary fishing areas (*qoliqoli*), Great Council of Chiefs' Development Trust Fund, and royalty and tax exemptions. The blueprint determined the system of funding Fijian administration and its programs, payment of rent arrears, education fund, grants to Fijian Holdings Limited and other Fijian-owned companies, government shares, rents and contracts, licences, loan schemes, royalties, land buy-back, assistance for business and cane farming and the discontinuation of the Lands Commission.

While the intention of the above-mentioned assistance programs was noble (Samisoni 2008), their implementation was shrouded in mystery. In 2001, Fiji was rocked by disclosure of corrupt practices in an agriculture scheme that was formulated to assist people in rural areas by providing tools, implements and equipment for farming and fishing. The scheme was aimed at the disadvantaged communities in rural areas, but in fact it was only available to some. No clear system was in use and little information was available on the way the assistance was handled. In the end, assistance was given to only those people who knew about it. There were records of people in urban areas receiving assistance. The scam was unearthed amidst allegations of corruption, nepotism and political vote buying (Shameem 2006), which cost approximately FJ\$60 million. It was never known how much of the money was used for the people targeted in the project and how much went to the suppliers and the civil servants who were in charge. The scheme resulted in the suspension, sacking and imprisonment of some senior civil servants. There was little evidence that the national objectives for the development project were achieved. No monitoring was undertaken. This was why better rural development procedures are required as the costs of not doing it properly are just too great.

Fiji experienced its fourth coup on 5 December 2006. On this occasion, an indigenous Fijian-dominated multiparty government was forcibly replaced under what the military called a 'clean-up campaign'. Laisenia Qarase's SDL government that had just won its second term in office was overthrown by Commodore Voreqe Bainimarama after a long and widely publicised stand-off amid allegations of blatant pro-Fijian nationalist interests promoted by the government at the expense of the welfare of the country's multiracial population, good governance and equitable development. Commentators remarked on Qarase's manipulation of the democratic processes to serve the interests of indigenous Fijian extremists (Baleinakorodawa et al. 2007; Shameem 2007). Policies such as affirmative action, the Qoliqoli Bill, the Reconciliation, Tolerance and Unity Bill and the Indigenous Land Claims Bill furthered indigenous Fijian interests at the expense of other groups. The 2006 coup redirected Fiji's development path to address the interests of all the people of Fiji, corruption and the mismanagement of the economy.

The interim administration of Commodore Bainimarama aims to provide better services to the people of Fiji. It revised the Budget, kept the value-added tax (VAT) level at 12.5 per cent and restructured the public service. Chief executive officers had their contracts and their posts reverted to permanent secretary positions with reduced salaries. Management and members of statutory organisations were overhauled, with many qualified indigenous Fijians on them implicated and replaced. The retirement age was reduced from 60 to 55 years to save over FJ$70 million in salaries (*fijilive* 2007). Efforts are under way to assist the 33 per cent of the population that lived below the poverty line and arrest the deteriorating state of the economy that continues to push people from rural areas into the towns and cities. Some major investments such as the development at Natadola and Momi have been readjusted to protect local interests.

Unresolved Issues

The main objectives of rural development emphasise the:

- creation of the necessary economic and social environment, which will stimulate and strengthen rural community development efforts
- provision of an effective institutional framework for consultation, cooperation and involvement at the community level
- coordination of the effort with existing agencies in rural areas at the most appropriate decentralised level
- stimulation of rural communities to seek their own improvement, through the satisfaction of people's needs, through their own effort and resources
- provision of advisory, technical, financial and other material assistance, particularly where economic benefits would result (Fiji Central Planning Office 1980:302; Fiji Ministry of Rural Development and Rural Housing 1987a:1, 1987b:2, 1992a:3, 1992b:9–10, 1994:1, 1995:2–3; Fiji Department of Rural Development 1996:2).

These objectives demonstrate the need for an enabling environment in Fiji if rural development is to be effective. The fact that the objectives remain untenable indicates the amount of work that has to be undertaken in rural Fiji. Rural development since the 1987 coups has been 'reactionary' and ineffective. It has been implemented haphazardly in places with trying conditions and has been associated with quick-fix and short-term solutions. The poor performance in rural development has deprived people of the opportunities to improve their living conditions as well as the chance to be a part of the modern economic system. Consequently, people in rural areas remain oblivious to the requirements of economic development and the role they must play to improve their situation.

Rural development is complex and needs to be well planned to ensure that each of the targeted features is addressed. This is an area where rural development has faltered in the last decade or so. Faced with the reality in rural Fiji after the honeymoon during the immediate post-independence years, the people quickly grew sceptical of their leaders and yearned for political change as if political leadership alone would improve their position. This, of course, does not work and is the reason why the approach must be altered and public education undertaken.

A new approach to rural development is needed to address some of the hindrances that are faced. A system for addressing rural development issues must be adopted. Lack of capital forces people to rely on government assistance, which is available only when the budgeted amount is available. People have few means of improving their position. Although the bulk of the land is owned by indigenous groups, it often is not leased and cannot be used to secure finance from lending institutions. A lot of the reserved native land is unutilised as people have only small gardens because they do not have the means to maximise their production. In other instances, rural dwellers who have tried to improve their productivity face problems of irregular transport to markets and the lack of market outlets in rural areas. These peculiar conditions restrict the opportunities to operate commercially viable ventures in rural areas. It is unlikely that rural development initiatives involving people in these areas will work given the existing lack of infrastructure and support services.

Development institutions are not available in rural Fiji. This deprives the people of the advice and support services they require. Since the untimely demise of the National Bank of Fiji, banking facilities have disappeared from rural areas; institutions such as the Fiji Development

Bank, the Rural Banking Scheme of the Australian and New Zealand Banking Group and government representatives carry out only periodic rural visits. In many cases, development activities in rural areas are undertaken only in exceptional circumstances.

The need to streamline the work of rural institutions is sorely required. Public education on important national issues such as the constitution, the rights and responsibilities of the people, the significance of elections, governance and rural development planning have not been adequately provided, and people who are poorly informed on these issues rely heavily on their provincial councils, which, by necessity, have unduly influenced national affairs. Although the councils meet regularly, there are serious questions about representation of people in rural areas. In addition, there is little systematic follow-up action.

The Rural Development Administrative Structure (Figure 1) has been in place since the pre-coup days and outlines the communication channels between government and the people. This structure coordinates development work at the national level between urban and rural areas and amongst different racial groups in different areas (Lasaqa 1984:146). While the structure enhances good coordination and prioritisation of the development initiative proposals, the approvals and implementation are time-consuming and cumbersome and do not cater for communities that seek immediate attention to their needs. The process demands longer-term planning of three to five years, which is often not undertaken at the community level, where the immediate needs exist (Nayacakalou 1978:15). Often, the enthusiasm for development initiatives is lost because of the long time taken to arrive at a decision. The process is also influenced by government officials, local elites and politicians, whose actions affect the distribution of aid and development assistance and its timing.

The structure does not always provide resources to support rural development activities proposed by the people. This support depends on the availability of finance. Moreover, the structure does not specify the government ministry responsible for implementing particular rural development activities. Thus, rural development initiative in an indigenous Fijian village may be undertaken by any of the government ministries individually or in association with others.

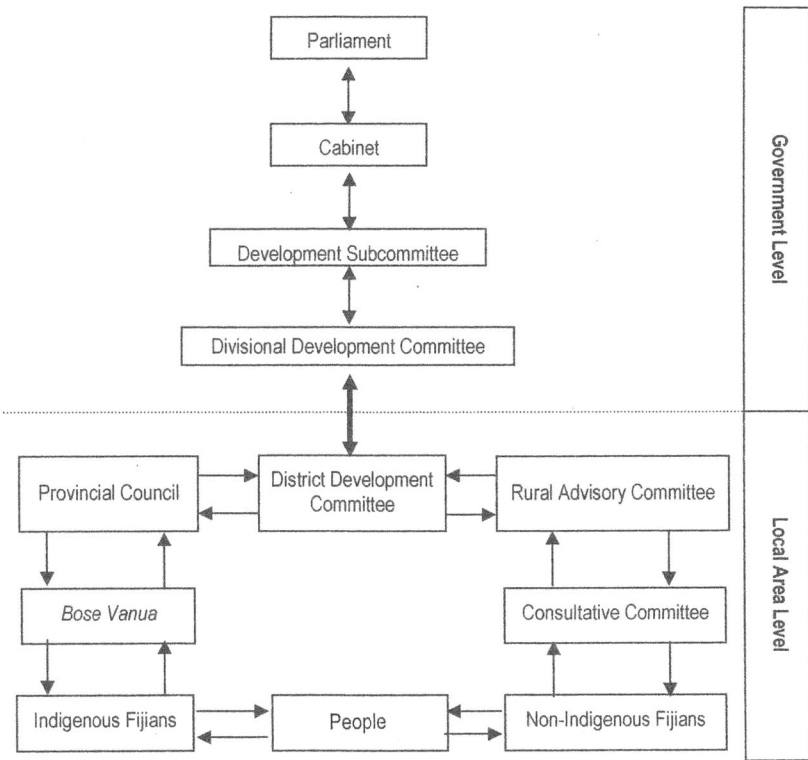

Figure 1. The Rural Development Administrative Structure.
Source: Lasaqa 1984:146–48.

Poorly planned rural development initiatives ultimately are damaging to the whole country. In a number of highly publicised cases, millions of dollars were spent on initiatives that were not effective in improving rural conditions. In many of these initiatives, there were short-term aims and gains accompanied by allegations of corruption, nepotism and of schemes benefiting people other than those who were targeted in the development activities. These costly initiatives have not only failed to improve living conditions in rural areas, they have also given rural dwellers false hopes. The recipe for trouble is set when people, who have least understanding of the economic development requirements and do not understand their own roles in the improvements of their conditions, mistakenly expect improvements in their lives when governments are usurped because they are dissatisfied with their present status.

Rural Development Issues

Pertinent rural development issues in Fiji include the types of activities introduced, the manner in which the rural development is undertaken and the effect on the people and their living conditions. Modernisation was promoted after independence in 1970 because indigenous Fijians' tradition, culture and social and cultural systems were regarded as hindrances to Fiji's economic progress (Spate 1959:1; Burns 1963; Belshaw 1964:282; Watters 1969:12; Fisk 1970:3). It was concluded that modernisation would stimulate the development of the country through a trickle-down process that would allow the rural hinterland to benefit from economic activities in the main centres.

Rural development initiatives, following the decentralisation approach, included the construction of townships, roads and airstrips and the establishment of junior secondary schools and commercial enterprises. These developments are meant to stimulate improvement in rural lives and reduce the movement of people to urban centres. However, people still leave their rural villages and settlements to seek education and employment in the main centres. In addition, the poor state of the markets and infrastructure, and people's customs and traditions hinder the operation of profit-making ventures in rural areas (Spate 1959:36; Fisk 1970:137; Nayacakalou 1978:40; Ravuvu 1988a:202, 1988b:8).

Rural development objectives in Fiji aim to improve the income of rural dwellers to reduce the economic gap between them and urban dwellers (Ravuvu 1988a:179, 1988b:70–71). This philosophy related to the thinking at the time that economic development would solve the problem of underdevelopment in rural areas. This position has been reviewed to acknowledge that economic development alone is not sufficient to solve underdevelopment in rural areas. In recent times, rural development programs have been designed to assist people to help themselves by encouraging those at the grassroots to define their development needs and to identify the resources available to meet them (Nayacakalou 1978:143; Lasaqa 1984:141). Given the poor state of the infrastructure, institutions and support services in rural Fiji, nothing is expected to occur unless the root causes of underdevelopment in rural areas are properly addressed.

The situation is closely scrutinised because indigenous Fijians, who were encouraged since the colonial days to remain in their villages, are demanding involvement in the economic sectors of the country's life

(Tupouniua et al. 1975:33). However, in trying to support the commercial aspirations of indigenous Fijians, the affirmative policy must emphasise the attainment of goals and results and not cause strife amongst racial groups, as summarised in *The Fiji Times* editorial on 2 November 1994:

> No one disputed the need to have more Fijians involved in commerce, but the practice of disadvantaging one group of traders to boost the stocks of another is like hobbling the fastest horse in a race so the rest can keep pace. The end result is that you go nowhere fast. Surely there is someone in the Government with the imagination and drive to come up with an effective, but fair, scheme to enhance the business prospects of indigenous Fijians without making half the country feel like lepers.

The argument that indigenous Fijian rights have been neglected has been used as a smokescreen in the political upheavals since 1987. The people who wanted to safeguard indigenous Fijian rights have not only extended these to include the right to govern and the improvement of living conditions in rural areas, but also to win public support. Ironically, these rights are more likely to be the outcome of effective rural development and not coups, which disrupt the economic activities that are crucial to the development of the country.

There has been little mention of the quality of the indigenous Fijian leadership over the years, nor of the fact that independent Fiji has always been under indigenous Fijian-led governments. These governments have not succeeded in meeting the expectations of development throughout the country and have not achieved much in providing for the rural populace in spite of all their affirmative policies. Ironically, political leaders have on most occasions easily convinced the populace that leadership must remain with Fijians *(fijilive* 2007). The experience in Fiji has demonstrated that rural development is more complicated than the provision of policies, strategies and project activities.

With the experience of the coups in the last 20 years, indigenous Fijians must accept that their disadvantaged position in rural areas is unlikely to improve with the illegal overthrow of governments. People's needs and aspirations can be satisfied only if they work hard and if their government supports their pursuit of development. Effective rural development needs good-quality government comprising leaders and people who understand the way the economy works and how it affects rural development. Indigenous Fijians must insist on having effective governance, regardless of its ethnic composition. People must demand results from their leaders and must withdraw their support if the quality of government is unacceptable. However, these changes must be instigated through the accepted political processes and not through coups.

Making the correct development decisions is critical, given Fiji's widely differing social and economic conditions. Indigenous Fijians in many parts of the country require capital, infrastructure, experience and skills, managerial expertise, and hard work and dedication to be successful. It is wrong to assume that indigenous Fijians will succeed in commercial activities if financial assistance is provided. This assumption ignores the obvious fact that commercial ventures require skills, business acumen and a certain level of infrastructure (Watters 1969:204). This has been demonstrated time and again when racially biased initiatives, aimed at uplifting indigenous Fijians, were eventually acquired through the market process by other ethnic groups who were more prepared to handle them. Implementing rural development is more demanding than providing development initiatives.

The Army Auxiliary Unit's Operation Veivueti operated a collection scheme to stimulate commercial activities in the villages after the coup in 1987. The unit, which was allocated FJ$20 million, reduced later to FJ$12 million, operated at a loss but appeased the villagers who benefited. The failure of the project was attributed to both the villagers and the project officials who were unprepared for the undertaking. The villagers lost interest after a while because of the vessels' irregular schedules. In addition, there were restrictions on what the villagers produced and sold. Project officials, who were mostly army personnel, lacked the entrepreneurial skills to operate the venture. The products were at times sold below the purchasing price due to deterioration in their quality because of the time taken to bring the product to the main markets. Furthermore, there were a lot of empty trips to rural areas because the people who were not ready for the visits did not provide enough produce.

The Equity Investment Management Company Limited (EIMCOL) was established to induce indigenous Fijian and Rotuman participation in commercial activities. Eight married couples were trained for six months and allocated a supermarket each through a joint Fiji Government and Fiji Development Bank (FDB) operation. EIMCOL failed because the participants in the scheme were ill-prepared to operate these commercial ventures (Qalo 1997:96, 196). The shops were in places where larger and well-established supermarkets provided competition to which these newly established businesses were unaccustomed. Moreover, there were allegations of careless buying and wastage by the people involved in the program.

The affirmative policy also was supported by special loans arranged with the FDB. In most of the cases, the people assisted were not always the most appropriate to undertake their chosen development activities but the ones in positions to benefit from these initiatives. This was illustrated in the sale of shares in the Fijian Holdings (Singh 2007) and the National Bank of Fiji saga (Grynberg et al. 2002), where the affirmative initiatives benefited the indigenous Fijian elites who could access these programs of assistance. The majority of the people—particularly those in rural areas—were not affected.

Experience in rural development also illustrated the inadequacy of government-led programs. The National Marketing Authority, the Fisheries Division and the Army's Auxiliary Unit all unsuccessfully tried the marketing concept that is now adopted successfully by some of the fish marketing companies buying fish in outer areas and islands and selling them in the main markets. Similarly, military involvements in commercial farming, rural development and commerce accumulated huge debts, which were all written off.

The Ministry of Agriculture Fisheries and Forests' Commodity Development Framework (CDF) was probably Fiji's largest rural development initiative. With a budget of FJ$69 million, the CDF was to revamp the agricultural, forestry and fisheries sectors and, hence, living conditions in rural areas. The concept emphasised production, value-adding and marketing activities to boost agricultural activities in the country.

The CDF emphasised diversification and the transformation of subsistence into commercial farming. Although the aims of the CDF were laudable, its targets were ambitious and its delivery inefficient and wasteful (Ragogo et al. 1999:3). The projection to increase the annual income from commodities through the CDF by more than FJ$745 million was excessive and questionable (*The Fiji Times* 1997; Ragogo et al. 1999:3).

The CDF promoted private-sector involvement but did not consult it. It was used to rescue ailing agriculture-based industries. The Pacific Fishing Company received FJ$5 million, Wonder Gardens received FJ$500,000, Yaqara Pastoral Company FJ$749,376, and the copra mills in Vanua

Balavu and Lakeba each were given FJ$200,000. There was no indication of how the CDF eased the financial problems of these companies, as there was no verification of whether the money was used for the required purposes and whether it made a difference to the status of the ventures. The handouts only prolonged the imminent failure of these operations; they made little difference to the lives of rural communities but provided welcome relief for the elite Fijian owners and stakeholders.

Crops such as yaqona, ginger, seaweed, taro, yam, pawpaw and cassava were allocated FJ$9.73 million up to December 1998, but the amount that actually reached the people involved in the project activities is uncertain. In a particular department, out of a total allocation of FJ$400,000 under the CDF, FJ$234,690 was spent on the purchase of 13 vehicles (Ragogo et al. 1999:3). An additional FJ$29,900 was earmarked for vehicle maintenance. A Squash Enterprises Limited was paid FJ$95,000 on the strength of a proposal that did not progress to the next stage. In addition, there were overseas trips and other purchases that were not part of the program's plans.

It was not surprising that one of the first things that Chaudhry's government did when it came into power in May 1999 was to suspend the CDF. This costly episode exemplified the need to make development more realistic and appropriate. The CDF has shown that monetary inputs alone cannot solve rural development problems and that poorly formulated projects are likely to be too costly for the country. One thing is certain: there were some people who did benefit from the project, but few of these were from rural communities.

People in Fiji continue to live between subsistence and a modern economy. The subsistence and informal economy is based in indigenous Fijian villages where community decision-making, resource allocation and management are founded on subsistence, limited technology and a high level of local environmental knowledge (Hunnam et al. 1996:49). The modern economy, on the other hand, is based on the economic activities that are part of the formal sector, largely based in towns and on the main islands.

People in rural areas, who have limited sources of income, are paying the highest prices for goods and services. For most of the consumables, people in rural areas pay much more than do those who earn regular incomes in the main centres and are periodically the beneficiaries of sales wars mounted by competing supermarket chains. In Kadavu and Gau, people pay more to move from one part of the island to another than to go there from Suva. Transportation is limited and linkages intermittent. The lack of services forces people to move from rural areas into the main centres where they contribute to the ever-growing poverty and squatter populations and where they are required to pay the same as their wage-earning colleagues and relations.

Alternative approaches have featured in rural development in recent times in attempts to improve it. Government policy to provide two-thirds of the total cost of any rural development activity if the community contributes the other third is a better arrangement than loan and repayment schemes, which have not been successful. The arrangement suits people who tend to slacken off after their initial enthusiasm wears off. Income-generating projects are encouraged in places where there are poor options, restricted markets and low buying power, and where the support services are limited.

Indigenous Fijians in villages own most of the land but produce subsistence outputs and cannot access financial resources. Consequently, people do manual work even with their commercial ventures. Life in villages seems relaxed and flexible but is in fact rigidly organised. Community work takes up a significant portion of time, which takes people away from their individual pursuits. The arrangement hinders individual initiatives and needs to be revised to suit contemporary considerations and aspirations.

The Way Forward

It is logical to deduce that the coup culture currently gripping Fiji will only be broken if the majority of the people deplore it as an unacceptable option to solve the nation's political problems. This position requires that people be educated that coups are wrong and must not be seen under any circumstance as justifiable. Unfortunately, all the successive coups to date protect themselves with immunity, providing lessons that coups and immunity are achievable.

The coup culture can be broken if rural development is effective so that people better understand the consequences of coups and why these are damaging to their interests. The people of Fiji must reject the propaganda that coups are mounted for them and must defend their democratically elected governments because they are relevant and effective. Moreover, indigenous Fijians need to decide what is best for them and not rely on the collective decisions of the provincial councils, which wield great influence based on the interpretations that the advisers provided.

Rural development activities must be based on understanding the requirements of development activities and the significance of local social and cultural conditions. Stakeholders must understand the life in villages, their value systems and needs because these influence the success of the development activities. Moreover, the support must include a minimum level of infrastructure and institutions. That is why a new system for rural development must be formulated.

Rural development must be under an authority that designs and fomulates, then implements and monitors successful rural development initiatives. The authority must formulate and enforce policies that minimise wastage and losses, and in doing so increase the positive impacts of rural development projects.

Rural development projects must provide opportunities for rural development that are not bound by project cycles and timelines but are undertaken because people want them as they make sense economically, socially, culturally and ecologically. The authority can also seek and secure its own resources and lead the drive to sustainability in rural development.

Project proposals need to be assessed on a case-by-case basis by competent officials. The local situation should be properly understood because it will determine the types of rural development activities people in the area get involved in. This will minimise projects that are doomed from the start because of factors that cannot be changed easily.

Rural development activities must maximise production, income and sustainable development. Simultaneously, development activities should be rewarding to those involved. The pursuit of rural development policies requires an integrated approach that uses quality databases and information for good decision-making. Government must improve its capacity for data collection and analysis to convince people of what it is doing.

Moreover, government departments must work closely with each other, local groups, NGOs and international development agencies to identify, formulate, implement, monitor and evaluate rural development initiatives. Government must provide the social and economic environment in which the private sector can participate (Nichols and Moore 1985:i). Government has to provide advice, the funds and the management guidelines. This cannot be realistically done by a particular line ministry and must be the responsibility of a body to facilitate the success of rural development within the country.

Conclusion

Waste of rural development resources and effort because of incompetence and corruption has badly affected the country and must be minimised. Hurriedly planned and implemented initiatives have robbed the country and the people not just of the money but more importantly of the opportunity to make a difference to their lives. Corruption has been a common reason behind each of the country's four coups. Operation Yavato (wood grub) was instituted by Rabuka in 1987 but was never completed because it involved many of the country's leaders and was judged too damaging to reveal. Given the events in the last 20 years, this was a costly mistake from which the country has not recovered.

George Speight accused Chaudhry's government of eroding indigenous Fijian rights through corrupt practices and controversial policies. In 2006, Commodore Bainimarama made the same justification for his 'clean-up campaign'. Indeed, corruption is the only consistent rationale behind the coups that have brought about the political, economic, social and cultural shocks in the country over the last 20 years. It must be quickly addressed because it cannot be allowed to continue. Under the new authority this has to be a major responsibility.

Improving rural development performance is one way of breaking the coup culture. Rural development must be made more effective to be relevant to people who have little understanding of economic principles. The performance of the economy will influence rural development, which must be suited to the conditions in different parts of the country and incorporate people's interests. These prerequisites are necessary because rural development is a commitment that requires hard work and perseverance. Furthermore, it is not an entitlement and it must be offered in a calculated manner.

The institutional structure to coordinate the requests from the people is in place but it must be strengthened and provided matching resources. There is a need to improve coordination within the different government ministries to ensure that appropriate assessments are undertaken for all development initiatives proposed. A review process is required to ensure that project plans are properly evaluated and thought through.

The resources committed to rural development must produce better results. People need to be committed to their chosen development activities because they have a good chance to succeed while government must provide a conducive environment that supports those people and groups that prove they are prepared and suited to undertake the development activities. This approach will enhance the design of appropriate rural development projects that reflect people's drive and commitment and the opportunities available in different areas. The results will improve conditions in rural areas, which will make the rural people realise the value of their governments and the high prices that are paid every time one is overthrown.

The coup culture in the country will be broken only if the people no longer see coups as viable options. The experience of the last 20 years has made people less gullible. They are aware that the coups will not enhance rural development and will not improve living conditions in the country. In addition, people are more critical of the propaganda that they used to accept in the past. The people of Fiji now know that to realistically address their needs and aspirations, they must focus on breaking the coup cycle they are a part of at present.

References

Baleinakorodawa, P., K. Barr and S. Qalowasa 2007. Time of Uncertainty, Opportunity. *The Fiji Times*, 19 December.

Belshaw, C.S. 1964. *Under the Ivi Tree: Society and Economic Growth in Rural Fiji*. Los Angeles: University of California Press.

Burns, A. 1963. *Fiji*. London: Her Majesty's Stationery Office.

Denoon, D., S. Firth, J. Linnekin, M. Meleisea and K. Nero 1997. *The Cambridge History of the Pacific Islanders*. Melbourne: Cambridge University Press. doi.org/10.1017/CHOL9780521441957

Government of Fiji 2000. *Blueprint for the Protection of Fijian and Rotuman Rights and Interests and the Advancement of Their Development.* Suva.

Government of Fiji 2002. *Strategic Development Plan 2003–2005: 'Rebuilding Confidence for Stability and Growth for a Peaceful Prosperous Fiji'.* Parliamentary Paper No. 72, November. Suva: Ministry of National Planning.

Fiji Central Planning Office 1980. *Fiji's Eighth Development Plan 1981–1985.* Suva: Government Printer.

Fiji Department of Regional Development 1996. Annual Report for the Year Ended 1995. *Parliamentary Paper No. 24 of 1996.* Suva.

Fiji Ministry of Rural Development and Rural Housing 1987a. Annual Report for the Years 1983–1984. *Parliamentary Paper No. 6 of 1987.* Suva.

Fiji Ministry of Rural Development and Rural Housing 1987b. Annual Report for the Year 1986. *Parliamentary Paper No. 20 of 1987.* Suva.

Fiji Ministry of Rural Development and Rural Housing 1992a and 1992b. Annual Report for the Year 1988. *Parliamentary Paper No. 3 of 1992.* Suva.

Fiji Ministry of Rural Development and Rural Housing 1994. Annual Report for the Year 1990. *Parliamentary Paper No. 14 of 1994.* Suva.

Fiji Ministry of Rural Development and Rural Housing 1995. Annual Report for the Year 1992. *Parliamentary Paper No. 43 of 1995.* Suva.

fijilive 4 February 2007.

Fisk, E.K. 1970. *The Political Economy of Independent Fiji.* Canberra: Australian National University Press.

Fisk, E.K. 1995. *Hardly Ever a Dull Moment.* Canberra: National Centre for Development Studies.

Grynberg, R., D. Munro and M. White 2002. *Crisis and Collapse of the NBF.* Suva: USP Book Centre.

Hunnam, P., K. Means and P. Chatterton 1996. Community Resource Conservation: WWF in Melanesia. In H. Wallace (ed.), *Developing Alternatives: Community Development Strategies and Environmental Issues in the Pacific.* Melbourne: Victoria University of Technology, 47–63.

Kick, C.G. 1998. Fiji Ministry of Rural Development Planning for the 'Regionalisation'. 30 January–14 February and 22–24 February. United Nations ESCAP-Pacific Operations Centre.

Lal, B.V. 1997. Towards a United Future: Report of the Fiji Constitution Review Commission. *Journal of Pacific History* 32(1):71–84. doi.org/10.1080/00223349708572828

Lasaqa, I. 1984. *The Fijian People Before and After Independence*. Canberra: Australian National University Press.

Nayacakalou, R.R. 1978. Tradition and Change in the Fijian Village. *The Fiji Times and Herald*.

Nichols, E.H and G.K.F. Moore 1985. *Report of the Review of International Arrangements of the Commercial Fisheries Sector, Fiji, 12 July–14 September*. Rome: FAO.

Qalo, R.R. 1997. *Small Business: A Study of a Fijian Family, the Mucunabitu Iron Works Contractor Cooperative Society Limited*. Suva: Mucunabitu Education Trust.

Ragogo, M., J. Hicks, R. Mafi and D. Turaga 1999. Stop the Rot: Jacobs. *The Fiji Times*, 25 June.

Ravuvu, A. 1988a. Development Communication: A Study of Two Beef Cattle Projects. In J. Overton and B. Banks (eds), *Rural Fiji*. Suva: Institute of Pacific Studies, 179–203.

Ravuvu, A. 1988b. *Development or Dependence: The Pattern of Change in a Fijian Village*. Suva: University of the South Pacific, 70–80.

Samisoni, M.T. 2008. Factors Influencing Entrepeneurial Success in Fiji: What Are Their Implications? DBA thesis, University of the Sunshine Coast.

Shameem, N. 2006. *State v Kunatuba* Sentence 15th November in the High Court of Fiji. Criminal Case No. HAC 018 of 2006.

Shameem, S. 2007. The Assumption of Executive Authority on December 5th 2006 by Commodore J.V. Bainimarama, Commander of the Republic of Fiji Military Forces: Constitutional and Human Rights Issues. Suva: Human Rights Commission.

Singh, T.R. 2007. Fijian Provinces Betrayed by Fijian Initiatives. www.fijibuzz.com/fiji-resource-ownership/Fijian-province (accessed 6 February 2007, site discontinued).

Spate, O.H.K. 1959. *The Fijian People: Economic Problems and Prospects*. A Report for the Legislative Council of Fiji, Council Paper No. 13. Suva: Government Printer.

The Fiji Times 1994. Editorial comment, 2 November.

The Fiji Times 1997. Editorial comment, 25 November.

Tupouniua, S., R. Crocombe and C. Slatter (eds) 1975. *The Pacific Way: Social Issues in National Development*. Suva: South Pacific Social Sciences Association.

Ward, R.G. 1998. Land Tenure. In R. Chandra and K. Mason (eds), *An Atlas of Fiji*. Suva: Department of Geography, University of the South Pacific, 92–97.

Watters, R.F. 1969. *Koro: Economic Development and Social Change in Fiji*. Oxford: Clarendon Press.

15

Urban Land in Solomon Islands: Powers of Exclusion and Counter-Exclusion

Joseph D. Foukona and Matthew G. Allen

Matthew Allen: Personal Journey

In the middle of 2017 I finally fulfilled my longstanding ambition of getting a job at the University of the South Pacific (USP). Balancing family and working life is never straightforward, but in 2016 the stars started to align, as they say. My wife was offered a diplomatic posting to Suva and my son graduated from high school in Canberra at the end of the year. I also became aware that a position at USP for which I was qualified would be advertised in 2017. The time was right. So we took the plunge and moved to Suva at the beginning of 2017. I became a visiting fellow at the School of Government, Development and International Affairs (SGDIA), where I now hold the position of Director of Development Studies, and I continued to work part time for The Australian National University (ANU) during 2017.

My engagements with SGDIA throughout 2017, including a six-week staff exchange with my colleague Gordon Nanau under the auspices of the USP–ANU Memorandum of Understanding (he went to ANU to focus on his research while I taught one of his courses at USP), very much strengthened my desire to work with the school. It is one of the most supportive and collegial work environments I have ever encountered—a testament to the outstanding leadership of Sandra Tarte and, before her, Vijay Naidu. I was absolutely delighted to be offered the position in the middle of 2017.

In many ways, arriving at USP has been the logical next step in my academic journey. Before joining USP, my entire scholarly career, both as a student and an academic, had been spent at ANU. With each successive research project in Pacific studies, my focus has, in a sense, jumped scales: from an MSc thesis investigating the human geography of a small island in Vanuatu (Malo) to a PhD study exploring the causes of the 1998–2003 conflict in Solomon Islands, to an Australian Research Council Discovery Early Career Researcher Award (DECRA) project looking at the political ecology of large-scale mining in Bougainville and Solomon Islands.

In coming to USP I have relished the opportunity to lift my gaze to the regional scale. This has been extraordinarily refreshing and invigorating, a wonderful learning experience. As the giants of Pacific studies—scholars such as Epeli Hau'ofa, Greg Fry and Margaret Jolly—have shown us, this vantage point is critically important, and it goes without saying that the view of Oceania from Suva could not be more different from the view from Canberra! Indeed, at times they appear irreconcilable.

This goes to the heart of why our USP–ANU relationships and partnerships are so vitally important. They work to bridge these different vantage points and conceptions of the region; to foster understanding, empathy and mutual respect. Now, arguably more than ever before, these two great centres of Pacific studies must work together to respectfully, ethically and competently provide the knowledge base required to assist our Pacific leaders to navigate the region through a rapidly changing and increasingly complex world.

Joseph Foukona: Personal Journey

I am a Solomon Islander of Malaitan heritage, a lawyer who has extensive knowledge and experience in land legislation and reform in the Pacific Islands. I am currently a senior lecturer and member of the editorial board for the *Journal of South Pacific Law*. I joined the University of the South Pacific's School of Law in Port Vila, Vanuatu, in 2004. My teaching, research and publications focus on land law, customary land tenure, Pacific legal history, land and development, traditional governance, climate change displacement and urbanisation in the Pacific Islands, especially Melanesia. I have been active as a facilitator of land and governance awareness programs in Solomon Islands.

I have worked with international organisations and the Solomon Islands government on a number of projects. These include working with the Solomon Islands Law Reform Commission on low- and high-water mark legislation. In 2011, I led a team of local researchers on a World Bank pilot research project on access to advisory resources by parties to customary land dealings and natural resources access agreements in Solomon Islands as well as being involved in a study on land law and the UN program on Reducing Emissions from Deforestation and Forest Degradation (REDD) in Solomon Islands. I completed a PhD at ANU on land reform and legislation in Solomon Islands, graduating in July 2018. During my time at ANU, I was involved in a number of research projects on Solomon Islands through the State, Society and Governance in Melanesia program (now Department of Pacific Affairs) such as land reform in 2015 and urbanisation in 2016.

Foukona, J. D. and M. G. Allen 2017. Urban Land in Solomon Islands: Powers of Exclusion and Counter-Exclusion. In S. McDonell, M. G. Allen and C. Filer (eds), *Kastom, Property and Ideology: Land Transformations in Melanesia*. Canberra: ANU Press.

Republished with the kind permission of ANU Press.

Introduction

Donovan Storey has observed that urban growth in Melanesia 'has created an unabated demand on services, shelter, infrastructure and land—all of which are in limited supply' (Storey 2003:259). There can be no doubt that the supply of, and demand for, land as a commodity is a salient driver of exclusion from land in urban Honiara, the capital of Solomon Islands. In keeping with this volume's mandate to engage with the *Powers of Exclusion* framework developed by Derek Hall, Philip Hirsch and Tania Murray Li (2011), we apply it, first, to an analysis of the processes by which people—both settlers and those 'indigenous' to the island of Guadalcanal, which hosts Honiara—are being prevented from accessing urban land; and second, to an analysis of the strategies that the subjects of this exclusion are employing to claim, or claim back, access to land within the city boundaries. In other words, we are interested in examining powers of both exclusion and counter-exclusion as they apply to contemporary Honiara. In doing so, we suggest that the powers of exclusion and counter-exclusion at play in Honiara can only be fully understood against the backdrop of an encompassing political economy characterised by patronage networks and personalised forms of political and administrative governance; and with reference to the particular histories and social relations of Solomon Islands.

That said, we find much of heuristic value in Hall, Hirsch and Li's framework. Of the four powers of exclusion they identify—regulation, force, the market and legitimation—regulation and the market (and, to a much lesser extent, force) provide useful lenses on the processes of exclusion that are playing out in Honiara. In the case of powers of counter-exclusion (Hall et al. 2011:170–91), we find that legitimation plays a central role, as evidenced by collective mobilisations around discourses such as indigeneity, customary landownership, nation-building and citizenship. While force has not, to date, emerged as a salient power of counter-exclusion in urban Honiara, contemporary urban land struggles are set against the backdrop of the so-called 'Ethnic Tension' of 1998 to 2003, which saw the violent eviction of settlers from rural and peri-urban areas immediately adjacent to Honiara at the hands of Guadalcanal militants whose agenda could be broadly characterised as 'ethno-territorial' (ibid. 175–80). In the contemporary post-conflict setting, lingering tensions and grievances, including in relation to the original alienation of the land that now hosts Honiara, cast a spectre of violence over the city. Moreover, the increasingly violent character of Honiara's settlements, most of which are organised along ethnic lines, and previous incidents involving the mobilisation of settlement youth in overt acts of collective political violence, raise the possibility that force could yet become more salient as a power of counter-exclusion in urban Honiara.

In applying the *Powers of Exclusion* framework to our examination of processes of exclusion in urban Honiara, and in particular to the interaction between regulation and the market, we arrive at a broadly similar set of conclusions to those reached by Hall, Hirsch and Li, namely that the formal rules often bear little resemblance to on-the-ground realities (ibid. 16); that public officials frequently 'act as tyrants' in the administration of land (ibid.:14); and that the market for land is not a product of 'some abstract space of supply and demand' (ibid.:18). We demonstrate how the abuse of discretionary powers vested in the Commissioner of Lands has seen property rights in urban land allocated in ways that distort the market and abrogate formal legal procedures. Once such allocations have been made, the courts have tended to rule in favour of registered titleholders, and, on occasion, these rulings have been enforced by the state's security apparatus. It is within this realm—the 'fuzzy zone of compromise, accommodation and bribery' (ibid.:16)—that Solomon Islands' distinctive political economy, characterised by patronage networks and highly personalised forms of political and administrative governance, becomes paramount in understanding how exclusion plays out in urban Honiara.

Moreover, this political economy is also evident in some of the powers of counter-exclusion. We shall elucidate cases in which settlers have been able to successfully mobilise political and patronage networks in order to secure their access to urban land. Counter-exclusion has also seen the deployment of discursive strategies that are familiar from Southeast Asia—for example, in competing narratives of settlers as citizens and nation-builders, on the one hand, and the rights of indigenous people on the other (Allen 2012). But again, these discourses are inflected by the particular histories and social relations of Solomon Islands. For example, the discourse of customary landownership (Filer 1997), which we conceptualise as sitting at a scale below indigeneity (which, in the case of Solomon Islands, is often nested at the scale of the island or province), has become a powerful ideology of both exclusion and counter-exclusion while settler narratives, especially those of the nation's largest group of migrant-settlers—Malaitans—are firmly rooted in histories of labour migration and workers' struggle. We also demonstrate how settler narratives of counter-exclusion have recently begun to invoke the colonial construct of 'waste lands', with its obvious connections to the overarching discursive themes of citizenship and nation-building.

We begin by discussing the historical context of Honiara and the rapid expansion of the city and its settlements that has occurred over the past several decades. We then examine the processes by which people have been excluded from accessing land in urban Honiara, focusing on the role of the Commissioner of Lands in both abrogating legal processes and distorting the urban land market. We then move to an analysis of the ways in which groups and individuals, including both settlers and indigenous landowners, have sought to counter their exclusion from the urban space. We conclude by reflecting upon the utility of the *Powers of Exclusion* framework in the case of urban Honiara and by discussing a recent change to the law designed to curb the discretionary powers of the Commissioner of Lands.

Historical Context of Honiara

The Honiara landscape once upon time was under customary land tenure. The tenure arrangements were in accordance with the rules of custom. The rights to customary land were exercised by individuals, a family or group who belong to a clan or tribe (Allan 1957). How a person accessed customary land was through membership of a line, tribe or clan. Access and use of customary land could also be allowed based on special arrangements such as compensation, marriage, warfare or gifts (Zoleveke 1979). However, in the case of Honiara, the customary landscape changed over time into an urban space as a consequence of land alienation prior to and during the colonial period.

The site of the present city of Honiara was 'partly occupied by the village of Mataniko which consisted of a group of leaf houses' (BSIP 1968:5). The alienation of this core landscape originates from three land transactions negotiated between traders and people categorised as landowners prior to the establishment of Solomon Islands as a British Protectorate in 1893 (Moore 2013). The core area from Lunga to Point Cruz, referred to as Mataniko, was alienated through sale by Woothia (or Uvothea), Chief of Lunga, Allea, Chief of Nanago, and the latter's son, Manungo, to Thomas Gervin Kelly, John Williams and Thomas Woodhouse (who were trading partners) for £60 of trade goods in November 1886 (Moore 2013; WPHC n.d.). The other area to the west, bordering on Point Cruz, referred to as Ta-wtu (or Mamara plantation), was alienated to Karl Oscar Svensen and his partner Rabuth. The third land transaction was the alienation of the 'area to the east, named "Tenavatu"' to William Dumply, an employee of Svensen (Moore 2013).

These land areas were further alienated by the traders to other commercial actors, such the Levers plantation company, following the introduction of a leasing system by the colonial government soon after 1893. This process of alienation resulted in the exclusion of the original landowners from their land because of the new owners asserting their property rights. These land alienation processes have been sources of contestation since the 1920s, which resonates with Colin Filer's concept of a 'double movement' of property rights in the context of Papua New Guinea. He argues that 'steps taken towards the partial or complete alienation of customary rights are continually compensated or counter-balanced by steps taken in the opposite direction, towards the reassertion of such rights' (Filer 2014:78). The double movement provides a useful framing for the ongoing assertion and reassertion of claims to land in and around Honiara.

The Kukum or Mataniko land, the core land area where Honiara is situated, was contested by landowners as an unfair purchase and this was investigated by Gilchrist Gibbs Alexander, who was appointed in 1919 as Lands Commissioner to investigate previous land alienations in the Protectorate.[1] The Lands Commission recommended that the land claim be settled as follows:

> (a) A survey should be made at the expense of Levers Pacific Plantation Ltd of all land to the east of the Matanikau River, all such land to be included in the title of the company, the Matanikau river to be the western boundary and the line run south west from Ilu to the back boundary of the Matanikau river; (b) the land to the west of the Matanikau River including all coconut trees planted by Levers Pacific Plantation Ltd to revert to native custom owners and to be excluded from the title of the [company]; (c) the natives to move the village of Matanikau to the west of the Matanikau river but to have the produce of the native gardens on the east side of the river so long as the present crops are bearing; (d) Levers to pay 50 pounds to the natives; (e) on completion of the survey a validating Regulation should be passed confirming the freehold title of Levers in the land shown on the survey plans as finally approved by the Resident Commissioner (WPHC 1922).

The Secretary of State confirmed this recommendation by publishing it in the *Pacific High Commission Gazette* in 1924, which gave it a force of law. This state-sanctioned process legitimated the property rights of Levers Pacific Plantation Ltd. It also authorised the return of land to the west of the Mataniko River to landowners.

Honiara did not exist prior to 1942. The decision by the colonial administration to relocate the capital from Tulagi to Honiara appeared to be influenced by a number of factors. One was the existence of critical infrastructure left behind by the departing United States forces in 1945, such as the airfield at Henderson. Another was the 'anticipated agriculture potential of the Guadalcanal Plains and the dry healthy nature of the climate' (Bellam 1970:70). During this period, Honiara was an

---

1   Alexander resigned towards the end of 1920 after investigating 29 out of 55 land claims. He was replaced by Frederick Beaumont Philips to complete the work of the Land Commission, which then became known as the Philips Commission.

'underpopulated and largely alienated hinterland' (ibid.). The land area on the east side of the Mataniko River, which was alienated by Levers Pacific Plantation Ltd and held as a freehold estate title known as Kukum, was acquired by the colonial administration in 1947 through a land acquisition process prescribed by law. The colonial administration acquired the land to the west of the Mataniko River through a process of negotiation with landowners who occupied it. Consequently, the landowners relocated to the fringes of the Honiara town boundary and the state assumed a 'monopoly of ownership of land in Honiara. On this clean new tenurial slate the capital was built' (ibid.:70).

However, in 1964, Baranamba Hoai of Mataniko village disputed the state's title to land comprising the Honiara town. He made a claim on behalf of himself and the Kakau and Hebata lines of Mataniko village, reasserting ownership rights over a part of the Honiara town land. Hoai and four others gave evidence to substantiate their land claim. But the Registrar of Titles rejected the claims on the basis of a lack of prima facie evidence and forwarded the case for decision by the Western Pacific High Court. In his ruling, Chief Justice G. G. Briggs also rejected Hoai's claim due to lack of reliable evidence. The High Court further held that Hoai's claim was the same claim that was settled in 1924, and remained binding on the parties concerned (Anon. 1964; Moore 2013). To this day, this remains the key court decision that legitimises the state's property rights to land in Honiara.

Post-War Migration and the Growth of Honiara's Settlements

Due to Honiara's status as a city situated on alienated land over which the state has proprietary rights, it has attracted migrants from other islands to be part of this state landscape. The pattern of internal migration was influenced by the uneven distribution of development and social and economic opportunities. The concentration of education, medical and employment opportunities in Honiara and the surrounding areas of north Guadalcanal was a major factor in attracting people to the island of Guadalcanal.

Although people from various islands have migrated and settled in Honiara, the largest number have come from Malaita (Gagahe 2000:53, 63–65). This is because it was Malaitan labour that was exploited in the development projects that took place on Guadalcanal, in the Western Solomons, and in other parts of the country. Part of the reason was that Malaita had a bigger population that could supply labour to the colonial plantations and, later, to the industries in Honiara. John Connell, in a study commissioned by the former South Pacific Commission (now the Secretariat of the Pacific Community), pointed out that migration to Guadalcanal and the Western Solomons was high in the period from 1978 to 1981 because of the employment opportunities available in these two provinces (Connell 1983). Nicholas Gagahe also noted that, according to the 1970, 1976 and 1986 national censuses, Malaita had a large number of out-migrants to Honiara, Guadalcanal, and Western and Central Provinces (Gagahe 2000:53, 63–65).

This has resulted in an increasing number of informal Malaitan settlements located in every corner of Honiara. Most of these settlements evolved from the temporary housing schemes that were introduced in the 1960s and their names reflect their ethnic composition based on either dialect or regions of Malaita. For instance, settlements in Honiara having Malaita dialect names are Ada'liua, Aekafo, Fera'ladoa, Matariu, Koa Hill, Lau Valley, Kwaio Valley, Fulisango and Tolo. Other settlements that comprise a mixture of people from various regions of Malaita include Burns Creek, Sun Valley, Borderline, New Mala, Kobito (1, 2 and 3), Green Valley, Gilbert Camp, Kaibia and Mamulele. While these settlements lack a guarantee of tenure security, with their residents therefore susceptible to processes of exclusion, some residents have built permanent houses and have subsequently successfully applied to the Commissioner of Lands to transfer the fixed-term estate title to them. We discuss this further in a later section of the chapter.

In 1960, the state introduced temporary housing area (THA) schemes on public or state land within the Honiara town boundary to cater for the influx of people to the town and to address the emergence of squatter settlements (Storey 2003). People were allowed to settle on public land and build temporary housing for a nominal fee of SB$5 or SB$10 per annum for a temporary occupation licence (TOL) (Tozaka and Nage 1981:115–18; Storey 2003). The system was intended to provide people some form of legal security in relation to urban land use while simultaneously discouraging 'large scale illegal settlement on other urban lands' (Storey 2003:269).

By the mid-1980s, 'THAs accommodated 23 per cent of Honiara's population … those THAs outside the town's boundaries numbered around 15, with an estimated population of 1,308 persons' (Storey 2003:269). Over the years, however, the THA system has broken down, due in part to the significant increase in rural–urban migration. Other factors that have contributed to its decline include inadequate town planning, unaffordable housing and the maladministration of urban land. A household survey in 2006, funded by AusAID through the Solomon Islands Institutional Strengthening Lands and Administration Project, reported that only 10 of the 3,000 households surveyed had a valid TOL.

During the Ethnic Tension, which was mainly restricted to the island of Guadalcanal, some 30,000 settlers, most of whom were of Malaitan origin, were violently evicted from their places of residence in the rural and peri-urban areas west and especially east of Honiara. These displaced people either returned to Malaita or sought refuge in Honiara, where the city boundaries were secured by police and Malaitan militias. In the wake of the Ethnic Tension, Malaitan settlers have been unwilling to return to their former homes in rural and peri-urban Guadalcanal, even in the case of those who had obtained legal titles to land (Allen 2012). Honiara, on the other hand, continues to be seen as a safe and legitimate space to take up residence—a factor that has contributed to the rapid growth of both the city and its settlements since the restoration of peace and law and order in mid-2003.

Occupying an area of only 22.73 square kilometres, Honiara is easily the largest urban centre in Solomon Islands, accounting for around 78 per cent of the total urban population. The 2009 census recorded the city's population as 64,606, which increases to around 80,000 when its peri-urban fringes are included (Allen and Dinnen 2015:391). Honiara's population has increased fivefold since Independence in 1978 (Moore 2015) and there are now around 30 informal settlements within the town boundary, six of which have encroached on customary land (Hou and Kudu 2012). Most of the residents in these settlements are considered as 'squatters' in the eyes of the state and city authorities because they 'lack legal title to the city land they occupy' (Englund 2002:141).

Powers of Exclusion in Contemporary Honiara

Drawing upon the *Powers of Exclusion* framework, we see regulation, the market and, to a lesser extent, force as the key drivers of exclusion in contemporary Honiara. However, as we shall demonstrate below, the two main powers of exclusion considered here—regulation and the market—can only be understood with reference to a political economy characterised by patronage relations and the personalised nature of political and administrative practices. Exclusion from land in Honiara is produced through a dynamic interaction between regulation, the market and social and power relations that resonates strongly with the observation that the formal rules governing land and property rights often bear little resemblance to on-the-ground realities (Hall et al. 2011). We now consider each of the powers of exclusion in turn, but within a cross-cutting context of political economy.

Regulation

Title to Honiara city land is vested in the state as perpetual estate regulated by the Land and Titles Act. Following the definition of regulation in the *Powers of Exclusion* framework, this legislation governs which 'individuals, groups or state agencies have rule-backed claims to any particular piece of land' (Hall et al. 2011:16). Under this legislation, the state has exclusive property right claims to Honiara city land by vesting perpetual estate titles in the Commissioner of Lands, who holds them in trust for the state.

This means that the Commissioner of Lands, as an agent of the state, has exclusive legal right to determine Honiara city land use, to benefit from the services of this land, and to transfer portions of the property rights at mutually agreeable terms. He has the legal right to dispossess people, or turn individual claimants without legal titles into squatters:

> Private property in land, other than customary land, is created by the Commissioner making a grant out of a perpetual estate over public land … [and the] derivate interests, technically terms of years, are called Fixed Term Estates. The Commissioner of Lands is also responsible for approving all transfers of Fixed Term Estates and for approving long subleases (Williams 2011:2).

This process of allocating private property rights depends entirely on the Commissioner of Lands' discretionary powers. These discretionary powers have been interpreted as giving him the authority to transfer or allocate plots of Honiara city land to private individuals, politicians or investors, regardless of the merits of such allocations. There have been numerous instances of the Commissioner of Lands exercising his discretionary powers in ways that appear to be beyond the textual legal meaning of how such powers should be exercised as prescribed by the Land and Titles Act. For example, the Honiara City Mayor, Andrew Mua, was reported on 7 June 2013 as complaining that the Commissioner of Lands had sold plots of land that were part of the Honiara dumpsite to Asian investors and other individuals (Namosuaia 2013).

The print media also reported that a small park in the centre of Point Cruz was allocated for transfer to a businessman. The Solo Environment Beautification Group claimed that they had started making a garden in the park after receiving assurance from the Permanent Secretary of the Ministry of Lands, Housing and Survey that the land would not be sold because drainage and sewerage lines lay under the area (Namosuaia 2013). Officers from the ministry, however, advised the group to stop any gardening work because the land had been sold for a commercial purpose. In August 2013, the media reported that a plot of land next to the Mataniko bridge, which had been set aside for possible future expansion of this urban transport infrastructure, was transferred by the Commissioner of Lands to an Asian businessman (Dawea 2013).

These examples show how the Commissioner of Lands' exercise of discretion, as provided by law, can easily be manipulated by 'uncodified and informal socio-political forces' (Pelto 2013). While the exercise of discretion by the Commissioner of Lands over urban land is often alleged to be an abuse of discretionary powers, there have been few court challenges or prosecutions. What is certain, however, is that the abuse of these discretionary powers has meant that a majority of Solomon Islanders find it challenging to acquire property rights in Honiara. This has seen the emergence over time of a range of strategies to acquire property rights in Honiara, which we discuss in the second part of this chapter as an instance of the powers of counter-exclusion.

The continual media reports and public complaints to the effect that the Commissioner of Lands has repeatedly abused his discretionary powers by leasing Honiara city land to politicians and investors for his own benefit has resulted in a recent amendment of the Land and Titles Act as part of the government's land reform program. This legislative amendment abolished the discretionary powers of the Commissioner of Lands and provides the Land Board with the 'powers and functions relating to the allocation of interest in land, the development of land and to ensure the administration of land is carried out in a fair, transparent and equitable manner'.[2] We return to this recent development in the conclusion.

The Market

The market as a process of exclusion establishes land as a commodity that can be bought and sold. The market depends on regulation to define the process of ownership and legal title to the city land that residents occupy. The land in Honiara has been accessed, controlled and leased for government and commercial offices, private homes, stores, hotels and small-scale business. With the rapid increase in rural–urban migration and population growth, land supply as a marketable commodity in Honiara has become a limited resource. As a result, within and around Honiara, people coming from other parts of the country continue to struggle to acquire private property.

One reason is that the government insiders, or those associated with the Ministry of Lands, Housing and Survey, have secured patches of land within the Honiara town boundary and are transferring their property rights to these lands at very high market values that are only affordable to the highest income earners and investors. There have been constant allegations from the public that numerous officers in the Ministry of Lands, including the office cleaner, have more than one fixed-term estate title to land in Honiara. This suggests that these lands officers know the system well and are heavily involved in land deals by inflating land market prices. The consequence of this is the exclusion of many low or middle-class Solomon Islanders—who make up the majority of the Honiara population—from acquiring property rights because they cannot afford the increasing price of urban land.

Individual market transactions in land are occurring in Honiara at price levels that many Solomon Islanders cannot afford. For example, in 2010, the Premier of Guadalcanal, when commenting on the sale of

---

2   Section 8A, *Land and Titles (Amendment) Act 2014.*

plots of land in the Lunga area, stated 'We learn that there are parcels of land sub-divided and registered and are ready for sale [that] are very expensive for potential individuals and business investors' (Palmer 2010). He recommended that Levers Solomon Limited, which holds the fixed-term estate title to the land in the Lunga area, 'reduce the current value of land sales at reasonable and affordable prices for individuals and businesses who would want to invest in Guadalcanal Province' (Palmer 2013). These land transactions are unregulated, so individuals or groups could easily be excluded by those with fixed-term estate titles due to unregulated market competition.

Force

Force, as a process of exclusion, concerns acts or threats of violence such as forceful eviction (Hall et al. 2011:4–5; see also McDonnell 2013). The Commissioner of Lands, as an agent of the state, and the Honiara Town Planning Board are the main actors who play an important role in determining people's access to, and development of, Honiara city land, including when to decide on the application of force as a process of exclusion.

Section 5 of the Town and Country Planning Act provides that there 'shall be a Town and Country Planning Board in each Province and in Honiara'. The Honiara Board has jurisdiction to establish a planning scheme and to regulate any development within the Honiara town boundary, including any material change of use of any building or land. The legislation prescribes that the Board must consider the planning scheme apart from any other material consideration when considering applications for building permits or any development within the Honiara town boundary (Foukona and Paterson 2013). However, 'the enforcement of planning requirements is, in practice, not very strong' (ibid.:75). This has given many people the impression that, as citizens, it is legitimate to first construct buildings on any vacant plot of land or any Honiara city land they have acquired and later apply for building permits if they are required by the Board to do so.

Due to the increase in informal settlements and the construction of houses without proper building permits, the Honiara City Council has recently started issuing notices to demolish such buildings as a measure to enforce its regulations (Namosuaia 2014). For example, an Asian businessman continued to build on a patch of land on the western side of the Mataniko bridge despite the Honiara Board turning down his proposed development application (Piringi 2013a). However, a Honiara city councillor challenged the decision of the Board, claiming that it was legitimate for the Asian businessman to develop the site because it was 'given by the Minister of Lands, Housing and Survey, Joseph Onika, who was one of the joint owners of that fixed term estate' (Piringi 2013b). The strategy used by the private businessman was to use the Honiara city councillor to challenge the decision of the board, and to highlight that the Minister of Lands, Housing and Survey was involved by leasing this land to the businessman, and thus it was legitimate. However, the board stood its ground and issued an order for the private business investor to demolish his building.

The decision of the board concerned the demolition of the private business investor's building rather than the title to the land. Once the Commissioner of Lands exercises his power in leasing urban land and a registered title is created, the property rights of the owner of registered title are indefeasible,[3] or 'not liable to be defeated except as provided by the Land and Titles Act'.[4] As highlighted by the Solomon Islands High Court:

> once a person becomes registered owner of an interest under the Act, he has absolute liberty to deal with that interest according to the title which attaches to it under the Act. An innocent party … is not bound to look beyond the register.[5]

Although the discretionary power of the Commissioner of Lands to create property rights has been questionable, and in some instances aggrieved settlers have challenged it, in most instances the courts in Solomon Islands have upheld the proprietary rights of the registered owner of land within the Honiara town boundary.

One example is the case of *Kee v. Matefaka*,[6] in which the defendants in this case were five families who had occupied and built semi-permanent houses on land the Commissioner of Lands had allocated to two Asian investors, Sia Kee Ching and Lau Khing Hung (Theonomi 2014).

---

3   The principle of indefeasibility and the conclusiveness of the register are covered under Parts VIII and IX of the Land and Titles Act.
4   *Lever Solomon Ltd v. Attorney General* (2013) SBCA 11. All court judgments cited in this chapter are available from www.paclii.org.
5   *Manepora'a v. Aonima* (2011) SBHC 79.
6   *Kee v. Matefaka* (2014) SBHC 112.

These two investors applied to the Solomon Islands High Court in order to evict the defendants from the land. The High Court upheld their application and a notice was issued to the families to vacate the land voluntarily, but they failed to do so. An enforcement order was subsequently issued, which the Sheriff of the High Court, with the assistance of the police, acted on to demolish the houses of the defendants and order them to vacate the land.

The defendants applied to the High Court seeking a stay of the enforcement orders due to 'maladministration by the Commissioner of Lands, no payment of stamp duty, and the issue of right of occupation'. The defendants claimed that they 'were not given sufficient time to prepare before vacation, and the manner in which the eviction orders were carried out was contrary to their rights and freedom from forced eviction' (*Kee v. Matefaka*). Edward Matefaka, a spokesperson for the families, claimed that they had 'submitted applications to the Commissioner of Lands', but while their 'applications are still pending before the Commissioner of Lands ... two foreigners' have come in and 'out rightly acquired the land' (Theonomi 2014). Matefaka questioned 'whether Solomon Islanders are entitled to apply for state land and why the two foreigners—is it because of money?' The actions of the agents of the state can easily translate into a conflict between the settlers and the state, particularly when the police are involved and perceived to be protecting the property interests of foreigners.

Despite the circumstances surrounding the way in which the land was acquired, the implicit force sanctioned by the court, as a process of exclusion, which was used by the agents of the state to evict the settlers, indicate that the Commissioner of Lands' land dealings are legal unless challenged otherwise on the basis of fraud or mistake.[7] The High Court upheld the property rights of the two investors, since they were the titleholders of the registered interest in the land, and ordered the eviction of the settlers.

Administration and management of Crown land is a function vested in the Commissioner of Lands and the Registrar of Titles. That function includes the allocation and grant of titles and can only be questioned through the Court challenging the validity of a title. Whoever is occupying Crown land

---

7   See Section 229, Land and Titles Act.

without going through the formal processes, and without the consent and approval of the Commissioner of Lands, occupies that land illegally and can be forced to vacate it in the event of resistance or unwillingness to do so.

Powers of Counter-Exclusion in Contemporary Honiara

Legitimation

Hall, Hirsch and Li describe legitimation as 'establishing the moral basis for exclusive claims' (Hall et al. 2011:5). They see legitimation playing a central role in counter-exclusions, which they define as 'collective mobilisation by groups of people seeking to counter their exclusion from land as territory or productive resource, and to assert their own powers to exclude' (ibid.:170). Attempts to counter the powers of exclusion that we have already elucidated, including the historical alienation of the land on which Honiara now sits, have seen the deployment of two overarching—and competing—discursive narratives, each of which seeks to establish a morally legitimate claim to property rights in Honiara. On one hand, Malaitan settlers cast themselves as 'workers and builders of the nation, thereby linking themselves to the legitimacy of the state and its broader modernising project' (Allen 2012:172), while on the other, 'a Guale "landowner" narrative invokes indigeneity as the paramount fount of legitimacy in the spheres of land and resource development' (ibid.:164). While Allen describes these competing discourses of legitimation in the context of the Ethnic Tension, with a particular focus on rural areas east and west of Honiara, we suggest that they are also discernible in the context of Honiara itself. Moreover, the strategies that are being deployed to counteract urban exclusion are inflected by Solomon Islands' political economy, as well as by local histories and social relations.

We have already seen that historical patterns of rural–urban migration explain why a significant proportion of settlers who have occupied land in Honiara are from Malaita. Allen (2012, 2013) describes how Malaitan identity narratives are embedded in the history of labour relations. Due to historical patterns of uneven development, and the lack of economic opportunities on Malaita, Malaitans have a long history of labour migration that stretches back to the international labour trade of the 19th and early 20th centuries. It is with some legitimacy, then, that Malaitans portray themselves as the workers and builders of Solomon Islands. In the wake of the Ethnic Tension, Malaitans have been reluctant to return to rural Guadalcanal. However, as Allen argues, their identity narrative nevertheless remains tied to the legitimacy of the state:

> The state underpins the rights of Malaitans to live within the Honiara town boundary—where they continue to comprise a significant proportion both of the urbanised elite and the town's overall population (Allen 2012:175).

A recent development that fits neatly into this nation-building and modernising narrative is the appeal by settlers in Honiara to the colonial concept of 'waste land'. This concept was introduced as part of the early colonial government's land policy, both to regulate land speculation and to make land available to investors. Section 10 of the Solomons (Land) Regulation No. 4 of 1896 defined waste land as 'land being vacant by reason of the extinction of the original native owners and their descendants'. Following the enactment of the Waste Land Regulation of 1900, as amended by Queen's Regulation No. 1 of 1901, repealed and consolidated by Queen's Regulation No. 2 of 1904, the definition of waste land was amended to mean land that was not owned, cultivated or occupied by any native (see Bennett 1987:131; see also Foukona 2007). The legal implication of this was that more land in the Protectorate became available for acquisition and alienation. This process contributed to the transformation of customary land into state land in Honiara.

Today the term 'waste land' is no longer recognised in law, but some settlers, mainly from Malaita, are still using the concept to assert their claim to vacant spaces in Honiara.[8] To some of these settlers, waste land is perceived as land that is not needed by Guadalcanal landowners or land in and around Honiara that is underdeveloped. In other words, some settlers justify their claims by asserting that, since the land is waste land, it is all right to occupy and build on it because it is not useful for any other development purpose. The fact that people continue to consider areas such as swampy places, valleys, river banks or steep gullies as waste land to legitimise their land claims is a basis for future land exclusion and contestation (Chand and Yala 2008).

---

8   This view is often expressed by settlers from Malaita who have recently built informal houses on undeveloped urban land situated in valleys and swampy areas, such as behind the King George and Panatina Ridge east of Honiara.

In many instances, the Commissioner of Lands has knowledge of these occupiers, who are usually defined in law as squatters, but the fact that they have remained on the land for a long period could constitute a possessory title.[9] Some of these occupiers have applied to the Commissioner of Lands for a grant of fixed-term estate title to the land. Others believe that, if they are ordered to vacate the land they have occupied for a long period of time, the Commissioner of Lands, as an agent of the state, and the Honiara Town Council would come up with a scheme to relocate them.[10]

In the post-conflict context, some settlers are also attempting to justify their claims to urban land over which they do not hold registered titles on the basis of being displaced by the Ethnic Tension: to evict them, they claim, would cause another displacement.[11] Such a strategy is reinforced by the fact that most informal settlements in Honiara are based on provincial or island affiliations, which creates a strong sense of group identity, security and protection.[12] Therefore, anyone who holds a legal title to a plot of land in Honiara that is occupied by settlers may find it difficult to assert their claim, either through legal means or by extrajudicial force. While going through the courts to obtain an eviction order is possible, as we have already seen, enforcing such an order in practice, and getting people to recognise it, is a difficult process that can create additional tensions.

The proposal by the Solomon Islands National Sports Council (NSC) to build a national sports stadium in the Burns Creek area is a case in point. The NSC acquired the perpetual estate title to land in this area that was occupied by settlers three years ago. The *Solomon Star* newspaper reported that in 2012 the settlers were 'given some time to leave their homes since the NSC took title over the proposed land but have not done so since then' (Anon. 2012). The settlers continued to reside on the land, and recently, with the financial help of their member of parliament (MP), they built a clinic right in the middle of the land that the NSC had earmarked for a playing field. This seemingly reinforced the settlers' perception that, if an MP can fund the building of a clinic on the land, then it is legitimate for them to continue occupying it. The NSC criticised the MP for failing to consult the Honiara City Council to ascertain the legal status of the land before funding the construction of the clinic

---

9   Section 225 of the Land and Titles Act deals with the principles of adverse possession.

10   See, for example, *Onika v. Sevesi* (2007) SBHC 57.

11   This was the view by some settlers who moved from the Guadalcanal Plains to Malaita during the Ethnic Tension and then relocated to the Burns Creek area, east of Honiara.

12   Connell and Curtain (1982:119–36, 127) made similar observations in Port Moresby and Lae.

building (Aruwafu 2012). In October 2013, the NSC revealed that the sport stadium's 'actual ground work could not eventuate as proposed, due to settlers refusing to leave the land earmarked for the stadium despite the call to relocate' (Anon. 2013).

Another example of an MP assisting settlers to assert their property rights concerned a block of public land opposite the White River betel nut market in 2013. Reef islanders from Temotu Province have occupied the land in question for the past 20 years and have named it Karaina settlement (Palmer 2013). The settlers were aware that they did not have tenure security and could be excluded from the land by any private person or company who acquires the legal title to it. The MP claimed that the settlers had asked him to register the land during his campaign in 2010, and he promised them that he would attempt to do so if he became an MP. The Commissioner of Lands made a grant out of a perpetual estate over the land by vesting a fixed-term estate title held in trust by three prominent members of the Karaina settlement: the ward councillor, the Honiara City mayor and the West Honiara MP (Palmer 2013). This land transaction was fast-tracked and enabled by the fact that an MP was engaged in the process, which suggests that the behaviour of the Commissioner of Lands is influenced by patronage politics.

Those people who do not have the requisite patronage networks to secure access to urban land have also adopted the strategy of building as fast as they can on any vacant plot of land that they identify in Honiara, even in the absence of any building permit approval from the Town and Country Planning Board (Diisango 2016). These vacant plots of land are public or alienated land for which the Commissioner of Lands holds perpetual estate titles from which fixed-term estates can be created.[13] Not many people who have built on these vacant plots of land have been able to acquire fixed-term estates due to a highly bureaucratic land transfer process and high land lease prices (see Keen and Kiddle 2016). Some settlers who can afford such high costs have paid brokers or middlemen, often referred to as 'land consultants', who are familiar with the system of transferring land or have connections with officers in the Ministry of Lands, Housing and Survey to fast-track the process of land transfer.

---

13   The Commissioner's power to deal with estates has now been transferred to a Land Board under the *Land and Titles (Amendment) Act 2014*.

Turning now to the strategies of counter-exclusion employed by indigenous people on Guadalcanal in relation to the land that hosts Honiara, we have already seen that the colonial-era land alienations that ultimately enabled the establishment of the city have been contested since the 1920s. In the postcolonial period, the return of, or compensation or rent for the use of, these lands—especially the area from Lunga to Tenaru—have featured prominently in a succession of formal demands that have been put to the national government by the Guadalcanal Provincial Government, most recently in the form of the 'demands by the bona fide and indigenous people of Guadalcanal' that were issued in January 1999 (see Fraenkel 2004:197–203; also Sasako 2003). These demands, and the discourses of indigeneity that have framed them, operate at the scale of the island of Guadalcanal. They can be interpreted as part of a broader ethno-territorial agenda that seeks to exclude the rights of outsiders, including the state, in matters of resource access and control on Guadalcanal (Allen 2012). This agenda was one of the key underlying causes of the violent land evictions that occurred during the Ethnic Tension.

However, this island-scale ethno-territorial project is deeply problematised by territorial ambitions and agendas that operate at lower scales of sociopolitical organisation, specifically at the scale of customary landownership. Originally postulated by Filer (1997), the 'ideology of customary landownership' has become an increasingly pervasive and powerful strategy of territorialisation and exclusion throughout post-colonial Melanesia. In the case of Honiara, there have been claims and counter-claims among Guadalcanal landowners and there have also been tensions between the Guadalcanal Provincial Government and individual landowner claimants.

For example, a chief called Andrew Kuvu, representing Guadalcanal indigenous tribal groups, asserted their ownership of land from Lunga to Tenaru (Anon. 2011), but another local man, Andrew Orea, alleged that Kuvu was illegally harvesting cocoa and coconut from this land and that another landowner, Jemuel Guwas, was selling plots of land from within this contested area (Orea 2009). Another landowner, George Vari, who was chairman of the Lunga-Tenaru Trust Board, challenged the claim by Guadalcanal provincial leaders that Lunga land belongs to the province and its people, and asserted that it belongs to the Malango people (Vari 2012). These claims and counter-claims demonstrate that Guadalcanal people, despite drawing on the 'ideology of customary landownership', are not one entity and, in any case, their ownership claims are without any legal basis. The property rights to the Lunga-Tenaru land, which is part of the Tenavatu estate, is vested in Levers Solomon Limited. With the consent of the state, Levers can sell the rights to this fixed-term estate to any private individual or investor, which entails the exclusion of Guadalcanal landowners.

Force

As previously discussed, there exist, both historically and in the contemporary context, multiscalar ethno-territorialising agendas in relation to Honiara. While there is no immediate evidence that these agendas will be pursued through some form of collective violence, the grievances that underscore them continue to be voiced by the Guadalcanal Provincial Government, by prominent Guadalcanal landowners and by a wider network of leaders throughout the province (see Babasia 2014; Leni 2014). Given the persistence of these grievances, and in the wake of the violent evictions that occurred on north Guadalcanal during the Ethnic Tension, a spectre of ethno-territorial violence hangs over all of Honiara. However unlikely a return to widespread violence may be, the possibility that these longstanding agendas may lead to collective violence aimed at reclaiming Honiara cannot be entirely discounted (Anon. 2014a, 2014b).

Moreover, within Honiara itself, settlements are widely perceived as violent spaces in which alcohol and drug abuse are widespread and acts of interpersonal and group violence are commonplace.[14] As mentioned previously, the threat of force is ever present and may act as a deterrent to those seeking to enforce property rights in settlement areas, including the state's security apparatus. In this sense, settlers' claims to rights of occupation or possession are backed by a spectre of violence. This threat of force is given greater weight, as well as an explicitly political dimension, by a number of well-documented cases of settlement youth being mobilised in overt acts of collective violence on the streets of Honiara. During the riots of April 2006, this collective violence effectively brought down the government of the day (see Dinnen 2007; Moore 2007). In this sense, Honiara's settlements are politically powerful spaces, at least for those political elites who are able to harness the energy and frustration of their younger residents.

---

14   One example would be the conflict between two ethnic groups in the Karaina settlement, situated in the White River area in western Honiara (Inifiri 2014).

Conclusion

In this chapter we have applied the *Powers of Exclusion* framework to an analysis of the processes by which both settlers and those 'indigenous' to the island of Guadalcanal have been prevented from accessing urban land, and to the strategies that the subjects of this exclusion have been employing to claim, or claim back, access to land within the city boundaries. We have found that the framework is broadly useful in explaining these dual processes and we arrive at a broadly similar set of conclusions as Hall, Hirsch and Li. With regard to the powers of exclusion: the formal rules have tended to bear little resemblance to on-the-ground realities; public officials have frequently acted as tyrants in the administration of land; and the market for land is not a product of some abstract space of supply and demand. In regard to the powers of counter-exclusion, legitimation has played a central role, as evidenced by collective mobilisations around discourses such as indigeneity, customary landownership, nation-building and citizenship. We have also argued, against the backdrop of the Ethnic Tension and the increasingly violent character of Honiara's settlements, that force, in the form of collective violence or the threat thereof, may yet become more salient as a power of counter-exclusion in this urban space.

However, just as the *Powers of Exclusion* framework is tailored to the particular political economy and social contexts of Southeast Asia, diverse as they are, so too, we have suggested, the powers of exclusion and counter-exclusion at play in contemporary Honiara can only be fully understood in the context of an encompassing political economy characterised by patronage networks and personalised forms of political and administrative governance, and with reference to the particular histories and social relations of Solomon Islands. Perhaps the most salient example of this political economy has been the abuse of discretionary powers vested in the Commissioner of Lands, which has seen property rights in urban land allocated in ways that distort the market and abrogate formal legal procedures. In many instances, the abuse of these powers has seen urban property rights granted to individuals on the basis of political patronage or to foreign investors for personal economic gain.

The circumstances surrounding the way that these land transactions are made are often perceived as dubious by members of the public and contrary to the expectations of occupiers. With the 2014 amendment to the Land and Titles Act, which abolishes the Commissioner's powers and establishes a Land Board to administer and lease land, it is anticipated that a more transparent leasing process will be introduced. It is hoped that questionable land dealings will be minimised since the discretionary power to create property rights vests in a board rather an individual who can easily be manipulated or bribed. The board came into operation in December 2014 and produced an annual report for 2015 that was tabled in parliament in May 2016 and has recently been made accessible to the public. The report provides a list of land allocations and the names of successful applicants (GoSI 2016). This demonstrates a degree of transparency in the board's deliberations. However, there are no records of minutes concerning how the board has dealt with the applications, including in relation to the criteria used to assess them. Furthermore, the issue of the high cost of land transactions has remained, which means that in most cases only those with money can afford to successfully apply for urban land in Honiara. Some of the applicants to whom the board has allocated land, as shown in the annual report, have revealed that they have not been able access the land. This is because boundary markers have been moved, the land is already occupied by someone else, or officers in the Ministry of Lands have been unhelpful in showing where the land is located and facilitating its transfer.

References

Allan, C.H. 1957. *Customary Land Tenure in the British Solomon Islands Protectorate: Report of the Special Lands Commission*. Honiara: Western Pacific High Commission.

Allen, M.G. 2012. Land, Identity and Conflict on Guadalcanal. *Australian Geographer* 43:163–80. doi.org/10.1080/00049182.2012.682294

Allen, M.G. 2013. *Greed and Grievance: Ex-Militants' Perspectives on the Conflict in Solomon Islands, 1998–2003*. Honolulu: University of Hawai'i Press (Topics in the Contemporary Pacific 2).

Allen, M.G. and S. Dinnen 2015. Solomon Islands in Transition? *Journal of Pacific History* 50:381–97. doi.org/10.1080/00223344. 2015.1101194

Anon. 1964. Native Claim to Honiara Land Rejected. *Pacific Island Monthly*, April.

Anon. 2011. Landowners Caution. *Solomon Star* (Editorial), 4 July.

Anon. 2012. NSC to Put in Work Plan. *Solomon Star* (Editorial), 27 June.

Anon. 2013. NSC Powerless. *Solomon Star* (Editorial), 30 October.

Anon. 2014a. Gov't Urged to Fix Boundary Issue. *Solomon Star*, 23 August.

Anon. 2014b. Tandai Landowners Slash Demarcation Proposal. *Solomon Star*, 17 September.

Aruwafu, C. 2012. NSC: Ete's Excuse Lame. *Solomon Star*, 24 October.

Babasia, E. 2014. Lunga Land. *Solomon Star*, 25 June.

Bellam, M.E.P. 1970. The Colonial City: Honiara, a Pacific Islands Case Study. *Pacific Viewpoint* 11(1):66–96.

Bennett, J.A. 1987. *Wealth of the Solomons: A History of a Pacific Archipelago 1800–1978*. Honolulu: University of Hawai'i Press (Pacific Islands Monograph 3).

BSIP (British Solomon Islands Protectorate) 1968. *BSIP News Sheet*, 1–14 February.

Chand, S. and C. Yala 2008. Informal Land Systems within Urban Settlements in Honiara and Port Moresby. In AusAID (Australian Agency for International Development) (ed.), *Making Land Work—Volume Two: Case Studies on Customary Land and Development in the Pacific*. Canberra: AusAID.

Connell, J. 1983. *Migration, Employment and Development in the South Pacific—Country Report 16: Solomon Islands*. Noumea: South Pacific Commission.

Connell, J. and R. Curtain 1982. The Political Economy of Urbanization in Melanesia. *Singapore Journal of Tropical Geography* 3:119–36. doi.org/10.1111/j.1467-9493.1982.tb00235.x

Dawea, E. 2013. Councillor Wants Development Stopped. *Solomon Star*, 2 August.

Diisango, S. 2016. Concern over Illegal Settlements. *Solomon Star*, 28 September.

Dinnen, S. 2007. A Comment on State-Building in Solomon Islands. *Journal of Pacific History* 42:255–63. doi.org/10.1080/ 00223340701461700

Englund, H. 2002. The Village in the City, the City in the Village: Migrants in Lilongwe. *Journal of Southern African Studies* 28:137–54. doi.org/10.1080/03057070120117015

Filer, C. 1997. Compensation, Rent and Power in Papua New Guinea. In S. Toft (ed.), *Compensation for Resource Development in Papua New Guinea*. Port Moresby: Law Reform Commission (Monograph 6).

Filer, C. 2014. The Double Movement of Immovable Property Rights in Papua New Guinea. *Journal of Pacific History* 49:76–94. doi.org/10.1080/0022334 4.2013.876158

Foukona, J. 2007. Legal aspects of customary land administration in Solomon Islands. *Journal of South Pacific Law* 11(1):64–72.

Foukona, J. and D. Paterson 2013. Solomon Islands. In D. Paterson and S. Farran (eds), *South Pacific Land Systems*. Suva: University of the South Pacific Press.

Fraenkel, J. 2004. *The Manipulation of Custom: From Uprising to Intervention in the Solomon Islands*. Canberra: Pandanus Books.

Gagahe, N.K. 2000. The Process of Internal Movement in Solomon Islands: The Case of Malaita. *Asia-Pacific Population Journal* 15(2):53–75.

GoSI (Government of Solomon Islands) 2016. Land Board Annual Report 2015. Honiara: Ministry of Lands, Housing and Survey.

Hall, D., P. Hirsch and T. Li 2011. *Powers of Exclusion: Land Dilemmas in Southeast Asia*. Singapore: NUS Press.

Hou, T. and D. Kudu 2012. Solomon Islands: Honiara Urban Profile. Nairobi: United Nations Human Settlements Programme (UN-Habitat).

Inifiri, J. 2014. Police Investigation in Karaina Row Start. *Solomon Star*, 27 August.

Keen, M. and L. Kiddle 2016. Priced Out of the Market: Informal Settlements in Honiara, Solomon Islands. *State Society and Governance in Melanesia Program In Brief 2016/28*. Canberra: The Australian National University.

Leni, N. 2014. Extension of City Boundary. *Solomon Star*, 22 September.

McDonnell, S. 2013. Exploring the Cultural Power of Land Law in Vanuatu: Law as a Performance That Creates Meaning and Identities. *Intersections* 33.

Moore, C. 2007. Helpem Fren: The Solomon Islands, 2003–2007. *Journal of Pacific History* 42:141–64. doi.org/10.1080/00223340701461601

Moore, C. 2013. Honiara. In C. Moore (ed.), *Solomon Islands Historical Encyclopaedia 1893–1978*. St Lucia: University of Queensland. www.solomon encyclopaedia.net/biogs/E000133b.htm (accessed 13 April 2014).

Moore, C. 2015. Honiara: Arrival City and Pacific Hybrid Living Space. *Journal of Pacific History* 50:419–36. doi.org/10.1080/00223344. 2015.1110869

Namosuaia, D. 2013. Land Risk. *Solomon Star*, 7 June.

Namosuaia, D. 2014. Mass City Clean-Up—Council Sets to Demolish Illegal Buildings. *Solomon Star*, 31 January.

Orea, A.S. 2009. Who is Kuvu? *Solomon Star*, 15 December.

Palmer, E. 2010. Land Row … Guadalcanal Wants to Be Part of Lungga Land Sale. *Solomon Star*, 31 March.

Palmer, E. 2013. Tran Acquire Title for Karaina Settlement. *Solomon Star*, 17 October.

Pelto, M. 2013. High Value Urban Land in Honiara For Sale—Deep, Deep Discounts Available to the Right Buyer. Devpolicy blogpost, 16 December. devpolicy.org/high-value-urban-land-in-honiara-for-sale-deep-deep-discounts-available-to-the-right-buyer-20131214/ (accessed 12 December 2016).

Piringi, C. 2013a. Defying Orders. *Solomon Star*, 10 October.

Piringi, C. 2013b. Maeli Hits Back. *Solomon Star*, 14 October.

Sasako, A. 2003. The Day and Forces that Changed Solomon Islands. *Fiji Islands Business*, July.

Storey, D. 2003. The Peri-Urban Pacific: From Exclusive to Inclusive Cities. *Asia Pacific Viewpoint* 44:259–79. doi.org/10.1111/j.1467-8373.2003.00214.x

Theonomi, B. 2014. More Houses Demolished: Families Left Homeless as Police Tear Down Homes. *Solomon Star*, 18 June.

Tozaka, M. and J. Nage 1981. Administering Squatter Settlements in Honiara. In P. Larmour, R.G. Crocombe and A. Taungenga (eds), *Land, People and Government: Public Lands Policy in the South Pacific*. Suva: University of the South Pacific, Institute of Pacific Studies, in association with Lincoln Institute of Land Policy.

Vari, G. 2012. Lunga Land Ownership. *Solomon Star*, 16 May.

Williams, S. 2011. Public Land Governance in Solomon Islands. Washington, DC: World Bank, Justice for the Poor Program (Briefing Note 6:1).

WPHC (Western Pacific High Commission) n.d. Land Claims, Register B. Auckland: University of Auckland (Special Collection WPHC MP 18/1/2).

WPHC (Western Pacific High Commission) 1922. British Solomon Islands Commission Claim No. 17—Matanikau, Kookom. Auckland: University of Auckland (Special Collection WPHC 4/IV, MP 450/1922).

Zoleveke, G. 1979. Traditional Ownership and Land Policy. In P. Larmour (ed.), *Land in Solomon Islands*. Suva: University of the South Pacific, Institute of Pacific Studies.

PART 5: INTO THE FUTURE

16

The Ocean in Us

Epeli Hau'ofa

Hau'ofa, E. 1998. The Ocean in Us. *The Contemporary Pacific* 10(2): 391–410.

Republished with the kind permission of the University of Hawai'i Press.

We sweat and cry salt water, so we know that the ocean is really in our blood.

—Teresia Teaiwa

In a previous essay, I advanced the notion of a much enlarged world of Oceania that has emerged through the astounding mobility of our peoples in the last 50 years (Hau'ofa 1993). [1] Most of us are part of this mobility, whether personally or through the movements of our relatives. This expanded Oceania is a world of social networks that crisscross the ocean all the way from Australia and New Zealand in the southwest to the United States and Canada in the northeast. It is a world that we have created largely

---

1   This paper is based on one that was delivered as an Oceania Lecture at the University of the South Pacific, Suva, in March 1997 and subsequently published in *Dreadlocks In Oceania* Vol. 1:124–48. A briefer, earlier version was delivered as a keynote address at the Third Conference of the European Society of Oceanists, Copenhagen, 13–15 December 1996. I am grateful to Greg Fry for his very insightful papers, 'Framing the Islands', 'The Politics of South Pacific Regional Cooperation', and 'The South Pacific "Experiment"'. Our recent conversation in Wainadoi helped to clarify a number of issues dealt with here.

through our own efforts, and have kept vibrant and independent of the Pacific Islands world of official diplomacy and neocolonial dependency. In portraying this new Oceania, I wanted to raise, especially among our emerging generations, the kind of consciousness that would help free us from the prevailing, externally generated definitions of our past, present and future.

I wish now to take this issue further by suggesting the development of a substantial regional identity that is anchored in our common inheritance of a very considerable portion of Earth's largest body of water, the Pacific Ocean. The notion of an identity for our region is not new; through much of the latter half of this century people have tried to instill a strong sense of belonging to an island's region for the sake of sustained regional cooperation. So far these attempts have foundered on the reef of our diversity, and on the requirements of international geopolitics, combined with assertions of narrow national self-interests on the part of our individual countries. I believe that a solid and effective regional identity can be forged and fostered. We have not been very successful in our attempts so far because, while fishing for the elusive school of tuna, we have lost sight of the ocean that surrounds and sustains us.

A common identity that would help us to act together for the advancement of our collective interests, including the protection of the ocean for the general good, is necessary for the quality of our survival in the so-called Pacific Century when, as we are told, important developments in the global economy will concentrate in huge regions that encircle us. As individual, colonially created, tiny countries acting alone, we could indeed 'fall off the map' or disappear into the black hole of a gigantic pan-Pacific doughnut, as our perspicacious friends, the denizens of the National Centre for Development Studies in Canberra, are fond of telling us. But acting together as a region, for the interests of the region as a whole, and above those of our individual countries, we would enhance our chances for a reasonable survival in the century that is already dawning upon us. Acting in unison for larger purposes and for the benefit of the wider community could help us to become more open-minded, idealistic, altruistic and generous, and less self-absorbed and corrupt in the conduct of our public affairs than we are today. In an age when our societies are preoccupied with the pursuit of material wealth, when the rampant market economy brings out unquenchable greed and amorality in us, it is necessary for our institutions of learning to develop corrective mechanisms such as the one proposed here, if we are to retain our sense of humanity and community.

An identity that is grounded in something as vast as the sea should exercise our minds and rekindle in us the spirit that sent our ancestors to explore the oceanic unknown and make it their home, our home.

I would like to make it clear at the outset that I am not in any way suggesting cultural homogeneity for our region. Such a thing is neither possible nor desirable. Our diverse loyalties are much too strong for a regional identity ever to erase them. Besides, our diversity is necessary for the struggle against the homogenising forces of the global juggernaut. It is even more necessary for those of us who must focus on strengthening their ancestral cultures in their struggles against seemingly overwhelming forces, to regain their lost sovereignty. The regional identity that I am concerned with is something additional to other identities that we already have, or will develop in the future, something that should serve to enrich our other selves.

A Regional Identity

The ideas for a regional identity that I express here have emerged largely from nearly 20 years of direct involvement with an institution that caters for many of the tertiary educational needs of most of the South Pacific islands region, and increasingly of countries north of the equator. In a very real sense, the University of the South Pacific is a microcosm of the region, and many aspects of its history, which began in 1968 in the era of decolonisation of island territories, mirror the developments in the regional communities it serves. The well-known diversity of social organisations, economies and cultures of the region is reflected in the student population that comprises people from all 12 countries that own the university, as well as a sprinkling from other regions. This sense of diversity is heightened by daily interactions—between students themselves, among staff, and between staff and students—that take place on our main campus in Suva, and by staff visits to regional countries to conduct face-to-face instruction of our extension students, summer schools, research and consultancy, and to perform other university duties.

Yet through these same interactions there has developed at our university an ill-defined sense of belonging to a Pacific Islands region, and of being Pacific Islanders. Because of its size, its on-campus residential arrangements for staff and students, and its spread, the university is the premier hatchery for the regional identity. Nevertheless, the sense of diversity is much more palpable and tangible than that of a larger common identity; students identify themselves much more with their nationality, race and personal friendships across the cultural divide than with the Pacific Islander identity. This is to be expected. Apart from primordial loyalties, students come to the university to obtain certificates for returning home to work for their respective countries. They do not come to the university in order ultimately to serve the region as such.

In the early years of the university's existence, there was a concerted attempt to strengthen the common identity through the promotion of the Pacific Way as a unifying ideology. But the Pacific Way was a shallow ideology that was swept away by the rising tide of regional disunity of the 1980s. While promoting the Pacific Way, the university was simultaneously sponsoring diversity through the support it gave to student cultural groups based on nationality and race. This support was manifest most clearly in the sponsorship given to Pacific Week, an annual festival during which students displayed, largely through music and dance, the cultural diversity of the region. The irony of promoting both the Pacific Way and the Pacific Week was lost in the hope that unity would somehow emerge from diversity. But any lasting sense of unity derived from the enjoyment of the variety of music and dances of the region was tenuous because no serious attempt was made to translate them or place them in their historical and social contexts. Audiences enjoyed the melodies, the rhythms and the movements; everything else was mystery. There is also a complete absence in the university's curricula of any degree program in Pacific studies. Anthropology, one of the basic disciplines for such a program, is not even taught at our university.

The development of a clear regional identity within this university was also hampered by the introduction in the early 1980s of neo-Marxism, which, as a global movement, was quite hostile to any expression of localism and regionalism. According to this ideology, Pacific people were part of a worldwide class structure based on an international division of labour. Nationalism and regionalism were bourgeois attempts to prevent the international unity of the working classes. The demise of the Pacific Way through natural causes, and that of neo-Marxism as a direct result of the 1987 right-wing military coups in Fiji, removed from our campus discourses the ideologies that transcended cultural diversity. The Pacific Week sputtered on for another 10 years as an affirmative expression of difference, with nothing concrete to counterbalance it.

Outside the University of the South Pacific, Pacific Islands regionalism, promoted by several other regional organisations, was facing parallel problems, together with a considerable degree of confusion. Much of this could be traced back to the colonial period. For example, our region has come under a variety of names that reflect not only confusion about what we are, but also the ways in which we have been slotted into pigeonholes, or juggled around for certain purposes. The earliest general name for the region was the South Seas, which became virtually synonymous with paradise, a false concept that we have not successfully shed because it is used to promote the hospitality industry. When I grew up in Papua New Guinea in the 1940s, we were still South Sea Islanders. We had not heard of the South Pacific or Pacific Islanders.

A much less used term for our region is Australasia, which is a combination of Australia and Asia, meaning south of Asia. According to the *Concise Oxford Dictionary*, it refers to Australia and the islands of the southwest Pacific. The term implies that the islands are in Australia's orbit. Not infrequently, however, Australians refer to the region as their 'backyard', the sort of area that has to be guarded against intrusions from behind.

Only after the Second World War did the term South Pacific come into general and popular use. It seems to have first spread through the Western Alliance military terminology during the war, and was popularised by James Michener's book *Tales of the South Pacific* and Rodgers and Hammerstein's hugely successful musical version of it. But the term is a misleading one. As used in our premier regional organisations, South Pacific comprises not just those islands that lie south of the equator; it covers the whole region, from the Marianas, deep in the North Pacific, to New Zealand in the south. Be that as it may, the term South Pacific has replaced South Seas, which today is confined almost totally to history books and old records.

Since the beginning of the postcolonial era, the term Pacific Islands region has emerged and is gradually replacing South Pacific as the descriptive name for our region. The South Pacific region was a creation of the Cold War era, and its significance was largely in relation to the security of Western interests in the Far East. South Pacific clearly included Australia and New Zealand, but the term Pacific Islands region excludes our larger neighbours and indicates more clearly than before the separation between us and them. This may reflect our contemporary political sovereignty, but in more recent times it has emerged to signify our declining importance to the West since the end of the Cold War, as well as the progressive movement by our neighbours toward Asia. The South Pacific of the Cold War, when our region was liberally courted by the West, is finished. Perhaps the best indication of this is the recommendation made at the last meeting of the South Pacific Conference to remove the term South Pacific from its secretariat, the South Pacific Commission. It will come as no surprise if the secretariat is renamed Pacific Islands Commission, or some other redesignation to be determined by the ever-shifting perceptions of what our region is or should be. Will the same change be made to the conference itself? And what of the South Pacific Forum or, for that matter, our very own University of the South Pacific? The point is that, as the Pacific Islands region, we are no longer as needed by others as we were; we are now increasingly told to shape up or else. The Forum Secretariat has been radically downsized, and the headship of the South Pacific Commission has recently been taken over by a non–Pacific Islander for the first time in about three decades.

Two other terms that include our region are significant indicators of our progressive marginalisation. The first is Asia-Pacific region as used by certain international agencies, such as those of the United Nations, to lump us together with hundreds of millions of Asians for the administration of services of various kinds. The other term is Asia-Pacific Economic Cooperation, APEC, which covers the entire Pacific Rim, but excludes the whole of the Pacific Islands region. Thus in the United Nations' Asia-Pacific region we are an appendage (or perhaps the appendix) of Asia, and in APEC we do not exist. It should now be evident why our region is characterised as the 'hole in the doughnut': an empty space. We should take careful note of this because if we do not exist for others, then we could in fact be dispensable.

This is not an exaggeration. Early this century the people of Banaba were persuaded to give up their island to a phosphate-mining company for the benefit of the British Empire. In the mid-century, the inhabitants of Bikini were coaxed into giving up their island for atomic tests that would benefit all mankind. Both groups of people consented to the destruction of their inheritance largely because they had no choice. They are today among the world's displaced populations; those who benefited from their sacrifice have forgotten or are doing their best to forget their existence. What does this bode for us in the 21st century and beyond? Banaba and Bikini were not isolated cases. The latter part of this century has made it clear that ours is the only region in the world where certain kinds of experiment and exploitation can be undertaken by powerful nations with minimal political repercussions to themselves. Modern society is generating and accumulating vast quantities of waste matter that must in the near future be disposed of where there will be least resistance. It may well be that for the survival of the human species in the next millennium we in Oceania will be urged, in the way the people of Banaba and Bikini were urged, to give up our lands and seas.

The older terms for our region were coined before any sense of regionalism on our part arose. In Africa and the Middle East, regionalism emerged from the struggle for independence. In our part of the world, regionalism first emerged as a creation of colonialism to preempt the rise of revolutionary, or even non-revolutionary, independence movements. This is the root of much of the problem of regionalism in the Pacific. We have not been able to define our world and ourselves without direct and often heavy external influences.

In summary, we could take our changing identities as a region over the last 200 years as marking the different stages of our history. In the earliest stage of our interactions with the outside world, we were the South Sea paradise of noble savages living in harmony with a bountiful nature; we were simultaneously lost and degraded souls to be pacified, Christianised, colonised and civilised. Then we became the South Pacific region of much importance for the security of Western interests in Asia. We were pampered by those whose real interests lay elsewhere, and those who conducted dangerous experiments on our islands. We have passed through that stage into the Pacific Islands region of naked, neocolonial dependency. Our erstwhile suitors are now creating with others along the rim of our ocean a new set of relationships that excludes us totally. Had this been happening elsewhere, our exclusion would not have mattered much. But in this instance we are physically located at the very centre of what is occurring around us. The development of APEC will affect our existence in fundamental ways whether we like it or not. We cannot afford to ignore our exclusion because what is involved here is our very survival.

The time has come for us to wake up to our modern history as a region. We cannot confront the issues of the Pacific Century individually as tiny countries, nor as the Pacific Islands region of bogus independence. We must develop a much stronger and genuinely independent regionalism than what we have today. A new sense of the region that is our own creation, based on our perceptions of our realities, is necessary for our survival in the dawning era.

Our present regionalism is a direct creation of colonialism. It emerged soon after the Second World War with the establishment (by Australia, France, Great Britain, the Netherlands, New Zealand and the United States) of the South Pacific Conference and, later, its secretariat, the South Pacific Commission. The 1950 South Pacific Conference at Nasinu, Fiji, was the first occasion ever in which indigenous island leaders from throughout Oceania met in a single forum to discuss practical issues of common interest to them. Needless to say, the agenda was set by the colonial powers. These authorities dominated the conference and the commission, which they had established to facilitate the pooling of limited resources and the effective implementation of regional programs in health, education, agriculture, fisheries and so forth, and to involve island leaders in the consideration of regional development policies. But behind all this was our rulers' attempt to present a progressive face to the United Nations, decolonisation committee and to unite the region, under their leadership, in the struggle against Marxism and liberation ideologies. It is not surprising then that, unlike other colonial regions of the world, our political independence (except in Vanuatu and Western Samoa) was largely imposed on us. It also came in packages that tied us firmly to the West.

Politics was not discussed at the South Pacific Conference, a policy that has survived more or less in regional organisations that have emerged in the postcolonial period. Although the Nasinu conference and subsequent South Pacific Conferences engendered a sense of regional identity, the ban on political discussions, which, at the time, were on the burning issues of decolonisation and communist expansionism, prevented the development of this identity beyond a vague sense of commonality.

The frustration with external domination of the South Pacific Conference led to the formation of the South Pacific Forum as an exclusive club by the leaders of the newly independent countries of the region. But the independence of the South Pacific Forum was compromised from the beginning with the inclusion, for financial considerations, of Australia and New Zealand in its membership. The membership of these countries in the South Pacific Conference and the South Pacific Forum has brought about complications in the development of a postcolonial regional identity. Australia and New Zealand are members of these regional bodies, not as nations but as patron governments. By mutual identification, their leaders who attend high-level regional meetings, and their representatives in regional secretariats, do not call themselves, nor are they considered,

Pacific Islanders. They are, however, our closest neighbours, with whom we have had historical and cultural connections that date back to the beginning of the European settlements of their countries. There is already an identity with these countries based on history, geography and numerous contemporary involvements, but this is fraught with ambivalence. New Zealand and especially Australia are not infrequently considered by us to be domineering, exploitative and in possession of the gentleness and sensitivity of the proverbial bull in a china shop, while we are often considered by the other side to be mendicant and mendacious, and our leading citizens woefully inept. Among ourselves, we do hold and express mutually uncomplimentary views, and occasionally act violently against each other, attitudes and conducts that are inimical to the development of regionalism. The point, however, is that, by virtue of their governments' membership in our premier regional organisations, Australia and New Zealand exert strong, if not dominant, influences in the conduct of our regional affairs and in the shaping of any Pacific Islands identity. At the same time, these countries display a strong chameleonic tendency; they have a habit of dropping in and out of the South Pacific region whenever it suits their national self-interests.

National self-interest and pride, the emergence of subregional blocks based on perceived cultural and ethnic affiliations, and the timidity and sheer lack of foresight on the part of our leaders, are examples of the numerous problems that beset Pacific Islands regionalism. Since these are commonly known, I will not discuss them here; suffice it to say that in general our regional organisations exist today mainly to serve national interests rather than those of the region as such.

Nevertheless, in the few instances when the region stood united, we have been successful in achieving our common aims. It is of utmost significance for the strengthening of a regional identity to know that our region has achieved its greatest degrees of unity on the issues of the threat to our common environment: the ocean. It should be noted that on these issues Australia and New Zealand often assumed the necessary leading roles because of our common sharing of the ocean. On issues of this kind, the sense of a regional identity, of being Pacific Islanders, is felt most acutely. The movement toward a Nuclear Free and Independent Pacific, the protests against the wall-of-death drift-netting, against plans to dispose of nuclear wastes in the ocean, the incineration of chemical weapons on Johnston Island, the 1995 resumption of nuclear tests on Moruroa, and, most ominously, the specter of our atoll islands and low-lying coastal regions disappearing under the rising sea level, are instances of a regional united front against threats to our environment. But as these issues come to the fore only occasionally, and as success in protests has dissipated the immediate sense of threat, we have generally reverted to our normal state of disunity and the pursuit of national self-indulgence. The problems, especially of toxic waste disposal and destructive exploitation of ocean resources, remain to haunt us. Nuclear-powered ships and vessels carrying radioactive materials still ply the ocean; international business concerns are still looking for islands for the disposal of toxic industrial wastes; activities that contribute to the depletion of the ozone continue; drift-netting has abated but not stopped; and the reefs of Moruroa Atoll may still crack and release radioactive materials. People who are concerned with these threats are trying hard to enlist region-wide support, but the level of their success is low as far as the general public is concerned. Witness the regionwide silence while the plutonium-laden Pacific Teal sailed through our territorial waters in March 1997. There is, however, a trend in the region to move from mere protests to the stage of active protection of the environment. For this to succeed, regionalism has to be strengthened. No single country in the Pacific can by itself protect its own slice of the oceanic environment: the very nature of that environment prescribes regional effort. And to develop the ocean resources sustainably, regional unity is required.

A Pacific Islands regional identity means a Pacific Islander identity. What or who is a Pacific Islander? The University of the South Pacific categorises its students and staff into regionals and non-regionals. A regional is someone who is a citizen of one of the member countries of the university's region. A regional is a Pacific Islander. But the issue is more complex than that. There are thousands of people with origins in Oceania who are citizens of Canada, the United States, Australia and New Zealand, and who consider themselves Pacific Islanders. In Fiji, about half the citizen population is of non-indigenous origin, and they are not considered or called Fijians. The term Fijian is reserved for the indigenous population, which still considers the rest as *vulagi*, or guests, even though their ancestors might have emigrated to Fiji a century or so ago. Fijians are Pacific Islanders. What of the rest? Given the mutual misunderstandings and suspicions between indigenous Fijians and, to some extent, most other indigenous Pacific Islanders on the one hand, and Indo-Fijians on the other, what proportion of the latter consider themselves Pacific Islanders? The view held by some people in the region is that only indigenous populations are Pacific Islanders. One of the reasons why many people disliked the Pacific Way ideology was their perceived exclusion from its coverage. There were, and perhaps still are, a few people in Tonga with full or part foreign ancestries who were or are stateless persons. Cook Islanders are citizens of their own country and simultaneously of New Zealand. French Polynesians and New Caledonians are French citizens, Guamanians are American citizens, and American Samoans have a leg each in the United States and eastern Samoa. To what degree are these people Pacific Islanders? Similar questions could be raised about the New Zealand Māori, Native Hawaiians and Australian Aborigines.

In anticipation of what I shall say later, I would like to make one point briefly. The issue of what or who is a Pacific Islander would not arise if we considered Oceania as comprising people as human beings with a common heritage and commitment, rather than as members of diverse nationalities and races. Oceania refers to a world of people connected to each other. The term Pacific Islands region refers to an official world of states and nationalities. John and Mary cannot just be Pacific Islanders; they have to be Ni-Vanuatu, or Tuvaluan, or Samoan first. As far as I am concerned, anyone who has lived in our region and is committed to Oceania is an Oceanian. This view opens up the possibility of expanding Oceania progressively to cover larger areas and more peoples than is possible under the term Pacific Islands region. In this formulation, the concepts Pacific Islands region and Pacific Islanders are as redundant as South Seas and South Sea Islanders. We have to search for appropriate names for common identities that are more accommodating, inclusive and flexible than what we have today.

At our university, the search for unity and common identity took on a new life following two incidents of violent confrontation in 1994 between inebriated students of different nationalities. In the aftermath of these incidents, which shook the university to its foundations, renewed efforts were made to bring about a sense of unity and common identity among our students in order to promote cross-cultural understanding and cooperation, and to forestall further outbreaks of violence. Measures were taken to minimise the deleterious consequences of diversity. Funding of cultural groups was drastically reduced, the Pacific Week was abandoned and the flag-raising ceremonies to celebrate national days were discontinued. Students were urged to regroup themselves into interest-based associations with memberships that cut across nationality and ethnicity. Our staff reexamined our academic programs, resulting in the introduction of a common course in Pacific studies, which itself is the beginning of a drive to introduce a Pacific studies degree program for the first time at this university, of all places.

The Oceania Centre for Arts and Culture

In 1996, the university finally acted on a decision made by its council in 1992 to establish an arts and culture program by creating the Centre for Pacific Arts and Culture, which opened in 1997.

As I was intimately involved in the planning for this centre, which deals directly with the issue of culture and identity, I became aware of two things. First, this new unit provides a rare opportunity for some of us at the university to realise the dreams we have had for many years. We have talked and written about our ideas and hopes, but only now have we been presented with an opportunity to transform them into reality. Second, if we were not careful, the programs being conceived for the centre would become a loose collection of odds and ends that would merely reflect the diversity of our cultures.

I began searching for a theme or a central concept on which to hang the programs of the centre. I toyed with the idea of Our Sea of Islands, which I had propounded a few years earlier, but felt uneasy about it because I did not wish to appear to be conspicuously riding a hobby horse. It is bad manners in many Oceanic societies to appear pushy. You do not push things for yourself. But it is a forgivable sin if you accidentally get someone else to do it for you. So I kept the idea at the back of my mind, and while in this condition I came across the following passage in an article written by Sylvia Earle (1996) for Time Magazine:

> The sea shapes the character of this planet, governs weather and climate, stabilises moisture that falls back on the land, replenishing Earth's fresh water to rivers, lakes, streams—and us. Every breath we take is possible because of the life-filled life-giving sea; oxygen is generated there, carbon dioxide absorbed. Both in terms of the sheer mass of living things and genetic diversity, that's where the action is. Rain forests and other terrestrial systems are important too, of course, but without the living ocean there would be no life on land. Most of Earth's living space, the biosphere, is ocean-about 97%. And not so coincidentally 97% of Earth's water is Ocean.

After I read Earle's account, it became clear that the ocean, and our historical relationships with it, would be the core theme for the centre. At about the same time, our journalism students produced the first issue of their newspaper, *Wansolwara*, a pidgin word that they translated as 'one ocean, one people'. Things started to fall into place and we were able to persuade the university to call the new unit the Oceania Centre for Arts and Culture.

Oceania

It also occurred to me that despite the sheer magnitude of the oceans, we are among the minute proportion of Earth's total human population who can truly be referred to as 'oceanic peoples'. Besides, our region is sometimes referred to as Oceania, a designation that I prefer above all others, for some very good reasons.

All our cultures have been shaped in fundamental ways by the adaptive interactions between our people and the sea that surrounds our island communities. In general, the smaller the island the more intensive are the interactions with the sea, and the more pronounced the sea's influences on culture. One did not have to be in direct interaction with the sea to be influenced by it. Regular climatic patterns, together with such unpredictable natural phenomena as droughts, prolonged rains, floods and cyclones that influenced the systems of terrestrial activities were largely determined by the ocean. On the largest island of Oceania, New Guinea, products of the sea, especially the much-valued shells, reached the most remote highlands societies, shaping their ceremonial and political systems. But, more importantly, inland people of our large islands are now citizens of Oceanic countries whose capitals and other urban centres are located in coastal areas, to which they are moving in large numbers to seek advancement. The sea is already part of their lives. Many of us today are not directly or personally dependent on the sea for our livelihood and would probably get seasick as soon as we set foot on a rocking boat. This means only that we are no longer sea travellers or fishers. But as long as we live on our islands we remain very much under the spell of the sea; we cannot avoid it.

Before the advent of Europeans in our region, our cultures were truly oceanic in the sense that the sea barrier shielded us for millennia from the great cultural influences that raged through continental land masses and adjacent islands. This prolonged period of isolation allowed for the emergence of distinctive oceanic cultures with no non-oceanic influences, except on the original cultures that the earliest settlers brought with them when they entered the vast, uninhabited region. Scholars of antiquity may raise the issue of continental cultural influences on the western and northwestern border islands of Oceania, but these are exceptions, and Asian mainland influences were largely absent until the modern era. On the eastern extremity of the region, there were some influences from the Americas, but these were minimal. For these reasons, Pacific Ocean islands, from Japan through the Philippines and Indonesia, which are adjacent to the Asian mainland, do not have oceanic cultures, and are therefore not part of Oceania. This definition of our region that delineates us clearly from Asia and the pre-Columbian Americas is based on our own historical developments, rather than on other people's perceptions of us.

Although the sea shielded us from Asian and American influences, the nature of the spread of our islands allowed a great deal of mobility within the region. The sea provided waterways that connected neighbouring islands into regional exchange groups that tended to merge into one another, allowing the diffusion of cultural traits through most of Oceania. These common traits of bygone and changing traditions have so far provided many of the elements for the construction of regional identities. But very many people on our islands do not share these common traits as part of their heritage, and an increasing number of true urbanites are alienated from their ancient histories. In other words, although our historical and cultural traditions are important elements of a regional identity, they are not in themselves sufficient to sustain that identity, for they exclude all those people whose ancestral heritage is sourced elsewhere, and those who are growing up in non-traditional environments.

The ocean that surrounds us is the one physical entity that all of us in Oceania share. It is the inescapable fact of our lives. What we lack is the conscious awareness of it, its implications and what we could do with it. The potentials are enormous, exciting, as they have always been. When our leaders and planners say that our future lies in the sea, they are thinking only in economic terms, about marine and seabed resources and their development. When people talk of the importance of the oceans for the continuity of life on Earth, they are making scientific statements. But for us in Oceania, the sea defines us, what we are and have always been. As the great Caribbean poet Derek Walcott put it, the sea is history. Recognition of this could be the beginning of a very important chapter in our history. We could open it as we enter the third millennium.

All of us in Oceania today, whether indigenous or otherwise, can truly assert that the sea is our single common heritage. Because the ocean is ever-flowing, the sea that laps the coastlines of Fiji, for example, is the same water that washes the shores of all the other countries of our region. Most of the dry land surfaces on our islands have been divided and allocated, and conflicting claims to land rights are the roots of some of the most intractable problems in virtually all our communities. Until very recently, the sea beyond the horizon and the reefs that skirt our islands was open water that belonged to no one and everyone. Much of the conflict between the major ethnic groups in Fiji, for example, is rooted in the issue of land rights. But the open sea beyond the nearshore areas of indigenous Fijian fishing rights is open to every Fiji citizen and free of disputes. Similarly, as far as ordinary people of Oceania are concerned, there are no national boundaries drawn across the sea between our countries. Just about every year, for example, some lost Tongan fishers, who might well have been fishing in Fijian waters, wash up in their frail vessels on the shores of Fiji. They have always, so far, been taken very good care of, then flown back home loaded with tinned fish.

It is one of the great ironies of the Law of the Sea Convention, which enlarged our national boundaries, that it is also extending the territorial instinct to where there was none before. As we all know, territoriality is probably the strongest spur for some of the most brutal acts of aggression. Because of the resource potentials of the open sea and the ocean bed, the water that had united subregions of Oceania in the past may become a major divisive factor in the relationships between our countries in the future. It is therefore essential that we ground any new regional identity in a belief in the common heritage of the sea. A realisation of the fact that the ocean is uncontainable and pays no respect to territoriality should spur us to advance the notion, based on physical reality and practices that date back to the initial settlements of Oceania, that the sea must remain open to all of us.

A regional identity anchored in our common heritage of the ocean does not mean an assertion of exclusive regional territorial rights, for the same water that washes and crashes on our shores also does the same to the coastlines of the whole Pacific Rim, from Antarctica to New Zealand, Australia, Southeast and East Asia, and right around to the Americas. The Pacific Ocean also merges into the Atlantic and the Indian Oceans to encircle the entire planet. As the sea is an open and ever-flowing reality, so should our oceanic identity transcend all forms of insularity to become one that is openly searching, inventive and welcoming. In a metaphorical sense, the ocean that has been our waterway to each other should also be our route to the rest of the world. Our most important role should be that of custodians of the ocean, and, as such, we must reach out to similar people elsewhere for the common task of protecting the seas for the general welfare of all living things. This may sound grandiose but it really is not, considering the growing importance of international movements to implement the most urgent projects in the global environmental agenda: the protection of the ozone layer, the forests and the oceans. The formation of an oceanic identity is really an aspect of our waking up to things that are already happening around us.

The ocean is not merely our omnipresent, empirical reality; equally important, it is our most wonderful metaphor for just about anything we can think of. Contemplation of its vastness and majesty, its allurement and fickleness, its regularities and unpredictability, its shoals and depths, and its isolating and linking role in our histories, excites the imagination and kindles a sense of wonder, curiosity and hope that could set us on journeys to explore new regions of creative enterprise that we have not dreamt of before.

What I have tried to say so far is that in order to give substance to a common regional identity and animate it, we must tie history and culture to empirical reality and practical action. This is not new; our ancestors wrote our histories on the landscape and the seascape; carved, stenciled and wove our metaphors on objects of utility; and sang and danced in rituals and ceremonies for the propitiation of the awesome forces of nature and society.

Some 20 years ago, Albert Wendt, in his landmark paper 'Towards a New Oceania' (1976), wrote of his vision of the region and its first season of postcolonial cultural flowering. The first two paragraphs read:

> I belong to Oceania—or, at least, I am rooted in a fertile part of it—and it nourishes my spirit, helps to define me, and feeds my imagination. A detached objective analysis I will leave to sociologists and all the other 'ologists' ... Objectivity is for such uncommitted gods. My commitment won't allow me to confine myself to such a narrow vision. So vast, so fabulously varied a scatter of islands, nations, cultures, mythologies and myths, so dazzling a creature, Oceania deserves more than an attempt at mundane fact; only the imagination in free flight can hope-if not to contain her-to grasp some of her shape, plumage, and pain.

I will not pretend that I know her in all her manifestations. No one ... ever did; no one does ... no one ever will because whenever we think we have captured her she has already assumed new guises-the love affair is endless, even her vital statistics ... will change endlessly. In the final instance, our countries, cultures, nations, planets are what we imagine them to be. One human being's reality is another's fiction. Perhaps we ourselves exist only in each other's dreams.

At the end of his rumination on the cultural revival in Oceania, partly through the words of the region's first generation of postcolonial writers and poets, Wendt concluded with this remark:

> This artistic renaissance is enriching our cultures further, reinforcing our identities/self-respect/and pride, and taking us through a genuine decolonisation; it is also acting as a unifying force in our region. In their individual journeys into the Void, these artists, through their work, are explaining us to ourselves and creating a new Oceania (ibid.).

This is very true. And for a new Oceania to take hold it must have a solid dimension of commonality that we can perceive with our senses. Culture and nature are inseparable. The Oceania that I see is a creation of countless people in all walks of life. Artists must work with others, for creativity lies in all fields, and besides, we need each other.

These were the thoughts that went through my mind as I searched for a thematic concept on which to focus a sufficient number of programs to give the Oceania Centre a clear, distinctive and unifying identity. The theme for the centre and for us to pursue is the ocean, and the interactions between us and the sea that have shaped and are shaping so much of our cultures. We begin with what we have in common and draw inspirations from the diverse patterns that have emerged from the successes and failures in our adaptation to the influences of the sea. From there we can range beyond the tenth horizon, secure in the knowledge of the home base to which we will always return for replenishment and revisions of the purposes and directions of our journeys. We shall visit our people who have gone to the lands of diaspora and tell them that we have built something, a new home for all of us. And, taking a cue from the ocean's ever-flowing and encircling nature, we will travel far and wide to connect with oceanic and maritime peoples elsewhere, and swap stories of voyages that we have taken and those yet to be embarked on. We will show them what we have, and learn from them different kinds of music, dance, art, ceremonies and other forms of cultural production. We may even together make new sounds, new rhythms, new choreographies and new songs and verses about how wonderful and terrible the sea is, and how we cannot live without it. We will talk about the good things the oceans have bestowed on us, the damaging things we have done to them, and how we must together try to heal their wounds and protect them forever.

I have said elsewhere that there are no more suitable people on earth to be the custodians of the oceans than those for whom the sea is home. We seem to have forgotten that we are such a people. Our roots, our origins are embedded in the sea. All our ancestors, including those who came as recently as 60 years ago, were brought here by the sea. Some were driven here by war, famine and pestilence; some were brought by necessity, to toil for others; and some came seeking adventures and perhaps new homes. Some arrived in good health, others barely survived the traumas of passage. For whatever reasons, and through whatever experiences they endured, they came by sea to the sea, and we have been here since. If we listened attentively to stories of ocean passage to new lands, and of the voyages of yore, our minds would open up to much that is profound in our histories, to much of what we are and what we have in common.

Contemporary developments are taking us away from our sea anchors. Most of our modern economic activities are land based. We travel mostly by air, flying miles above the oceans, completing our journeys in hours instead of days and weeks and months. We rear and educate our young on things that have scant relevance to the sea. Yet we are told that the future of most of our countries lies there. Have we forgotten so much that we will not easily find our way back to the ocean?

As a region we are floundering because we have forgotten, or spurned, the study and contemplation of our pasts, even our recent histories, as irrelevant for the understanding and conduct of our contemporary affairs. We have thereby allowed others who are well equipped with the so-called objective knowledge of our historical development to continue reconstituting and reshaping our world and ourselves with impunity, and in accordance with their shifting interests at any given moment in history. We have tagged along with this for so long that we have kept our silence even though we have virtually been defined out of existence. We have floundered also because we have considered regionalism mainly from the points of view of individual national interests rather than the interest of a wider collectivity. And we have failed to build any clear and enduring regional identity, partly because, so far, we have constructed edifices with disconnected traits from traditional cultures and passing events, not basing them on concrete foundations.

The regional identity proposed here has been constructed on a base of concrete reality. That the sea is as real as you and I, that it shapes the character of this planet, that it is a major source of our sustenance, that it is something that we all share in common wherever we are in Oceania, are all statements of fact. But above that level of everyday experience, the sea is our pathway to each other and to everyone else, the sea is our endless saga, the sea is our most powerful metaphor, the ocean is in us.

References

Earle, S. 1996. The Well of Life. *Time Magazine*, 28 October.

Fry, G. 1991. The Politics of South Pacific Regional Cooperation. In R. Thakur (ed.), *The South Pacific: Problems, Issues, Prospects*. London: Macmillan, in association with the University of Otago. doi.org/10.1007/978-1-349-12519-7_11

Fry, G. 1996. Framing the Islands: Knowledge and Power in Changing Australian Images of 'The South Pacific'. *The Contemporary Pacific* 9:305–44.

Fry, G. 1997. The South Pacific 'Experiment': Reflections on the Origins of Regional Identity. *Journal of Pacific History* 32(2):180–202. doi.org/10.1080/00223349708572837

Hau'ofa, E. 1993. Our Sea of Islands. In E. Waddell, V. Naidu and E. Hau'ofa (eds), *A New Oceania: Rediscovering Our Sea of Islands*. Suva: School of Social and Economic Development, University of the South Pacific. Reprinted in *The Contemporary Pacific* 6(1994):147–61.

Wendt, A. 1976. Towards a New Oceania. *Mana Review* 1:49–60.

17

The 'New Pacific Diplomacy': An Introduction

Sandra Tarte and Greg Fry

This chapter is the introduction to another book published by ANU Press, listed below. It is republished in this collection as it is the best analysis we have of the 'new Pacific diplomacy', an assertion of Pacific countries' diplomatic independence in recent years on a wide range of issues from oceans management to fisheries and climate change.

— Stewart Firth and Vijay Naidu (eds)

Sandra Tarte: Personal Journey

As an early career scholar at the University of the South Pacific (USP), I was drawn to The Australian National University for my PhD studies by its reputation in the fields of Pacific studies and international relations. It was Greg Fry who directed me to the Australia-Japan Research Centre at ANU, where I subsequently completed my PhD under the supervision of Professor Peter Drysdale. After completing my degree, I returned to my position as a lecturer in history/politics at USP. But my links with ANU continued. My PhD, 'Japan's Aid Diplomacy and the Pacific Islands', was published jointly by ANU's National Centre for Development Studies and USP's Institute of Pacific Studies in 1998. That same year I spent part of my sabbatical with the State, Society and Governance in Melanesia program at ANU, writing an article on multilateral fisheries negotiations in the Pacific. This was later published in the *Journal of Pacific History* (Vol. 34, No. 3, 1999).

In more recent years, I have had the privilege of working at USP with a number of scholars from ANU (past and present) who have provided me with inspiration, collegiality and friendship. They include Stewart Firth, Scott MacWilliam, Greg Fry and, more recently, Matthew Allen. I am particularly proud of the collaboration with Greg that produced *The New Pacific Diplomacy*, a joint ANU/USP publication. Another recent ANU collaboration was with Matthew Dornan and Tess Newton-Cain from the Development Policy Centre at ANU, together with Wesley Morgan from USP, on green growth in the Pacific islands. I continue to contribute articles to the *East Asia Forum* blog, published by ANU.

Greg Fry: Personal Journey

I have had a very close connection with the University of the South Pacific (USP) over the last 43 years. It began in 1975 when I stayed on the USP campus as part of my field research for my master's thesis on Pacific regionalism. At this time, the campus was the vibrant centre for 'Pacific Way' activism in academia, the arts and literature, and political protest on nuclear activities. It was also the home of the new South Pacific Bureau for Economic Co-operation working on regional cooperation on trade, law of the sea and economic development. This exciting experience sparked my interest in the study of regionalism and Pacific politics, which I then continued at The Australian National University (ANU) in teaching and research. In 1981, I jumped at the opportunity to return to USP for a short-term appointment to teach politics in the School of Social and Economic Development. Even though I had to return to my position at ANU, this experience inspired me to spend a few weeks each subsequent year at USP engaging with regional scholars. I found this to be an invaluable support for my research and teaching of Pacific politics at ANU. In 2011, I was fortunate to be able to return to USP for five years. It was a very exciting time to be at the regional university and to be with colleagues who shared my interest in regional politics. It resulted in the production of a book, *The New Pacific Diplomacy*, co-edited with Sandra Tarte and jointly published by ANU Press and USP Press. It brought together a number of Pacific Island voices on the key issues in the changing regional landscape. I continue my involvement with USP as an adjunct associate professor involved in teaching postgraduate courses as required.

Tarte, S. and G. Fry 2015. The 'New Pacific Diplomacy': An Introduction. In G. Fry and S. Tarte (eds), *The New Pacific Diplomacy*. Canberra: ANU Press.

Since 2009 there has been a fundamental shift in the way that Pacific Island states engage with regional and world politics. The region has experienced what President Anote Tong of Kiribati has aptly called a 'paradigm shift' in ideas about how Pacific diplomacy should be organised, and on what principles it should operate. Many leaders have called for a heightened Pacific voice in global affairs and a new commitment to establishing Pacific Island control of this diplomatic process. This change in thinking has been expressed in the establishment of new channels and arenas for Pacific diplomacy at the regional and global levels, and new ways of connecting the two levels through active use of intermediate diplomatic associations.

This shift to a 'new Pacific diplomacy' is as fundamental as the move by the independent Pacific Island states four decades ago to create a postcolonial diplomatic system through the establishment of the South Pacific Forum (renamed Pacific Islands Forum in 2000) (Fry 1994). Indeed, in many ways, the current activity is reminiscent of that time—in its assertive attitude, the emphasis on Pacific Island control of the diplomatic agenda, the creation of new institutions, its appeal to regional identity and its concern with negotiating global agendas that are impacting Pacific societies. It is not, in our view, too dramatic to see this as a time of transformation of the regional diplomatic culture equivalent to the move from the colonial to the postcolonial era, a time that represents a transformation of regional order.[1]

This book brings together a range of analyses and perspectives on these dramatic new developments in Pacific diplomacy at sub-regional, regional and global levels, and in the key sectors of global negotiation for Pacific states: oceans management, fisheries, climate change, sustainable development, decolonisation, seabed mining and trade.[2] It also examines state and non-government roles in this new Pacific diplomacy. The book also focuses on the question of the significance of these new developments in negotiating global issues of key importance to the Pacific, and the implications for the future of the regional diplomatic architecture. Some of these perspectives are analyses of new developments, others are proposals that can be seen as part of the new Pacific diplomacy. Examples of the latter include the call by Cook Islands Prime Minister Henry

---

1   Sandra Tarte makes the detailed case for seeing the new Pacific diplomacy as constituting a shift in regional order (Tarte 2014).
2   Most of these chapters were first delivered as papers to the New Pacific Diplomacy Workshop organised by the School of Government, Development and International Affairs, the University of the South Pacific, Suva, 4–5 December 2014.

Puna to 're-imagine' the region, President Tong's appeal for the Pacific to 'chart its own course' and Ambassador Kaliopate Tavola's proposal for a Pacific-controlled Pacific Islands Forum (without Australia and New Zealand) to better meet the strategic necessities of the Pacific Island states in global diplomacy.

To create a context for considering these perspectives, this introductory chapter explores five questions. First, what do we mean by 'Pacific diplomacy'? Second, what are the expressions of the new Pacific diplomacy? Third, how significant is the new Pacific diplomacy? Fourth, how should we understand its emergence? Fifth, what are the implications of the new Pacific diplomacy for the negotiation of Pacific Island interests and for the future regional architecture?

'Pacific Diplomacy'

As employed in the following chapters, the 'Pacific' refers to the thousands of islands and island societies scattered across the Pacific Ocean, stretching from the Micronesian islands just south of Japan and east of the Philippines, south to Papua New Guinea and down the Melanesian chain of islands to New Caledonia, then east across the Polynesian Pacific to Tahiti. These societies are politically organised into 14 postcolonial states (Cook Islands, Federated States of Micronesia, Fiji, Kiribati, Marshall Islands, Nauru, Niue, Palau, Papua New Guinea, Samoa, Solomon Islands, Tonga, Tuvalu and Vanuatu) and the remaining dependent territories of France (New Caledonia, Wallis and Futuna and French Polynesia), Britain (Pitcairn Island), New Zealand (Tokelau) and the US (American Samoa, Guam and the Commonwealth of the Northern Mariana Islands). Taking into account its sea area (largely made up of 200 nautical mile exclusive economic zones of the constituent states and territories), this region is roughly the size of Africa.

By 'Pacific diplomacy', we mean the diplomacy pursued by Pacific states in global forums, or in multilateral arenas in which the Pacific bloc is negotiating with just one external power (as in the case of tuna negotiations with the US). This includes negotiations within the Pacific group to determine joint positions to be taken to global talks. It refers to their engagement in the joint negotiation of such matters as trade, sustainable development, climate change, nuclear issues, decolonisation and fisheries. We also include the diplomatic activity concerned with establishing the diplomatic institutions in which regional diplomacy is carried out and a Pacific joint position is negotiated. Finally, we include in our definition of Pacific diplomacy the accepted principles, norms and practices that underpin regional diplomacy and might be usefully described as constituting a regional diplomatic culture.

The history of Pacific diplomacy, so defined, begins in a concerted way in the mid-1960s as the first Pacific Island states became independent from colonial rule. The new Pacific states conducted their own foreign policies, but as small island states their capacity for extensive unilateral diplomacy was limited.[3] From the start, there was a commitment to regional diplomacy and joint diplomatic approaches in global forums to effect diplomatic outcomes. In this volume, Transform Aqorau refers to this as 'the diplomacy of the past, the "Pacific Way", and doing things by consensus'.

The key vehicle for this Pacific diplomacy was the South Pacific Forum. It was established partly to promote cooperation on regional ventures, but, just as importantly, also to take a Pacific voice to the world. The Pacific Island states were preoccupied with working together to advance their interests in global diplomacy as well as integrating their economies. They did so by creating a regional organisation, the South Pacific Forum. In the 1970s and 1980s, the forum was very active in expressing a Pacific diplomacy on key issues. Their successful joint diplomacy, which took place under the auspices of the forum, culminated in a series of international treaties on resource protection, environmental issues and tuna access, and prohibitions on drift-net fishing, the dumping of radioactive wastes in Pacific waters, nuclear testing and trade (Fry 1994). They also collectively achieved the reinscription of New Caledonia on the list of territories falling under the oversight of the United Nations (UN) Decolonisation Committee. These were notable achievements for joint diplomacy by the Pacific states as they took on the world's most powerful countries on issues of great concern to the national interest of those powers.

From the mid-1990s, the forum was much less active in global diplomacy. Led by an Australian and New Zealand concern with promoting regional integration and a new regional economic order along neoliberal lines, the forum became focused on regional integration (Fry 2005). This was joined by a War on Terror security agenda from 2001, focusing on countering

---

3 These constraints are explored in Boyce and Herr (1974).

transnational organised crime and terrorism. While there were examples of the earlier diplomacy being pursued by the forum secretariat—on trade negotiations with Europe, and with Australia and New Zealand, for example (as described by Wesley Morgan in this volume)—this had largely disappeared by 2000. By then, the forum appeared to have moved away from its founding objective of assisting Pacific states to negotiate jointly on global issues impacting the region.

The New Diplomatic System

The most dramatic expression of what we are calling the new Pacific diplomacy has been associated with Fiji's activist foreign policy since its suspension from the Pacific Islands Forum (PIF) in 2009. The Bainimarama Government enunciated several new foreign policy principles aimed at circumventing its isolation in regional and global diplomacy: that Fiji should garner and represent a Pacific voice that could be heard in global forums; that Fiji should promote itself as the hub of the Pacific and as a leader of Pacific Island states; that it should engage in south–south cooperation in the Pacific and the wider world; that regional diplomacy and regional institutions should be firmly controlled by Pacific Island states and not constrained by metropolitan powers (especially Australia and New Zealand); and that the Pacific should be better organised to engage in global diplomacy. The Fiji Government also introduced the idea of including civil society, the private sector and dependent territories, alongside independent governments, as equal partners in a new kind of 'network diplomacy'.

Fiji expressed these ideas in a series of major initiatives: in giving leadership to a renaissance of the Melanesian Spearhead Group (MSG); in creating the Pacific Islands Development Forum (PIDF); and by invigorating the existing Pacific Small Island Developing States at the UN as a Pacific Island–only bloc to a point where it replaced the PIF as the main representative of the Pacific voice at the UN. These developments in Fiji's new Pacific diplomacy are described and examined in the chapters by Ambassador Mawi and Makereta Komai.

It is, however, a central premise underlying the approach of this book that it would be a mistake to see the new Pacific diplomacy as solely a Fiji phenomenon. Fiji policy and leadership has obviously been the key catalyst, but it is important to note the wider support for these new institutions and ideas across the region as evidenced in the support for a new array of Pacific-controlled institutions.

Significantly, the new Pacific diplomacy has been expressed in the actions of the Pacific Island states since 2009 in developing a new diplomatic architecture outside the PIF system, both to conduct some important aspects of regional affairs and to represent the Pacific Islands region to the world on the key issues of concern such as climate change and fisheries management. For Pacific leaders, these moves do not represent a wholesale rejection of the PIF; rather they suggest recognition of a need for complementary forums to undertake diplomatic functions and pursue needs that can no longer be met in the PIF system.[4] The new Pacific diplomatic system now handles the core global diplomatic needs of the Pacific Island states in relation to key issues such as trade, climate change, decolonisation, fisheries management and sustainable development. This new system has worked well to meet those needs, and is widely supported by Pacific Island states.

Pacific Small Island Developing States

One significant institutional development has been the rise of the Pacific Small Island Developing States Group (PSIDS) at the UN. Although this group had existed since the early 1990s in relation to global sustainable development negotiations in the Rio process, the PSIDS has taken on a dramatically new diplomatic role for the Pacific Island states since 2009, to the point where it has all but replaced the PIF as the primary organising forum for Pacific representations at the global level.

The PSIDS has also become the key diplomatic vehicle for Pacific participation in global southern coalitions such as the Alliance of Small Island States (AOSIS) and the Group of 77. It is, for example, the main organising arena for determining and prosecuting Pacific positions on climate change mitigation in the UN Framework Convention on Climate Change, and also in relation to the Rio+20 UN Conference on Sustainable Development in 2012, and the Third International Conference on Small Island Developing States in Apia, Samoa, in 2014. It is important to

---

4   This refers to the forum itself and the other institutions in the Council of Regional Organisations in the Pacific (CROP), such as the Forum Fisheries Agency, Secretariat of the Pacific Regional Environment Programme and the Secretariat of the Pacific Community.

note that while the enhancement of PSIDS was undoubtedly a Fiji-led initiative, it has been strongly supported by all Pacific Island state UN members. Fulori Manoa explores the significance of this development of the PSIDS at the UN in this volume.

Melanesian Spearhead Group

A second major expression of the new Pacific diplomacy has been the reinvigoration of the MSG and its emergence as a major forum for sub-regional integration, and for diplomacy on decolonisation. Again, although Fiji leadership provided the catalyst for its reinvigoration, it is important to note that all Melanesian countries embraced the new and deeper integration proposed as part of the new MSG since 2009. Papua New Guinean leadership was also very important in this reinvigoration. The achievements have been significant. Most prominent has been the achievement of significant free trade in goods and services, including the movement of skilled labour, which is explored by Sovaia Marawa in this volume. The MSG has been able to achieve a level of integration not yet achieved in the wider PIF grouping in relation to trade and movement of professional workers.

The Pacific Islands Development Forum

The third and perhaps most controversial element in the new regional diplomatic architecture is the PIDF, which was a Fiji-led initiative established in 2013. It developed out of the Engaging with the Pacific meetings, which Fiji organised from 2010 as a means of building ties with its Pacific neighbours following suspension from the PIF. While clearly the flagship of the Fiji Government's efforts to lead regional diplomacy after suspension from the PIF, the new kind of regional diplomacy it represented also appealed to many other Pacific leaders. This is described in the chapter by Sandra Tarte.

There were three novel elements of the PIDF that particularly seemed to capture the imagination of Pacific Island leaders. The first was that the new institution emphasised inclusivity, a connection between leaders and society, which had been lacking in the PIF. It brought together civil society groups, the private sector, international agencies and governments in a process that stressed partnerships and network diplomacy. Second is its focus on 'green growth', which seemed to offer hope of overcoming the stalling of regional action in key areas such as climate change and sustainable development. Finally, the PIDF was motivated by the desire for self-determination. At the PIDF secretariat opening in 2014, Prime Minister Bainimarama said the Fiji-based group had a single purpose:

> It is not a question of prestige or establishing yet another talkfest, it is about creating an organisation that is more attuned to our development needs as Pacific countries. It is about creating an organisation that is relatively free of interference from outsiders (Cooney 2014).

Although Prime Minister Bainimarama has said that the PIDF was not intended to compete with the PIF, he seemed to give a different impression in other statements about the organisation's purpose:

> Why do we need a new body, a new framework of cooperation? Because the existing regional structure for the past four decades —the Pacific Islands Forum—is for governments only and has also come to be dominated only by a few (Pareti 2013).

Parties to the Nauru Agreement

The fourth institutional development was the establishment of the Parties to the Nauru Agreement (PNA) Headquarters in 2009. The PNA represented the island states with the region's largest tuna stocks and served as a vehicle for gaining greater control over their shared resource. The tiny but effective Majuro-based secretariat has been highly successful in implementing novel ideas in fisheries management, which have translated into dramatic increases in revenue to the member countries. This development is independent of Fiji's suspension from the PIF, since Fiji is not a member of PNA, and therefore demonstrates a broader assertion of Pacific control over regionalism. The role and impact of the PNA are described in the chapters by Transform Aqorau and Jope Tarai.

New Trade Negotiation Agencies

Finally, Pacific Island states have created new Pacific-run institutions outside the PIF to negotiate trade and economic relationships with Australia, New Zealand and Europe. In the case of negotiations with Australia and New Zealand on the Pacific Agreement on Closer Economic Relations (PACER) Plus (described in the chapter by Wesley Morgan), they argued for an independent office outside the PIF to provide advice on the negotiations. The Vila-based Office of the Chief Trade Adviser was established in 2009, despite Australian and New Zealand efforts first to oppose its creation, then to dictate who the adviser would be, and finally to sideline it. In the case of negotiations with the European Union over a regional economic partnership agreement, and in relation to developing Pacific positions to take to African, Caribbean and Pacific (ACP) meetings, the Pacific Island states decided in 2012 to create a Pacific ACP Office based in Port Moresby. The Pacific Islands Forum Secretariat had previously been the responsible agency for this function (Komai 2014).

Pacific Islands Forum

It could be argued that we are now seeing evidence of new Pacific diplomacy ideas in developments within the PIF. Dame Meg Taylor's chapter talks about inclusivity, and making the forum fit for purpose and responsive to critical reviews (allowing the leaders to make effective decisions). Significantly, the forum has also begun to redefine its mandate to include joint diplomacy, rather than just integration and cooperation as in the recent past, and has made new claims to diplomatic agendas, which it had seemingly abandoned in the previous decade. This is partly in response to the new Pacific diplomacy, and indicates the influence of the thinking and ideas shaping the new diplomacy. Whereas the new Pacific diplomacy is in many ways a response to what was seen as the limitations of the PIF (that it was elitist, statist and unable to act on key diplomatic needs such as climate change), the forum has now sought to remedy some of these areas. As Dame Meg Taylor asserts, 'The forum secretariat must engage with civil society and the private sector more routinely in its work. We need to recognise the important role that civil society plays in the regional space'.[5] As Claire Slatter argues in this volume, the new Pacific framework goes a long way in addressing the key concerns of civil society about inclusion and openness, although she argues it is still too early to judge how substantive these moves are.

---

5   Address by Secretary-General of the Pacific Islands Forum Secretariat, Diplomacy Roundtable, School of Government, Development and International Affairs, Faculty of Business and Economics, the University of the South Pacific, 27 May 2015.

A Paradigm Shift?

Underpinning these institutional changes is a new set of ideas about how the Pacific should engage in global and regional diplomacy. The coherence and novelty of these ideas and their departure from prevailing ideas suggests that President Tong of Kiribati was prescient in calling this a paradigm shift. First and foremost of these ideas is that the Pacific should, in President Tong's words, 'chart its own course'. This is reflected in various calls for the development of an effective Pacific voice, in Prime Minister Puna's call for reimagining Oceania, and in the founding ideas of the PIDF. This call for regional self-determination is expressed in the creation of new institutions and ventures.

Second, there is the claim that the Pacific needs to engage assertively in global diplomacy in relation to key challenges impacting the region; that it should indeed aspire to global diplomatic leadership in key areas such as climate change, tuna diplomacy, and oceans management. Third, it is claimed that there should be effective representation of a genuine 'Pacific voice' in global forums and that Pacific Island states need to work together in joint diplomacy at the global level. Fourth, there is growing recognition and acceptance of the role of sub-regional groupings and initiatives, in line with the view that a 'one-region' approach need not be the best approach. As Aqorau notes in his contribution to this volume, 'Having a single region arrangement is useful for some purposes but not for others'. Chapters by Dame Meg Taylor and Tess Newton Cain also make this argument.

Fifth, there should be a capacity to participate in southern diplomatic alliances and to leverage Pacific Island positions on the global agenda through these intermediaries. Specifically, Pacific diplomatic architecture needs to be configured to provide the capacity to participate in middle level 'southern' diplomatic alliances, such as AOSIS, the ACP and Group of 77 plus China. Sixthly, the generation of the Pacific voice needs to be inclusive (of civil society, private sector and governments).

The Significance of the 'New Pacific Diplomacy'

How then should we assess the significance of this new Pacific diplomacy? As already suggested, we argue that it represents a fundamental transformation in diplomatic ideas, institutions and practices. The transformative nature of this new paradigm and its institutional expression in a new diplomatic system is seen more clearly if we compare the current developments with other stages in the history of Pacific diplomacy. Seen in this historical context, the significance of the current changes is clearly of the order of the shift from the colonial to the postcolonial diplomatic system in 1971.

Those developments set up a regional diplomatic culture with certain assumptions about who should belong, who should speak and how diplomacy should be conducted. This prevailed until the early 1990s. In the 1990s and 2000s there was a slow unravelling of this regional diplomatic culture, and a move away from the assumptions of equality and respect for self-determination. When compared with the regional diplomatic culture that developed in the 1990s and early 2000s, which was hierarchical and disrespectful to the self-determination principle, the new Pacific diplomacy represents a new regional diplomatic culture. At the same time, because it represents the same values and principles of the original regional political settlement of 1971, it could also be represented as a restoration of the original regional diplomatic culture established by the forum in 1971 (Fry 2015). More broadly, the new Pacific diplomacy can be seen as effecting a fundamental change in the contemporary regional order, given its impact on the pattern of power and the transformation of dominant ideas and institutions (Tarte 2014).

The significance of the new Pacific diplomacy is also accentuated by the lack of attention to the joint diplomacy side of regionalism within the PIF for the last two decades, seemingly encouraged by a definition of regionalism focused on regional integration. This emphasis had overlooked that the forum was established to do both—support regional integration and represent the Pacific interests in global diplomacy. In the first two decades it was not doing well on regional integration, but it was highly successful in collective diplomacy. In the next two decades it focused more on regional integration and less on its role of representing the region in global diplomacy. This makes the emergence of the new Pacific diplomacy, from around 2009, an even more marked development.

Finally, significance is derived from the fact that support for this new paradigm, and the new institutions, has come from across the Pacific. Thus this is not just to be seen as only Fiji-supported, and as therefore disappearing once Fiji re-enters the forum system. The PSIDS, for example, is supported by all Pacific Island states (including Samoa), and the significant MSG achievements since 2009 could only be achieved with the support of all Melanesian states and the joint leadership of Fiji and PNG. There is widespread Pacific support for the principles and objectives of the PIDF. They are not about to be wound back to the status quo ante with Fiji's return to democracy.

Why the New Pacific Diplomacy?

How then to explain this transformative development in Pacific diplomacy since the late 2000s? For many observers, the answer is Fiji. Fiji foreign policy post-2009 was the catalyst for many of the key institutional developments. Suspended from the forum, and from forum trade talks with the European Union, Fiji sought other ways of linking to the world and alternate regional arenas. It obviously had the key role in initiating the reinvigoration of the MSG and the establishment of the PIDF, and the development of the Pacific group at the UN was a Fiji initiative. However, other leaders and countries supported Fiji's initiatives and nearly all Pacific Island states signed on to these initiatives.

Other observers have emphasised China's influence or the support of other geopolitical influences as being behind these developments. As argued by Michael O'Keefe in this volume, while the heightened global interest in the Pacific, particularly from China, acted as a facilitating environment for some of these developments, the driving force is provided by Pacific agency.

The changing geopolitics of the region since 2009 have created an enabling context to promote alternative diplomatic initiatives without relying on Australian or New Zealand funding. Chinese, Russian, Indonesian and United Arab Emirates funding is important for PIDF operations, for example.

The driving force for the wider support for the new Pacific diplomacy lies outside these explanations. It lies in a shared perception of an increasing strategic necessity to develop effective diplomatic strategies to deal with key issues of concern to regional leaders around trade, fishing, climate change, and decolonisation. This has been coupled with a realisation that the PIF was not meeting this need.

There were several reasons for this. One was the involvement of Australia and New Zealand in forum deliberations, making it hard to take strong positions on climate change or trade and decolonisation when their positions were antithetical. There has been a building resentment that the forum is no longer a place where the Pacific diplomatic voice can be developed and promoted, and that the regional diplomatic culture has reverted to the kind of hierarchical diplomatic culture that the forum was established to overcome. Rather than a diplomatic forum in which Australia and New Zealand are guests at the diplomatic table of the Pacific Island states, as originally conceived, the forum is now seen as one in which the interests of Australia and New Zealand prevail, to the detriment of island interests, in engaging the global negotiations which matter to them.

The most obvious case is climate diplomacy in relation to carbon emissions targets, where the interests of Australia and New Zealand could not be more divergent from that of the island states. Indeed, in many ways climate change has become the nuclear testing issue of the 21st century. It has brought an urgency and united front to island collaboration. Where the Pacific states might in the past have tolerated some frustration with the domination of the regional agenda in the PIF by Canberra and Wellington (to pursue the War on Terror or to promote a regional neoliberal economic order), this tolerance may have reached its limit on the climate change issue.

One can see the rising anger, among the atoll states in particular, on the lack of action by the PIF in representing a joint position on this question because of the restraining influence of Australia and New Zealand on regional positions on emissions targets. For the Pacific Island states, it is simply not possible to pursue an AOSIS position on emissions targets through an organisation in which Australia and New Zealand are present and determined to water down any positions that might affect their interests. This concern has been accentuated by the Australian Government's extreme position on the issue. Marshall Islands Foreign Minister Tony de Brum was reported in September 2014 as saying:

> He and the leaders of other Pacific Island nations were bewildered by what he called 'backsliding' on climate change by Australia, which the region had considered to be its 'big brother down south'. Probably one of the most frustrating events of the past year for Pacific islanders is Australia's strange behaviour when it comes to climate change ... Island nations had watched with dismay not only the abolition of the carbon tax in Australia, but also the defunding of scientific advisory bodies ... Pacific Island nations no longer have time to debate climate change or even to engage in dialogue about how it might be mitigated—they need immediate action. Failure to act for us would mean disappearance under the sea by the turn of the century (O'Malley 2014).

A second reason is that the presence of Australia and New Zealand in the PIF creates a logistical problem for the Pacific Island states in seeking to use southern global coalitions (such as AOSIS and the G77) to leverage their joint position on key issues such as climate change. With Australia and New Zealand being full members and the main financiers of the forum, the forum is not recognised as a southern grouping by these coalitions. This unnecessarily limits the bargaining power of Pacific states.

Third, as we have seen, since the mid-1990s the forum had largely abandoned the field of joint diplomacy for a focus on regional integration. This emphasis culminated in the Pacific Plan of 2003 to 2013, which was a technocratic plan around an Australia–New Zealand agenda of pooling and integration either to secure the region in the War on Terror or to lower tariff barriers and harmonise laws in accordance with a neoliberal economic agenda. This was a far cry from the assertive Pacific voice of the 1980s dealing with the big issues confronting the region. Significantly, 'joint diplomacy', or representing a Pacific voice, no longer appeared as part of the forum's definition of regionalism and its mandate.

A fourth explanation of a region-wide commitment to the new Pacific diplomatic network was the emergence of a more vocal Pacific leadership with a commitment to engage in regional debates more like the 1970s and 1980s. This has partly been due to Fiji's commitment to overcome the isolation imposed by the forum, but just as important have been the efforts of Marshall Islands leaders and President Tong of Kiribati to give leadership in climate change diplomacy in the region, and even globally, and the political will of the O'Neill Government in Papua New Guinea to work with Fiji in promoting the MSG, and an independent Pacific ACP secretariat.

Implications of the New Pacific Diplomacy

The new Pacific diplomacy represents an assertion of regional independence as well as a means for achieving more effective outcomes in regional and international forums. This has seen some marked successes: unprecedented financial returns from tuna access agreements as described by Transform Aqorau and Jope Tarai; reinscription of French Polynesia on the UN list of non-self-governing territories (see Nic Maclellan's chapter); the inclusion of 'stand-alone' sustainable development goals on oceans and climate change by the UN (as described by Fulori Manoa); and more coordinated advocacy on global climate policy by Pacific states (see George Carter's chapter). Meanwhile, members of the MSG continue to take significant steps towards regional integration (described in chapters by Sovaia Marawa, Wesley Morgan, and Tess Newton Cain) and the promotion of south–south cooperation. Pacific states have also successfully navigated what Dame Meg Taylor describes as 'a crowded and complex geopolitical landscape',[6] in order to leverage recognition for their own development agenda (as evident, for example, in the broad support for the establishment of the PIDF).

These successes and achievements vindicate and validate the shifts that are underway in Pacific diplomacy, including the use of alternative, island-only groupings, and the forging of closer relationships with non-traditional partners. They also lend momentum to President Anote Tong's call to 'engage even more aggressively internationally'.[7] Perhaps most significantly, given the current trends in Pacific regionalism, these successes can inspire greater political commitment to 'act regionally'. Ultimately, it is not frameworks or plans that matter to the leaders and their people, it is the results of regional endeavours that count.

---

6 Address by Secretary-General of the Pacific Islands Forum Secretariat, Diplomacy Roundtable, School of Government, Development and International Affairs, Faculty of Business and Economics, the University of the South Pacific, 27 May 2015.

7 Keynote Address by President of Kiribati at the Launch of the Pacific International Relations Forum of the School of Government, Development and International Affairs of the University of the South Pacific, Holiday Inn, Suva, 9 October 2012.

The transformation of the regional architecture is central to the new Pacific diplomacy, but it remains an unfinished journey. As various chapters in this volume indicate, it is by no means obvious where this journey will end. Dame Meg Taylor refers to 'a complex regional architecture where geopolitics and finance play an important part'. The influence of these factors will continue to challenge Pacific regionalism, whether or not Australia and New Zealand play a different role in the PIF in future, and whatever role the PIDF assumes in the regional system. Tensions over policy positions on issues such as decolonisation and climate change are also likely to deepen in the future.

What the contributors to this volume all point to, from their various perspectives and positions, is the way the new Pacific diplomacy is creating opportunities and avenues for island countries to influence the regional order, in line with their own interests and aspirations. This will perhaps have most impact and resonance on future efforts to shape an approach to regional integration and diplomacy that will deliver fully on the expectations of the people of the Pacific.

Organisation of the Book

The book begins with an overview vision statement by President Anote Tong of Kiribati, which expresses many of the key ideas that motivate the new Pacific diplomacy. His plea for the Pacific to 'chart its own course' reflects the central importance of the promotion of regional self-determination at the centre of the new developments. A second theme with wider resonance is that the Pacific states should pursue this in unison. There is, he argues, a need for Pacific solidarity. Third, he contends that Pacific leaders need to act from necessity and survival to confront new global forces threatening their way of life. They need to not only assert themselves 'aggressively' but to aspire to 'global leadership' in key diplomatic domains such as climate change, oceans management and sustainable development. To achieve this, they need to change their mindset away from the view that small island states are necessarily dominated by developed countries and find confidence in the fact that they are large ocean states. He both recognises and calls for a paradigm shift in Pacific diplomacy.

The importance of President Tong's vision is reflected in the recognition given to it by Australia's Foreign Minister Julie Bishop when she argued that any review of regional architecture needed to take this sentiment into account. During her visit to Papua New Guinea in December 2014, she said, 'It was time for Pacific leaders to chart their own course … I really think it's time the Pacific leaders determine what they want for the 21st century and I'm hoping that Australia will be able to host that' (Wroe 2014).

The first section of the book focuses on the recent developments in the regional diplomatic system. These institutional developments and their underlying principles are what have caught peoples' imagination that something significant has been under way. Kaliopate Tavola's chapter presents the case for a radical restructuring of the Pacific Islands Forum without Australia and New Zealand. His considered case for an all-island state forum provides the economic and political logic for the Fiji Government position that it will only return to forum membership if Australia and New Zealand are asked to leave.

The New Pacific diplomacy was initially seen as in opposition to the Pacific Islands Forum system dominated by Australia and New Zealand. But as evident from Dame Meg Taylor's chapter, the forum is also undergoing major change consistent with many of the principles of the new Pacific diplomacy. This is recognised by Claire Slatter's critical examination of the claims surrounding the new Pacific framework, which she argues do seem to treat seriously the earlier critique of the forum in such areas as inclusion of non-government organisations (NGOs). Maureen Penjueli offers a more trenchant critique of both the forum and the PIDF (despite its claims of inclusion) based on the past difficulties of civil society to be heard in Pacific regionalism.

Sandra Tarte then introduces the most prominent expression of the new Pacific diplomacy, the Pacific Islands Development Forum. As seen by many, this is potentially a competing organisation with the Pacific Islands Forum and is to be the heart of a Fiji-led alternative regional system. Fulori Manoa demonstrates that, while less well known, the dramatic rise of the PSIDS at the United Nations since 2009 has in many ways been the major success story of the new Pacific diplomacy.

The second section focuses on Fiji's key role in the new Pacific diplomacy showing its major role as a catalyst in key developments since 2009. Ambassador Mawi provides a government perspective emphasising the south–south aspect of this new regional foreign policy, while Makereta Komai provides an analysis of the origins and implications of Fiji's new policies since 2009.

The third section deals with the geopolitical context in which the new Pacific diplomacy emerged and developed. Michael O'Keefe argues that the changing geopolitical context, including the rise of China and the entrance of new interests such as Russia and the United Arab Emirates, has provided an enabling environment for the new Pacific diplomacy but does not devalue 'the issues, trends and agendas that have shaped the evolution of a new approach to diplomacy from within the region' (O'Keefe 2015). Nicola Baker explores the dominant managerial role of Australia and New Zealand in Pacific regionalism, which is seen by many to provide the major stimulus to the development of a reactive new Pacific diplomacy. She argues that it is a mistake to lump together these two influential neighbours as if they are a joint actor or to assume that New Zealand simply follows Australia's lead.

The fourth section focuses on developments in sub-regionalism and the question of how they articulate with the broader regional diplomatic system. Tess Newton Cain explains the nature of the renaissance of the Melanesian Spearhead Group and highlights the issues provoked by its new prominence. Sovaia Marawa examines what is arguably the most impressive achievement in this recent renaissance—the negotiation of a Melanesia Free Trade Area—and why this was successful in contrast to the experience in the broader Pacific Islands region. Suzanne Lowe Gallen reviews the untold story of Micronesian diplomacy at the sub-regional level and how this complements Pacific regional diplomacy.

In the final three sections, the authors examine the key areas of contemporary Pacific diplomacy. Nicollette Goulding and George Carter introduce us to the complexity of Pacific approaches to climate diplomacy on the road to the 2015 Paris conference; Transform Aqorau and Jope Tarai examine new developments in tuna diplomacy; Wesley Morgan explores the assertive Pacific diplomacy in relation to Europe and Australia and New Zealand on trade; and Nic Maclellan examines the recent record of Pacific diplomacy on pushing for decolonisation in the case of French Polynesia and West Papua.

References

Boyce, P. and R.A. Herr 1974. 'Microstate Diplomacy in the South Pacific'. *Australian Outlook* 28(1):24–35. doi.org/10.1080/10357717408444489

Cooney, C. 2014. Fiji Shuns Pacific Forum Membership Unless Australia and New Zealand are Expelled. *ABC News*, 29 April. abc.net.au/news/2014-04-29/fiji-shuns-forum-membership/5418014 (accessed 23 February 2015).

Fry, G. 1994. International Cooperation in the South Pacific: From regional integration to collective diplomacy. In W.A. Axline (ed.), *The Political Economy of Regional Cooperation*. London: Pinter Press, 136–77.

Fry, G. 2005. Pooled Regional Governance in the Island Pacific: Lessons from history. *Pacific Economic Bulletin* 20(3):111–19.

Fry, G. 2015. Recapturing the Spirit of 1971: Towards a New Regional Political Settlement in the Pacific. DPA Discussion Paper 2015/3. Canberra: The Australian National University.

Komai, M. 2014. Reconfiguring Regionalism in the Pacific. *PACNEWS*, 9 April. pina.com.fj/?p=pacnews&m=read&o=137809727550b7cea62a2839b85457 (site discontinued).

O'Keefe, M. 2015. The Strategic Context of the New Pacific Diplomacy. In G. Fry and S. Tarte (eds), *The New Pacific Diplomacy*. Canberra: ANU Press. doi.org/10.22459/NPD.12.2015.11

O'Malley, N. 2014. Australia is a Pacific Island: It has a responsibility. *The Canberra Times*, 21 September.

Pareti, S. 2013. Fiji Pushes for Alternative to Pacific Islands Forum. *ABC News*, 6 August. abc.net.au/news/2013-08-06/fiji-forum/4867748

Tarte, S. 2014. Regionalism and Changing Regional Order in the Pacific Islands. *Asia and the Pacific Policy Studies* 1(2):312–24. doi.org/10.1002/app5.27

Wroe, D. 2014. Foreign Minister Julie Bishop Backs Summit to Plan New 'Regional Architecture' in the Pacific. *The Canberra Times*, 14 December. canberratimes.com.au/politics/federal/foreign-minister-julie-bishop-backs-summit-to-plan-new-regional-architecture-in-pacific-20141214-126wh0.html

18

Niu Mana, Sport, Media and the Australian Diaspora

Katerina Martina Teaiwa

Katerina Teaiwa: Personal Journey

I grew up on the Laucala campus of the University of the South Pacific (USP) as my mother, Joan Teaiwa, worked there as a course developer in extension services from 1980 to 2000, and my elder sister, Teresia Teaiwa, as a lecturer in history/politics from 1994 to 2000. We took music lessons on campus from the wonderful Mr Ueta Solomona, played tennis at the USP courts, swam regularly at the USP pool, did exercise classes at the USP gym and I played on the White Fire basketball team led by USP Professor Randy Thaman and Bob Tuxon.

My mother had started a ballet school in Suva in the 1980s and my sisters and I were avid dancers. In the mid-1990s, Professor Epeli Hau'ofa was expanding the Oceania Centre for Arts and Culture and looking for artists and performers to develop their work at the centre. He introduced me to the very talented Allan Alo and together we founded the Oceania Dance Theatre (ODT) with Letava Tafuna'i. I danced for years with Allan in various shows including USP's early dance theatre productions, collaborating with musicians and visual artists. ODT travelled to Honolulu where I had completed my MA in Pacific Islands Studies and to Canberra where I was doing my PhD at The Australian National University (ANU). I discovered that the anthropology department had been recycling name tags on the doors for years and Epeli's name was still there from the 1970s on the back of a label being used in the late 1990s.

It is amazing to see where the ODT dancers are today after Allan's and Peter Espiritu's guidance and mentorship. I am now an associate professor at ANU. I serve on the advisory board for the Oceania Centre for Arts, Culture and Pacific Studies and have continued to collaborate with staff and artists over the years. Pacific studies was greatly influenced by Epeli, Allan and Teresia, who have sadly all passed away, leaving tremendous legacies in the arts and scholarship at USP and across the region.

Teaiwa, K.M. 2016. *Niu Mana*, Sport, Media and the Australian Diaspora. In M. Tomlinson and Ty P. Kāwika Tengan (eds), *New Mana: Transformations of a Classic Concept in Pacific Languages and Cultures*. Canberra: ANU Press, 107–30.

Republished with the kind permission of ANU Press.

Prelude

In the trailer for *In Football We Trust*, a documentary directed by Tony Vainuku and produced by Erika Cohn of Idle Wild films, several young Polynesian men identify themselves as playing high school football. An inter title appears stating that approximately 150,000 Samoans and Tongans now live in the United States and are 56 times more likely to make it into the National Football League (NFL) than any other 'race' despite one in four of the same group living in poverty. And why is their success rate so high? Words like faith, talent, culture, warrior and family flash across the screen, followed by 'it's the only option' (IFWT Productions and ITVS 2014).

Former running back Vai Sikahema appears, stating that it is unfair for kids growing up to be told they will make it into the NFL. But then a series of players and a mother make it clear that football is seen as a 'door', a pathway to major success, not just for the individual but for the whole family. A young man says that all his mother's brothers are in prison, and all his father's brothers are in prison as well. The soundtrack for the trailer is a bombastic chorus that increases in tempo as the final words proclaim the film title encapsulating a spirit of American patriotism, faith, even blind faith, and also a worrying edge. What if you don't make it? Or what if you do make it and life just gets more challenging? The suicide of Samoan All-Pro NFL player Junior Seau by gunshot in 2012 hangs like a spectre over this trailer. His autopsy showed he had suffered from numerous head injuries. He left no suicide note but a page was found handwritten with the lyrics of his favourite country song 'Who I Ain't'. Co-written by his friend, Jamie Paulin, it describes a man who regrets the person he has become (Steeg 2012).

Introduction

In this chapter I present some preliminary thoughts on 'new *mana*' and a discussion of how globalisation and the Pacific diaspora might compel us to reimagine key Pan-Pacific concepts such as *mana, tapu, talanoa, va, Moana*, Oceania and *Solwara* (salt water) in new or, to use 350Pacific.org's play on words, *niu* ways.[1] By 'key' I don't mean that these words are the same or even exist in every Pacific language, but rather that a sense of spiritual efficacy, agency and authority or power; sacred or taboo things, people and places; relational space; the ocean as material, pragmatic, connective and sacred; and the Pacific as a region shaped by shared kinship, are important across most contemporary Pacific cultures and contexts. Some call this the 'Pacific Way' (Crocombe 1976), an idea still relevant in spite of the critiques of Pacific political scientists over the years (Lawson 2010).

In spite of many scholarly assumptions about the differences between Melanesians, Micronesians and Polynesians, the concepts I have mentioned are relevant across communities who care about what they see as destructive global forces affecting the lives of people in the diaspora, in small islands, and in the highlands of the Pacific's largest islands. This is seen vividly in 350Pacific.org's climate change protests across the region and in the Madang Wansolwara Dance gathering in August 2014 of artists, activists, scholars, civil society and church leaders in Papua New Guinea, for example.[2] These concepts are thus transformed, reimagined and applied according to historical, political, environmental and economic contexts, and increasingly drive regional activism. At the heart of it is, as scholars

---

1   *Niu* is a common word for coconut across many Pacific languages. In Mallon and Pereira's work (see Mallon and Pereira 2002), and in popular parlance in Aotearoa New Zealand, *niu* converts any negative connotations of the word coconut, signalling race or ethnicity negatively or implying an islander is non-modern or 'fresh off the boat', into a positive term marking Pacific flavours or styles that have infused New Zealand national identities.

2   350Pacific.org is a global climate movement for promoting grassroots climate change activism and information. 350Pacific.org is represented by the 'Pacific Climate Warriors' in various actions and events. See more at 350Pacific.org.

such as Margaret Jolly have argued, an enduring sense of collective and relational personhood shaped by both indigenous heritage and Christian values and concepts (Jolly interviewed by Giggacher 2014).

While many have explored *mana* in either specific cultural and linguistic contexts such as Hawaiian, Fijian, Māori, Tongan and Samoan, and in what I would call new age gaming (Golub and Peterson 2016) and intense spiritual remix mode (Morgain 2016), I would like to consider *mana* through an interdisciplinary Pacific Studies lens, and in diverse Pan-Pacific (intercultural or regional), Pasifika, diasporic and postcolonial contexts. While it is beyond the scope of my discussion here on diaspora and sport, I also have questions about how far we can take a discussion of *mana* and commerce or industry, *mana* and the commodity sign, and *mana* in the context of indigenous traditions, such as faʻa Samoa, or anga fakatonga, and sexuality, given the often conservative, Christian, heteronormative and ethno-nationalist values within Pacific communities. *Mana* is about both limits and possibilities, applications and denials within a system of specific contemporary Pacific values and ideas.

The Australian Context

The topic of *mana* and sport is not something I sought out for research but rather something that developed as I created the undergraduate teaching program in Pacific Studies at The Australian National University (ANU) over the past seven years. We currently run the only Pacific studies teaching program at any level in Australian higher education and there is very little visibility for the field as a potential area of study in the primary or secondary school system (Rose et al. 2009). As I was trying to imagine how to expand the program and attract students, I was forced to think more broadly about how the Pacific featured in the national Australian consciousness (Teaiwa 2007). Several things became clear very quickly.

Aside from the obvious and dominant pragmatic and policy context— tied primarily to Australia's regional aid, development and governance agenda—there is very little content on the Pacific in the school system in any Australian state. And while there is a wealth of writing about the Pacific Islands, very little of it is available as teaching material and most of it does not engage the Pacific diaspora (Rose et al. 2009). There are just a handful of scholars who do research on Pacific communities in Australia, including research on South Sea Islanders, the descendants of Melanesians and other Pacific Islanders forced to work on Australian sugar plantations (see, for example, Banivanua-Mar 2007; Boucher 2012; Lee and Francis 2009; Rose et al. 2009; Vasta 2004). Thus, in Pacific studies in Australia, which is geographically in Oceania and where there is significant Pacific research and policy work, there is a preference for engaging the Pacific out there in the Islands, not the Pacific within Australian cities and neighbourhoods. And neither the domestic nor the island context are seen as relevant for Australian education (Rose et al. 2009; Teaiwa 2007).

Furthermore, compared with New Zealand, and increasingly the United States, Pacific Islanders are not a recognised equity category or community. Statistics on the exact numbers of Islanders in Australia are not readily available, although a reasonable estimate based on census reports for ancestry, including Māori and Indo-Fijians, would put the total around 2 per cent or 400,000, which would be half a percentage less than the estimated Indigenous Australian population (see Pryke 2014; Pryor 2013; Queensland Health 2013). Pacific communities are primarily resident in New South Wales (NSW) and Queensland and are growing in Victoria, the Australian Capital Territory (ACT), South Australia, Western Australia and the Northern Territory.

Despite Australia's long history of engagement with the south-west Pacific, particularly Papua New Guinea, and with Nauru and Kiribati, most 21st-century Pacific migrants are not Melanesian or Micronesian but Polynesian (Pryke 2014). The majority of migrants do not come straight from the Islands, but take advantage of the Trans-Tasman Agreement and move from New Zealand to Australia, drawn by the possibilities of employment within the strong Australian economy. This is certainly the case for the large Māori Australian population, sometimes referred to as 'Mozzies' in the media (Pryor 2013). Many trans-Tasman migrants regularly identify as New Zealander, and many Māori, duplicating structural relations with Pacific migrants back in New Zealand, prefer to be counted or imagined separately from Pacific Islanders (see Teaiwa and Mallon 2005). These factors make it difficult to get a sense of the real Pacific population size in Australia.

Because I expected that future students in Pacific studies would include Pacific Islanders of the diaspora, I sought as much information as possible about Pacific communities in Australia and soon realised there were two dominant and highly visible arenas for positive Pacific participation in the Australian social and cultural landscape: sport and popular culture. Within these arenas, it is the Pacific Islander male, and more specifically Polynesian male, who is the most visible (Lakisa et al. 2014). The Melanesian diaspora by contrast is almost invisible despite the fact that there are increasing numbers of mixed heritage Papua New Guinean (PNG) Australians who often come from families with PNG mothers and Australian·fathers because it is still difficult to migrate from Melanesia to Australia, compared with, for example, central and eastern Polynesia to New Zealand (see Lewis-Harris 2011; Pryke 2014).

There is a corresponding arena of negative visibility for Pacific communities, again dominated by Polynesian males, within the criminal justice system at all levels. For example, in 2008 the community liaison officer at the Woodford correctional facility in Queensland, a maximum security prison, told me that 10 per cent of their population consists of young Pacific males. And stories on Pacific Islander gangs and crime abound in Australian and New Zealand newspapers, television and online platforms (see, for example, Ansley 2012; Betz 2013; Hill 2013). The Woodford officer, however, also stressed that the Pacific population was the most organised and positive, fostering links with other inmates, especially Indigenous Australians, and creating cultural programs to connect with their families (personal communication, November 2008).

In a context where Pacific communities migrate to Australia for strong economic reasons, and where their visibility is often shaped by negative representations in the media, the corresponding 'positive' arenas of sport and popular culture become even more important as spaces in which Pacific people can counter negative stereotypes with narratives of cultural pride, agency and citizenship (Lakisa et al. 2014; Uperesa 2014). Such positive participation and citizenship is captured by the notion of communal *mana*. Brendan Hokowhitu usefully frames this convergence of *mana* and sport in the New Zealand context in terms of a history of colonialism, sport and European settlement:

> For a culture on the brink of extinction and subjected to explicit racism in nearly all walks of society, sport offered *tāne* a sort of salvation. Furthermore, given the national hysteria for rugby throughout the twentieth century and the consequent status of the game, it is not surprising that, for Māori men, the rugby and rugby league field was a site where they could gain their community's respect and thus mana. One need only look at the obituaries in *Mana Magazine* to recognize that *tāne* are eulogized for their sporting feat (Hokowhitu 2004:269–70).

Vince Diaz, in his discussion of American gridiron or football, similarly describes this phenomenon as 'beating the colonizer at his own game' (Diaz 2011:97). While he acknowledges the positive potential of sport, Hokowhitu is critical of dominant, hypermasculine representations of what he calls the 'naturally physical' Māori man epitomised by sports such as rugby and American football circulated by mass media, and he challenges Māori men to live beyond these dominant constructs (Hokowhitu 2004:266, 278).

While Hokowhitu was not describing a Māori diasporic context, I became interested in the idea of gaining *mana* through sport both in the islands and overseas and the differences between those contexts. The word *mana* has become quite common with a taken-for-granted meaning in English as a kind of spiritual power or potency that can manifest in persons, objects, places or acts. Mei Winitana, who does write about the Māori diaspora, describes the *mana* in 'Mana Wahine Māori' in Australia, with reference to the works of Maori Marsden in the 1970s and Paul Tapsell in the 1990s:

> Mana can be likened to the Greek equivalent of 'dunamai', indicating a 'capability' towards power ... This capability may be described as charisma, an indefinable 'X factor' that some people possess that influences and inspires others. Charismatic people are telegenic, that is, they project a certain look, particular warmth in their smile, and a personal aura or presence. They communicate in ways that touch the minds and hearts of people for both positive and negative purposes (Winitana 2008:2).

Media influence can enhance this telegenic quality, promoting both a provocative and reactive image for public consumption (ibid.:2). The prominence of sport and popular culture across all forms of media, and the rise in Pacific Islander and Māori participation within these fields, coupled with the expectations of family and community (Besnier 2012; Uperesa 2014), dramatically increase the pressures on athletes and popular artists to be responsible for not just their own, but everyone's image, everyone's hopes and everyone's *mana*. The expectations can be unbearable and coupled with other factors including injury or loss of contract, the suicide or attempted suicide rates of rugby league players are growing at a worrying rate, similar to their football counterparts (Cadzow 2013; Massoud 2013).

The backlash from Tongan and other Pacific communities in Australia and the United States towards Australian comedian Chris Lilley's ABC and HBO-syndicated show *Jonah from Tonga* (Lilley 2014), underscores this widespread aversion to negative public representation. In reaction to Lilley, in controversial brownface and playing a young, misunderstood, delinquent Tongan teenage male with a propensity for swearing, scholars and church leaders protested, and young people mounted the counter-campaign #MyNameisNOTJonah across Twitter and Facebook. Leitu Havea's selfie, circulated widely on social and regular media, proclaimed:

> I am a proud Tongan
> I've NEVER spent time in prison
> I was NEVER suspended from school
> I am currently studying for my university degree
> #MyNameisNOTJonah
> #ChangeStartsHERE #ProudPoly
> (SBS 2014).

Theorising *Mana*

In his article 'Rethinking Mana', Roger M. Keesing (1984) critiques the predominant notion—a notion based on Robert Henry Codrington's work, which he says came to dominate anthropological writing— of *mana* as a spiritual essence or power that could be gained or lost (compare with Kolshus 2016). He re-examined *mana* by taking a comparative linguistic perspective, arguing that it is not classically a noun but rather a stative verb. Things and human enterprises are *mana* rather than have *mana*. He argued that we can speak of the *mana*-ness of a thing or act, and things that are *mana* are efficacious, potent, successful, true, fulfilled and realised. In short, they 'work' (ibid.:138). So, for example: a stone used magically that actually works, a fisherman's abundant catch, and a potion that heals, all are *mana*. In all contexts, ancestors, spirits and the gods help make people and things *mana*. But the notion of *mana* as a noun denoting substantive power is, as many have observed, prominent in and beyond Polynesia and it is this definition of *mana* that has come to dominate our application of the term.

In 'Retheorizing Mana', Matt Tomlinson (2006) points out that Keesing did not include Christian visions of Oceanic *mana* and that Christianity might be the key to rethinking *mana* in the contemporary Pacific. He argues that *mana* became a standard noun not just in English-language anthropological literature but in Fijian and as used by Fijians too. The concept underwent transformation in the process of the missionary transcription of Pacific languages, and particularly in the translation of the Bible. It is now typically used as a noun, associated not only with ancestors and chiefs but also with church leaders (see also Tomlinson and Bigitibau 2016).

Tomlinson argues that Christian transformations of *mana* 'were not simply grammatical, nor simply a matter of substantivizing mana … The transformations of mana were metonymic of wider political processes' (2006:180). For example, the creation of a permanent elite chiefly class in Fiji via British colonial policy reified custom and as such this class was rationalised accordingly—they, the chiefs, must have *mana*. He further argues that by the same token, *mana* can slip away or be lost: he quotes Christina Toren's observation that 'a chief's mana is not what it was … because they are all Christians, and so the power of the ancestor gods has diminished' (Tomlinson 2006:180). One particular area where this is observed is in effective speech: only God can speak with automatic effectiveness, not chiefs.

On a relevant point for my argument about masculinity and sport, Tomlinson also argues that for Fijians, when configuring *mana* negatively, there is seen to be a loss in male physical strength and prowess compared with the past. And while he does not mention it explicitly, I imagine this has something to do with the transformation of the warrior class into the modern institutions of sport, military and police. So Fijian *mana* today is often configured negatively, in terms of its disappearance, but it is clear that male sporting heroes and soldiers are viewed to an extent, in Ty P. Kāwika Tengan and Jesse Markham's (2009) terms, as contemporary warriors signalling a pre-colonial masculinity.

Diaz takes this point further, echoing the sentiments of the documentary *In Football We Trust* by stating:

> The key Polynesian concept that best captures … what is at stake in Samoan and other Polynesian performances on the American gridiron is mana. Mana is what accounts for this remarkable and unrivalled success as an ethnic or even demographic group—no other racial or ethnic group and no other similarly-sized community in the world has ever produced the number of major college and professional football players per capita. In the simplest terms possible to understand in English, mana is a powerful presence or force to be found in people, animals, and even inanimate

objects, and as might be imagined in post-missionary Christianity, mana also gets ultimately linked with God, and service and obligation to God … Precisely when it is hitched to warrior traditions in powerful ways, American football can be viewed as a virtual stage for the performance of Samoan manhood and masculinity and the broader values in fa'a Samoa through mana (Diaz 2011:101).

The stakes of the *mana* of elite players in the context of the broader community are well illustrated by Diaz's analysis of gay NFL star Esera Tuaolo's public coming out on national TV (after his retirement), which resulted in a tsunami of criticism and abuse from his Samoan community. People were happy when his football enhanced their perceived collective *mana* but when he publicly announced his sexuality, the response from one blogger was:

Talofa Esera, You are a disgust and menace to Samoan culture! I guess you're out of your mind! God hates gays as stated in the bible. What is wrong with you? Do not associate God with these filthy faggots and maggots. Tell your parents that you are gay and see what their reactions might be (Diaz 2011: 97).

Setting aside my own personal judgement about such nasty comments, my question is: what happens when we add sport, the diaspora and mass media to this discussion of *mana*? The hysteria comes partly from the social significance and great visibility of sport and, like popular culture, its potential to uplift as well as demonise entire communities while simultaneously exposing certain values, or revealing a diversity of values, including homophobia. If *mana* is potency, whether individual or collective, physical or spiritual, then the immense presence of sport and media in countries where Pacific diasporic groups are most prominent means that social values—uplifting ones like strength and courage, and degrading ones like homophobia and intolerance—will necessarily be pulled into any discussion of *mana*.

Success in sports helps reinstate a male efficacy perceived to be lost through colonialism, migration, minority status in the diaspora, and class status (Uperesa 2014). Tengan and Markham discuss similar issues, stating that football:

becomes a site for the practice and fulfilment of family and spiritual values of faith and loyalty, especially for islanders in the diaspora. At the same time, the Polynesian male warrior becomes a commodity image to be sold for big business (2009:2414).

Sport is marketed as a hypermasculine spectacle for society as a whole. Furthermore, they discuss how the black super-athlete reinforces racial hierarchies and both glorifies and demonises primitive hypermasculinity. They argue, 'Within the present configuration of the sports-media complex, islander men, like African American and Native American men, have become commodified and consumed as racialized and hypermasculine spectacle' (Tengan and Markham 2009:2414; see also Lakisa et al. 2014). There is a complex relationship between the commodified spectacle and notions of leadership, status or authority and the interpretation and significance of sport, popular culture and political icons for Pacific audiences. Within all this are both internally generated and externally integrated biases, racism, sexism, homophobia and notions of class.

In the Australian diaspora, participation in sport and popular culture is a particular area of visibility and success for Pacific peoples that holds great meaning for minority communities (Lakisa et al. 2014; Uperesa 2014). And this is key for Australia because the spheres of politics and higher education are not currently arenas in which Islanders are visible compared with New Zealand and the United States where there are politicians and PhDs of Pacific descent who are nationally celebrated. Sport is not just an athletic opportunity but an economic one that allows successful players class mobility, and to fulfil cultural obligations, what Fa'anofo Lisaclaire Uperesa describes as 'the opportunity to give back … [and the] privilege of performing *tautua* (service, in this case expanded and transnationalized)' (2014:294–95). The achievements of elite players bring *mana*, as it were, not just to their corresponding Pacific communities but to their clubs and associated, and often multicultural, Australian fan base.

Revisiting Hokowhitu's analysis of why sport is seen as so significant:

> My father, like many Māori of his generation, lived for sports. He grew up in an era when sport was one of the few spheres where tāne could achieve success and compete with Pākeha men on an 'even playing field' and, accordingly, could gain mana in the Pākeha world. My father's enthusiasm for sport carried over to me, along with a definition of masculinity based on the noble, physically tough, staunch, and emotion-less Māori men we witnessed on the local, provincial, and national rugby fields (Hokowhitu 2004:260).

The commodification and fetishisation of Pacific bodies by diverse audiences through the sports/media complex adds another dimension to the issue. Media and the diaspora are deterritorialised spaces where agency, expression and meaning are constructed in articulation with the 'offline' sociopolitical context. And this offline sociopolitical context has its own particular sets of challenges and opportunities. Being a Pacific Islander in New Zealand or the United States, where there are named Pacific Islander agencies, programs and statutory bodies, is very different from being a Pacific Islander in Australia, where issues such as Pasifika education, health and welfare are dealt with, fairly inconsistently, at the state level. And within Australia, being a Pacific Islander in Canberra, with smaller, dispersed Pacific populations, is different from being a Pacific Islander in Campbelltown, Western Sydney, or Logan, Queensland, where they are concentrated and visible. While Pacific peoples across the globe celebrate their football, rugby union and rugby league stars, what that means to communities on the ground in their particular social and political circumstances varies considerably.

Location shapes how different agents participate and make meaning, and Australia is a particular kind of national, cultural, economic, political and geographic context compared with the United States, New Zealand or even Fiji as a migration destination. Expressions of difference, for example through distinct ethnic identities in Australia, do not always convert into social or cultural capital in the same way they might in other countries, including the United States where categories such as Native American, Asian American and Pacific Islander American exist and mean something structurally.

While there are still similar experiences of structural marginalisation and economic disadvantage, there is less to be gained, socially, for example, by being a Samoan or Tongan in a school in Melbourne, compared with being a Samoan or Tongan in a school in Auckland or Utah with their high, concentrated Polynesian populations. So while the strategies to integrate or assimilate into dominant cultures are strong in all of these contexts, the pressures and tactics in Australia are particular to this country's racial and indigenous politics. These are historically shaped by the protracted denial of Indigenous Australian rights; the White Australia policy focused on populating the country with white migrants from 1901 to 1973, and a current prioritisation of 'skilled' migration. Compared with New Zealand and the United States, and in spite of relying on blackbirder labour from Melanesia on Queensland plantations from 1863 to 1904, Australia actively discouraged migration from the Pacific, including from its former colonial territories of Papua New Guinea and Nauru. Well aware of the inflow of Pacific migrants now via New Zealand, Australian policymakers continue to be concerned with the Trans-Tasman Agreement (see Lee 2009:7).

Given this environment and the absence of a federal portfolio for domestic Pacific issues, Pacific Islanders in Australia have to be extra proactive in carving out safe spaces where they can celebrate their cultures and pass on their languages and values to their children. *Mana* is easily diffused in Australia and potentially rendered irrelevant where the pressures to assimilate, for example on sporting fields from primary school to elite levels, are strong. Pacific rugby union and rugby league players, with their large Australian fan bases, could easily play as just brown bodies in a white game, grateful they or their parents made it to Australian shores, playing in Australian professional sporting codes with all of the challenges of the migration experience. But they do not always just play the game. I propose, in a preliminary way, that there is more to the agency of elite Pacific athletes than the commodity sign. When Pacific players do not just play as brown bodies, when they draw media attention to their Pacific heritage and the centrality of 'family, faith and culture' (Lakisa et al. 2014:347), the effect can be powerful.

Body Pacifica and the NRL

In January 2012, I conducted a workshop with a team of ANU Pacific Studies staff working in collaboration with the National Rugby League (NRL) education and welfare office, particularly with former star and now welfare officer Nigel Vagana. Something one of the players said to me has helped me think about players' agency and transformative potential in what is regularly viewed as a violent game that epitomises dominant notions of Australian hypermasculinity and was replete with scandals over drugs, alcohol and gender-based violence (Hutchins and Mikosza 1998).

The player told me that the Pacific players on his team would regularly get together to pray before the game and in order to do this they would have to step out of the larger group, go into their own corner and pray together before returning to finish the rest of the pre-game ritual. After a while, the team coach and management flagged this as very non team-like behaviour and stressed that players needed to be strong and cohesive and not highlight their differences before the game. However, rather than asking the Pacific men to stop praying, they instead decided that if the Islanders were going to pray, everyone was going to pray. This is quite a decision in a country which is far less publicly religious than, say, the United States, but a similar thing has also happened in rugby union (see Moloney 2008).

A few years ago, sports journalist John-Paul Moloney contacted me at ANU to ask why Pacific people had to pray all the time. It was becoming quite evident within the Brumbies that their new Pacific players had very different values from the Anglo-Australian players; values that were expressed quite visibly by conducting prayers at training sessions and before games. Moloney wrote:

> Faith in a football team is no new thing. But its presence within the Canberra Super 14 team is greater than ever. Its rise has corresponded with an influx into the club of Pacific Island footballers, who almost to a man believe in Christianity, which has been indigenised within Tongan, New Zealand Māori, Fijian and Samoan communities. Flyhalf Christian Lealiifano wears his faith visibly on the field, drawing a crucifix in marker pen on strapping tape around his wrist (Moloney 2008).

One of the main reasons the rugby league team decided to go with the Pacific Islanders' prayer ritual, and why teams like the Brumbies will have to get used to prayer, is because of the current demographic realities of both sporting codes. These were announced in *The Sydney Morning Herald* in 2006:

> Forget new rules, expansion teams and codes of conduct—the biggest influence on Australia's rugby codes has been the influx of Pacific Islanders. Some even say that it's inevitable the NRL and senior rugby union will soon be dominated by players with Tongan, Samoan or Māori blood (Lane 2006).

The sheer numbers of Pacific players, 50 per cent of the whole junior game and over 20 per cent of the top tier, means that by demographics alone these players have the potential to transform the game from the inside and make some of their cultural values and practices mainstream, particularly if they resist the impetus to assimilate into dominant Australian culture (Lakisa et al. 2014; Horton and Zakus 2009; Lakisa 2011). While I agree with many of Diaz's, Tengan's and Markham's critiques in the context of the NFL in the United States, I have observed some positive and proactive efforts by Pacific rugby and especially rugby league players in Australia to infuse the game more broadly with their own values. This is also more possible in a country the size of Australia compared with that of the United States.

While some forms of fundamentalist Christianity and homophobia, for example, are hardly mutually exclusive, between sport, popular culture and this particular Australian context, new possibilities for transforming perceptions of Pacific men and Pacific communities are possible. If (*niu*/new) *mana* is about a state of being strong, efficacious, prosperous, successful, having 'status and prestige' (Palmer and Masters 2010), and doing mighty or even miraculous acts, especially when they score tries, tackle, run fast and help win games, then I wonder if, in both senses of the word, whether noun or verb, and as 'force', players truly have the potential to increase their own and the more general *mana* of Pacific communities, many of whom are struggling in the Australian system. Revisiting Diaz's observations about the stakes of *mana*, what are the direct links between *mana*, masculinity and sport? Is 'new *mana*' dependent on a still hypermasculine 'new warrior' to reinstate authority lost in the process of colonialism and migration? Or is there another possibility within the sphere of men's sport to enhance this shared *mana*?

Let us take a look at three very different players who represent the most visible masculine Pacific types within the game. Someone like Samoan–New Zealander Sonny Bill Williams may not have as much potential for gaining or conferring *mana* as he is sometimes viewed as someone who follows the paycheck, switches back and forth between rugby league and union codes, and changes clubs at a regular rate. This is not to disconnect *mana* from a concept of rational economics; financial success is important to Pacific communities, as are values of stability and loyalty. But Williams' potential to be viewed as a leader, rather than just a brown body with high athletic prowess in a white game, has been undermined by a range of factors including the regular sexualisation of his image.

Tongan player William Hopoate, whose father also played league and was viewed as a 'bad boy' of the game, is practically the opposite of his dad. In spite of being one of the youngest players ever drafted into the professional tier, Hopoate gave up a AU$1.7 million contract with the Parramatta Eels to go on a two-year mission for the Church of Jesus Christ of Latter-day Saints. His decision confounded many fans and the NRL community as it was fairly unimaginable to the general public that anyone would choose the life of a missionary over being a highly paid star athlete. To Islanders, however, one could argue his choice signalled the kind of *mana* seen in 'a great deed', in this case, an act of Christian faith and sacrifice.

Retired Fijian player Petero Civoniceva, whose father also played rugby, is viewed as someone with incredible *mana* who is senior, humble, well-respected and leads by example. I observed this first hand in meetings with Civoniceva, current players and other stakeholders at the NRL education and welfare office in Sydney. While his Fijian surname has never been pronounced correctly—he is called 'Sivonisiva' instead of the correct 'Thivonitheva' by his teammates, fans and sports journalists—when Petero speaks, other players listen.

While Civoniceva is respected in the game, he has not always been respected by fans. In 2008, during a game against Parramatta, an Eels fan sitting very close to the field shouted that he was a 'fucking monkey'. The fan, who was later banned for five years from attending rugby league matches, said yes he'd called him a 'fucking monkey' but it wasn't meant to be racist (Read 2008). But racism is rampant within Australian sport and Pacific and Indigenous Australian players have long been targets of verbal abuse. After his incident, the usually quiet Civoniceva decided to speak up and gave several media interviews where he denounced racism within the sport and called for a change in attitudes through an NRL anti-racism campaign. Initially the NRL agreed, but apparently no campaign ever emerged, much to his disappointment. The Australian Football League (AFL), however, championed an anti-racism campaign inspired by their outspoken Indigenous players such as 2014 Australian of the Year Adam Goodes, and drew in sporting heroes from other codes (Australian Human Rights Commission 2013). Goodes experienced racism throughout his career and particularly towards the end. In 2015, after crowds booed an Indigenous post-goal 'war dance', he took leave and subsequently retired. This sparked a national dialogue on racism in sport which was prominent in mainstream media.

After this incident, Civoniceva and other senior Pacific players decided to get together regularly to talk about some of these problems and the group has been a catalyst for a number of new initiatives. Led by NRL education and welfare officer and former League star Nigel Vagana, they have come up with projects that are specifically designed to help players become better leaders and role models within and beyond the game.

The 2010 *Body Pacifica* initiative, for example, was one such project. Players used their status and popularity to promote Pacific art, culture and tangible and intangible heritage with many flow-on effects for Pacific communities in and beyond New South Wales. Produced by rugby league player turned curator Leo Tanoi and Carli Leimbach, *Body Pacifica* ran from June to August 2010 at the Casula Powerhouse Arts Centre in Liverpool, Western Sydney, and involved a diverse program of exhibitions, live performances, workshops, digital displays and sales of a very successful calendar.

The *Body Pacifica* calendar, which sold out in advance, was art-directed by celebrated New Zealand-born photographer of Samoan heritage Greg Semu in collaboration with graphic designer Frank Puletua, a former player and the only Pacific player with a degree in fine arts. It featured NRL players of Pacific heritage: Jarryd Hayne, Fuifui Moimoi, Paul Alton, Roy Asotasi, Dene Halatau, Frank Puletua, Nathan Cayless, Petero Civoniceva, Michael Jennings, Ruben Wiki, Manu Vatuvei, Jared Waerea-Hargreaves and Nigel Vagana, dressed in costumes sourced from the Pacific collection of the Australian Museum.

At the photo shoot a variety of objects was put out for them to choose from and then the photography session followed. Some players selected items that were not from their island of heritage and some players, like Jarryd Hayne (who is Fijian, born and raised in Australia), displayed the items, such as the *tabua*, in what most Fijians would view as an incorrect manner. A *tabua* or whale's tooth is not a necklace, but is something that is held and presented ceremonially.

The players' photographs were displayed in larger-than-life—dare I say god-like—images, which lined the first floor gallery of Casula Powerhouse. And like benevolent gods they seemed to watch over the three months of activities and over the many crowds that gathered during the opening and closing events. Some of them, however, did not actually show up in person; they instead lent their *mana* or spirit to the event and this was recognised and celebrated by the audience.

Body Pacifica was very well received by Pacific communities and the general public with Casula Powerhouse winning a NSW IMAGine award in public engagement for the exhibition. Thousands of people from the Pacific community, most of whom were not regular museum or gallery patrons, visited Casula during *Body Pacifica*. This helped inspire Vagana, Civoniceva and other players to take another initiative. In 2011, after almost two years of on-and-off discussions between my school's director at the time, Kent Anderson, the co-owner of the South Sydney Rabbitohs Peter Holmes à Court, and Vagana, I was asked to join the new NRL

Pacific Council as a Pacific Studies expert to help the education and welfare office come up with ideas for new ways to enhance education, leadership and positive role modelling for Pacific players.

Kent Anderson saw this collaboration as an important opportunity for Pacific Studies to strategically expand its research, education and outreach goals. We designed a Pacific Studies leadership camp where elite players from 13 professional clubs would engage with Pacific history, religion, literature and the performing arts. They went through a series of lectures and workshops and put together final performances that reflected their learning. A team of Pacific Islander scholars and Papua New Guinean choreographer Julia Gray facilitated the three-day event with additional mentoring and inspiration from visitors to the camp such as Tofiga Fepulea'i of the internationally acclaimed comedy duo Laughing Samoans, former NFL player Richard Brown and Australian Idol contestant and Māori pop singer Stan Walker.

At the end of the camp, the players reported that the history and leadership modules had had a significant impact on their sense of Pacific history, identity and culture and they were motivated to spread this throughout their club communities. At this point, I handed the project over to other members of the team for further collaboration but I was struck by how this very short exposure to many of the core aspects of Pacific Studies learning had a reported impact on elite athletes, most of whom—unlike their NFL counterparts who play college football and therefore study throughout a significant period of their careers—had received little higher education, technical or academic. It is well known within the NRL that Pacific Islander players do not take advantage of higher education opportunities compared with their Anglo-Australian counterparts.

While the *Body Pacifica* exhibition had catalysed a much needed public display of Pacific pride, the NRL education and welfare office was keen to take this further and deepen the historical and cultural knowledge of their players. In Hokowhitu's terms, they had enhanced the *mana* of their communities and potentially increased their own *mana* by gaining respect through the lending of their regularly commoditised bodies and images to celebrate Pacific culture instead. Now Vagana wanted to ensure that they did indeed have a deeper knowledge of that culture via education.

Reflection

Migrant Pacific Islanders are transforming and applying new interpretations of both *mana* and *tapu* (taboo) in their diasporic contexts. For example, diasporic groups will apply these notions to sacred Pacific objects in museums in their new countries of residence. While they may not always understand the meaning of the objects in their original contexts, such objects have come to signify an important link to the ancestors and the Islands, bridging that distance in both time and space (Singh and Blake 2012). It is that distance from the home island context and the ways in which publicly visible bodies, acts or objects become infused with the potential *mana*—efficacy and image—of whole communities which requires a rethinking of the stakes of *mana* compared with earlier studies focused on understanding its formal linguistic properties and application in the islands.

What I have done here is lay out some questions, reflected on what others such as Tengan, Markham, Hokowhitu, Diaz and Uperesa have signalled already in their research, and presented the Australian diasporic context as offering further opportunities for critical examination of the concept or effect of *mana*. I do not believe the word itself needs to be present or regularly utilised in Pacific diasporic discourse for its essential qualities or effects to be relevant. As argued by Diaz, *mana* is still the best concept to capture what is at stake in the relationship between Pacific sporting icons and the communities they represent. The deeds, words and images of an elite Pacific athlete can uplift or shame their entire cultures. This is the nature of Pacific, and especially Polynesian, relational personhood. As writer Sia Figiel has poignantly offered in her succinct characterisation of Samoan collective identity: '"I" is "we"… always' (1996:136).

Australia is a new and certainly less understood or researched diasporic space compared with the United States and New Zealand, and one that has deeply unresolved racial politics, but it is also a kind of open field for Islanders to transform and claim in their own ways. The kind of *mana* created by something like *Body Pacifica* or the NRL leadership camp is both individual and collective, noun and verb, human and object, and also fleeting. A chief's or God's *mana* might need to be proven but is supposed to be durable, but an athlete's power is often short term and almost always ends in one kind of defeat or another by virtue of the fact that retirement or injury means they cannot exercise athletic prowess any more in the same way.

Currently, while there are concentrations of Pacific communities and inspiring personalities and deeds evident within suburbs across several states, it remains to be seen what kind of *niu* space Australia will become for Pacific Islanders. That is, a space infused with and informed by Pacific flavours, styles and values regardless of gender, artistic talent or athletic prowess. At the moment, in spite of the seasonal explosion of male Islander bodies across the sporting fields and flat screen televisions of countless Australian homes, Pacific peoples and the Pacific Islands still occupy the edges of Australian consciousness, especially with the intense and strategic economic, educational and political turn within the last 20 years towards Asia.

References

Ansley, G. 2012. Australia's Pacific Gangland. *New Zealand Herald*, 21 January. www.nzherald.co.nz/world/news/article.cfm?c_id=2&objectid=10780126 (accessed 11 October 2015).

Australian Human Rights Commission 2013. *Racism: It Stops with Me*. YouTube, 23 May. www.youtube.com/watch?v=ASsZ-u9YV3c (accessed 4 April 2014).

Banivanua-Mar, T. 2007. *Violence and Colonial Dialogue: The Australian-Pacific Indentured Labor Trade*. Honolulu: University of Hawai'i Press.

Besnier, N. 2012. The Athlete's Body and the Global Condition: Tongan Rugby Players in Japan. *American Anthropologist* 39(3):491–510. doi.org/10.1111/j.1548-1425.2012.01377.x

Betz, E. 2013. Unemployment not the cause of Pacific Islander violence in Logan. *The Conversation*, 18 January. theconversation.com/unemployment-not-the-cause-of-pacific-islander-violence-in-logan-11650 (accessed 3 September 2014).

Boucher, D. 2012. On Finding our Own Voices: Australia's Samoan Diaspora, Representation and Identity. BA Honours thesis, Griffith University.

Cadzow, J. 2013. The Quiet One. *The Sydney Morning Herald*, 30 May. www.smh.com.au/rugby-league/league-news/the-quiet-one-20130422-2i948.html (accessed 9 September 2014, site discontinued).

Crocombe, R. 1976. *The Pacific Way: An Emerging Identity*. Suva: Lotu Pacifica.

Diaz, V. 2011. Tackling Pacific hegemonic formations on the American gridiron. *Amerasia Journal* 37(3):90–113. doi.org/10.1111/j.1548-1425.2012.01377.x

Figiel, S. 1996. *Where We Once Belonged*, Auckland: Pasifika Press.

Giggacher, J. 2014. Kindred Spirits (Interview with Margaret Jolly). Original, abridged article in the *ANU Reporter*, Autumn:28–29. pasifika.anu.edu.au/news-events/all-stories/kindred-spirits (accessed 8 September 2014).

Golub, A. and J. Peterson 2016. How Mana Left the Pacific and Became a Video Game Mechanic. In M. Tomlinson and Ty P. Kāwika Tengan (eds), *New Mana: Transformations of a Classic Concept in Pacific Languages and Cultures*. Canberra: ANU Press. doi.org/10.22459/NM.04.2016.12

Hill, B. 2013. Maori/Pacific Gang Violence in Australia. *Radio Australia*, 15 May. www.radioaustralia.net.au/international/radio/program/pacific-beat/maori pacific-gang-violence-in-melbourne/1131308 (accessed 12 October 2015, site discontinued).

Hokowhitu, B. 2004. Tackling Māori Masculinity. *The Contemporary Pacific* 16(2):259–84. doi.org/10.1353/cp.2004.0046

Horton, P. and D. Zakus 2009. Pacifica in Australian Rugby: Emanant (sic) Social, Cultural and Economic Issues. *Sporting Traditions* 26(2):67–86.

Hutchins, B. and J. Mikosza 1998. Australian Rugby League and Violence 1970–1995: A Case Study in the Maintenance of Masculine Hegemony. *Journal of Sociology* 34:246–63. doi.org/10.1177/144078339803400303

IFWT Productions and ITVS 2014. *In Football We Trust* (documentary film). Trailer online: www.youtube.com/watch?v=0I6vb4XwV0o (accessed 9 October 2015, site discontinued).

Keesing, R.M. 1984. Rethinking 'mana'. *Journal of Anthropological Research* 40(1):137–56. doi.org/10.1177/144078339803400303

Kolshus, T. 2016. Mana on the Move: Why Empirical Anchorage Trumps Philosophical Drift. In M. Tomlinson and Ty P. Kāwika Tengan (eds), *New Mana: Transformations of a Classic Concept in Pacific Languages and Cultures*. Canberra: ANU Press. doi.org/10.22459/NM.04.2016.06

Lakisa, D. 2011. The Pacific Revolution: Pacific & Māori Players in Australian Rugby League. MA thesis, Southern Cross University, New South Wales.

Lakisa, D., D. Adair and T. Taylor 2014. Pasifika Diaspora and the Changing Face of Australian Rugby League. *The Contemporary Pacific* 26(2):347–67. doi.org/10.1353/cp.2014.0029

Lane, D. 2006. Islanders in Junior Leagues, it's a Really Big Issue. *The Sydney Morning Herald*, 16 July. www.smh.com.au/news/league/islanders-in-junior-leagues-its-a-really-big-issue/2006/07/15/1152637922188.html (accessed 12 October 2015).

Lawson, S. 2010. 'The Pacific Way' as Postcolonial Discourse: Towards a Reassessment. *Journal of Pacific History* 45(3):297–314. doi.org/10.1080/00223344.2010.530810

Lee, H. 2009. Pacific Migration and Transnationalism: Historical Perspectives. In H. Lee and S.T. Francis (eds), *Migration and Transnationalism: Pacific Perspectives*. Canberra: ANU E Press, 7–42. doi.org/10.22459/MT.08.2009.01

Lee, H. and S.T. Francis (eds) 2009. *Migration and Transnationalism: Pacific Perspectives*. Canberra: ANU E Press. doi.org/10.22459/MT.08.2009

Lewis-Harris, J. 2011. Dancing on the Weekend: Papua New Guinea Culture Schools in Urban Australia. *Intersections: Gender and Sexuality in Asia and the Pacific* 27 (November). intersections.anu.edu.au/issue27/lewis-harris.htm (accessed 2 September 2014).

Lilley, C. 2014. *Jonah from Tonga* (television series). Melbourne: Princess Pictures.

Madang Wansolwara Dance 2014. Papua New Guinea Mine Watch blog. ramumine.wordpress.com/2014/09/01/madang-wansolwara-dance/ (accessed 3 September 2014).

Mallon, S. and P.F. Pereira (eds) 2002. *Pacific Art Niu Sila: The Pacific Dimension of Contemporary Arts in New Zealand*. Wellington: Te Papa Press.

Massoud, J. 2013. Reni Maitua Has Revealed how He Hit Rock Bottom and Attempted to Take His Own Life. *The Sunday Telegraph*, 14 December. www.foxsports.com.au/nrl/nrl-premiership/reni-maitua-has-revealed-how-he-hit-rock-bottom-and-attempted-to-take-his-own-life/news-story/1c4068cf09570e0f574e8fb81a8e6fcf? (accessed 9 September 2014).

Moloney, J.P. 2008. New Brumbies Profess the Faith. *The Canberra Times*, 17 December. www.smh.com.au/rugby-union/union-news/new-brumbies-profess-the-faith-20091124-j902.html#ixzz3CDkMEuI3 (accessed 2 September 2014, site discontinued).

Morgain, R. 2016. Mana for a New Age. In M. Tomlinson and Ty P. Kāwika Tengan (eds), *New Mana: Transformations of a Classic Concept in Pacific Languages and Cultures*. Canberra: ANU Press. doi.org/10.22459/NM.04.2016.11

Palmer, F. and T. Masters 2010. Māori Feminism and Sport Leadership. *Sport Management Review* 13(4):331–44. doi.org/10.1016/j.smr.2010.06.001

Pryke, J. 2014. Pacific Islanders in Australia: Where are the Melanesians? DevPolicyBlog, 28 August. www.devpolicy.org/pacific-islanders-in-australia-where-are-the-melanesians-20140828/ (accessed 2 September 2014).

Pryor, N. 2013. Maori in Oz: Living the Good Life. *Stuff*, 19 July. www.stuff.co.nz/national/8937746/Maori-in-Oz-Living-the-good-life (accessed 12 October 2015).

Queensland Health 2013. Pacific Islander and Maori Population Size and Distribution. www.health.qld.gov.au/multicultural/health_workers/pac-island-pop (accessed 11 October 2015).

Read, B. 2008. Petero Civoniceva Racial Abuser Banned from League Games. *The Australian*, 9 July. www.theaustralian.com.au/archive/news/civoniceva-racial-abuser-banned-by-nrl/story-e6frg7mo-1111116859701?nk=c707862ddd0d4ad38c5ee30ad197f35b (accessed 3 September 2014, site discontinued).

Rose, S., M. Quanchi and C. Moore 2009. *A National Strategy for the Study of the Pacific*. Brisbane: Australian Association for the Advancement of Pacific Studies.

SBS 2014. Chris Lilley Facing Social Media Backlash over 'Racist' Jonah from Tonga, 15 May. www.sbs.com.au/news/article/2014/05/15/chris-lilley-facing-social-media-backlash-over-racist-jonah-tonga (accessed 3 September 2014, site discontinued).

Singh, S. and M. Blake 2012. The Digitization of Pacific Cultural Collections: Consulting with Diasporic Pacific Communities and Experts. *Curator: The Museum Journal* 55(1): 95–105. doi.org/10.1111/j.2151-6952.2011.00132.x

Steeg, J.L. 2012. Junior Seau: Song of Sorrow. *The San Diego Union-Tribune*. www.utsandiego.com/news/2012/Oct/14/junior-seau-real-story/ (accessed 2 April 2014, site discontinued).

Teaiwa, K. 2007. Aussie Islanders Fight Ignorance. *The Fiji Times*, 30 October (original article in *The Canberra Times*, 29 October 2007). www.fijitimes.com/story.aspx?id=73247 (accessed 3 September 2014, site discontinued).

Teaiwa, T. and S. Mallon 2005. Ambivalent Kinships: Pacific People in New Zealand. In J.H. Liu, T. McCreanor and T. McIntosh (eds), *New Zealand Identities: Departures and Destinations*. Wellington: Victoria University Press, 207–29.

Tengan, T.P. Kāwika and J. Markham 2009. Performing Polynesian Masculinities in American Football: From 'Rainbows to Warriors'. *International Journal of the History of Sport* 26(16):2412–31.

Tomlinson, M. 2006. Retheorizing Mana: Bible Translation and Discourse of Loss in Fiji. *Oceania* 76(2):173–85. doi.org/10.1002/j.1834-4461.2006. tb03043.x

Tomlinson M. and S. Bigitbau 2016. Theologies of *Mana* and *Sau* in Fiji. In M. Tomlinson and Ty P. Kāwika Tengan (eds), *New Mana: Transformations of a Classic Concept in Pacific Languages and Cultures.* Canberra: ANU Press. doi.org/10.22459/NM.04.2016.09

Uperesa, F.L. 2014. Fabled Futures: Migration and Mobility for Samoans in American Football. *The Contemporary Pacific* 26(2): 281–301. doi.org/ 10.1353/cp.2014.0045

Vasta, E. 2004. Community, the State and the Deserving Citizen: Pacific Islanders in Australia. *Journal of Ethnic and Migration Studies* 30(1):195–213. doi.org/10.1080/1369183032000170231

Winitana, M. 2008. Contemporary Conceptions of Mana Wahine Māori in Australia: A Diasporic Discussion. *Mai Review* 3, Research Note 4:1–8.

Afterword

Stewart Firth

When I was at the University of the South Pacific (USP), 1998–2004, themes for Pacific research by those of us in the Department of History/Politics suggested themselves from the events that were unfolding around us—the politics of Fiji above all: the coup of 2000, the prolonged detention of parliamentarians by rebels, the military mutiny, the 2001 election that brought to power Laisenia Qarase and the years of contestation between government and military leading to the coup of 2006 and a permanently influential military role in the government of Fiji. At the same time, we were highly conscious of the breakdown of law and order in Solomon Islands—something that directly affected the Solomon Islanders at USP—and the coming of the Regional Assistance Mission to Solomon Islands in 2003, a major regional intervention that was to last for the next 14 years. Wider global forces played their part in the decision to intervene in Solomon Islands, above all 9/11 and the Bali bombings, which prompted Australia to consider the security of the region in a new and threatening context.

The international economy and globalisation were a second major context that informed the interests of staff and students across many disciplines at USP. As the bandwagon of free trade advanced, special arrangements that favoured small countries were ruled inconsistent with the requirements of the World Trade Organization, spelling the end of Fiji's garment industry as a growing sector of the economy and large employer. The ideology of international competitiveness—that every country should do what it does best and then trade—might have applied to the fast-growing economies of East Asia, but it did not apply to the Pacific Islands, whose small size and remoteness consigned them to the rank of bit players on the stage of the global economy. This simple point—that some regions are different from others—was missing from the understanding of the global bureaucrats who prescribed identical versions of neoliberal economic policy the world over.

A third context, emphasised officially by USP as the theme of all we did, was the Pacific Islands region itself, the home of most students and their likely destination after graduation. Whether it was Randy Thaman leading a group of USP students into the interior of Fiji; the geography staff decamping en masse to study Niue; history students heading for a visit to Bau or Levuka; the economists and development experts examining squatter settlements; the tourism academics testing the possibilities of eco-tourism; the marine studies students studying mangroves and coastal fisheries; or literature students delving for the first time into the work of Albert Wendt, Konai Thaman, Pio Manoa and Sia Figiel, the subject was close to students' interests and hearts because it was in the Pacific.

Regionalism was another context for those of us at what is, after all, a regional institution. Regionalism will be more than ever a focus of teaching and research at USP in the years ahead: an era of climate change, better management of fisheries and new regional agendas such as the Blue Pacific. Regionalism binds the Pacific together in common ambition for development. Greg Fry and Sandra Tarte, in their contribution to this volume, see the current changes taking place in Pacific Islands regionalism and diplomacy as 'of the order of the shift from the colonial to the postcolonial diplomatic system in 1971'.

The future will have its own contexts, and one of them will be the shift in the geostrategic situation in the Pacific Islands. The rapid rise of China in the region as a commercial partner, investor and aid partner with Pacific countries has unsettled the calculations of Australia, New Zealand, France, Japan and the US, all of them long accustomed to unchallenged Western dominance. Australia in particular has shifted course, announcing a step up in its Pacific engagement and a raft of policy initiatives, including a high-speed communications cable between Australia and Solomon Islands so as to ensure that the business did not go to the Chinese company Huawei, as well as a new infrastructure fund for the entire region. The visit by Australian Prime Minister Scott Morrison to Vanuatu and Fiji in 2019 symbolised the new Australian mood, and the importance of the University of the South Pacific in the future of the region was recognised by Morrison's announcement that Australia would fund a new Australia–USP partnership worth AU$84 million to 2025. China's rising presence in the region, then, has given Pacific Island states new leverage in their dealings with old development partners such as Australia.

What Australia does not have to offer the Pacific, at least at present, is action on climate change. For atoll states such as Kiribati, the Marshall Islands and Tuvalu, climate change is an issue not merely of importance but of survival, and the urgency of their situation is reflected in the role they now play in global climate change diplomacy. Referring to the coal mining industry in Australia, the Fijian Prime Minister Frank Bainimarama reminded the Australian Prime Minister that, 'From where we are sitting, we cannot imagine how the interests of any single industry can be placed above the welfare of Pacific peoples—vulnerable people in the world over' (Dziedzic and Handley 2019). Climate change—causes, dimensions, solutions, diplomacy—is already a key theme in USP teaching and research in many disciplines and will continue to be so.

Another future theme can be seen in the work of a remarkable group of younger USP scholars who are examining the role of social media and the internet in Fiji and the rest of the Pacific. In a groundbreaking article published in 2014, Glen Finau, Romitesh Kant, Jope Tarai and Acklesh Prasad from USP and Sarah Logan and John Cox from ANU analysed 'Social Media and e-Democracy in Fiji, Solomon Islands and Vanuatu' (Finau et al. 2014). The researchers compared political social media Facebook pages in the three countries, concluding that social media is making government more accountable. Much more such research has followed and a recent joint article by USP and ex-USP scholars Jope Tarai, Glen Finau, Romitesh Kant and Jason Titifanue, together with Tait Brimacombe from the University of Adelaide, extends its horizons by focusing on digital feminism in Fiji (Brimacombe et al. 2018).

The University of the South Pacific stands at the threshold of a new era of leadership under Vice Chancellor and President Professor Pal Ahluwalia, who believes USP has 'a real opportunity to become a truly world-class institution by building upon the promise of its mission and values' (USP 2018). For its part, The Australian National University, which has enjoyed such a close relationship with USP for half a century, remains as much a centre of expertise about the Pacific Islands as ever and looks forward to another 50 years of cooperation with the premier institution of learning in the Pacific Islands region.

References

Brimacombe, T., R. Kant, G. Finau, J. Tarai and J. Titifanue 2018. A New Frontier in Digital Activism: An Exploration of Digital Feminism in Fiji. *Asia and the Pacific Policy Studies* 5(3):508–21. doi.org/10.1002/app5.253

Dziedzic, S. and E. Handley 2019. Climate Change Is 'No Laughing Matter', Fiji's PM Frank Bainimarama Tells Australia during Scott Morrison's Pacific Trip. *ABC News*, 19 January. www.abc.net.au/news/2019-01-18/climate-change-is-no-laughing-matter-fiji-pm-says/10724582

Finau, G., R. Kant, J. Tarai, A. Prasad, S. Logan and J. Cox 2014. Social Media and e-Democracy in Fiji, Solomon Islands and Vanuatu. Paper presented at 20th Americas Conference on Information Systems, AIS (Association for Information Systems), Savannah, 7–10 August.

University of the South Pacific (USP) 2018. New USP Vice-Chancellor and President Appointed. *News@USP*, 6 June. www.usp.ac.fj/news/story.php?id=2800